Repertoires
of Terrorism

Columbia Studies in Terrorism and Irregular Warfare

Columbia Studies in Terrorism and Irregular Warfare

BRUCE HOFFMAN, SERIES EDITOR

This series seeks to fill a conspicuous gap in the burgeoning literature on terrorism, guerrilla warfare, and insurgency. The series adheres to the highest standards of scholarship and discourse and publishes books that elucidate the strategy, operations, means, motivations, and effects posed by terrorist, guerrilla, and insurgent organizations and movements. It thereby provides a solid and increasingly expanding foundation of knowledge on these subjects for students, established scholars, and informed reading audiences alike.

John Horgan, *Terrorist Minds: The Psychology of Violent Extremism from Al-Qaeda to the Far Right*

Harrison Akins, *The Terrorism Trap: The War on Terror Inside America's Partner States*

Rita Katz, *Saints and Soldiers: Inside Internet-Age Terrorism, From Syria to the Capitol Siege*

Tricia L. Bacon and Elizabeth Grimm, *Terror in Transition: Leadership and Succession in Terrorist Organizations*

Daveed Gartenstein-Ross and Thomas Joscelyn, *Enemies Near and Far: How Jihadist Groups Strategize, Plot, and Learn*

Boaz Ganor, *Israel's Counterterrorism Strategy: Origins to the Present*

Arie Perliger, *American Zealots: Inside Right-Wing Domestic Terrorism*

Erin M. Kearns and Joseph K. Young, *Tortured Logic: Why Some Americans Support the Use of Torture in Counterterrorism*

Lorenzo Vidino, *The Closed Circle: Joining and Leaving the Muslim Brotherhood in the West*

Aaron Y. Zelin, *Your Sons Are at Your Service: Tunisia's Missionaries of Jihad*

Mariya Y. Omelicheva and Lawrence P. Markowitz, *Webs of Corruption: Trafficking and Terrorism in Central Asia*

Bryan C. Price, *Targeting Top Terrorists: Understanding Leadership Removal in Counterterrorism Strategy*

Wendy Pearlman and Boaz Atzili, *Triadic Coercion: Israel's Targeting of States That Host Nonstate Actors*

Stephen Tankel, *With Us and Against Us: How America's Partners Help and Hinder the War on Terror*

Bruce Hoffman, *Inside Terrorism*, third edition

For a complete list of books in the series, please see the Columbia University Press website.

Repertoires of Terrorism

Organizational Identity
and Violence in Colombia's
Civil War

ANDREAS E. FELDMANN

Columbia
University
Press
New York

Columbia University Press
Publishers Since 1893
New York   Chichester, West Sussex
cup.columbia.edu
Copyright © 2024 Columbia University Press
All rights reserved

Library of Congress Cataloging-in-Publication Data
Names: Feldmann, Andreas E., author.
Title: Repertoires of terrorism in civil war : organizational identity and
   violence in Colombia's Civil War / Andreas E. Feldmann.
Description: New York : Columbia University Press, [2024] |
   Series: Columbia studies in terrorism and irregular warfare |
   Includes bibliographical references and index.
Identifiers: LCCN 2023048874 (print) | LCCN 2023048875 (ebook) |
   ISBN 9780231213745 (hardback) | ISBN 9780231213752 (trade paperback) |
   ISBN 9780231560009 (ebook)
Subjects: LCSH: Terrorism—Colombia—History. | State-sponsored
   terrorism—Colombia—History. | Civil war—Colombia—History. |
   Paramilitary forces—Colombia—History. | Political violence—Colombia—
   History. | Human rights—Colombia—History. | Colombia—Politics and
   government—1974–
Classification: LCC HV6433.C6 F45 2024 (print) | LCC HV6433.C6 (ebook) |
   DDC 363.32509861—dc23/eng/20240108
LC record available at https://lccn.loc.gov/2023048874
LC ebook record available at https://lccn.loc.gov/2023048875

Cover design: Chang Jae Lee
Cover image: © AP Photo/Javier Galeano

A la familia Olea

Contents

Acknowledgments ix
List of Abbreviations xiii

Introduction 1

1. Theorizing Armed Parties' Repertoires of Terrorism During Civil Wars 26

2. The Evolution of the Colombian Civil War: From Conventional to Criminal Warfare 53

3. The Mighty FARC and the Use of Terrorism 71

4. The ELN: From *Foquismo* Warfare to Terrorism 99

5. Paramilitary Terrorism: The Fusion of Counterinsurgency and Criminality 126

6. State Terror in the Colombian Civil War 157

7. Terrorism in Criminal Wars 186

Conclusion 208

Appendix 1: The Use of Terrorism by Colombian Armed Parties 219
Appendix 2: Interviewees 229
Notes 231
Bibliography 289
Index 315

Acknowledgments

This book is the culmination of more than ten years of work. I began the journey while teaching at the Instituto de Ciencia Política (ICP) of the Catholic University of Chile in my hometown, Santiago de Chile. I continued after moving with my family back to my second home, Chicago, in the summer of 2014. Although often daunting, this intellectual expedition has been meaningful and humbling. I learned many things about Colombia's captivating history, myself, academia, and, more significantly, human nature. The kindness I have encountered along the way from my Colombian family, colleagues, students, friends, sources, and strangers, contrasts with the inhumanity I write about in this book. I confess that during the many trips I have taken over the years to Colombia, this would perplex me: the great historian David Bushnell hints at this feeling in his magisterial book, *The Making of Modern Colombia: A Nation in Spite of Itself*, widely cited in my work, in which he recounts how foreigners investigating the country all too often wrestle with how to make sense of the violence raging in a land inhabited by the warmest of people.

This book was possible thanks to a significant number of individuals who, in different capacities, helped me along the way. I begin by acknowledging the faculty who mentored me at Notre Dame, especially two giants in the field of human rights, the late Gil Loescher and Juan E. Méndez. I was fortunate to be trained by such talented, humane scholars, from whom I learned that we owe our work and best efforts to the victims we write about. From them, I also learned to rely on human rights as a compass to avoid getting lost in our preconceptions and biases.

Several organizations provided support for this research. ICP founded part of my early fieldwork. Several former colleagues and students at the *Católica* helped during the initial phases of the project, including Umut Aydin, Tomás Chuaqui, Paula Lekanda, Rodrigo Mardones, Alex Micic, Nicolás Palacios, Dania Straughan, and especially Mauricio Ortegón, an exceptional research assistant who worked with me analyzing the Noche y Niebla data.

I am also grateful to the University of Illinois Chicago (UIC) School of Liberal Arts and Sciences (LAS) for its generous support. In addition to resources, UIC provided a stimulating working environment to conduct research. Esteemed colleagues at the Latin American and Latino Studies Program and the Department of Political Science and other units offered advice, feedback on concrete chapters, or simply words of encouragement and support. I am grateful to Soledad Álvarez, Marco Boccece, Christopher Boyer, Ralph Cintrón, Joaquín Chávez, Jonathan Inda, Petia Kostadinova, Evan McKenzie, Amalia Pallares, Maria Schechtman, Astrida Tantillo, Nena Torres, Bruce Tyler, and Yue Zhang. My dear friend and colleague Xóchitl Bada deserves special credit for her always sound advice and support at the later stages of the project. And so does Adam Goodman, who helped me by leading my book workshop with his accustomed charm and skill. Many outstanding UIC students helped me, too, including Héctor Alarcón, Cruz Bonlarrón, Alexandra Fryer, and Sebastián Tobón. Three of them deserve special mention: Michael Tremesky, whose diligent work wrestling with the database was invaluable; Jorge Mantilla, whose insight and knowledge helped me to make sense of many challenging facets of the research; and Marc Lopez, who worked with me on the shadow case demonstrating excellent research instincts.

UIC should also be credited for helping me organize a book workshop that proved critical to the book's success. I owe a colossal debt of gratitude to the workshop's participants, Carla Alberti, Angélica Durán-Martínez, Juan Esteban Montes, and Hillel Soifer. All of them offered fantastic feedback and suggestions on ways to strengthen the quality and overall appeal of the manuscript. Two colleagues warrant special mention. I have no words to describe Gustavo Duncan's collegiality: his incredible knowledge is only surpassed by his generosity and willingness to help colleagues and students. Few people understand Colombia better than he, and even fewer are willing to share their knowledge as he does. Juan Pablo Luna is arguably one of my generation's most talented Latin American political scientists and a dear friend and colleague who provided priceless advice on a topic far away from his comfort zone. I am incredibly grateful to him.

Part of the last iterations of my extensive fieldwork was possible through the support of the Carnegie Endowment for International Peace and the Bosch Stiftung, which commissioned a series of studies on the impact of the Colombian peace process with FARC (2016). Special thanks to Henry Alt-Hacker, Richard Youngs, and especially Tom Carothers for his generosity and vision, which also contributed to making this book possible. I also acknowledge my wonderful colleagues and partners in crime in the *Rising Democracy Network*, Federico Merke, and Oliver Stuenkel.

Over several years of fieldwork in Colombia, I met wonderful colleagues who gracefully shared their wisdom. Special thanks to Felipe Botero, Álvaro Camacho, Camilo Echandía, Diana Guiza, Francisco Leal, Carlo Nasi, Román Ortiz, Mónica Pachón, Angelika Rettberg, Renata Segura, and, especially Fernando Cubides, Pedro Díaz, Gustavo Gallón, Eric Lair, and Iván Orozco, who on repeated occasions shared their wisdom. Many other colleagues also provided critical and generous feedback on diverse parts of the book or helped me tackle thorny questions. I am grateful to Juan Albarracín, Alejandro Anaya-Muñoz, Ana Arjona, Sara Doskow, Carlos Guevara Mann, Christoph Kleber, Ben Lessing, Cristián Pérez, Aníbal Pérez-Liñan, Jonathan Rosen, and Guillermo Trejo. I also acknowledge both the role Victor Hinojosa played in the initial phases of this book and the Honors College of Baylor University for financial support during the early stages of the project.

I presented chapters of the manuscript in workshops and conferences in Latin America, Europe, and the United States, including the Catholic University of Chile, the Watson Center of Brown University, the Center of Latin American Studies at the University of Chicago, University College Dublin, and the University of Illinois, Chicago. Chapters 4 and 5 draw on a previously published article, "Revolutionary Terror in the Colombian Civil War," *Studies in Conflict and Terrorism* 48, no. 10 (2018): 825–846. The shadow case in chapter 8, in turn, represents an expanded version of a co-authored piece with Marc Lopez titled "Repertoires of Terrorism in the Mexican Criminal War," *Perspectives on Terrorism* 16, no. 2 (2022): 4–13.

Much of the writing and polishing of the book was done at UIC Richard J. Daley Library and the Regenstein Library at the University of Chicago, where I benefited from access to a wealth of sources and to Mansueto, the most beautiful and stimulating of places for any writer. To my gracious hosts at the Reg, many thanks.

Two individuals helped improve the manuscript through their careful copyediting and suggestions. Especial thanks to Nikolai Stieglitz for his outstanding work in the early stages of the project. Matt Seidel took the relay from Nikolai and worked on several later iterations of the manuscript, demonstrating great professionalism and skill.

I owe a debt of gratitude to the team at Columbia University Press. It is a great honor to publish my work in a series I have always loved. I am thankful to Bruce Hoffman, a prominent terrorism studies scholar and one of the kindest editors I have encountered in my career, who believed in the project and encouraged me to publish it in this fine series. Special thanks too to Caelyn Cobb for piloting the book with such efficiency, Monique Laban, Caelyn's competent and kind assistant, and Kathryn Jorge. I also owe a huge debt of gratitude to Glenn Court for her most professional and splendid work copyediting the manuscript. I also appreciate the three anonymous reviewers of the manuscript for the quality and constructive nature of their comments. The feedback I received from them and their concrete suggestions to improve parts of the book were invaluable.

Finally, I could not end without mentioning my family. Unfortunately, my parents, Pedro Feldmann and Marita Pietsch, are not around anymore. However, in so many ways, this journey bore fruit due to their unwavering and nurturing love and wisdom for sending me to the Swiss School in Santiago, where my intellectual journey started. I dedicate this book to my Colombian family, beginning with my wife, Helena Olea, the best partner anyone could dream of, and my son, Martín Feldmann-Olea, who will soon embark on his professional journey in Poitiers and New York. For their love and support, thanks from the bottom of my heart. My appreciation also goes to my endearing political family, the Oleas (Agapito, Helenita, Camilo, Carmencita, Piña, Lisa, Roberto, Andrés, Doriana, Oswaldo, Clelia, Bianca, Josefina, Liliana, Miranda, Antonio, Isabella, and Juan Esteban), who welcomed me with an open heart and taught me to understand their wonderful country just a little bit better.

Abbreviations

ACCU   Peasant Self-Defense Forces of Córdoba and Urabá (Autodefensas Campesinas de Córdoba y Urabá)
ACDEGAM   Peasant Association of Cattle Ranchers and Agriculturalists of Magdalena Medio (Asociación de Campesinos y Ganaderos del Magdalena Medio)
AUC   United Self-Defense Forces of Colombia (Autodefensas Unidas de Colombia)
CINEP   Research Center for Investigation and Popular Education (Centro de Investigación y Educación Popular)
CSSF   Colombian state security forces
DAS   Administrative Security Department (Departamento Administrativo de Seguridad)
DNS   Doctrine of National Security
DTOs   drug trafficking organizations
ETA   Basque Homeland and Liberty (Euskadi Ta Askatasuna)
ELN   National Liberation Army (Ejército de Liberación Nacional)
EPL   Popular Liberation Army (Ejército Popular de Liberación)
FARC   People's Alternative Revolutionary Force (Fuerza Alternativa Revolucionaria del Común); Revolutionary Armed Forces of Colombia (Fuerzas Armadas Revolucionarias de Colombia)

FMLN	Farabundo Martí Liberation Front (Frente Farabundo Martí para la Liberación Nacional)
GAULA	Personal Liberty Unified Action Groups (Grupos de Acción Unificada por la Libertad Personal)
GTD	Global Terrorism Database
IHL	international humanitarian law
M-19	April 19 Movement (Movimiento 19 de abril)
MAS	Death to Kidnappers (Muerte a Secuestradores)
PEPES	Persecuted by Pablo Escobar (Perseguidos por Pablo Escobar)
PPW	prolonged popular war
RCI	Independent Peasant Republics (Repúblicas Campesinas Independientes)
TSC	Cali Supreme Tribunal (Tribunal Superior Cali)

Repertoires of Terrorism

Introduction

On July 15, 1997, a group of one hundred heavily armed individuals belonging to a paramilitary squad entered the small municipality of Mapiripán, Colombia, in the southeastern Meta department. Considered a strategic corridor for moving supplies to clandestine laboratories deep in the jungle, Mapiripán was disputed by paramilitaries of the United Self-Defense Forces of Colombia (Autodefensas Unidas de Colombia, or AUC) and guerrillas of the Revolutionary Armed Forces of Colombia (Fuerzas Armadas Revolucionarias de Colombia, or FARC). Dressed in Colombian Army fatigues, the commandos stormed several villages, selectively retrieved civilians from their homes, and then proceeded to torture and execute them. No shots were heard, and witnesses related that the executions were carried out with knives, machetes, and chainsaws, the bodies dismembered and later thrown into the mighty Guaviare River. In the six-day rampage, dozens of civilians accused of collaborating with guerrillas were brutally murdered. State agents enabled the operation by covering up the massacre and providing logistical support to the perpetrators.[1] Consequently, in the aftermath, a case was brought before the Inter-American Court of Human Rights, which found that the Colombian state had violated the victims' fundamental rights, including life, human dignity, liberty, freedom of movement, and judicial protection.[2]

Two years later, in 1999, guerrillas of the National Liberation Army (Ejército de Liberación Nacional, or ELN) carried out two high-profile mass abductions. In April, ELN guerrillas kidnapped all forty-six passengers aboard a commercial Avianca flight: soon after the plane took off from Bucaramanga, the guerrillas forced the captain to land at a clandestine airstrip in the small town of Simití, eighty miles away in the department of Bolívar. They eventually released all hostages, but many were held for twenty months and one died in captivity. In May, the ELN struck again, this time kidnapping hundreds of churchgoers in a middle-class suburb of Cali. Guerrillas arrived unexpectedly at a church during a service and snatched all those in attendance, including dozens of children and the priest, forcing them to board two buses that ferried them to a nearby town, Jamundí, where they were kept for several months before being released unharmed.[3] A few years later, in an event that caused consternation across the country, FARC operatives bombed the exclusive El Nogal Club, a symbol of Colombian power located in the heart of the capital, Bogotá. The 330-pound explosive device was placed underneath a car and killed thirty-two people, including six children, and injured another 160. The daring attack marked the FARC's decision to bring the war to Colombian cities in what constituted a major escalation of the conflict.[4]

These vignettes describe coldhearted acts of violence perpetrated by diverse actors, from guerilla groups with Cold War origins and right-wing paramilitary groups representing the interests of the landed elite and narcotraffickers to the Colombian state security forces (CSSF).[5] These incidents took place in vastly different locations, from sophisticated urban centers such as Bogotá and Cali to rural hamlets known as *veredas* in remote areas. Similarly, the victims came from diverse backgrounds: peasants, grassroots and community organizers, human rights defenders, intellectuals, well-to-do churchgoers and club members, minors, the elderly, and people with disabilities. Some were chosen randomly; others were selected because the perpetrators suspected, most often without any concrete evidence, that they supported a rival faction; still others were targeted because in their attackers' minds they represented a particular way of thinking or a certain social group.

Although seemingly dissimilar, these acts of violence have an important commonality: they constitute acts of terrorism carried out in the context of Colombia's long and bloody civil war, which dates to the decision of guerrillas to take up arms against the central state in the mid-1960s. This work understands terrorism as an inhumane tactic in which actors deliberately target civilians in open defiance of the cardinal principles of international humanitarian law (IHL)—distinction—with the objective of spreading fear among a wider population (a more detailed conceptual definition follows).[6]

Terrorism has occurred frequently throughout the Colombian conflict. Data compiled for this book cover twenty-five years of the war and show that all actors have used terrorism. All in all, the sample registered 29,672 incidents, of which 12,760 could be directly traced to the central protagonists of the conflict: the two main guerrilla groups, the CSSF, and paramilitary groups (see figure 0.1).[7] Figure 0.2 shows that even though all these groups systematically used the same violent tactic, they developed markedly distinct repertoires or blueprints.

As figure 0.2 makes clear, paramilitaries predominantly carried out massacres and summary executions, limiting their use of abductions and avoiding bombings altogether. The CSSF engaged primarily in summary executions and, to a lesser extent, in massacres and abductions; like

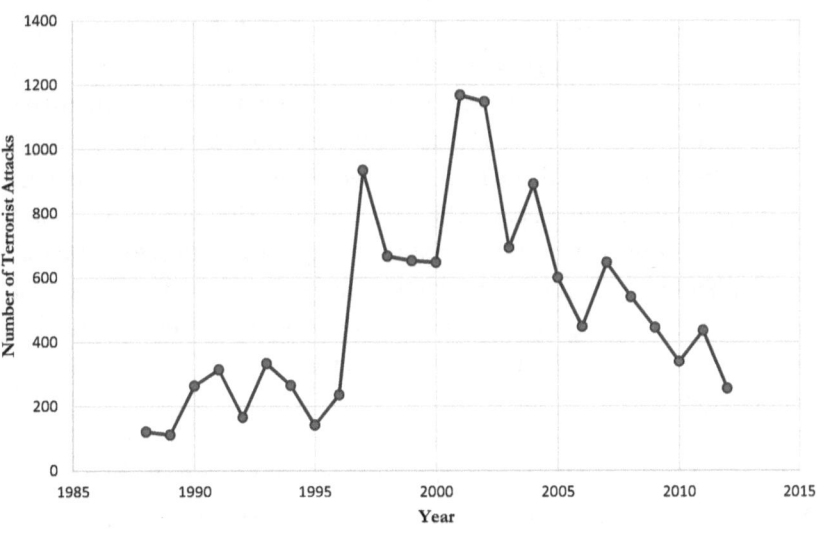

FIGURE 0.1 Terrorist attacks in the Colombian civil war, 1988–2012.

Source: Author's tabulation based on CINEP data.

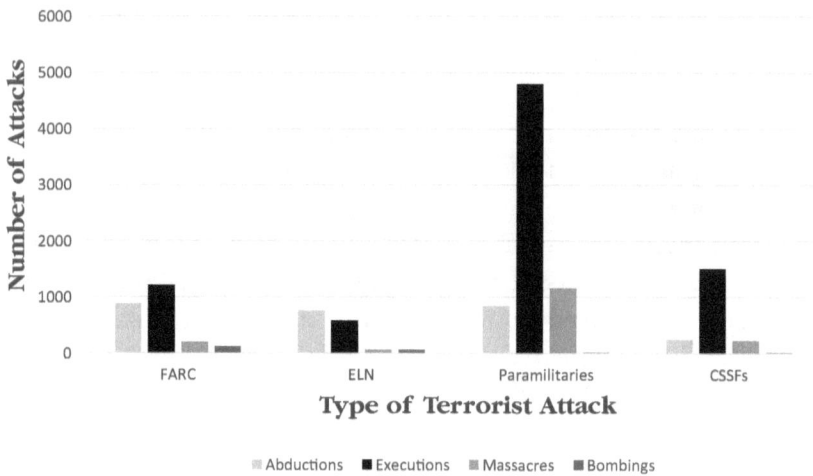

FIGURE 0.2 Colombian armed groups' repertoires of terrorism, 1988–2012.

Source: Author's tabulation based on CINEP data.

paramilitaries, they steered clear of explosive attacks. As for the FARC, they consistently used all forms of terrorism; the ELN concentrated on abductions, executions, and, to a lesser extent, bombings and massacres. Moreover, even when carrying out the same type of attack, parties did so in strikingly different ways. Paramilitaries were more inclined than other actors to rely on summary executions and massacres in which they practiced overkill, or *sevicia*, a Spanish term for violently marking the victims' bodies, which would be later displayed to maximize fear among the population. For the most part, the CSSF and guerrilla groups, especially the ELN, shied away from such graphic displays of violence. As for abductions, whereas guerrillas perpetrated these acts to attract attention, paramilitaries—and especially the CSSF—were more discreet, because their main objective was not to garner publicity but to maintain plausible deniability.[8]

Throughout the conflict, armed parties in Colombia repeatedly clung to terrorist tactics that proved counterproductive, often doubling down on them. For example, guerrillas' stubborn reliance on kidnappings created a major pushback from powerful landed elites, narcotraffickers, and other victimized groups and received widespread societal condemnation. Similarly, paramilitary insistence on massacres, which often included acts of barbarism, prompted general repudiation and alienated important allies—including members of the Colombian Armed Forces and conservative politicians.[9]

Testimonies from the protagonists of Colombia's civil war further illustrate how various groups preferred certain forms of terrorism and rejected others. For example, when confronted by a member of a humanitarian organization over whether his group had "disappeared" a young woman and her toddler in a town in northeastern Colombia, an ELN commander replied in an unyielding tone, "Por favor compa, si no somos paracos . . . devolvimos al chino a su familia" (Come on bro, we are not paramilitaries . . . we returned the boy to the family).[10] In the same vein, Carlos Castaño, the influential paramilitary commander and one of the founders of the AUC, explains in his memoirs, "I never ordered a kidnapping for economic reasons, only for political ones,"[11] alluding to paramilitaries' reluctance to use abductions for financial gain or publicity.[12]

Profuse data and scores of testimonies underline the extent to which Colombian armed parties developed singular *repertoires of terrorism*. By this is meant the distinct and recognizable combination of particular types of terrorist attacks employed by an armed party over an extended period. This conceptualization draws on classical studies in political sociology on repertoires of action, in particular Tilly's seminal work on repertoires of contention, which he defines as learned cultural experiences arising from political struggle.[13] Such variation in the types and forms of terrorism used by Colombian armed parties seems puzzling. Why did these groups rely on such markedly different terrorist practices during the civil war? Why did they prefer certain kinds of attacks to others? Why did some seek publicity and others prefer secrecy? Finally, why did some actors resort to committing graphic displays of violence and others avoid such spectacles? This book systematically investigates this intriguing variation in the context of the Colombian civil war.

How Parties Use Terrorism in Civil War

Across the world, terrorism occurs regularly and systematically in civil wars (e.g., Afghanistan, Mali, Syria, Yemen). This violent tactic is also witnessed in international wars, as the shocking images from the Russian onslaught in Ukraine remind us of and features prominently in so-called criminal wars in countries such as Mexico and Brazil.[14] Despite the persistence of armed conflicts and the depressing regularity with which terrorism arises in them, our understanding of the ways terrorism unfolds in them and how armed groups use it remains limited.[15]

Classical work within terrorism studies—which explores organizational traits such as ideology, group composition, and leadership choices, among others—provides important clues regarding how violent organizations select specific repertoires of action.[16] This literature, however, has for the most part eschewed discussions of civil war, and only a few works devote attention to the matter.[17] Meanwhile, the comparative politics work on civilian victimization during civil wars has convincingly advanced a series of hypotheses concerning armed parties' behavior. However, this literature does not conceptualize these attacks as terrorism, subsuming them into the broader category of civilian targeting. In addition, most studies within this literature base their explanations on strategic military considerations[18] (i.e., achieving territorial control, weakening the enemy, reducing the costs of fighting).[19] To the extent that their microlevel analyses are predicated upon a strategic logic, these scholars assume that actors' behavior is homogeneous, thus failing to account for the vast ideological and behavioral gulfs differentiating armed parties.

To a significant degree, limitations in our understanding of the use of terrorism in civil wars result from a lack of dialogue and cross-fertilization between these literatures.[20] Recent work has begun to address this problem by integrating insights from these and other literatures and has consequently broadened our understanding of this phenomenon not only conceptually but also in terms of the strategic uses of terrorism in the context of civil wars.[21] Yet, although these studies generally concentrate on unpacking why parties resort to terrorism in civil war, they pay little attention to how exactly they employ this tactic or to what accounts for operational differences among the various parties.

In seeking to explain variation in the use of terrorism in civil war, this work develops an organizational approach that investigates armed parties' tactics and questions their behavior rather than taking it as a given. I argue that although terrorism is driven by strategic considerations of a political and military nature, the manifestations of this practice, or the repertoires of terrorism, result from armed parties' *organizational identities*, defined as the central, distinctive, and enduring attributes distinguishing an armed group from other warring parties. Organizational identity represents a social category; that is, it is a form of collective identity constituted and shaped by norms, goals, purposes, and cognitive models (i.e., worldviews).[22] Far from monolithic, organizational identities tend to be multifaceted, often combining seemingly incompatible features. Repertoires of terrorism, this works posits, are concrete manifestations of such organizational identities, which armed parties use as a method of communication and to assert their relevance and presence in a given space.

Although repertoires of terrorism are an expression of distinct organizational preferences, they are not immutable and can change over time. Armed parties often incorporate tactical innovations and refine their terrorism tactics. Moreover, they can adopt some of their rivals' successful tactics and adapt them to fit their specific organizational preferences and constraints. This flexibility is particularly relevant in the fluid, ever-changing context of civil wars. Like the repertoires of terrorism they use, organizations' identities are not fixed and can evolve. As explored later in this book, particularly in chapter 7, the identity of certain armed parties—especially guerrillas—altered as groups relaxed their ideological views and became increasingly involved in criminal practices. These changes prompted slight shifts in their terrorist tactics.

The argument in this work combines insights from comparative politics and international relations as it engages with work on organizational identity. By linking organizational identity to group interests and, ultimately, to behavior, this formulation offers a sound alternative to rational accounts that tend to artificially standardize actors' behavior.[23] Organizational identity, it is claimed, offers a more plausible interpretation than excessively rigid accounts that are ill equipped to explain certain outcomes, in this case variation in armed parties' behavior.[24] This work also draws on insights from constructivism, an international relations framework offering a social theory for understanding international behavior, and state behavior in particular.[25] Constructivism argues that interests are not simply the result of rational preferences but instead intersubjectively constructed.[26] It posits that actors' interests can be traced to particular identities defining their stance on several issues (e.g., security, the economy, the environment).[27] Although constructivism eschews using identity as an explanatory variable, many authors within this school embrace identity as the functional equivalent of an independent variable.[28]

Drawing on the insights of organizational theory and constructivism, I assume that armed parties, like nations and firms, develop particular identities, and that this unique character informs their repertoires of action, including their use and selection of distinct forms of terrorism. In other words, repertoires of terrorism reflect armed parties' character and preferences. The development of a singular repertoire of terrorism is thus a distinctive marker of a group's presence and plays an important communicational role, distinguishing the organization from its enemies and rivals.

The process of translating organizational identity into concrete repertoires of terrorism is complex and influenced by the organization's unique history, leadership, and overall institutional features and processes. The origins of the group, specifically the historical context in which it evolved and its formative years, are crucial in shaping identity. Of particular importance are what Francesco Moro calls *foundational myths*, by which he means the narratives detailing how a group came to be and that bestow on it a distinct character and sense of purpose.[29]

The development of organizational identity is also inextricably related to a group's ideational aspects. Different worldviews inform the emergence of groups in reaction to historical moments (e.g., the Cold War). Ideology represents a critical element in this process. Following Francisco Gutiérrez-Sanín and Elisabeth Wood, ideology is understood as "a more or less systematic set of ideas that includes the identification of a referent group (a class, ethnic of other social group), an enunciation of the grievances or challenges that the group confronts, the identification of objectives on behalf of that group (political change or defense against its threat) and a (perhaps vaguely defined) program of action."[30] Whether secular, religious, or focused on a single issue (e.g., the environment), ideology is not only key in nurturing group identity but also informs actors' goals and guides their actions.

A related factor shaping armed parties' identity concerns their involvement in or relationship with criminal enterprises. Armed groups can display an overt criminal composition, be directly enmeshed in illicit industries, or engage in criminal activities for pragmatic reasons that seem at odds with their ideological stance; in each case, incorporating a *criminal ethos* partly determines the group's identity.³¹ A criminal ethos may surface in terrorism repertoires that include graphic displays of violence and acts that seek to maximize fear.³²

Ideational aspects and other markers influence how armed parties, and their leaders—who arguably play the most vital role in identity formation—understand and perceive reality.³³ Within armed organizations, leaders occupy a multiplicity of roles, from developing military, operational, and logistics capacities to devising funding strategies to recruiting members and overseeing internal disciplinary and socialization mechanisms.³⁴ An important aspect of leadership concerns creating protocols for the groups' behavior toward the civilian population. When it comes to developing and selecting concrete repertoires of violence, leaders strive to align military and ideational considerations, mindful that such an alignment enhances the organization's cohesiveness. For example, leaders tend to adopt military tactics that not only match their organizations' main objectives but, following constructivist thought, also reflect their organizational preferences and identity. For leaders, their milieu, personal experiences, socialization, and exposure to ideology around their particular political struggle all are important factors shaping this process.

Once leaders choose repertoires of terrorism, these repertoires become institutionalized through socialization (i.e., a process whereby actors acquire and internalize norms and rules in a given setting).³⁵ In the case of military organizations, socialization includes formal mechanisms such as training and informal ones such as hazing and initiation rituals, which are strikingly similar across groups.³⁶ Political training (indoctrination) and the creation of disciplinary regimes to regulate behavior are also critical in this process.³⁷ These are not solely top-down mechanisms (e.g., training, indoctrination) but may also arise from bottom-up dynamics such as peer learning, imitation, and group pressure.

These group dynamics are all observable in the Colombian civil war. As the empirical chapters of this book discuss in detail, Colombian armed parties forged their unique identities in a highly fluid scenario and displayed consistency in the type and nature of attacks they perpetrated over the years. This consistency reveals how the terrorism tactics used in civil war can be clearly traced to organizational preferences derived from parties' unique identities. Arguments linking civilian victimization to breakdowns in discipline—groups pursuing personal vendettas, commanders, or rank-and file soldiers going on violent rampages—or to mere irrationality simply cannot explain the considerable empirical regularity observed in the particular forms of terrorism employed by all Colombian armed parties over twenty-five years.[38]

Defining and Operationalizing Terrorism in Civil War

Terrorism is notoriously difficult to define and is considered by many to be a contested concept. Problems reaching a definitional common ground stem in part from the politicized nature of the term, encapsulated by the old saying that one person's terrorist is another's freedom fighter. Kalliopi Koufa, the former UN Special Rapporteur on Human Rights and Terrorism, underscores that defining the term is difficult given the tendency to conflate actions with value judgments.[39] Beyond the politicization of the term, terrorism poses conceptual challenges stemming from its complex nature and heterogeneity.[40] Acts of terrorism can take many forms: the bombing of an airplane or a mass transit system, a suicide bomb detonated in a crowded marketplace, or a massacre carried out in a rural village. Yet all these acts have two fundamental features in common. First and foremost, they intentionally target noncombatants.[41] Second, they are designed to generate fear and spread a message to an audience beyond the immediate victims of the violence.[42] The goal of terrorism is to intimidate a (target) population or adversaries, be they a specific group (e.g., union members, human rights activists) or a much broader collection of people (e.g., oligarchs, the "bourgeoisie"). Terrorism can also be used to coerce governments to change their policies and to do so it harnesses the power of spectacle.[43] It is often claimed that terrorists do not need many people to die but instead many people to watch.[44] The real objective of terrorists, therefore, are those who witness the attack or its aftermath.

This works draws on the conceptualization advanced by Alex Schmid, Albert Jongman, and Michael Stohl that enjoys broad appeal in the academic community and defines terrorism as

> An anxiety inspiring method of repeated violent action employed by (semi-) clandestine, individual, group or state actors for idiosyncratic, criminal, or political reasons, whereby—in contrast to assassination—the

direct targets of violence are not the main targets. The immediate human victims of violence are generally randomly (targets of opportunity) or selectively (representative or symbolic) targets from a target population and serve as message generators. Threat- and violence-based communication processes between terrorist (organisation), (imperiled) victims, and main targets are used to manipulate the main target audience(s), turning it into a target of terror, a target of demands, or a target of attention, depending on whether intimidation, coercion, or propaganda is primarily sought.[45]

Another complexity in this area of research concerns the divide between state and nonstate terrorism. The terrorism literature has traditionally addressed these questions separately because they present theoretical challenges.[46] Nonstate terrorism, it is generally agreed, involves different types of nonstate actors (nationalist, religious, revolutionary). State terrorism is a more controversial matter that usually involves states' illegal use of force and has received comparatively less attention despite being arguably as important a phenomenon and even more lethal.[47]

Christopher Mitchell and his colleagues define state terrorism as purposeful coercion and violence (or the threat thereof) used with the intent of inducing extreme angst in observers identifying with the target of violence such that they perceive themselves as likely future victims. Fear, they explain, compels viewers to consider changing their behavior according to the perpetrator's wishes.[48] Under state terrorism, terrorist acts are perpetrated by state agents or by private groups acting on orders from or on behalf of a state; this tactic is usually used by authoritarian or totalitarian regimes to terrorize their population and propagate fear among citizens to curb political opposition.[49] An important subcategory of state terrorism is state-sponsored terrorism, whereby a state relies on illicit and clandestine terrorist actions through proxy actors to undermine both domestic and external enemies.[50] Although it seems counterintuitive, democratic regimes might also rely on state terrorism, particularly when confronting domestic insurrection or a foreign attack that rises to the level of armed conflict,[51] as the Colombian case illustrates.

Concerning the differences between state and nongovernmental types of violence, Charles Tilly distinguishes between *state-sponsored* violence (in which the perpetrators are authorized by and benefit from the protection and material support of the state) and *state-incited* violence (in which the offending groups have no direct connection to state power but explicitly claim to be working for state interests).[52] Authors such as Bruce Hoffman also differentiate between *terror,* understood as violence and intimidation by states against their own population, and *terrorism,* understood as violence associated with nonstate groups.[53] This work, however, does not make this distinction and prefers to use the term terrorism regardless of the perpetrator.

Furthermore, and as spelled out at length in chapter 2, this book views terrorism as a distinct form of violence perpetrated in civil wars. It argues that terrorism is a particular subset of civilian targeting, often shocking and inhumane, characterized by a *communicative logic* seeking to instill fear beyond the victims of the attack (e.g., foes, rivals, the public). Such acts may be used to undermine the legitimacy of the state and demonstrate its failure to protect its population (for further discussion of this agitational strategy, see the following section). Conversely, with state terrorism, the state attempts to shore up its legitimacy by showing its determination and capacity to root out challenges to its power.[54] Thus, as discussed in chapter 2, terrorism coexists with other common forms of violence used in civil war that entail civilian victimization such as ethnic cleansing, dispossession, or extermination. These are guided by tangible, concrete purposes and not, as terrorism is, by a communicational logic.

REPERTOIRES OF TERRORISM IN CIVIL WAR

To achieve their objectives, armed groups participating in civil wars rely on diverse forms of violence and terrorism (targeted assassinations, bombings, abductions, massacres, disappearances, torture, forced recruitment, and sexual violence).[55] Drawing on existing typologies of terrorism,[56] this study distinguishes among three broad categories of terrorist attacks perpetrated during civil wars (see table 0.1).

The first category, insurgent, refers to anti-regime terrorism. This modality entails spectacular forms of violence, carried out with a propagandistic intent, by groups seeking to transform the sociopolitical and economic status quo. These groups resort to terrorism to increase the visibility of their cause and, relatedly, to undermine the legitimacy of the state by underscoring its inability to protect the population. Gregory Raymond

TABLE 0.1 Terrorist Attacks in Civil War

Insurgent	Territorial	Pro-regime
Explosive attacks	Massacres	Enforced disappearance
Abduction		Torture

Source: Author's tabulation.

explains how various groups using such terrorist tactics to change sociopolitical and economic conditions pursue different strategic objectives. On the one hand, groups adopt what Raymond calls agitational strategies, that is, committing violent acts that help them increase their stature, advertise their political agenda, and discredit their rivals.[57] Agitation also involves an element of provocation in that it seeks to elicit disproportionate response from the state, a reaction further undermines its legitimacy.[58] On the other hand, groups also adopt coercive strategies, using shocking attacks as leverage to extort authorities; these can reinforce their propagandistic efforts and again undermine the state's legitimacy in public opinion.[59] That these acts challenge state legitimacy explains, in part, why states are reluctant to negotiate with entities using terrorism.[60] The prototypical attacks of this category include abductions and bombings.[61]

In selecting repertoires of terrorism, anarchist, nationalist, religious, and revolutionary groups have weighed the benefits of such coercive and (in particular) agitational strategies.[62] For example, revolutionary theorists such as Carlos Marighella, leader of the Brazilian Action for National Liberation (Ação Libertadora Nacional), whose *Mini Manual of the Urban Guerrilla* became a bible of sorts among leftist groups in the 1970s, explicitly recommends tactics with high propagandistic value such as the abduction of notable targets, explosive attacks against symbols of power, magnicides, and public executions.[63] He claims that such actions can destroy a state's aura of invincibility and ignite a massive popular uprising. These tactics became the hallmark of most radical leftist organizations in Latin America, including Colombian insurgent groups.[64]

A second category, pro-regime terrorism, refers to actions seeking to buttress—not undermine—the status quo by enhancing the state's coercive capacity. This practice is linked to state terrorism, which, as indicated, involves state agents seeking to spread fear among citizens to curb political opposition.[65] With pro-regime terrorism, the main objective is to inhibit the ability of civil society to carry out collective action and confront the existing government and its power. A vast literature demonstrates how states, in particular authoritarian and totalitarian regimes, resort to extreme terrorist measures such as torture, enforced disappearance, or summary executions in their zeal to suppress potential threats to their power.[66] These tactics have been widely employed in so-called dirty wars by dictatorial and at times democratic regimes enmeshed in civil wars and also by extralegal groups (death squads, paramilitaries, vigilantes) fighting alongside states against those challenging the governmental monopoly of force.[67] To the extent that these acts of violence can be attributed to the state and its allies, the fear they generate reinforces the perception that the state is firmly in control.

The third category, territorial terrorism, refers to actions by parties for military purposes to exert territorial control. As the literature has established, the targeting of civilians, whether selective or indiscriminate, is generally to subvert and possibly destroy the production and logistical capacities of the enemy and deter potential civilian collaboration.[68] Critically, such acts deny enemies and challengers the needed resources and information to maintain military control over contested zones during an armed conflict.[69] Such territorial terrorism displays a different logic than insurgent and pro-regime terrorism does. As a tactic, its message is more restricted and calibrated to a smaller audience within a restricted geographic area: it merely seeks to convey to the population that the state or nonstate actor is in control and communicate the risks involved in challenging that actor.[70] Specifically, state and nonstate actors alike have commonly used massacres to cement territorial control.[71]

It is critical to emphasize that these conceptual categorizations describe ideal types: on-the-ground tactics cannot always be classified so neatly, and terrorist practices often involve multiple goals.[72] For example, the use of abductions, as noted, has been linked to agitational motivations on the part of insurgent groups, yet this practice is often also used for financial purposes.[73] Furthermore, multiple groups can each practice similar tactics. Disappearances and torture, though generally linked to state repressive strategies, are also undertaken by insurgent and criminal groups. However, ample evidence presented in the following chapters shows that certain practices are more prevalent among certain parties, depending on their organizational identity and goals. Relatedly, armed groups can adapt their practices to their distinct identity to distinguish themselves from rivals and enemies, as the use of abductions by paramilitaries and state agents illustrates (i.e., they do not use it for agitational purposes, but to coerce their enemies).[74]

These distinct categories of terrorism prove useful while considering the modus operandi of Colombian armed parties. When expanding their operations throughout the late 1970s—a period in which they were heavily influenced by revolutionary doctrines in vogue—the FARC, the ELN, and other Colombian guerrillas incorporated bombings, abductions, and summary executions into their repertoires of terrorism. Such attacks, characterized by an agitational and coercive logic, became hallmarks of their presence in an area and powerful instruments for disseminating their revolutionary goals. In the case of the FARC, during the Seventh National Conference in 1982, a watershed moment in the organization's history, its leaders explicitly incorporated a mix of military and agitational terrorist tactics into its strategy.[75] The ELN, similarly, adopted kidnapping as a central tactic, later adding summary executions and explosive attacks. These acts (especially kidnappings) served agitational purposes by disrupting the normal functioning of local economies.[76]

Paramilitary organizations, conversely, resorted to pro-regime forms of terrorism such as torture and disappearance to distinguish themselves and counter the actions of guerrillas. These groups also systematically used territorial forms of terrorism (in particular massacres), enforced disappearances, and summary executions to eradicate guerrilla presence in several important productive sites such as the Magdalena medio region. Paramilitary groups counted on the support of the CSSF, which embraced similar tactics, provided logistical support and cover for paramilitary terrorism, and—most crucially—furnished military training in counterinsurgency; this training directly incorporated quid pro quo terrorist tactics, many of which involved staging graphic displays of violence.[77] Throughout the conflict, other groups adapted their own practices to these developments. With the irruption of paramilitary groups in the late 1970s and their subsequent strengthening in the mid-1990s, guerrillas (especially the FARC) added territorial terrorism (e.g., summary executions and massacres) to their repertoires. Their massacres followed a strategic logic informed by military necessity as parties began fighting for the control over populations in several strategic areas. Paramilitaries, meanwhile, incorporated abductions into their repertoires, which, as we have seen, were originally informed by an insurgent logic. Yet these groups did not use abductions for agitational purposes but instead much more discreetly, targeting the families of guerrilla members, and never for financial purposes.

In sum, Colombian armed parties selected terrorist tactics that represented their organizational identities and used them to announce or solidify their presence in a given area. Guerrilla groups displayed a preference for insurgent terrorism such as abductions and bombings, seeking to erode the legitimacy of the state by exposing its inability to protect ordinary citizens. As such, these tactics displayed an agitational or anti-status quo character. The terrorism repertoires used by the CSSF and paramilitaries displayed a clear preference for pro-regime attacks. They relied on disappearance, torture, and especially territorial terrorism such as massacres and summary executions as part of a counterinsurgency strategy of shoring up the state's legitimacy by demonstrating its capacity to control, even if violently, the rise of armed challengers. As the war raged on, however, groups incorporated new modalities, adapting them to their organizational preferences in accordance with their group identities.

Research Design

This exploration of repertoires of terrorism in the Colombian civil war is part of a long intellectual tradition seeking to understand frequent manifestations of political violence in what is arguably one of the most sophisticated and cultured societies in Latin America.[78] This book investigates one specific angle of violence, terrorism, a practice long considered one of the most significant, and regrettable, expressions of human brutality. The Colombian civil war is an exceptional laboratory for investigating this matter. Even though this conflict has been marked by terrorist attacks devised to instill fear in the population, little is known about the nature, logic, and manifestations of this tactic, notwithstanding the vast production of work on the war. Indeed, only a handful of studies have directly explored terrorism in the Colombian civil war.[79]

Colombia represents a fascinating case study for exploring the relationship between terrorism and civil war.[80] Several points warrant this assertion. First, dehumanizing practices, including terrorism, have been a particularly salient aspect of this conflict. Colombians have withstood decades of systematic and widespread human rights violations, including massacres, abductions, executions, bombings, sexual violence, torture, enforced disappearance, forced recruitment, and population uprooting. Many of these abuses were part of a deliberate terroristic strategy, as underscored in the monumental work of the Colombian Truth Commission (Comisión para el Esclarecimiento de la Verdad la Convivencia y la No Repetición).[81] Colombia, indeed, boasts one of the highest rates of terrorism in the world, as the data compiled for this book and many other sources shows.[82]

Second, the long duration of the conflict, fifty-eight years and counting, allows researchers to analyze the evolution of this practice synchronically over several decades, specifically, how armed parties adapted this tactic throughout the civil war's shifting dynamics. Third, its complex configuration permits scholars to investigate variations in the use of terrorism among diverse actors. Colombia is a unique context in this regard given the variety of armed groups, each with its own ideological orientation, ranging from guerrillas (Marxist, Cuban-inspired, Maoist) to paramilitary groups with dissimilar origins and from diverse units within the state security forces. To the extent that state and nonstate parties have systematically relied on terrorism during civil wars, Colombia also allows researchers to explore both sets of actors and thus avoid the common tendency to study state and nonstate terrorism in isolation. Fourth, and relatedly, Colombian human rights organizations have painstakingly chronicled the abuses perpetrated during the conflict, providing an invaluable source of information.[83] Although certainly not perfect,[84] these data are more case specific (and accurate) than data from existing large databases, such as the Global Terrorism Database, which, though informative, are not attuned to national contexts.[85]

Finally, the Colombian case study is particularly compelling on normative grounds. The country's civil war has had a lasting and pernicious impact on society. According to the recently published final report of the Truth Commission on the conflict, 450,000 people have lost their lives, 121,000 have disappeared, and up to 20 percent have been victims of IHL breaches. As many as six million people have been forcibly displaced from their communities, condemned to destitution and a liminal life.[86] As expected, the conflict has had disastrous effects on the country's social fabric as well, sowing the seeds of distrust in communities afflicted by violence, giving rise to profound cynicism throughout society, and vastly increasing levels of political polarization.[87]

By considering the central question—how is terrorism employed in civil wars? —this investigation aims to develop novel hypotheses regarding the importance of organizational features, in particular identity, in the production of terrorism during civil war. In his discussion on case studies, Jack Levy makes a distinction between works that generate hypotheses and those that test or apply them.[88] The hypotheses generated by this study, in turn, could be tested by scholars in other relevant cases. Moreover, to the extent that answering its central question requires looking at armed parties' behavior and the evolution of terrorist practices in close detail, the work also tests existing hypotheses developed by the comparative politics literature about terrorism used for strategic purposes.

Studies on the use of dehumanizing techniques during civil war, such as terrorism, pose important methodological challenges. Because parties and individuals are reluctant to admit that they use terrorism—a tactic that draws widespread condemnation—gathering evidence on the phenomenon and its logic is understandingly complex.[89] Fortunately, as indicated, researchers and human rights organizations have for more than thirty years done commendable work chronicling human rights abuses and recording the testimonies of victims in Colombia. This information has proven invaluable for this and many other studies of violence.[90]

This study uses mostly qualitative methods and relies on data compiled over more than a decade. Most of the information collected for the book is the result of extensive field research in Bogotá but also during short trips to the departments of Antioquia, Cundinamarca, Meta, and Norte de Santander. Evidence is drawn from several sources. These include semistructured interviews with relevant players including human rights activists, humanitarian workers, diplomats, journalists, representatives of international organizations, and prosecutors, as well as scholars and other experts on armed conflict.[91] Information was also gathered during efforts to establish a historical memory of the conflict (e.g., workshops, roundtables, encounters with victims) in which perpetrators reflected on their experiences and volunteered information about their deeds.[92] Their accounts revealed important information about groups' internal dealings, discussions, modi operandi, and strategies. Also critical were exchanges with humanitarian workers including delegates of the International Committee of the Red Cross, protection officers of the UN High Commissioner for Refugees and the Office of the United Nations High Commissioner for Human Rights, and international and local nongovernmental organizations working in the field. In their efforts to assist and protect victims, humanitarian workers had regular interactions with armed parties. As a result, they acquired a firsthand knowledge and understanding of armed groups' practices and rationales. Given the sensitive nature of many of these testimonies, several interviewees requested confidentiality.

The investigation is complemented by extensive archival research and an exhaustive treatment of other sources. It looks at judicial records, many containing critical testimonies from perpetrators of terrorism acts who, under oath, confessed to their deeds and furnished vital insights regarding their rationale and motives. The work reviewed dozens of publicly available case files, judicial rulings, and prosecutors' investigations against armed parties' commanders, including cases brought before the Justice and Peace (Justicia y Paz) proceedings and the recently created Special Tribunal for Peace (Tribunal Especial para la Paz).[93] Judicial records also include cases brought before regional human rights mechanisms such as the Inter-American System on Human Rights (Court and Commission). Furthermore, this book makes abundant use of secondary sources, including testimonies of protagonists compiled by the National Center of Historic Memory (Centro Nacional de Memoria Histórica), memoirs by and interviews with participants in the conflict over the years, and internal organizational documents—memoranda, letters, and communiqués detailing internal discussions—many of which are documented in biographies and historical accounts in Spanish.

Additionally, to trace the evolution of terrorism empirically, I have built an extensive database on terrorist actions. The work systematically reports data on four key indicators of terrorism: massacres, summary executions, abductions, and bombings of civilian targets.[94] Data are compiled from two collections of human rights data: Noche y Niebla and Justicia y Paz. Noche y Niebla is generally considered the most expansive and reliable database on political violence in Colombia.[95] Published by the Research Center for Investigation and Popular Education (Centro de Investigación y Educación Popular, or CINEP) and drawing from the journalism of nineteen newspapers with national or regional coverage, accounts from diverse nongovernmental organizations, official reports released by the Colombian state, testimonies of victims and on-site visits, Noche y Niebla tracks all reported incidents of political violence each year.[96] From 1988 to 1995, reports were also collected by Justicia y Paz. This group uses a similar methodology, drawing on reporting from ten national or regional newspapers and the output of a variety of nongovernmental organizations.[97]

In addition, in its discussion of the latest phase of the Colombian civil war following the Peace Accord with FARC in 2016, the book also presents some preliminary reflections on the case of Mexico (see chapter 7). Mexico is used here as a shadow case to complement the book's discussion on whether armed parties' repertoires of terrorism can also be traced to organizational identities during so-called criminal wars.[98] Besides secondary sources such as databases on violence and human rights reports, I draw on information collected during three short field trips to Mexico City and Michoacán. While in Mexico, I conducted fifteen semi-structured interviews with relevant players including human rights activists, humanitarian workers, journalists, representatives of international organizations, and mayors, as well as scholars and other experts on armed conflict.

Road Map

The book develops its argument over eight chapters. Chapter 1 offers a theoretical explanation of the use of terrorism in civil war. It underlines that terrorism constitutes a subset of civilian targeting characterized by a strategic logic seeking to instill fear in adversaries and the general population. It thus differs from other forms of civilian targeting characterized by a tangible, noncommunicational logic. Based on this contextual analysis, the chapter subsequently offers a theoretical analysis to explain what accounts for armed parties' diverse repertoires of terrorism. It posits that variation results from groups' organizational identities, which stem from their history, ideological predilections and doctrinarian interpretations, and leadership, identities that are later socialized within the organizations through institutional mechanisms. This chapter also addresses how the evolution of a group's organizational identity might impact its repertoires of terrorism.

Chapter 2 presents a brief historical account of the evolution of the conflict, discussing its nature, configuration, and progression. It traces the development of guerrilla and paramilitary groups and outlines their origin, main goals, and strategies as well as the state policies informing the behavior of government security forces. This overview seeks to familiarize readers with critical historical aspects useful for understanding the main argument of the book and its empirical chapters.

Chapters 3 and 4 cover the evolving terrorist practices of Colombian guerrilla groups. The first centers on the FARC, the strongest and most consequential of the two insurgent organizations participating in the civil war. The chapter posits that the FARC's terrorism practices evolved over time, driven by a combination of ideational preferences derived from the group identity as a peasant revolutionary organization guided by the charismatic leadership of Manuel Marulanda and other prominent commanders. The FARC's terrorism tactics followed a clear progression: influenced by revolutionary ideologies in vogue in the 1970s such as urban guerrilla warfare, the group gradually began to incorporate terrorist tactics such as abductions into its repertoire. The importation of revolutionary doctrines from other Latin American groups and the Viet Cong was critical in reshaping the FARC's overall strategies, in particular the commitment to using all forms of struggle to achieve their revolutionary objectives. The FARC incorporated terrorism as an agitational tool, seeking to erode the legitimacy of the state by exposing its inability to protect ordinary citizens. The group's ideology fostered the idea among its fighters and leaders that, though extreme, terrorism was a legitimate weapon to be deployed in the struggle. The group's leaders justified the deliberate victimization of certain civilians—considered enemies of the people either in terms of their class (landowners, executives) or because they opposed the group (informants, bureaucrats)—as an inevitable outcome of class warfare. As to the forms of terrorism used, the FARC adopted an anti–status quo strategy and embraced bombings and abductions to demonstrate state weakness. As paramilitary groups multiplied and subsequently strengthened in the mid-1990s, the FARC embraced new tactics that followed a strategic logic informed by military necessity (massacres and executions) as it began to engage in territorial disputes with right-wing rivals.

As for the ELN, chapter 4 shows how the group also deliberately resorted to terrorism with the objective of spreading fear among the population, undermining state power, and pressuring state representatives and civil society to yield to its demands. Like the FARC's, the group's terrorist practices evolved over time, initially fueled by ideological preferences and later, responding to changing military conditions in the theater of war. Influenced by revolutionary doctrines imported from urban revolutionary groups in the 1970s, the ELN, like the FARC, incorporated agitational forms of terror such as abductions into its repertoires of action. Also just like their FARC competitors, ELN commanders (e.g., Gabino), played a key role in selecting repertoires of insurgent terrorism, justifying targeting civilians in the name of class warfare. The chapter shows that the ELN's reliance on terrorism displays some relevant differences with the FARC's. Despite important organizational similarities and ideological proximity, the ELN perpetrated fewer attacks than the FARC; the former specialized in abductions and executions, relying less on bombings and especially massacres. These differences, it is posited, arise from the ELN's unique ideology that amalgamates Marxism, a nationalistic, anti-imperialist discourse, and a Christian outlook toward the poor. This last element derived from the influence that progressive clergymen commanders exercised within the group, an influence predicated on liberation theology. This ethos, I argue, shaped the group's position on the proper use of violence and terror. In this regard, its violent methods and harsh rhetoric notwithstanding, the group did exercise restraint, limiting some of the most egregious forms of violence (massacres, bombings, targeting civilians). Last, the chapter shows how the irruption of paramilitary groups in the 1980s forced the ELN to vary its tactics when forced to dispute and defend territory.

Chapter 5 looks at the terrorist practices of paramilitary organizations, which were behind the greatest number of attacks during the war. The chapter argues that, like guerrilla groups, paramilitary organizations resorted to terrorism as a strategic device to advance their military and political objectives. Paramilitary groups deployed this tactic to decimate guerrillas' civilian support system, calibrating their terrorist tactics in accordance with changing conditions in the theater of war. Although the logic behind the use of terrorism (to advance political and military goals) resembles that of guerrilla groups, the nature of the terrorism reveals important differences. Paramilitaries' terrorism blueprint derives from their identity as pro-regime groups and a counterinsurgency doctrine fueled by anticommunist ideology. Influenced by urban counterrevolutionary doctrines developed in France and the United States, paramilitaries mastered certain terrorist repertoires characterized by a pro–status quo logic and justified by ultraconservative views that sought to maintain the existing political and social order. The shape of paramilitary terrorism was also informed by a criminal ethos stemming from the incorporation of drug and emerald traffickers, who rose within the ranks of the organizations to become some of their most influential commanders. This criminal ethos made paramilitaries prone to predatory behavior and to overkill tactics to maximize fear among rivals and punish those who stood in their way. Like their guerrilla rivals, paramilitaries justified terrorism as a legitimate way of maintaining social order and averting a collapse of the Colombian state. Also just like guerrillas, paramilitary groups rationalized terrorism as necessary if extreme—in their case, an inevitable outcome of counterinsurgency warfare. Targets included people considered enemies of the state who aided and abetted guerrillas (e.g., sympathizers, informants, so-called useful fools) and who displayed progressive political views (e.g., leftist organizers, union and grassroots leaders, intellectuals).

Chapter 6 traces the use of terrorism by the CSSF, showing how diverse parts of the Colombian security apparatus also relied extensively and systematically on terrorism tactics including torture, enforced disappearance, forced displacement, targeted assassinations, abductions, and massacres. The CSSF's terror blueprint differs in several ways from that of nonstate actors in the civil war, however. The chapter argues that the CSSF resorted to terrorism as a strategy to advance military and political objectives while confronting insurgent groups. Like their paramilitary allies, the CSSF, especially the Colombian Army, used terrorism to deprive guerrillas of civilian support, calibrating attacks in accordance with changing conditions in the conflict (i.e., guerrilla offensives, truces, and tactical retreats). State terrorism resembled paramilitary terrorism in that it was directed most prominently against guerrillas' civilian support structures in territories either controlled by or disputed with insurgent groups. Yet, in contrast to many Latin American countries where states used terrorism against the general population in times of peace, in Colombia state terrorism was for the most part employed during counterinsurgency operations. The democratic nature of Colombia's regime partially constrained CSSF actions, preventing more widespread excesses and creating perverse incentives for the externalization of counterinsurgency operations to paramilitary groups. State terrorism, it is also posited, was not uniform across the country, some units within the CSSF being more predisposed to adopt this strategy. The chapter describes how state terrorism resembles the pro-status quo logic of paramilitary groups, inspired by a harsh ideological view that regarded insurgency—and the socialist ideas inspiring it—as an existential threat to the country. Such a view stemmed from the CSSF's self-promoted image as the protectors of the nation and was heavily influenced by the doctrine of national security and its internal enemy thesis in vogue during the Cold War. State forces, which enjoyed significant degrees of autonomy, justified terrorism as a legitimate means to avert a national tragedy and rationalized this tactic as a necessary, inevitable outcome of counterinsurgency warfare.

Chapter 7 presents a brief reflection on the use of terrorism in the latest phase of the Colombian civil war following the 2016 Peace Agreements between the Colombian government and the FARC. The chapter examines whether armed parties' repertoires of terrorism have changed in this new period of the conflict marked by the growing role of criminality. It assesses whether changes in parties' identities have affected their repertoires of terrorism, engaging with the recent literature on criminal politics to do so. The chapter argues that Colombia remains in a situation of internal armed conflict that can be thought of as a criminal war. Insofar as repertoires of terrorism are concerned, evidence shows that armed parties' tactics have remained stable despite a notable decrease in the intensity of violence; this data point to a surprising degree of organizational inertia. The analysis is complemented by considering Mexico as a shadow case and discussing how terrorism arises in new settings characterized by widespread criminal violence, which is increasingly common throughout Latin America. This preliminary consideration of the Mexican case supports the finding that armed parties display important differences in their repertoires of terrorism because of their distinct organizational identities in criminal wars.

The final chapter—the conclusion—discusses the implications of the book's main empirical findings for studies on civil war, terrorism, and criminality. It underscores the need to continue working on cross-fertilizing these areas with a view to refining our understanding of diverse violent strategies used during civil war. It also argues that the book's findings will be helpful in considering new forms of violence, in particular those deployed in criminal wars. The concluding section also discusses this study's implications in the realm of public policy.

All in all, these chapters show the critical role that organizational identity plays in producing and rationalizing violence, underlining that its manifestations, including terrorism, are by no means uniform. This insight challenges extant explanations attributing armed groups' behavior exclusively to rational motivations. Such a view, which offers convenient parsimony, tends to homogenize the behavior of actors and to disregard critical historical, ideational, and human factors (i.e., leadership) that clearly differentiate groups from one another. Beyond accounting for diverse forms of armed parties' repertoires of violence, organizational identity offers important clues for understanding the motivations of armed groups, thus opening a fruitful avenue for devising interventions to protect populations affected by war.

1

Theorizing Armed Parties' Repertoires of Terrorism During Civil Wars

This chapter offers a theoretical explanation of the use of terrorism in civil war. It underscores that terrorism constitutes a subset of civilian targeting characterized by a strategic logic seeking to instill fear in adversaries and the general population through violence. It thus differs from other forms of civilian targeting characterized by a tangible, noncommunicational logic (e.g., ethnic cleansing, dispossession, or genocide). Subsequently, and based on this contextual groundwork, the chapter offers a theoretical discussion regarding variations in armed parties' repertoires of terrorism. It argues that these differences result from organizational identities, defined as the central, enduring, and distinctive organizational attributes distinguishing warring parties. Organizational identity reflects an organization's history, ideological predilections and doctrinarian interpretations, and leadership. Leaders play a critical role in developing repertoires of terrorism as they select and promote tactics that derive from and conform with the group's singular identity (revolutionary, religious, nationalist, pro–status quo, and so forth). Such repertoires are distinctive markers of a group's presence and play an important communicational role distinguishing it from its enemies and rivals. These repertoires are socialized through institutional mechanisms such as training, indoctrination, and internal disciplinary mechanisms. Rather than being fixed, repertoires of terrorism evolve over time as parties change or adapt their tactics to the ever-changing conditions in civil wars and embrace some of their rivals' tactics.

The discussion proceeds as follows. The first section discusses the relationship between civil war and terrorism, examining their similarities, differences, and overlaps. In so doing, it probes whether it is analytically possible to distinguish between civilian targeting and terrorism. Building on this discussion, the chapter subsequently discusses how organizational identity accounts for armed groups' different repertoires of terrorism. Following a brief conceptual discussion of organizational identity, the chapter next elaborates on how this notion informs the development of singular terrorist repertoires and their evolution in time. The chapter concludes with some brief reflections.

Conceptualizing Terrorism During Civil War

Although knowledge on the dynamics of violence in civil war has advanced significantly in the last two decades, researchers have only recently begun to explore the use of terrorism in these contexts.[1] The civil war literature, whose yield is abundant,[2] has for the most part omitted terrorism, preferring instead on a broader category, civilian targeting. Terrorism studies, for their part, have concentrated on mostly peaceful contexts, seldom looking into how this practice arises in situations of armed conflict.[3] Partly because of these gaps in the literature, the relationship between civil war and terrorism remains fuzzy and often misunderstood.

A consensus in the literature is that, though interconnected, civil war and terrorism are different forms of violence. Nicholas Sambanis thus claims that civil war and terrorism are adjacent, interlinked phenomena often arising together and sharing the same root causes (i.e., territorial disputes, ideological, religious, and self-determination struggles).[4] Civil wars, moreover, provide ideal conditions for terrorism to emerge beyond igniting such an armed conflict, terrorism can prolong or derail attempts to end it.[5]

In unpacking the relationship between the two forms of violence, Stathis Kalyvas stresses that civil war and terrorism differ significantly in terms of their nature, logic, and purpose.[6] As to their nature, civil wars—and wars in general—refer to situations in which parties, unable or unwilling to find a negotiated or nonviolent solution to their differences, turn to violence to force their will on their adversaries.[7] Extant definitions on civil war conceptualize it as a conflict whose sources are normally political or territorial, one in which organized parties under a responsible command clash and where violence exceeds a given threshold of battle-related deaths over a specified period.[8] As for terrorism, as discussed in the introduction, it is best conceptualized as a violent tactic in which armed parties intentionally attack civilians to generate fear in a target audience to further their goals.[9] Two crucial attributes characterize terrorism: purposeful harming of innocent civilians and deliberately using extreme, dramatic violence against defenseless targets to attract publicity.[10]

The logic behind these two forms of violence also differs. To the extent that wars involve significant levels of organization, legal and international relations scholars have long argued that wars themselves can be conceptualized as institutions. In his seminal work, Hedley Bull conceptualizes war as one of the constitutive institutions of international society (alongside other foundational elements such as the balance of power, law, diplomacy, and the great powers) and argues that war contributes to the emergence of a particular order.[11] Work on civil war also advances the idea that such conflicts are governed by a certain order. Kalyvas posits that the logic of violence in civil war follows a graspable logic; Ana Arjona in her remarkable account of the Colombian civil war shows how, far from being chaotic, civil wars display a surprising degree of order in which people have clear expectations of what may occur, what actions are or are not permissible, and how to go about their daily lives during the conflict.[12] In a similar vein, Paul Staniland illustrates how civil war contexts shape state-rebel relations to produce a wartime order that differs from the peacetime one.[13]

The idea that war produces a certain order informs the emergence of norms and rules regulating the use of force in such contexts. Modern warfare is regulated by international humanitarian law (IHL), a set of rules codified in treaties and conventions dating back to the nineteenth century striving to ameliorate the most pernicious effects of armed conflicts.[14] IHL, which is partly based on the principles of distinction and proportionality, aims to protect civilians and the *hors de combat* (i.e., combatants not taking part in hostilities, such as wounded and shipwrecked soldiers and prisoners of war) who enjoy immunity.[15] IHL also regulates hostilities with a view to curbing warfare's most cruel and inhumane methods.[16] Even though most civil wars are characterized by systematic and widespread violations of IHL, the expectation is that nonetheless parties will abide by them.[17] Violators may be held accountable for their crimes in domestic and international arenas such as the International Criminal Court. Terrorism, conversely, blatantly rejects existing humanitarian rules and regulations: civilians, considered protected people under IHL, are deliberately targeted to generate fear in the society at large. Terrorism thus entails the premeditated violation of the principle of distinction, one of IHL's cardinal rules, and therefore lies outside the purview of civilized, socially constructed norms of behavior.[18]

Most significantly, the primary purpose of civil war and of terrorism also differs. In civil wars, parties use violence to militarily defeat an adversary, either through conventional warfare, whereby parties with similar military capabilities fight each other in open battles, or through unconventional or irregular warfare, where lightly armed groups (e.g., guerrillas) confront a stronger party—normally a state—via hit-and-run operations against military targets.[19] In either case, civil wars entail organized armed entities militarily confronting their adversaries.[20] Thus the nature of violence tends to be direct in that parties attempt to overwhelm their enemies and impose their will on them.[21] The logic behind terrorism is manifestly different: it is symbolic and communicational rather than military.[22] Attacks are used as a communicational device to spread fear in the population or coerce an adversary, or both.[23] Put differently, terrorism targets civilians to intimidate and frighten other people and thus can be seen as an indirect use of violence.[24] To the extent that it deliberately avoids open military engagement, terrorism is better conceptualized as a guerrilla-like form of warfare though guerrilla warfare explicitly uses force only against military targets.[25]

Distinguishing Between Forms of Violence During Civil War

A second, relevant analytical question concerns whether terrorism constitutes a distinct form of violence within the broad category of civilian targeting. During civil wars, civilian targeting often takes multiple forms, including lethal (e.g., mass killings, abductions, ethnic cleansing, terrorism, and genocide) and nonlethal (e.g., rape, forced recruitment) violence. Scholars are divided over whether terrorism constitutes a distinctive form of violence used in civil war.

Most work on civil wars within the comparative politics literature makes no real distinction between terrorism and other forms of violence used against civilians in these contexts. For example, in his analysis, Kalyvas argues that although violence (including civilian targeting) exercised in civil war should be distinguished from terrorism, which he describes as a form of violence used by weaker parties and restricted to the operation of nonstate actors in times of peace, he does not agree that terrorism should constitute its own category.[26] His characterization thus subsumes terrorism within a broader category of civilian targeting.[27] Some terrorism studies research, however, attempts to distinguish between different forms of violence against civilians, including terrorism. Luis de la Calle and Ignacio Sánchez Cuenca, for example, argue that terrorism in civil war occurs when nonstate parties attack civilians in areas they do not physically control. These groups practice spectacular acts of violence (e.g., bombings) to increase their visibility and compensate for their incapacity to project coercive power. Conversely, in areas where they have more power and control, nonstate actors opt for military actions (ambushes, villages seizures, small battles).[28]

Recent work has explored this question further and advanced the view that civilian targeting during civil war constitutes a specific, multipronged strategy deployed by armed parties. These studies conceptualize terrorism as a distinct form of civilian targeting.[29] In sync with such a view, this work posits that to the extent that terrorism is characterized by unique attributes, it is best conceptualized as a subcategory of civilian targeting. The question thus arises: how exactly does terrorism differ from other forms of civilian targeting?

As indicated in the previous section, the logic behind terrorism essentially entails using violence as a symbolic way to advance political or criminal motives. The critical element distinguishing terrorism from other forms of violence is its communicational purpose. Reflecting such a stance, Erica Chenoweth distinguishes terrorism from civilian targeting by arguing that the former is "characterized by its randomness and its attempt to convey a political message beyond the targets themselves."[30] Agreeing with such a view, most studies commonly underscore that terrorism is best conceptualized as a tactic whose principal goal is to spread fear in an audience to produce a desired outcome.[31]

Distinguishing terrorism from other forms of civilian targeting is difficult because all share a critical feature: the inhumane, purposeful targeting of defenseless people. I argue, however, that it is precisely the nature of this targeting that sets terrorism apart: terrorism deliberately targets civilians because such blatant disregard of basic principles of humanity maximizes fear. If innocent people (children, the elderly, and so forth) can be targets, then everyone is at risk. In other words, as Eugen Victor Walter reminds us, the logic of terroristic violence is indirect: groups use terrorism to promote a cause, not to harm individuals per se.[32] Unlike other forms of civilian targeting, the harm done to the victims is ultimately less important that what the violent act symbolizes. Discussing this matter, Jessica Stanton insightfully points out that what differentiates terrorism from other forms of violence is precisely the target audience, which she defines as an oppositional third party.[33] The logic is simple: armed groups target civilians in shocking ways to force a third party to make concessions and ultimately further their political goals. Terrorism is also used to induce civilians to behave in accordance with armed parties' objectives. Scorched earth policies, whereby armed parties cleanse territories of purported opponents or undesired populations, exemplifies this mechanism. Here again, violence is used indirectly: victims are used as instruments to compel others to abandon zones groups seek to control.[34]

Conversely, many other forms of intentional civilian violence carried out during civil wars entail concrete goals, such as dispossessing people for economic gain. David Keen's work has shown how atrocities during civil wars can often be explained by what he calls the "economic functions of violence."[35] Keen persuasively shows how across the most diverse conflicts, armed parties (leaders or followers) have victimized civilians for economic gain. Here, the logic of violence is not symbolic or communicational but tangible. Another example of civilian targeting with concrete objectives is mass violence, defined as the large-scale intentional killing of civilians, including cases of genocide.[36] In mass killings, parties deliberately attack civilians with the objective of exterminating them for a variety of reasons (e.g., religious, ethnic, cultural, social, economic, or political). Extremist worldviews reduce victims to one "oppositional" identity (e.g., Tutsi in Rwanda, bourgeois in Cambodia, Armenian in Turkey, Jew in

Nazi Germany, Indigenous in Guatemala) and are used to justify violent behavior.[37] Yet, regardless of the motives behind the targeting, this violence has a clear goal: extermination.

Admittedly, the line dividing different forms of violence against civilians is often hard to discern. One problem is that violent actions seeking to dispossess or eliminate people naturally generate fear, regardless of whether this was the offending party's original intent. Indeed, human rights advocates and victims rightly point out that from the victims' standpoint, the difference is minimal between being targeted for concrete or for symbolic purposes. For researchers and policymakers, however, the distinction is important because it helps sharpen our understanding of the logic and modi operandi of groups in armed conflicts.[38]

Variation in Armed Parties' Repertoires of Terrorism

Having clarified some important conceptual points concerning the use of terrorism in civil war, this section discusses the main theoretical puzzle inspiring this work. As usually happens when researching a complex topic, the question arose inductively. While conducting field work in Bogotá and Villavicencio, the gateway to the stunning oriental llanos (lowlands), I spoke with several humanitarian workers with vast experience on the ground. Their accounts coincided in suggesting that it was possible to identify the party behind an attack by the type of violence deployed. After the long, painstaking work of compiling and analyzing a database on the use of terrorism in Colombia, I confirmed this anecdotal observation, because the data revealed that parties do indeed develop their own distinct violent blueprints, to borrow the apt coinage of Francisco Gutiérrez-Sanín and Elisabeth Wood.[39]

This puzzling variation in the repertoires of terrorism has not been addressed satisfactorily in the specialized literature. As is often the case, this shortcoming derives in part from analytical biases, blind spots, and a notable lack of cross-fertilization across literatures covering related topics. Work in comparative politics has advanced a series of hypotheses regarding why parties target civilians during civil wars.[40] Kalyvas's seminal study, which sought to engage with studies on ethnic conflict and refute Mary Kaldor's influential but controversial new wars thesis, is a key reference point for this discussion.[41] Kalyvas develops an argument based on a military logic. Shifting the parameters from macro factors to the micro foundations of violence, Kalyvas argues that civilian targeting, whether selective or indiscriminate, is driven by territorial considerations resulting from a party's rational decision to reduce its vulnerability in the extremely fluid and uncertain context of civil war. Violence against civilians follows the logic of contestation and not only subverts and possibly destroys the production and logistical capacity of the enemy but also deters potential civilian collaboration and information sharing with the enemy.[42]

Although Kalyvas and others taking a similar line offer important insights into the logic informing civilian targeting, in their zeal to develop an overarching theory based on rationality, they assume that parties' behavior is homogeneous.[43] Yet evidence from many conflicts around the world and Latin America demonstrates that this is hardly the case. In Peru, for example, the repertoires of violence of the different parties involved (the Shining Path, the Tupac Amaru Revolutionary Movement, the civilian self-defense forces, and security forces) varied significantly.[44] Furthermore, as I discuss in chapter 7, variation in repertoires of terrorism also arise in criminal wars.[45] One example is the ongoing conflict in Mexico—these repertoires vary not only among different categories of armed groups (drug trafficking organizations, self-defense forces, and security forces) but even within the same types of groups.[46]

Seeking to complement existing accounts, a stream of investigations within comparative politics into civil war have advanced explanations on civilian targeting based on organizational features. These works have covered discipline and principal-agent problems resulting from the absence of enforcement mechanisms, recruitment tools, and lower-ranking personnel's desire for personal gain or revenge.[47] Although these studies have been gaining ground and broadening our understanding of victimization patterns, most have also assumed a strictly rational logic that discounts ideational factors and assumed that, *ceteris paribus*, parties behave uniformly.[48] Jeremy Weinstein's influential study on the organizational patterns of civilian victimization—in which he argues that such targeting is related to the social endowments held by recruits prior to joining an organization—reflects this approach.[49]

Another important body of work addressing civilian targeting looks at the informal institutional and arrangements in the wartime social order.

These studies center their attention on unpacking the nature and development of informal arrangements and institutions, but touch on civilian victimization only tangentially. As alluded to earlier, they posit that different wartime orders are more prone to violence than others depending on the parties' resources, links with the population, and strategies (i.e., a predisposition to fight or cooperate).[50]

Some recent work within this literature has addressed armed parties' variation in the use of violence more directly. Two strands stand out. First is scholarship looking at whether parties rely on direct or indiscriminate violence, such as Laia Balcells' study on the Spanish civil war.[51] Next are studies investigating what factors produce restraint. One of these is Jessica Stanton's comparative analysis of armed parties' behavior.[52] Another is Hyeran Jo's study on rebel compliance.[53] Although helpful, these works indirectly address the question at hand: Balcells concentrates on one overarching pattern (direct versus indiscriminate attacks), whereas Stanton and Jo investigate restraint rather than specific repertoires of violence and terrorism. Amalia Green's excellent study of the Salvadoran civil war, which looks specifically at repertoires of violence, is probably closest in spirit to this current work.[54] However, her analysis is much broader, in that it incorporates a broader range of attacks (lethal and nonlethal), does not distinguish between terrorism and more general forms of civilian victimization, and offers a different argument (see following).

For their part, terrorism studies offer some useful medium-range theories to account for civilian victimization. There are two predominant explanations within this literature: ideology and rational-strategic thinking. Classical work in this area underscores the role of ideology in motivating the use of terrorism by armed organizations, and target selection.[55] Ideological beliefs have played a pivotal role in groups incorporating terrorism into their repertoires of violence since the late nineteenth century. Terrorism studies have linked ideology to diverse dynamics including radical social movements,[56] right-wing radicalism,[57] and state terror.[58] David Rapoport's wave theory,[59] which argues that terrorism occurs in cyclical waves fed by distinct, time-specific ideologies (e.g., anarchism, decolonization, leftist radicalism, religious fundamentalism), is particularly important and offers a powerful lens through which to interpret the trajectory of several Latin American insurrectionist groups such as the Colombian guerrillas.[60]

A second camp in this field interprets terrorism from a rational perspective, claiming that groups deploy the tactic for instrumental reasons.[61] In this view, terrorism is seen as communicational strategy that seeks to modify behavior by coercion or, alternatively, as a way to sap the state's energy to fight or compensate for power imbalances in the conflict.[62] These explanations underscore Tilly's assertion that most acts of terrorism ought to be seen as complementary to or by-products of struggles in which parties deploy simultaneous forms of political claims making.[63] A particularly significant contribution in this vein is Martha Crenshaw's groundbreaking analysis of revolutionary terrorism in the Algerian civil war, which considers ideological and strategic factors to explain why Algerian rebels victimized civilians. She posits that terrorism is an unpredictable, socially unacceptable form of violence designed to modify the targeted population's behavior to align with organizational goals.[64] Terrorism studies also offer crucial insights on armed groups' internal dynamics and how such preferences account for their repertoires of terrorism. Within this literature, the work on suicide terrorism and outbidding is particularly relevant given that it directly traces variation among parties' use of terrorism to organizational trajectories.[65]

Though relevant, the arguments these two literatures offer fail to nail down what accounts for variation in parties use of terrorism. This book's central thesis is that explaining these variations requires an approach that directly traces armed parties' tactics and inquiries to the causes of their behavior rather than viewing groups as predictable, easily classifiable actors. Drawing on organizational behavior theory and constructivism in international relations, I argue that armed parties' repertoires of terrorism are the product of *organizational identity,* defined as the central and enduring attributes distinguishing an armed group from other warring parties.[66] Armed groups develop singular identities over time that shape their behavior: repertoires of action, including the selection and development of violent (and nonviolent) tactics, are one of the many concrete manifestations of such an identity. In the case of terrorism, organizational preferences derived from groups' nature (revolutionary, nationalist, reactionary) determine singular modus operandi and the specific types of attacks deployed. Repertoires of terrorism function as an identity marker, a communication device with which a group can announce its presence and goals, assert its relevance, and distinguish itself from enemies and rivals in the eyes of the population.

In developing this argument, this work engages with studies in political science that use organizational identity as an explanatory variable.[67] Rawi Abdelal and his colleagues conceptualize organizational identity as a social category, that is, a form of collective identity.[68] In their analysis, they explain that organizational identity comprises two dimensions: content and contestation. The former refers to elements like norms (i.e., formal, and informal rules), goals (i.e., shared purposes), relational components (i.e., what distinguishes a group from other groups and how groups perceive one another), and cognitive models (i.e., worldviews or perceptions regarding material or political conditions and interests). Contestation, in turn, refers to the degree of group cohesion.[69] By linking organizational identity to group interests and, ultimately, behavior, this formulation offers a sound alternative to rational accounts that tend to artificially standardize actors.[70] Organizational identity thus presents a more plausible interpretation than excessively rigid accounts that seem ill equipped to explain certain outcomes such as case variation in armed parties' behavior.[71]

The emergence of identity as a major explanatory tool owes a great deal to the international relations literature, in particular insights from constructivism, which offers a social theory for understanding state behavior and international life.[72] According to this theory, identity is the fundamental pillar of international society and a critical dimension shaping state behavior. A social theory of international relations, constructivism posits that preferences and interests are not simply the result of rational preferences but instead intersubjectively constructed.[73] States' interests can be traced to particular identities developed over long periods that ultimately define their stance on a host of issues (i.e., security, the economy, the environment) and their behavior toward other states.[74] Identity results from the confluence of historical processes, domestic configurations, philosophical views (e.g., liberalism, Marxism), traditions (e.g., isolationism, cosmopolitanism), and institutional manifestations and preferences (e.g., for democracy).[75] Although constructivism does not deploy identity as an explanatory variable, many authors within this school embrace identity as a "functional equivalent" of an independent variable.[76]

Work on ethnic conflict in comparative politics has also explored the role of identity in civil war.[77] In the same vein, Wood's seminal study on insurgent collective action in El Salvador traces how the war influenced peasants' identities.[78] She further explores identity transformation in the context of civil war by expanding her analysis to other cases, including Peru, Sri Lanka, and Sierra Leone.[79] She shows how the violent nature of civil war, along with its concomitant political mobilizations and military socialization, often polarizes and transforms local identities. She explains how external armed actors' attempts to mobilize the local population and their attacks on residents alter the nature of local grievances, linking them to broader national cleavages that were not salient in rural communities beforehand. This process, Wood outlines, significantly influences residents' identities. The creation and development of Colombian guerrilla forces were clearly influenced by this process, as the empirical chapters will show. Ann Fujii Lee's account of the Rwandan genocide, which uses a constructivist lens, also traces how local identities are shaped by civil war. She shows how a deliberate attempt to radicalize people turned amicable neighbors into perpetrators of civilian violence, and demonstrates how a state-sponsored construction of ethnicity serves as a "dramaturgical blueprint of violence" that radically alters peoples' identities.[80] Similarly, identity plays a vital role in Anastasia Shesterinina's work on the Georgian civil in the breakaway region of Abkhazia, in which she interrogates participants about their decision to join the warring parties.[81] Taking issue with rational explanations attributing mobilization to individual risk assessments, Shesterinina argues that such decisions result from the collective conflict identities people developed before the war through observation and political participation; these identities, in turn, influence their perception and understanding of violence.

Armed Parties' Identities

Referencing this literature, and drawing on some of its insights, this work assumes that armed parties, such as nations or firms,[82] have distinct identities that result from a complex process (i.e., identity formation) driven by mutually reinforcing historical, institutional, and contextual processes.[83] These social processes influence warring parties (and other actors) in the context of civil wars. Armed parties' central, distinctive, and enduring attributes develop over time, arising from a complex progression involving ideology and other doctrinal interpretations, leadership preferences, and constitutive elements of the group such as membership profiles. These factors mold the character, ethos, institutional bases, and practices of an armed party in a unique way over the lifetime as an organization. Klaus Schlichte, who describes these evolutions as organizational trajectories, argues that groups pursue diverse strategies in their efforts to legitimize and institutionalize a given internal order, and that a failure to do that could lead to their demise.[84] Organizational identity thus not only creates a sense of unity and purpose but also informs linkages with communities that can provide logistical support and recruits.[85] Consistent with constructivist thinking, identities are not stagnant and may evolve in the fluid context of civil war. On occasion, and especially during long-term conflicts, repertoires can evolve due to internal changes that modify central elements of the group's identity. For example, when groups with strong ideological views become gradually enmeshed in criminal activities in order to finance their operations, these entanglements may alter their core identity and consequently influence their use of terrorist tactics. Conversely, armed parties in which criminals participate, such as paramilitary groups in Colombia, may develop a greater awareness of and concern over political issues, adopting a more ideological identity over time.

Figure 1.1 presents a stylized scheme of the complex process linking organizational identity with repertoires of terrorism. Repertoires of terrorism arise over time as part of a intricate dynamic that begins with the creation of an armed group. The historical context under which an organization emerges, its ideological allegiance, and—depending on the group—the existence of a criminal ethos shapes the group's initial preferences. The amalgamation of these factors, often mediated by the transnational diffusion of ideas, influences leaders' preferences and guides their selection of repertoires of action, including the use of terrorism. Leaders play a critical role because they select tactics that match their organization's worldviews and purported goals. Later, they disseminate these preferences within the group through institutional means, including military training and socialization mechanisms. This process entails a certain degree of endogeneity in that socialization and action repertoires arise simultaneously; as constructivist scholars have argued, behavioral practices result from an intersubjective process in which decisions reinforce practices and vice versa.[86] In other words, although leaders choose and develop

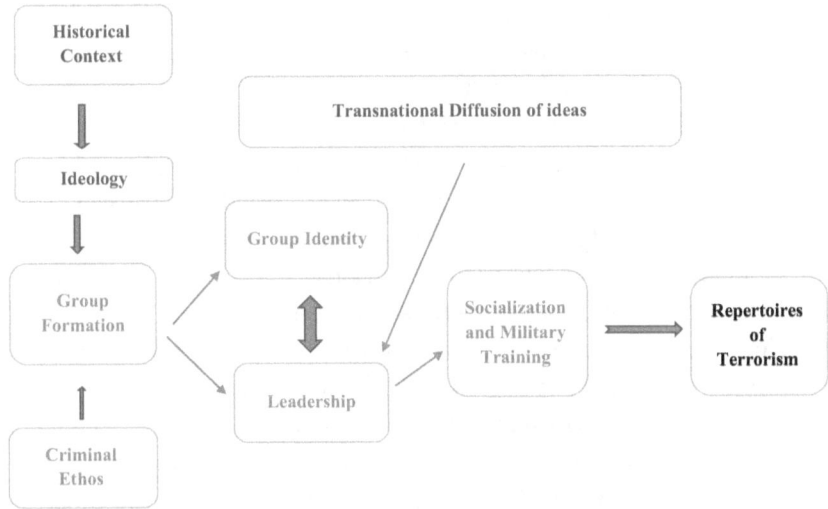

FIGURE 1.1 How organizational identity translates into repertoires of terrorism.

repertoires of action, such repertoires once selected also shape (and reinforce) leaders' views and perceptions. In what follows, the chapter unpacks this process step by step.

HISTORICAL CONTEXT

The historical context and overall conditions in which armed parties emerged and developed constitute crucial elements shaping group identity.[87] Borrowing from organizational behavior theory, Francesco Moro argues that many armed groups' foundational myths are fundamental to developing a distinctive character, building legitimacy, mobilizing resources, and creating a sense of belonging and commitment for their members. Stories detailing how a group originated and overcame challenges "become the backbone of organizational cultures (and norms) and thus often drive their actions."[88] Such sagas create an affective link nurturing group identity and ensuring "boundary maintenance and ascription to the reference group."[89]

As the empirical chapters of this book detail, foundational myths contribute to the development of organizational identity. The Colombian military's can be traced to the country's war of independence, in which its members were hailed as liberators from colonial power and defenders of the motherland from domestic and foreign foes. As for the Revolutionary Armed Forces of Colombia (FARC), their historical trajectory was shaped by the Colombian state's destruction of the Independent Peasant Republics and, more broadly, on the traumatic experience during La Violencia, in which peasants were brutally targeted. These episodes helped galvanize a strong sense of unity predicated on victimhood and fostered its distinct peasant character as an armed organization.[90] The foundational myth of the National Liberation Army (ELN) is unmistakably linked to the Cuban Revolution and its almost mystical power that inspired repeated revolutionary waves across the region.[91] Finally, in the case of paramilitary groups, theirs can be traced to years of chaos and violence in Colombia's rural regions caused by guerrilla groups, which paved the way for the formation of self-defense militias. Paramilitaries view their emergence as the story of common people courageously rising up against the existential threat of Marxist guerrillas seeking to rip apart the existing order and destroy their traditional ways of life. Context also matters, in that the acute polarization brought about by the Cold War was critical in the emergence of both guerrilla and paramilitary groups.

IDEOLOGY

The emergence of armed organizations is also inextricably related to ideational aspects, which play an enormously important role in the development of organizational identity. Group ideologies emerge in reaction to historical moments and, once established, critically influence armed parties' understanding and perception of reality. Following Gutiérrez-Sanín and Wood, this work defines ideology as "a more or less systematic set of ideas that includes the identification of a referent group (a class, ethnic of other social group), an enunciation of the grievances or challenges that the group confronts, the identification of objectives on behalf of that group (political change or defense against its threat) and a (perhaps vaguely defined) program of action."[92]

Whether secular, religious, or issue-related, ideology not only fosters group identity but also informs actors' goals and guides their actions. Rather than being monolithic, however, ideologies often arise from an amalgamation of superimposed doctrines reflecting an organization's primary (and unique) identity traits. Such ideas often display remarkable degrees of internal inconsistency.[93]

Adherence to ideology varies among armed parties, some organizations being much more zealous and rigid and others much more pragmatic. Gutiérrez-Sanín and Wood make an important distinction between groups relying on ideology for instrumental reasons and those that adhere to deep normative commitments, classifying them as having weak or strong programs, respectively.[94] The former refers to groups that pragmatically use ideology to enhance their appeal, buttress recruitment, and reduce principal-agent problems related to maintaining discipline and motivation. The latter refer to groups displaying sincere convictions for a particular cause.[95]

The link between ideology and the production of violence and terrorism has been widely acknowledged,[96] but it is imperative to establish how exactly ideas translate into different forms of violence. In simple terms, ideology motivates, stimulates, and rationalizes the use of terrorism.[97] Ideologies matter because they provide a framing and justification for actions and prescribe ways to achieve certain goals.[98] Extremist views, for example, can lend intellectual justification to acts of extreme brutality that defy basic human norms. A critical part of this process is the *dehumanization* of the other.[99] As Ehud Sprinzak underscores, radicals embrace ideologies that dehumanize the other to justify their use of violence, including terrorism.[100] Group belief systems shape the perception of right and wrong and their members' understanding of security, including whom they consider to be rivals and enemies. In this regard, Jeff Goodwin's theory of categorical terrorism, which posits that parties target civilians because their ideologies reduce them to a broad category of "complicit" beneficiaries and supporters of an order they seek to destroy, is particularly illuminating in explaining how overarching views inform civilian victimization.[101] In an important contribution to our understanding of how ideology translates into decisions to employ violence, Jonathan Maynard elaborates on the concrete mechanisms informing this process. He identifies two principal causal accounts, both linked to organizational dynamics: the *internalization* of worldviews and social environments or *structures* within groups.[102]

Terrorism is often the product of a radical worldview calling for the destruction of an existing order considered decadent, corrupt, and unjust. Rapoport's historical account of successive waves of modern terrorism linked, in chronological order, to anarchism, self-determination, ultra-leftism, and radical religion show how diverse ideologies (secular, religious, nationalist) have historically served as inspiration for the tactic.[103] Interestingly, radical views based on defending the existing social order have also often motivated terrorism, particularly state terrorism.[104] In his analysis of repression in Argentina, for example, Adam Scharpf shows how military officers espousing fierce nationalist and anticommunist views were more prone to practicing terrorism than officers with liberal views.[105]

Viewing the issue through a psychological lens, Jerrold Post asserts that polarizing, absolutist ideologies create a narrative without nuance among armed parties in which rivals are perceived as a source of evil. Such views create a distorted, self-righteous perception that morally justifies destroying rivals by any means necessary. Extreme ideology, therefore, may turn into "the scripture of a group's morality." Post explains: "What the group, through its interpretation of its ideology, defines as moral becomes moral—and becomes the authority for the compliant members. And if the ideology indicates that 'they are responsible for our problems,' to destroy 'them' is not only viewed as justified but can be seen to be a moral imperative."[106]

In his interesting overview of the rationale behind civilian targeting in war, Hugo Slim argues that some particularly egregious acts are motivated by totalizing ideologies that reduce human beings to a distinctive attribute that warrants their targeting, even their extermination.[107] Although Slim's account mostly explains the rationale behind genocide, its logic certainly applies to that of organizations relying on terrorism, which reduce victims to a single identity and dehumanize them to the point of justifying their destruction. In providing a justification for the September 11 attacks, for instance, al-Qaeda leader Osama bin Laden mentioned that those killed in the attack should not be considered innocent civilians because, as taxpayers, they were helping finance the United States' imperialist policies in the Middle East.[108]

An additional component linking ideology to violence is radicalization, which Ted Robert Gurr defines as a process in which groups unsuccessfully mobilize in the pursuit of a given objective (social, political). As members (whom he calls "activists") of the group lose patience with conventional tools, they begin to experiment with more unconventional, extreme methods. Exasperation and dissatisfaction, Gurr goes on to explain, offer the motivation (anger) and rationale leading for employing terrorist tactics.[109]

The empirical chapters of this book show that ideology played a critical role in the production of terrorism among Colombian armed parties. Like most left-wing insurgent groups, the ELN and the FARC rationalized extreme forms of violence as inevitable outcomes of class warfare. Paramilitary groups and the Colombian state security forces (CSSF), for their part, justified their widespread use of terrorism by citing the need to contain dangerous, unpatriotic elements adamant on destroying Colombia's existing order. Both espoused strong anticommunist views and rationalized terrorism as an extreme but necessary resort. Targets included people considered enemies of the state who aided and abetted guerrillas (e.g., sympathizers, informants, useful fools) and those displaying progressive political views (e.g., leftist organizers, union and grassroots leaders, intellectuals).

The analysis also reveals the extent to which a group's Weltanschauung could combine seemingly incompatible views. The identity of Colombian armed parties comprises a kaleidoscope of contrasting and at times inconsistent views over time. The ELN adheres to a mixture of Cuban-inspired socialism, liberation theology, and nationalism; the FARC to a conventional pro-Soviet brand of socialism and a peasant self-governing culture; paramilitary groups to strong anticommunist views derived from a counterinsurgency doctrine blended with pro-market liberalism and a criminal ethos inherited from the drug trafficking world; and, finally, the CSSF to a mixture of conservative and nationalist views predicated on national security doctrines imported from American, Brazilian, and French counterinsurgency ideologues.

LEADERSHIP

In addition to historical context and ideology, leadership is a critical component linking organizational identity to repertoires of terrorism. Leaders guide and interpret organizational preferences and therefore play a crucial role in generating repertoires of action, including violence.[110] As pointed out earlier, leaders are themselves influenced by group dynamics because the organization's identity is intersubjectively constructed by all members of the group. However, their role in identity construction is paramount because they use their power and influence to direct the trajectory of the organization in ways that reinforce existing beliefs.

Even though leaders are important in all organizations, their influence is particularly significant in armed parties, given the hierarchical nature of these groups and the dangerous, uncertain context in which they operate.[111] Leaders' responsibilities within armed groups are manifold, ranging from developing military, operational, and logistics capacities to devising funding strategies to overseeing recruitment and internal disciplinary and socialization mechanisms. They also establish the concrete protocols regarding group behavior toward the civilian population. Green, for example, argues that leaders define repertoires of violence, including civilian targeting, according to organizational preferences and goals (as they see them). This process, she posits, can also entail curbing a group's propensity to use violence by internalizing restraint through political education[112]

Repertoires of terrorism are developed by leaders through socialization, the process whereby actors acquire and internalize norms and rules in a given setting. Jeffrey Checkel underscores that socialization's goal is not simply behavioral adaptation but "a degree of change in an actors' sense of self."[113] In the case of military organizations, as Elisabeth Wood explains, socialization includes formal mechanisms (i.e., rigorous training, what she calls "boot camp") and informal ones such as hazing and initiation rituals, which, she underscores, bear formidable resemblances across groups.[114] Military sociology, an extensive field looking at different elements of military culture, similarly underlines the importance of organizational features (procedures, training, careers, and so forth) in shaping professional armies' repertoires of action.[115] Terrorism studies have also established how groups' social environments can determine organizational strategies.[116] Furthermore, classical work tracing the influence of radical organizations in Europe in the 1970s and 1980s reveals the role of indoctrination and socialization in the production of terrorism.[117] Political training (indoctrination) and disciplinary regimes that regulate behavior are critical in this process.[118] These mechanisms are not solely top-down (training, indoctrination) but may also arise from bottom-up dynamics such as peer learning, imitation, and group pressure. Dennis Rodgers shows how similar practices take place among criminal groups in his analysis of street gangs in Central America.[119]

The argument advanced in this work emphasizes the interface between ideational and operational aspects within armed groups. It claims that apart from the strategic military considerations that inform leaders' viewpoints (as Green underscores), top commanders perform a more immaterial yet important task: instilling a distinctive identity and sense of direction within the organization that fosters group commitment and esprit de corps. When it comes to developing and selecting concrete repertoires of violence, leaders strive to align military and ideational considerations, mindful that such blending buttresses the organization's cohesiveness. Leaders design military tactics that not only match their organizations' main objectives but, following constructivist thought, reflect their organizational preferences and identity. Put differently, leaders select from a menu of options tactics that represent their groups' core values and narratives (revolutionary, national, religious) while discarding others perceived as antithetical or unworthy. For example, as mentioned in the introduction, Colombian paramilitaries rejected the use of extortive kidnappings because they were associated with revolutionary groups they loathed, whereas both FARC and ELN leaderships rejected disappearances and avoided graphic displays of violence, actions they considered at odds with their core revolutionary principles. Once tactics are identified, commanders design training programs in which members acquire concrete technical skills to deploy them, thus internalizing their use.[120] To the extent that commanders' choices entrench specific tactics within the group, especially as these behaviors become socialized (learned, perfected, and routinized), a degree of inertia often sets in over time. Chapter 7 examines this intriguing trend and provides evidence for how organizational inertia derived from the early choices of their leaders makes groups cling to certain terrorist repertoires even as internal changes alter their identity.

This book engages with but ultimately discards extant arguments in the literature positing that civilian victimization results from a breakdown of social norms and armed group discipline.[121] On this point, Wood advances the view that armed parties engage in systematic rape not because it is deliberately adopted as a tactic but because low-ranking combatants act opportunistically and often disobey orders.[122] However, the empirical chapters offer evidence to support a top-down explanation of repertoires of terrorism in civil war: leaders chose distinct repertoires during the embryonic years of their armed parties, repertoires later incorporated and refined through training and socialization mechanisms. I also illustrate that armed parties' repertoires of terrorism remain consistent over time despite changes in leadership and group composition. This finding therefore does not support an explanation based on the choices or will of rank-and-file combatants. If that were the case, one would observe less regularity in the use of terrorism across organizations and over time. Similarly, I show that parties stubbornly cling to specific tactics even when such actions seem counterproductive, as illustrated in discussions on the use of abductions in the case of guerrillas and massacres in the case of paramilitaries.

Contextual and historical conditions naturally influence leaders' worldviews.[123] Rapoport's theory of historical terrorism waves, alluded to previously, reveals distinct periods characterized by a concrete set of terrorist repertoires. Highly relevant for this study is the third wave of rebel terrorism (1960–1990) and the subsequent repressive wave across Latin America. Reacting to major setbacks, in particular the killing of Ernesto "Che" Guevara by Bolivian security forces in 1967, several revolutionary leaders advocated for a major overhaul of the prevailing Cuban *foco* doctrine.[124] Against this backdrop, they embraced the urban warfare doctrine originally developed by Abraham Guillén and Carlos Marighella, a neatly crafted narrative linking a unique ideational worldview with a concrete set of terrorist tactics.[125] Marighella was convinced that the revolutionary fight should move from rural spaces to urban power centers, where most of the population resided. Terrorist attacks such as indiscriminate bombings and kidnappings against targets considered symbols of the exploitative bourgeoisie and imperialist regime (conservative politicians and intellectuals, entrepreneurs, executives of multinational companies) soon became associated with leftist organizations across Latin America.[126] These agitational attacks were embraced and perfected by multiple revolutionary and nationalist organizations in Latin America and beyond. Highly publicized kidnappings of commercial airliners, for example, constituted an important tactical adaptation in the 1970s and were mostly employed by radical leftist and nationalist organizations outside Latin America such as the Italian Red Brigades, the Japanese Red Army, the Palestinian Liberation Organization, the German Red Army Faction, and the U.S. Weather Underground.

At the opposite end of the ideological spectrum, right-wing groups (paramilitary groups and death squads) with anticommunist tendencies and some states embraced violence and terrorism to counter the perceived threat posed by leftist factions. These actors would develop their own distinctive repertoires (e.g., disappearances, torture). Such tactics were influenced by military doctrines developed by the French, American, and Brazilian militaries based on the notion of prescribing the use of specific counterinsurgency techniques aimed at neutralizing the threat of insurgent groups in the name of national security.[127] These doctrines, which often incorporated specific training in tactics such as torture, massacres, disappearance, and targeted killings, were devised to force civilian compliance and deprive insurgent groups of civilian support ("drain the sea to catch the fish," in Mao Tse-Tung's famous dictum).

TRANSNATIONAL DIFFUSION OF IDEAS

Views justifying the use of violence are often diffused transnationally. This dynamic was particularly critical during the Cold War, when the two global superpowers furnished ideological guidance and military support and training to their allies.[128] Armed groups then and now often incorporate repertoires of action, including terrorist tactics, from external (usually ideationally proximate) parties. James Forest explains that organizations purposefully seek to acquire such knowledge, which they view as important to their long-term success and prospects.[129] As Michael Horowitz documents in the case of suicide terrorism, organizations can share expertise and experiences, often through direct exchanges.[130]

In the Colombian case, tactical diffusion was closely linked to Cold War dynamics, a pivotal but often overlooked contextual dimension of the conflict. The superpower rivalry during this period affected diverse aspects of civil wars (e.g., their onset, termination, financing) across the globe as well as the use of terrorism in democratic settings. Radical leftist groups including guerrillas were heavily influenced by the transnational revolutionary doctrines in vogue during those years,[131] such as Marighella's urban warfare manual, Maoist warfare tactics, and the Vietnamese *dau tranh*. On the other side of the political spectrum, permutations of the national security doctrine informed counterinsurgency policies that incorporated repertoires of terrorism. Transnational collaboration played an important role throughout the conflict, as several concrete cases show. Members of the Provisional Irish Republican Army, a splinter group of the Irish Republican Army, traveled to Colombia to train FARC operatives in the use of explosives.[132] Meanwhile, retired members of the Israeli and British armies trained paramilitary operatives in counterinsurgency techniques that amounted to terrorism or torture, such as "enhanced interrogation" methods.[133] Members of the Colombian Army, themselves trained by foreign advisors (mostly American), taught paramilitaries counterinsurgency techniques that also often incorporated terror tactics (e.g., disappearance, torture).[134]

CRIMINAL ETHOS

A final factor informing repertoires of terrorism involves links between groups and the criminal underworld. Terrorism has historically been considered political in nature, but criminal groups are increasingly incorporating this tactic into their repertoires of action.[135] Walter Laqueur asserts that thirty years ago, the line dividing organizations that used terrorism to advance political goals and organized criminals was more clear, but that this division has blurred, leading in some cases to a symbiosis between criminal and politically oriented organizations.[136]

This symbiosis stems from two concomitant dynamics. First, often deprived of traditional sources of funding, politically motivated groups espousing terrorism have sought new ways to finance their operations, often through illicit activities (e.g., drug trafficking, smuggling, racketeering, money laundering).[137] Second, and more critical to my argument, even though the use of terrorist tactics by criminal organizations can be traced back to the Sicilian mafia in the early twentieth century, this phenomenon is becoming more widespread today.[138] The behavior of criminal groups in Latin America—including Brazilian, Ecuadorian, and Mexican drug trafficking organizations, which have consistently used terrorism tactics to combat rivals, including the state—reflects a broader pattern among criminal groups operating as far afield as in Russia, India, and Afghanistan. Chris Dishman asserts that criminal organizations are increasingly utilizing terrorism to neutralize the power of authorities and destroy rivals.[139] Violence is directed at a specific "anticonstituency" rather than at the public at large and is generally divorced from a political rhetoric. Criminals do not seek changes in state policy or regime change but rather to limit the state's intervention in certain spaces and transactions related to their business.[140]

Interdisciplinary work in terrorism studies and criminology has unpacked the relationship between crime and terrorism.[141] One of the best theoretical articulations is Tamara Makarenko's notion of the crime-terrorism nexus. She argues that the relationship between these two types or organizations can be conceptualized as a continuum, with one ideal type at each extreme and diverse permutations in between. This framework shows how, under certain circumstances, political and criminal organizations engage, cooperate, or merge with one another.[142] Because of this dynamic process, Makarenko explains, in some cases groups "no longer retain the defining points that had hitherto made them a political or criminal group."[143] As discussed in chapter 7, Mexican cartels have long used and honed terrorist practices. Political organizations, for their part, have developed significant expertise in conducting criminal activities. Colombian guerrillas increasingly developed expertise in the drug industry and other clandestine activities such as smuggling, money laundering, extortion, and racketeering.[144] On occasion, politically and criminally motived groups may converge as ideological groups relax their views and become more pragmatic, perhaps meeting criminal groups that have adopted more political views halfway. The Taliban in Afghanistan, who combine dogmatic religious views with a criminal ethos developed through years of involvement in the opium industry, are an emblematic case.[145]

When it comes to the use of violence in civil war, including terrorism, scholars have posited that groups' modi operandi may be at least in part influenced by criminal codes. Armed parties whose leadership has a criminal background often incorporate repertoires of terrorism originating in the underworld. Criminal organizations carry out terrorism campaigns to secure their operational environment by neutralizing opponents, law enforcement officials, and hostile politicians.[146] Studies of violence in the Bosnian civil war established how atrocities amounting to terrorism were committed by paramilitary groups comprising former members of Yugoslavia's criminal underworld.[147] Similarly, in Sierra Leone, many of the distressing terrorism practices deployed against civilians, such as deliberate maiming and sexual violence, was neither wanton nor senseless but instead sprung from the diverse political and criminal motivations of the Revolutionary United Front.[148]

More broadly, terrorism is to a significant degree linked to the logic underpinning organized crime or mafia-like behavior.[149] Organized crime entails selling and controlling the supply of private protection.[150] Classic criminological work characterizes the mafia as a form of behavior or mode of power.[151] The mafia emerges in areas where the state has limited capacity to provide public goods (i.e., security); these regions are normally characterized by high levels of uncertainty and limited trust in the state, with criminals filling the void with their offer to supply protection.[152] Protection is usually delivered and maintained through violent arrangements that are nonetheless guided by internal rules and a distinct logic shaping expectations and behavior.

Private protection offered by the mafia is predicated on the idea of exclusivity. Criminals rarely tolerate competition and seek to violently impose their will upon competitors, whom they consider adversaries. As the Sicilian adage goes, "Your enemy is a businessman like you."[153] Reputational considerations are one of the most salient aspects of this criminal ethos in that demonstrations of toughness provide credibility both in the eyes of clients and criminal members. Weakness, conversely, creates doubts and thus open the way for competitors.[154] Among all reputational considerations, the ability and willingness to kill are paramount in the mafia code of conduct. Federico Varese asserts that one of the leaders of the Italian mafia once explained that mafiosi must be prepared to kill and be relatively proficient at it.[155] The idea of a division of labor within criminal organizations, according to which members could restrict their role to nonviolent endeavors, is simply not viable. People learn to kill from the day they join the organization and develop considerable expertise over the length of their involvement.

Ruthlessness is another critical reputational aspect, reflecting a group's determination to achieve its goals and inclination to use gruesome methods to instill fear in competitors and punish deviant behavior.[156] Symbolic uses of violence, including maiming victims, desecrating and displaying bodies, and unusually cruel methods of torture are trademark features of organized crime.[157] In his detailed analysis of mafia behavior, Roberto Saviano argues that such cruelty is not inherent but always learned, usually needing to be channeled through a process of socialization.[158] Similarly, Ricardo Vargas attributes this behavior to what he calls the *esprit mafioso*,[159] a code of conduct resembling ancient criminal mores adapted to the modern drug trade, which contributed to introducing forms of para-institutionality to their repertoires of violence. Studies in criminology, similarly, establish how organizational features mold members in accordance with organizational goals and views.[160] Recent work on gangs are particularly insightful in demonstrating how extreme forms of violence are transmitted through socializing mechanisms including rites of passage, peer pressure, and incentives that in essence socialize individuals to become a part of the group.[161]

Contemporary studies on criminal war have also touched on this reputational dynamic. Looking at situations in which drug trafficking organizations decide to confront the state, Benjamin Lessing argues that these organizations use violence, including terrorism, as a form of lobbying to try and force authorities to change their policies.[162] Pablo Escobar's total war to combat extraditions or the Familia Michoacana cartel's shocking displays of violence to force the Mexican government to reconsider deploying troops into Michoacán are cases in point. Relatedly, Angélica Durán-Martínez's work shows that criminal groups often opt to engage in, and claim responsibility for, high-visibility violence. The author presents evidence of how groups broadcast or hide their violent acts depending on their incentives, arguing that this strategy arises in scenarios of high uncertainty characterized by the fragmentation of state security apparatuses. She claims that in circumstances in which the incentives for concealing violence decrease, criminals may rely on visible displays of violence to "eliminate rivals, to retaliate or pressure the state or to *scare away civilians*" [emphasis added].[163] The empirical evidence offered in this book supports such a view, in showing how the modi operandi of Colombian paramilitaries are permeated by a criminal ethos that has merged with a counterinsurgency doctrine fueled by anticommunist ideology.

Conclusions

This chapter offers a theoretical discussion of the use of terrorism in civil war. It begins by conceptualizing the relationship between civil war and terrorist actions, underscoring the differences, similarities, and overlapping elements. It shows that though the line between the two can be blurry, they are analytically different. Violence against civilians constitutes a regular occurrence during civil war; however, it is not a constitutive element in that wars are defined by sustained operations (i.e., battles) among militarily organized parties. In the case of terrorism, conversely, the deliberate targeting of civilians represents a conditio sine qua non.

The discussion then looks at the relationship between terrorism and civilian targeting. It underlines that terrorism represents a particular subset of civilian targeting characterized by a communicative logic that uses violence to instill fear beyond the immediate victims of the attack and intimidate foes, rivals, and the public. As a result, terrorism is qualitatively different from civilian targeting with its noncommunicational, tangible purpose such as ethnic cleansing, dispossession, or genocide. Terrorism, I argue, differs from other forms of violence perpetrated in civil war in that it deliberately violates cardinal IHL principles in having the clear intent to spread fear among a wider audience.

Finally, the chapter discusses the sources of variation in the specific repertoires of terrorism that diverse groups use during civil war. It argues that these differences stem from organizational identities, defined as the central, enduring, and distinctive attributes characterizing armed parties. Organizational identity arises because of unique evolutionary processes involving a group's history, ideological predilections and doctrinarian interpretations, leadership, and socialization mechanisms. Leaders play a critical role in developing repertoires of terrorism given that they select and promote distinct types and attacks that derive from and conform with the group's unique identity. The selection and adaptation of repertoires of violence, it is further posited, are socialized through institutional mechanisms such as training, indoctrination, and discipline—all practices that reinforce organizational identity and members' sense of belonging. The development of a singular repertoire of terrorism thus becomes a distinctive marker of a group's presence and plays an important communicational role, distinguishing the group from its enemies and rivals.

2

The Evolution of the Colombian Civil War

From Conventional to Criminal Warfare

Colombia's history as an independent republic has been marked by repeated cycles of violence and turmoil, including several civil wars characterized by widespread human rights violations and the systematic use of terrorism. Partisan warfare between Conservatives and Liberals unleashed massive outbursts of violence during the nineteenth and the first half of the twentieth centuries, antecedents of existing armed conflict. Even though in the recent past, powerful armed parties including paramilitary groups and the People's Alternative Revolutionary Force (the political successor to the rebel group) demobilized, raising hopes that the country was moving past its prolonged and costly civil war, the truth is that violence rages on, although in different guises.

This chapter offers a brief overview of the Colombian civil war from 1964 to the present. Detailed accounts of the conflict are numerous.[1] This shortened version seeks to familiarize readers with Colombian history and critical aspects of its evolution that should prove useful for understanding the main argument and the empirical chapters of the book. The discussion is organized into five parts, reflecting the distinct phases of the conflict. It begins with an examination on the conditions that informed the rise and development of guerrilla groups in the 1960s and the initial reaction of the Colombian state. It then looks at the emergence of paramilitary groups in the late 1970s, whose rise marks a turning point in the conflict due to the steep deterioration of violence they brought about. A third section describes the most intense period of the civil war, which coincides with the apex of guerrilla power and the creation of the United Self-Defense Forces of Colombia, or Autodefensas (AUC), a confederation of paramilitary groups with national reach. This is followed by a brief discussion on the so-called democratic security policy undertaken by former president Álvaro Uribe (2002–2010) and its impact on overall security conditions. The last section examines contemporary conditions following the signing of the 2016 peace accord with the FARC and the conflict's transformation from a conventional into a criminal war.

The Rise of Insurgency in Rural Colombia (1964–1978)

The emergence of guerrilla groups such as the FARC and the National Liberation Army, or Ejército de Liberación Nacional (ELN), reflect the endemic turmoil that has plagued the Colombian countryside since the country achieved independence in the early nineteenth century. From a geographical point of view, Colombia presents ideal conditions for guerrilla warfare, including a huge, fragmented geography crisscrossed by rugged mountain chains, extensive swampy lowlands, and impenetrable, sparsely populated jungle areas.[2] Rural unrest stemmed from a malign combination of disputes between peasants and landlords, partisan struggle over control of the countryside, and pervasive *bandolerism*. Agrarian conflicts were widespread and revolved around three axes: labor conditions, disputes concerning the use and ownership of the land, and indigenous grievances over encroachment on what was regarded as ancestral land and forced acculturation efforts. A small percentage of peasants managed to break free from the hacienda system and claim their own land, either as squatters or by colonizing remote areas such as the Andean piedmont (settling on its steep slopes), Colombia's jungle regions, and the vast eastern lowlands toward Venezuela.[3] Such moves led to a campaign of systematic repression by landlords, who resisted their emancipation or tried to seize their land. Catherine LeGrand reports more than 450 confrontations between landlords and peasants between 1875 and 1930.[4]

Repeated insurrections were clearly linked to a problematic state-building process in which the fragile central government was incapable of fulfilling many basic functions, including guaranteeing security and providing basic public goods (e.g., infrastructure, social services). A critical, exacerbating element was the acute political cleavage between Liberals and Conservatives, the two main political forces in Colombia. Beginning after the country gained independence from Spain, violent competition between these parties undermined early efforts to centralize power.[5] Moreover, the emergence of several poles of economic development (Bogotá, Antioquia, and the Atlantic coast) reinforced regional autonomy at the expense of power accumulation at the central level. This process was informed by an elite consensus favoring a laissez faire model that was not necessarily favorable to the development of a strong central state.[6] Tensions between the capital and local authorities, who often perceived the former as a menace rather than a source of legitimate authority, were common and further fueled conflict. Although usually claiming allegiance to one of the two main parties, regional leaders enjoyed significant autonomy and acted in accordance with their perceived interests, often resorting to brute force to maintain order in areas under their influence. These conditions paved the way for the emergence of a frontier justice system administered by local *caciques* (strongmen). Against this backdrop, the state's legitimacy was predictably low in the eyes of the population, a lack of confidence that further eroded state strength.[7] State fragility was worsened by its often patrimonial and despotic exercise of power characterized by corruption, excesses, and internecine fighting.[8]

This problematic process of state formation had a strong impact on the socioeconomic conditions of the peasantry. In the absence of a strong central government regulating economic affairs, a steady process of land accumulation by rich *hacendados* (landlords) led Colombia to become one of the countries with the most skewed land distribution in the Americas.[9] The origins of this troublesome pattern, however, can be traced to Spanish colonial rule, which created a stratified social order configured according to class and ethnic lines, with landlords at the top and a vast mass of subservient peasants working on haciendas.

Such were the political and economic contexts in which twentieth-century violence would flourish. In a country accustomed to high levels of turmoil and bloodshed, the period known as La Violencia (1948–1964) stood out for its colossal levels of turmoil and inhumanity.[10] Violence was sparked by the assassination of the charismatic Liberal leader Jorge Eliécer Gaitán in April 1948, which plunged the country, particularly rural areas, into communal violence along party lines. The turmoil started to gradually recede following a military coup by General Gustavo Rojas Pinilla (1953–1957), who relied on a mix of incentives and harsh measures to stymie interparty violence. The slow process of pacification continued after democracy was restored with the creation of the National Front (1958–1974), a power-sharing agreement between the country's two main parties.[11]

The National Front succeeded in diminishing violence but ultimately proved unable to address, let alone remedy, deep socioeconomic cleavages, in particular land claims, and left out vast sectors of the population, such as the peasantry and pauperized urban dwellers. Their feeling of marginalization was critical to the rise of modern insurgent groups.[12] Peasants and disgruntled progressive urban youth, frustrated that their demands were not being met by the ruling political order, founded the FARC and the ELN between 1964 and 1966. In the case of the former, peasants from the Tolima region took up arms following the Colombian Army's destruction of the so-called Independent Peasant Republics.[13] These self-governed enclaves had become sanctuaries for peasants and their families fleeing the excesses of armed militias, state security forces (the army and police), and common bandits vying for control of rural areas during La Violencia.[14] Historian Eric Hobsbawm describes how, during this period, renegades and outlaws swarmed the Colombian countryside wreaking havoc on the population.[15] The leaders of peasant self-defense groups who survived the assault, including legendary chief commander Pedro Antonio Marín (aka Tiro Fijo, or "Sure Shot"), founded the FARC.

Relatedly, the ELN was part of the first wave of insurgent movements that sprung up across Latin America after the 1959 Cuban Revolution. As such, it is a prime example of the *foquista* guerrilla model in vogue in Latin America during the 1960s (see chapter 4). The ELN was founded by a heterogeneous group of leftist militants flowing from two main sources: a dissident wing of the Liberal Revolutionary Movement associated with Alfonso López Michelsen, an influential Liberal politician who opposed the National Front; and former members of Rafael Rangel's self-defense group, a peasant force associated with the Liberal Party that had been active in small municipalities in the Magdalena Medio (San Vicente del Chucurí, Simacota, and Barrancabermeja) during La Violencia.[16] Influenced by the revolutionary fervor of those days, several other revolutionary groups espousing alternative doctrinal tendencies like Maoism also emerged, most prominently the Popular Liberation Army (Ejército Popular de Liberación, or EPL), founded in Urabá and lower Cauca around 1967.[17]

In their early years, the FARC and the ELN carried out limited operations seeking to "liberate" small swaths of territory from the control of the central state. Most of their activities were in sync with guerrilla precepts, which entailed harassing the military in hit-and-run operations and generally sparing civilians from harm. Drawing on the Cuban revolutionary tradition, the ELN in particular relied on highly symbolic, guerrilla-like attacks with the hopes of awakening the peasantry's revolutionary consciousness.[18] At the beginning, the Colombian state reacted in a relatively measured way to the emergence of these groups despite growing concerns about communist advances in the Western Hemisphere following Fidel Castro's triumph, fears that would be magnified by U.S. geostrategic concerns.[19] To the extent that in their early years the FARC and ELN had few fighters, poor and outdated arsenals, and a limited operational range circumscribed to isolated areas in the countryside (Tolima and eastern Santander), the Colombian state security forces (CSSF) adopted a cautious counterinsurgency approach seeking mostly to contain them.[20] This state indulgence is often regarded as a missed opportunity to destroy guerrillas during their embryonic phase when they were weak and vulnerable.[21]

Over time, the state's timid stance allowed guerrillas not only to survive but also to thrive, increasing their influence and power across the country.[22] Further, as is often the case, insurgent adherence to strict guerrilla tactics gradually mutated into more brazen tactics like terrorism.[23] In their newly established operational bases, guerrillas began to harass and target cattle ranchers and landowners, both influential and humble, extorting them for money and terrorizing them with attacks and kidnappings when their demands were not met. They also both pressured peasants living in areas under their control to follow their orders or face dire consequences and developed a set of institutions and informal rules that regulated various aspects of peasant life (justice, freedom of movement, economic activities, and so forth).[24]

The Emergence of Paramilitary Groups (1978–1990)

Growing insecurity in the countryside led to the emergence of paramilitary groups in the late 1970s.[25] Paramilitary groups are large mobile organizations characterized by a unified command and formal structures; they are composed of full-time members and capable of conducting wide-scale, complex military operations over a prolonged period (see chapter 5). Their rise contributed to a dramatic deterioration of security conditions in Colombia.[26] They multiplied the number of actors participating in the war, thus rendering the conflict more complex and intractable, but also influenced the methods employed in the war.[27]

Three main groups contributed to the emergence of Colombian paramilitary organizations: landowners and cattle ranchers, members of the armed forces, and criminals. As to the first group, economic elites—in particular regional bosses, landowners, and cattle ranchers in the southern Magdalena Medio region around the municipality of Puerto Boyacá—were critical. Although many were powerful individuals owning large estates, many others were common people who, following years of sacrifice, became small landowners and were subsequently targeted by guerrilla groups.[28] Concerned about rising peasant unrest linked to unresolved agrarian demands, these individuals organized lightly armed groups, often recruiting local ruffians to curb peasant mobilization and deter the forceful occupations of their properties.[29]

In their efforts to stem potential peasant unrest, landed elites were aided by the Colombian state, which, concerned about the emergence of revolutionary groups, viewed the newly created, landowner-backed militias as a welcome partner in its counterinsurgency efforts. The Colombian state promoted legislation and a string of executive decrees authorizing the creation of self-defense groups during the administration of Guillermo León Valencia of the Conservative Party (1962–1966) and Carlos Lleras Restrepo of the Liberal Party (1966–1970).[30] Regardless of a growing consensus that paramilitaries constituted an autonomous force with significant degrees of agency that at times came into conflict with the state, most accounts highlight that the state also played a pivotal role in the emergence and subsequent strengthening of these groups. Some members of the armed forces, including active high-ranking officials, not only turned a blind eye to paramilitaries' illegal operations but also actively endorsed their activities by supplying weapons, training, and logistical support; sharing intelligence; and conducting covert joint operations. Given the informal links between paramilitary groups and some members of the army, paramilitaries often operated with impunity in areas of high military presence.[31]

Criminals, including emerald smugglers and especially narcotraffickers, are the third component of paramilitary groups. In the 1980s, operators of the Medellín Cartel such as Pablo Escobar and Gonzalo Rodríguez Gacha (aka El Mexicano) bought large swaths of land to launder their vast illicit earnings. Drug barons saw a profitable business opportunity in these transactions as many landowners, fatigued from guerrilla kidnappings and extortion, decided to sell their properties at a fraction of the market price.[32] Drug barons, however, soon faced the same guerrilla harassment as landowners, though they used their considerable resources and expertise to protect themselves and their newly acquired properties. Facing a common enemy, drug barons quickly realized the strategic value of joining forces with traditional landowners and other regional political elites and members of the security forces.[33]

Paramilitaries made localized forms of terrorism the centerpiece of their military struggle.[34] Their strategies often included targeted assassinations, torture, abductions, intimidation, and massacres. Violence was directed against those deemed as a threat to their interests, ranging from purported guerrilla supporters and leftist sympathizers (intellectuals, labor union members, journalists, human rights activists, even comedians) to the politicians and state officials who opposed them, including majors, governors, and judges.[35] As the introduction points out, some attacks were accompanied by gruesome acts of cruelty in which the defaced bodies of victims were publicly displayed to heighten fear and paralyze potential resistance.[36] In zones under their control, moreover, paramilitary groups started to regulate the activities of the population, repressing any attempts to defy their authority.[37] They also infiltrated state institutions (police, military, judicial system), corrupting and threatening officials.[38]

The deterioration in Colombia's security conditions took an ominous turn following two developments: the unexpected strengthening of guerrilla groups and a rise in narcotrafficking violence. During the Seventh National Conference in 1982, the FARC officially adopted *dau tranh*, a three-pronged insurgency method pioneered by Vietnamese rebels.[39] The strategy complemented military operations with actions in the political realm. Militarily, the FARC unveiled plans to escalate the conflict from conducting guerrilla warfare to confronting security forces in open battle.[40] The group gradually expanded its presence from its traditional strongholds in central Colombia and ventured into new territories, including urban areas. The FARC sought to render these areas ungovernable and thus force

Colombian security forces to overextend themselves. As part of this plan, the group gradually increased its reliance on terrorism, incorporating summary executions and bombings against detractors and antagonists who were formally declared enemies of the people.[41] These actions aimed to undermine opposing groups and coerce civilians into supporting their insurgency.[42] In the political realm, the FARC attempted to spread its ideology throughout popular neighborhoods and universities with a view toward building a network of sympathizers and informants.[43] In a critical component of this push, the FARC formed its own party, the Patriotic Union, which would allow the group to complement its military efforts with electoral campaigns. The Patriotic Union was created in 1985 as part of the peace negotiations the FARC opened with the administration of Conservative President Belisario Betancur (1982–1986). The party, however, ended up being destroyed through the shady maneuverings and violence attacks of right-wing groups and this political sabotage would profoundly shape the political mentality of the FARC going forward.[44]

Similarly, after almost being destroyed by security forces in the early 1970s, the ELN regrouped following the success of the Domingo Laín front, which was formed by a small group of militants who struck out and moved into the Sarare jungle, a remote region linking the department of Santander with the eastern lowlands in the departments of Boyacá and Meta.[45] Thanks to methodical campaigns of persuasion and peasant indoctrination, the front grew steadily and, more important, reaped vast sums of money through extortion and kidnappings.[46] Domingo Laín's successful strategic model made it into the ELN's most successful unit. Indeed, by 1986 the ELN fully restructured its operations following the front's blueprint and flexible combat model.[47] Adopting this new strategic formula paid huge dividends for the ELN, inaugurating an important period of growth for the organization. Before 1980, the group's force amounted to some 250 to 300 combatants, and its presence was limited to the departments of Santander, Antioquia, and southern Bolívar. From 1983 on, though, the ELN began a rapid expansion, reaching approximately 2,500 operatives by the early 1990s; these combatants were divided across five major war fronts and subdivided into thirty-five smaller fronts, each comprising seventy-five to eighty-five combatants on average. This astounding growth, particularly between 1986 and 1989, allowed the ELN to expand its presence to most parts of central and northern Colombia.[48]

Pressured by ever-intensifying attacks by the Colombian Army and paramilitary groups, which made use of brutal tactics to obliterate their support bases, guerrilla groups—especially the FARC—responded in kind by stepping up attacks against civilians, including carrying out massacres. This move responded to their growing need to hold on to strategic territory, protect their economic interests, and keep civilians under their control through fear.[49] Insurgent violence worsened with the irruption of the April 19 Movement (Movimiento 19 de Abril, or M-19). Incorporating the revolutionary formula developed by urban revolutionary groups in Brazil and the Southern Cone,[50] M-19 carried out a string of terrorist attacks in major metropolitan areas.[51]

This phase of worsening violence in the countryside and urban areas, in turn, caused the Colombian state to ramp up its counterinsurgency efforts further, a response informed by the doctrine of national security, which gained traction under Liberal President Julio César Turbay Ayala (1978–1982). In a pattern reminiscent of Southern Cone dictatorships, the Colombian state implemented harsh repressive measures to neutralize the challenge posed by guerrillas. The state conferred important judicial powers on the Colombian military, most notably jurisdiction over "many 'political' crimes" committed by civilians, and the authority to try those cases in its own courts.[52] Marco Palacio notes that up to sixty thousand people were detained in the first year of Turbay Ayala's administration and that intimidation and torture were systematically practiced. Targets included leftist militants, students, intellectuals, labor unionists, and anyone suspected of belonging to guerrilla groups.[53]

Against this worrisome deterioration of security conditions, an unexpected and highly unusual wave of violence exacerbated the country's already turbulent situation in the mid-1980s. The violence spiked after the Medellín Cartel—a loose conglomerate of drug smugglers that included Pablo Escobar, Gonzalo Rodríguez Gacha, Jorge Luis Ochoa Vásquez, and Carlos Lehder—decided to militarily defy President Belisario Betancur's (1982–1986) decision to extradite drug dealers to the United States to face justice for their alleged crimes. The cartel leaders initiated their violent campaign by assassinating Justice Minister Rodrigo Lara Bonilla in a daring attack in broad daylight on the streets of Bogotá in 1984. To pressure the government to yield to their demands, the so-called extraditables then unleashed a harsh terrorist campaign that included bombings, executions, and the kidnappings of members of prominent families and public servants.[54]

Between 1989 and 1990, the group carried out further attacks, including sixty bombings against newspapers, shopping malls, an airliner (Avianca Flight 203, with 109 passengers, exploded midflight), and other soft targets, more abductions, and targeted assassinations against a plethora of soft targets, including politicians, judges, intellectuals, and journalists.[55] The campaign, which sought to soften the government's resolve to extradite kingpins, is one of the earliest and most acute displays of terrorism on the part of organizations with criminal intent. Gustavo Duncan and his colleagues explain that the Medellín Cartel deployed terrorism as a political weapon more than to maximize profits, thus demonstrating how such an organization can shift along the terrorism crime nexus.[56] This decade-long struggle (1984–1993) claimed the lives of thousands of Colombians, injured many more, destroyed vital infrastructure, and further undermined the state's legitimacy because of its inability to protect Colombians from the drug traffickers' wrath.

Showing significant flexibility, Escobar, Rodríguez Gacha, and their associates borrowed both pro-state and insurgent terrorist tactics and took them to a new level, profoundly affecting how terrorism would be employed in Colombia. Daniel Pécaut argues that the violent campaign unleashed by the Medellín Cartel was an inflection point in the use of terrorism and that several groups refined their repertoires of violence using Escobar's playbook. On this point, he asserts, "Nothing similar had ever occurred in the previous long history of violence in Colombia. Key figures were assassinated like Gaitán in 1948, but none of the earlier protagonists of violence had aimed to attack the very operation of the state itself.... A sort of taboo had been broken and the whole realm of violence was redefined."[57]

The Zenith of Violence (1994–2005)

The demise of the Medellín Cartel put an end to a dark period characterized by a unique blend of narco-related terrorism that left a traumatic imprint on the country. Yet, far from opening the way for the peace yearned for by exhausted Colombians, the cartel's collapse was in fact the overture to the worst period of the war, one in which stronger and emboldened guerrillas clashed with a new, more aggressive generation of paramilitary groups. The strengthening of paramilitary groups owes much to the so-called Persecuted by Pablo Escobar (Perseguidos por Pablo Escobar, or PEPES) group, a shadowy, powerful alliance of the capo's long list of enemies, which included the Cali Cartel, former Medellín Cartel operatives who fell out of favor with the kingpin, the Colombian state, and the United States. The PEPES were critical in the fall of the mighty Escobar, who was shot dead by security forces in 1993.[58]

Paramilitarism's new phase is inextricably linked to former lieutenants of Escobar who joined PEPES, such as Diego Murillo (aka Don Berna) as well as Fidel Castaño and his two brothers, Vicente and Carlos. Following Escobar's death, Fidel Castaño seized part of the now-defunct Medellín operation and utilized the resources and expertise he had acquired during his power struggles with Escobar to build a powerful army. In 1993, the Castaños founded the Peasant Self-Defense Forces of Córdoba and Urabá (ACCU). The ACCU, which played a seminal role in articulating a national paramilitary project, was partly demand driven, responding to the growing clamor for security by cattle ranchers and banana growers exasperated by EPL and FARC activity in Urabá. Urabá, and later Córdoba, would replace Puerto Boyacá as the epicenter of paramilitarism because of its privileged position as a strategic corridor for the transshipment of drugs, a main source of revenue.[59] The paramilitary experiment in Córdoba and Urabá would soon be exported to various regions of the country. The movement spread quickly to areas including the eastern lowland region, the eastern areas bordering Venezuela, the highlands of Boyacá, and the Cauca Valley.[60] This expansion cemented the emergence of the United Self-Defense Forces of Colombia (AUC), a national paramilitary umbrella organization created by Carlos Castaño, Fidel's younger brother, who took over the ACCU following Fidel's disappearance in 1994. At its zenith, the AUC comprised approximately thirty-one thousand armed combatants divided into scores of units.[61]

The growth of paramilitary groups was buttressed by various state-sanctioned civilian self-defense force known as Asociaciones Comunitarias de Vigilancia (Surveillance and Private Security Associations). These groups dated to the Liberal presidency of César Gaviria, but they were officially sanctioned only in 1994 during the administration of President Ernesto Samper, also of the Liberal Party (1994–1998), and would come to be called Cooperatives of Rural Security (CONVIVIR). Originally conceived as lightly armed groups, these civilian forces would eventually support the anti-subversive project of the state. Unlike conventional paramilitary groups operating in Colombia, however, the Colombian Armed Forces openly and legally supported the CONVIVIR. By 1997, CONVIVIR groups across the country numbered almost four hundred, totaling 120,000 members nationally, though only 10 percent were armed. Contrary to initial plans, the CONVIVIR project ended up further strengthening paramilitary groups when the latter absorbed many of them into their ranks.[62]

The growth of these paramilitary groups occurred alongside and was influenced by political negotiations between the state and guerrillas. Several scholars contend that the AUC's national project was inadvertently bolstered by the Conservative administration of Andrés Pastrana (1998–2002), who opened peace negotiations with the FARC in 1998.[63] His surprising announcement was met with consternation by wide sectors of the armed forces, who considered the move risky and unwise. Concern grew when, as a goodwill gesture to move negotiations forward, Pastrana granted the FARC a demilitarized zone in the southern department of Caquetá but failed to secure a ceasefire. As many within the state security forces worried would occur, the FARC strategically used these conditions to increase its strength. During the three years negotiations lasted, the group took advantage of the sanctuary to recruit and train new operatives, stage attacks, and develop military expertise, including terrorist tactics.[64] The FARC also established a presence in major metropolitan areas, where it staged highly visible attacks, kidnappings in particular. The FARC reached its apex in 2002 following its brief capture of Mitú, capital city of the department of Vaupés, which sent shockwaves through Colombia's military establishment.[65]

Against this backdrop, the AUC embarked on a plan to confront the FARC—and the ELN—at the national level. Under the leadership of Carlos Castaño, paramilitaries perfected a business model that made the AUC into a formidable force. Duncan asserts that the AUC's evolution marked a qualitative transformation in paramilitary groups as they morphed from informal militias into much larger, well-organized private armies capable of waging territorial conflicts with guerrillas and characterized by a command structure, group iconographies, and a clearly articulated doctrine. Some small militias intent on remaining independent were incorporated into the AUC's project by force.[66] These groups would soon discover that their military might not only allowed them to control large areas of the country but could also be leveraged to transform themselves into important political players.⁶⁷

Paramilitary groups used their growing coercive power to consolidate their control of coca cultivation, drug processing and production zones, and transshipment routes along border areas. They also expanded their influence in profitable legal businesses (cattle ranching, mining). One of the most formidable and long-lasting effects of paramilitarism's second phase was the reconfiguration of power in rural Colombia. Mimicking the Marxist strategy of combining all forms of struggle, paramilitary groups developed political outlets.⁶⁸ To achieve their goals within zones under their control, paramilitaries began to regulate the activities of the population, repressing any attempts to defy their authority. To that end, they threatened or bought off elected local authorities and infiltrated state institutions such as the police, the military, and the judiciary. Paramilitaries became the dominant actor in many rural areas across the country, replacing traditional elites, who now served as links between their new patrons and the central state. As their grip over these zones strengthened, paramilitaries reshaped existing regional orders and replaced them with new regimes characterized by unaccountability and violent enforcement.⁶⁹

THE DEMOCRATIC SECURITY POLICY (2002–2010)

Paramilitaries' meteoric rise was buttressed by the ascendance to power of Álvaro Uribe, the governor of Antioquia who launched a successful bid for Colombia's presidency in 2002. A cunning politician, Uribe identified the electorate's frustration with the peace process and its craving for security, campaigning on the promise to fight the FARC head-on to restore security and the rule of law. One of the cornerstones of Uribe's two terms in office was the so-called Democratic Security Policy, which sought to ameliorate the country's critical security situation by boosting the state's infrastructural capacity, particularly in the realm of security.⁷⁰ This aggressive policy was buttressed by Plan Colombia, a counterinsurgency assistance initiative underwritten by the United States.⁷¹ The administration justified the policy by claiming that militarization was the only answer to insecurity, and that the military build-up was crucial not only to enforce the rule of law but also to promote economic and social development.⁷²

The policy rested on three basic pillars. First, it called for carrying out counterinsurgency activities aimed at neutralizing the growing power of the FARC as well as the smaller ELN. The Colombian state's main objectives were to dislodge guerrillas from areas deemed critical for economic development and political governability, to regain control of the country's main highways—which had been seriously compromised by guerrilla attacks and sabotage—and to destroy the FARC's strategic rear guard in the southern departments of Meta, Guaviare, and Caquetá. Second, it sought to curb the production and commercialization of narcotics by measures including aerial interdiction, crop eradication, destruction of clandestine laboratories, and aggressive prosecution and extradition of narcotraffickers. Third, it attempted to defuse the threat posed by paramilitary groups by opening formal peace negotiations with the AUC in 2003. After lengthy negotiations, the Colombian state and paramilitary groups signed the Santafé de Ralito Peace Accord in 2006, under which 30,915 combatants formally demobilized.[73] In accordance with the terms of the agreement, top commanders and mid-ranking officers agreed to lay down their arms in exchange for lighter sentences as part of a contentious law outlined in the accord. Rank-and-file combatants, for their part, entered a reintegration program that would provide them vocational training, financial assistance, and psychological support to ease their transition back to civilian life.[74]

The peace agreement proved highly controversial, however. The transitional justice section of the accord was criticized because in the view of many detractors, it granted impunity for heinous crimes, as chapter 5 of this book recounts.[75] More important, the design and execution of the accord failed to fully extirpate paramilitarism. For example, many former paramilitary organizations refused to participate in the process, unwilling to relinquish their power or fearing state retaliation. These apprehensions proved well founded in 2008, when, after refusing to honor the terms of the agreement, the Uribe government proceeded to extradite several top paramilitary commanders to the United States. More worryingly, many paramilitary groups that purportedly demobilized remained active. Some participated in the demobilization process only to reappear later under different guises in other regions of Colombia. Sarah Daly Zukerman reports that half of all paramilitary groups remilitarized within five years after the signing of the peace accord.[76] Other groups cheated the treaty conditions by fraudulently recruiting civilians to pose as combatants while keeping a core segment of their fighters active. Furthermore, opportunists—including common criminals—posed as AUC combatants to claim the reintegration benefits the state offered.[77]

Notwithstanding these flaws, President Uribe's policies did achieve some positive security results. The FARC suffered heavy blows at the hands of the CSSF, which captured or killed senior and mid-ranking officers and wrestled strategic areas from FARC control. Between 2004 and 2010, the FARC's fighting force dwindled from sixteen thousand to approximately seven or eight thousand combatants following heavy military losses and massive desertion.[78] The ELN also endured heavy casualties and was forced to limit its operations and relocate part of its leadership to Venezuela.[79] As for paramilitary groups, the combination of demobilization, arrests, prosecutions of mid-ranking lieutenants, and the extradition of top commanders to the United States severely weakened them. The debilitation of guerrillas and paramilitary groups contributed to diminish overall levels of violence and to temporarily reduce drug cultivation and production because of an aggressive campaign of aerial fumigation.[80] Yet, despite these ostensible successes, Uribe and his polices were unable to promote lasting conditions of peace and were marred by several scandals. The two most damaging were the so-called *falsos positivos*, in which civilian killings were staged by state security forces to look as if they had lawfully occurred during combats with insurgent operatives; and *parapolítica*, instances of paramilitaries infiltrating the ranks of the president's party.[81]

Post-Conflict Phase (2016–Present)

In 2012, the center-right administration of President Juan Manuel Santos, who served as President Uribe's defense minister, surprisingly reopened peace negotiations with the FARC. Following a lengthy and tortuous process that included a referendum about the terms of the Peace Accord, the Colombian state and the FARC signed a treaty in Havana in 2016. Under the terms of the agreement, the bulk of the FARC's force, estimated at ten thousand fighters, agreed to demobilize and transition into a political party, the FARC, in exchange for promises regarding rural land reform, special political representation,[82] and the creation of a transitional justice mechanism known as Special Jurisdiction for Peace (Jurisdicción Especial para la Paz) that would hear cases against FARC commanders for their alleged crimes.[83]

The accord created enormous expectations that the country would finally put an end to the conflict, but violence has continued (see chapter 7). The long ideological struggle for power has morphed into a conflict marked by localized pockets of violence. In this new period, highly sophisticated criminal organizations and guerrillas increasingly involved in illegal business vie for power among themselves and with state security forces.[84] This phase of violence resembles the conditions of so-called criminal wars, that is, contexts where parties with strictly economic motivations seek to constrain their enemies, including the state, through violence.[85]

Remaining armed camps include FARC dissidents, the ELN, and a plethora of regionally based paramilitary successor groups (see chapter 7).[86] Following the demobilization of the FARC, these groups moved in and began to dispute strategic territory formerly held by the disbanded organization.[87] Groups have since engaged in ferocious battles to control strategic areas for the transshipment and production of drugs sites where they exploit natural resources (mining, timber) and the profitable business of human smuggling along the Venezuelan border.[88] Meanwhile, landholding elites, many with ties to paramilitary groups, have fomented violence in their attempts to block land distribution reforms. Armed groups have gained control of significant swaths of territory where the state has little presence in the departments of Arauca, Cauca, Chocó, Nariño, Norte de Santander, and Valle del Cauca, among the most prominent.[89]

To a significant degree, these dynamics are related to shortcomings in the implementation of the peace accord.[90] Domestic and international actors, including facilitators and brokers of the peace deal, have expressed their frustration at the difficulties experienced throughout the implementation phase.[91] One critical shortcoming concerns security conditions. Even though the bulk of the FARC demobilized, between 5 and 8 percent remained armed, and the accord did not formally include FARC militia members, its so-called strategic reserve of seven thousand to eight thousand active combatants.[92] Claiming that the Colombian state had not complied with the terms of the agreement, an estimated five thousand former FARC fighters remain active.[93]

In sum, as a recent report observes, "the territorial vacuum left by the old insurgency, and the absence of many promised government reforms, has unleashed a criminal morass as new groups form, and old groups mutate, in a battle to control flourishing illicit economies."[94] Despite changes in the composition and goals of armed groups, the post-conflict context has preserved many of the violent conditions that characterized the ex-ante period, including massive human rights violations and the widespread use of terrorism. According to human rights organizations, between November 2016 and December 2020, 972 social leaders were assassinated in Colombia.[95] Colombia's ombudsperson explains that these leaders were killed by armed parties with the intent to paralyze communities and neutralize potential challenges to their power.[96] Finally, terrorist attacks such as abductions, executions, bombing attacks, massacres, and other type of actions have continued to afflict the country.

After securing a win in the 2022 presidential elections, the new administration of President Gustavo Petro, who presides over the first left-wing government in the history of Colombia, announced plans to embark on a comprehensive peace initiative. The plan, known as Total Peace (Paz Total), seeks to reach a negotiated solution with all armed parties still operating in the country (twenty-six in total). The plan partly follows the logic of the 2016 peace accord with the FARC in that it purportedly tackles several interconnected challenges (drug trafficking and cultivation, land tenure, illicit mining, and environmental issues) simultaneously. The government has promised to put on hold plans to capture the leaders of armed parties and to offer incentives (reduced sentences, suspended extradition) in exchange for their demobilization and information on illegal operations.[97]

Conclusions

This chapter provides a brief account of the evolution of security conditions in Colombia, showing how from its independence from Spain in the nineteenth century, the country's history has been marked by repeated cycles of civil war in which terrorism has been systematically employed by warring parties. The latest phase of violence in an ongoing conflict dating back to a peasant insurrection in the mid-1960s is characterized by a complex, multidimensional configuration in which a plethora of armed parties—including guerrilla groups, paramilitary forces, and state security forces—have practiced massive violence.

The conflict has grown concentrically as the growth of guerrilla power was matched by the significant mobilization of influential civilian sectors in the countryside, often with links to illicit industries and supported by the Colombian state. Despite repeated attempts to find a military and negotiated solution to this multipronged conflict—such as the partial demobilization and weakening of the AUC in 2005 and the FARC in 2016—the war rages on. In this respect, the chapter underlines how what began as an ideological conflict has morphed into a criminal war where powerful organizations involved in illegal business vie for power and where security forces create localized pockets of violence. Today, these parties continue to use similarly dehumanizing tactics as in the past, including the systematic and widespread use of terrorism.

3
The Mighty FARC and the Use of Terrorism

In a sober ceremony held in a hotel in downtown Bogotá on May 20, 2017, demobilized Revolutionary Armed Forces of Colombia (FARC) members involved in the bombing of the El Nogal Club met with survivors and relatives of the those killed or wounded. The meeting, organized by Bertha Lucía Fríes, one of the victims of the attack, was part of a series of interventions organized across the country to promote truth and reconciliation following the 2016 peace accord between the FARC and the Colombian state. The conversation was candid and often very difficult: victims and their relatives shared their ordeal of losing loved ones or carrying the physical and emotional scars of the attacks; guerillas spoke about the hardship they faced and the inhumanity of war. In the most emotional moment of the gathering, guerrillas expressed their deep remorse for the attack and asked for forgiveness. The bombing against the exclusive private club, a symbol of Colombian upper-class power, was one of the most emblematic of FARC's terrorist strikes and one of the deadliest episodes in the country's civil war. The attack, which entailed detonating 200 kilograms of C4, a highly powerful plastic explosive hidden in a car, was carried out by the Teófilo Forero Mobile Column but masterminded by the group's high-ranking commanders.[1]

In pursuit of its revolutionary goals, the FARC used terrorism systematically and with a clear agitational intent: indiscriminate bombings such as the attack on El Nogal in which thirty-six people died and two hundred more were injured, were meant to terrorize the public and undermine trust in the Colombian state by showing its inability to protect its citizens, not even the most powerful, thereby conveying that nobody was safe. General agreement that the FARC relied extensively on terrorism during the Colombian civil war aside,[2] several questions concerning this group's use of this tactic remain unanswered. For example, how exactly did the FARC employ terrorism and what elements informed its choices? Why was the FARC more prone to certain types of attacks? How does its repertoire vary from that of other armed parties, including fellow guerrilla groups? Did its tactics evolve over time? Finally, are terrorist patterns geographically uniform or do they vary subnationally?

This chapter unpacks the methods and motives behind the FARC's repertoire of terrorism. To do so, it traces the historical development of the group, the role of its leadership, and its internal organizational practices. The database assembled for this study contains 2,409 terrorist attacks ascribed to the FARC between 1988 and 2012, which correspond to 18.9 percent of the total number registered in this book's sample, which could be traced to a culprit (12,760). Figure 3.1 presents a chronological display of the FARC's use of terrorism on four selected indicators found in the sample. It shows that the group relied systematically on this tactic throughout the duration of the conflict, with terrorist attacks ebbing and flowing in accordance with periods of intensification and deescalation in the civil war. The group perpetrated on average forty attacks per year between 1988 and 1996. Terrorist acts surge after 1998 following the creation of a demilitarized zone controlled by the group under the terms of the negotiation process during the presidency of Andrés Pastrana (1998–2002) and the inception of Plan Colombia. The years 2001 and 2002, with 276 and 325 attacks per year, respectively, saw the highest incidence of FARC terrorism. After 2003, attacks decreased, especially around 2007, when the group started to feel the squeeze of the military offensive under the so-called Democratic Security Policy that led to the group's final demobilization in 2016.

From a comparative perspective, the FARC perpetrated less than half of all paramilitary terrorist attacks, but substantially more than the Colombian state security forces (CSSF). Among insurgent groups, the FARC accounted for 57 percent of the terrorist attacks found in the sample: the

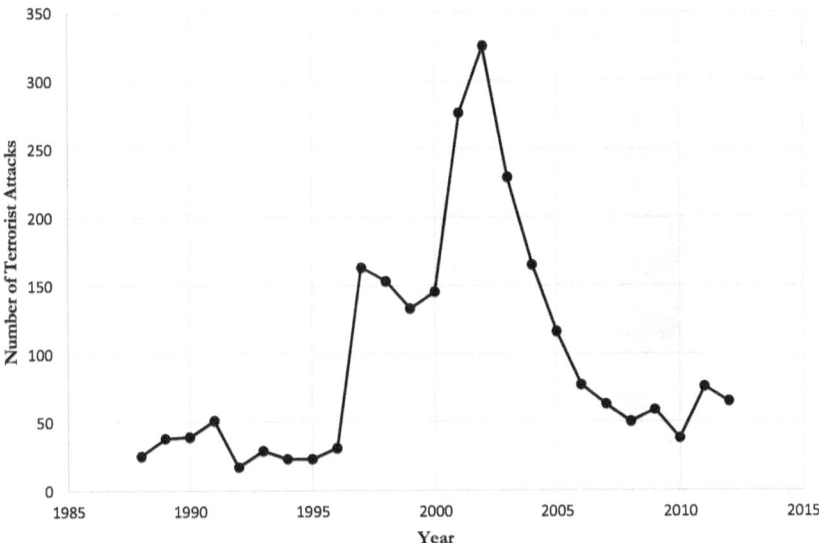

FIGURE 3.1 FARC's use of terrorism, 1988–2012.

Source: Author's tabulation based on CINEP data.

group indeed perpetrated more such acts than all other guerilla groups combined.[3] As to the FARC's repertoire of terrorism, figure 3.2 displays the use of this tactic according to the most prevalent forms of attacks the group used, which can be disaggregated as follows: 1,204 executions, 884 abductions, 200 massacres, and 121 indiscriminate bombing attacks. This group also engaged in other terrorist tactics, including torture and disappearance.[4]

The FARC's use of terrorism follows a clear sequence. Influenced by revolutionary doctrines and praxis in vogue in the 1960s and 1970s, leaders gradually embraced insurgent terrorist strikes like abductions and bombing attacks as cornerstones of their repertoire of action. Summary executions were also sporadically incorporated, often targeting "enemies of the people" (infiltrators, traitors, and even common thieves).[5] These were agitational actions designed to erode the legitimacy of the state by exposing its inability to protect ordinary citizens. Years later, and influenced by trends in Vietnam and Central America, the group adopted a dual military-political strategy and sought to project its presence into urban areas. The new strategy coincided with a period of state military expansion, which

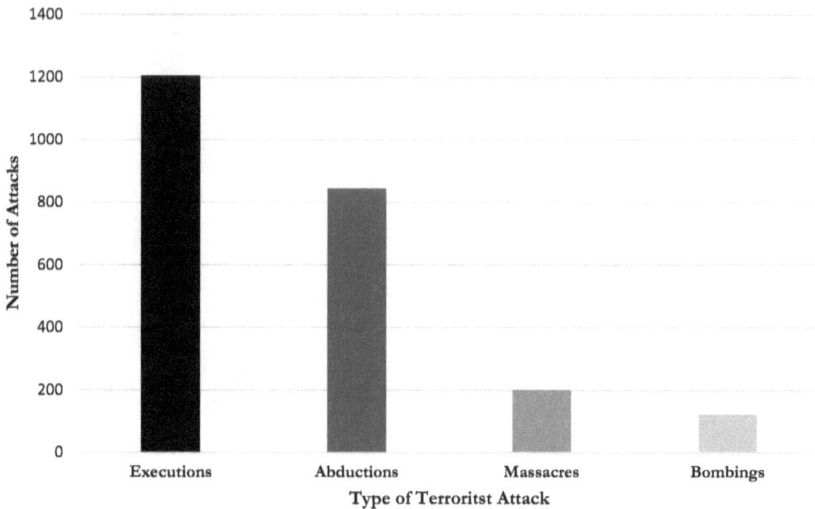

FIGURE 3.2 FARC's repertoires of terrorism, 1988–2012.

Source: Author's tabulation based on CINEP data.

would be intensified by the irruption of paramilitary groups. Responding and adapting to paramilitaries' extreme methods, the FARC incorporated into its repertoire territorial forms of terrorism, in particular massacres, while disputing territory with right-wing foes. Although the FARC relied extensively on territorial terrorism during the most intense period of war, for the most part it steered clear of sacralized forms of violence (overkill), which did not align with its revolutionary ethos.

This chapter argues that the FARC's repertoire of terrorism is the product of its unique organizational identity as an autonomous, pragmatic, and highly militarized group characterized by orthodox revolutionary thinking and strong connections to the peasant class. The FARC's identity was critically influenced by the tumultuous period of La Violencia, most relevantly by the destruction of the Independent Peasant Republics, a foundational moment that would instill within the group a sense of victimization and mistrust toward the Colombian state and society at large. FARC terrorist practices evolved over time, driven by a combination of ideological preferences and strategic military thinking from the Secretariat, a seven-member panel overseeing all activities. The group's leadership, which remained stable over time, promoted the idea that, though extreme, terrorist acts were a legitimate way of conducting its class warfare and were justified against certain civilians considered enemies of the people, either because of their class or because they opposed the group. One event that significantly influenced the FARC's reliance on terrorism was the decimation of thousands of Patriotic Union militants at the hands of right-wing paramilitary groups in the mid-1980s, which further sowed mistrust and propelled hawkish views within the organization. This experience propelled FARC leadership to embrace a more aggressive military strategy, which was often complemented with terrorist tactics.[6]

A note of caution around conceptual terms is required when examining the FARC's use of terrorism. As alluded to in the introduction, the difference between guerrilla warfare and terrorism is often misunderstood. This confusion stems from the fact that guerrilla groups often rely on terrorism as part of their repertoire of action and because states are prone to characterizing guerrillas and other antagonistic groups as "terrorist organizations" when seeking to delegitimize them. Ian Beckett defines guerrilla warfare as "a set of military tactics utilized by a minority group within a state or an indigenous population in order to oppose the government or foreign occupying forces."[7] Timothy Wickham-Crowley explains that it is an ancient form of warfare generally used by weaker parties facing superior forces. Guerrilla warfare, he explains, is better defined in military than in social or political terms. It involves avoiding direct confrontation in pitched battles and concentrating on "slowly sapping the enemy's strength and morale through ambushes, minor skirmishes, lightning raids and withdrawals, cutting off communications and supply lines, and similar techniques."[8]

Guerrillas normally set up small military units and seek to establish liberated zones that can be used to militarily challenge the state. Guerrillas use these areas to mount attacks against the state, often creating a parallel state structure.[9] These areas are generally located in the countryside, but on rare occasions guerrillas have also "liberated" urban areas.[10] Terrorism, by contrast, relies on a totally different logic in that it purposefully avoids military confrontation and deliberately targets civilians to create widespread commotion.[11] Consequently, the principal difference between terrorism and guerrilla warfare is the nature of the violent act itself, irrespective of the organization or individual carrying it out.

Guerrilla operations are directed principally against the members of the enemy's security and armed forces as well as their infrastructure, particularly strategic installations, whereas terrorism entails the deliberate targeting of civilians.

The chapter proceeds as follows. This first section provides a detailed overview of the creation and evolution of the FARC, underlining the importance of historical antecedents in shaping distinctive identity traits within the organization. The second section details how ideology evolved within the group and influenced commanders' views on how best to carry out their revolutionary endeavor. Relatedly, this section also looks at the institutional mechanisms, such as training and indoctrination, that give rise to a singular repertoire of terrorism. The chapter then describes how the adoption of an aggressive military strategy, coupled with the emergence of paramilitary groups, pushed the FARC to embrace territorial forms of terrorism as it disputed strategic sites with its enemies. The chapter concludes with reflections on the FARC's use of terrorism and its role within Colombia's civil war.

The Historical Foundation of the FARC

The FARC's organizational identity is inherently tied to Colombia's turbulent rural development throughout the twentieth century, a process marked by violence and shattered expectations that created fertile ground for peasant radicalization. The emergence of the group can be traced to the arrival of the Communist Party of Colombia (PCC) to the countryside during the 1920s. Up to that point, the PCC was only present in urban areas, where it sought to influence politics and lay the foundations of a modern political party. The PCC, which strictly adhered to a Marxist Soviet line, played an important role in an embryonic urban labor movement. Yet, facing mounting repression in the cities, the party eventually sought refuge in the countryside, thinking—rightly—that the oppressive conditions endured by peasants were ideal for developing a revolutionary consciousness.[12] Thus the PCC developed strong links to agrarian resistance movements from its early days: its cadre provided ideological blueprints for resistance and helped peasant communities to develop critical organizational know-how as part of a nascent movement protesting their harsh living conditions. During the 1930s, the peasant resistance was not violent, reflecting the moderation exhibited by the PCC, which was then a close ally of the progressive wing of the Colombian Liberal Party.[13]

This would change during La Violencia, when the commotion that engulfed the country, threatened the very existence of several peasant communities, and forced them to organize self-defense groups.[14] According to Eduardo Pizarro, La Violencia inaugurated a long period of conflict (1949-1964) characterized by proliferating self-defense forces and guerrillas.[15] In 1949, the PCC, which had rejected the use of violence as a viable instrument for attaining power, reversed course and embraced a strategy based on the principle of self-defense for the masses, arguing that Colombia had become ripe for revolution. Although many peasant self-defense groups claimed allegiance to the PCC, others remained ideologically closer to the Liberal Party. Indeed, for a while Communists and Liberals cooperated in confronting menacing Conservative forces and bandits during La Violencia. This tactical alliance, however, broke down as strategic differences and discord stemming from personal rivalries emerged.[16]

A pivotal development in the formation and trajectory of the FARC was the emergence of independent republics to which peasants and their families flocked in search of protection during the worst periods of La Violencia; at their zenith, they hosted up to four thousand people. These enclaves emerged in a region between Cundinamarca and Tolima known as Tequendama and the phenomenon was described by Eric Hobsbawm as the Colombian version of the Swiss popular uprising led by Wilhelm Tell.[17] The first republic, Viotá, was followed by many other enclaves in the early 1950s.[18] The most emblematic of these was Gaitania—later named Marquetalia—founded by Fermín Charry Rincón. Although suspicious of these emancipatory moves, the central state, which was then controlled by Conservatives, refrained from moving against these sanctuaries given the country's critical security situation. Moreover, peasant republics received a boost after the junta led by General Rojas Pinilla, who deposed the Conservative government in 1953, was able to reduce violence across the country and offered a general amnesty to revolting peasants.[19]

The fervor sparked by the 1959 Cuban Revolution, however, emboldened leaders and supporters of peasant republics, prompting fear among members of the newly created National Front—led by President Lleras Camargo (1958–1962)—that the enclaves could incubate a massive insurrection. These fears were in part stoked by the John F. Kennedy administration, which had begun to implement the Alliance of Progress, a policy that combined economic assistance and counterinsurgency measures with a view to containing Cuban-inspired insurrections across the region.[20] Pressured by members of Colombia's armed forces and by the United States, Lleras Camargo's successor, Conservative President Guillermo León Valencia (1962–1966), instructed Colombian security forces to infiltrate the enclaves in 1964 in an attempt to destabilize them from within. When this plan failed, he ordered the army to destroy them one by one.[21]

The FARC rose from the ashes of this failed socio-communitarian experiment. Pedro Antonio Marín (aka Tirofijo, "Sure Shot"), the legendary commander who ruled the group for forty-two years (1966–2008), founded the FARC in 1964 alongside other survivors of the Colombian army's assault on Marquetalia.[22] The destruction of the peasant republics became a foundational moment that would significantly shape the FARC's identity and ethos.[23] It left scars among its defiant survivors, who nurtured a deep sense of animosity against the existing institutional order and a distrust of the outside world. FARC founding members resented what they regarded as a betrayal by both the Colombian government and the Liberal Party, which did nothing to help them. This bitter experience also instilled within the group a strong sense of autonomy and a fierce commitment to social change.[24] Elaborating on the nature of the FARC's values, José Juvenal Velandia (aka Iván Ríos), a commander of the powerful Central Bloc who would become the youngest member of FARC's High Command, asserts, "We can talk about a *fariana* culture, a culture of resistance or equality. These are values that identify our organization."[25]

Ideology

As explained in chapter 2, ideology plays a critical role in the development of armed parties' repertoires of terrorism. Ideology offers an intellectual justification for acts of violence committed in the service of a given cause or worldview. In the case of the FARC, it drew on a radical, Manichean view that interprets society strictly in terms of class struggle to articulate and rationalize violence, including attacks on civilian targets. Manuel Marulanda described this viewpoint in a 1984 interview: "Our enemies," he said, "are all those reactionary sectors who do not want to see a process of social, economic, and political change in Colombia."[26] According to this outlook, those belonging to the bourgeoisie are seen as enemies of the people and thus deemed legitimate targets. Marulanda's articulation of the FARC's justification offers a pristine example of Goodwin's theory of categorical terrorism in that people are reduced to a broad category of "complicit" beneficiaries or supporters of an order that needs to be destroyed to create a more just society.[27] The FARC thus systematically targeted members of the upper class ("oligarchs"), state officials ("lackeys"), foreign dignitaries and executives ("imperialists"), and common people accused of being informants (*sapos*). Even though the FARC tolerated mild forms of dissent and resistance from the communities it ruled,[28] the group was implacable when declaring—with or without evidence—that someone was collaborating with the enemy. Such a label often carried a death sentence, justified on ideological grounds.[29]

In his insightful analysis, Jorge Giraldo asserts that two ideas were critical in constructing the identity of Colombian guerrilla groups: revolutionary maximalism and the fatality of class contradiction. The former, characterized by a steadfast commitment to revolution in which determination trumped rationality, prevented these groups from considering any concession (e.g., land reform). Guerillas' sole purpose became overthrowing ruling governments and replacing them with a new regime, and this maximalist view was used to justify their decision to perpetrate inhumane practices during the entrenched conflict. Likewise, the groups' fatal view of class contradictions contributed to their notion that class warfare was inevitable and thus also justified many forms of violence. Such a vision, borrowed from Lenin's hyper-realist doctrine within Marxism, convinced guerrillas that the bourgeoisie would only yield power through violence.[30]

Reflecting its rigid ideological position, the FARC openly rejected the main principles of international humanitarian law, claiming they constituted an unrepresentative and ultimately illegitimate "bourgeois" construct that often ignored the messy reality of war.[31] The group's inclination to use extreme measures, including terrorism, was further galvanized by state repressive policies, such as President Turbay Ayala's crackdown on leftist organizations and sympathizers (1978–1982). As underlined in chapter 6, the widespread use of state-sanctioned violence (disappearances, torture, executions) reinforced the ideological discourse within the FARC justifying violence as a suitable reaction to oppression and injustice.[32]

Due to the influence of the PCC during its formation, the FARC internalized many of the highly dogmatic views that characterized communist parties at the time.[33] During its early years, the FARC adhered to a pro-Soviet Marxist-Leninist position. Although purportedly aligned with these orthodox ideologies, the group maintained an independent stance, reflecting a peasant tendency to trust nobody but their own. In the words of commander Julián Garcés, peasant culture was central to the organization's decision-making and identity, which often led to clashes with other groups within the leftist camp, including fellow guerrilla organizations and the PCC.[34]

Even though nominally adhering to strict Marxist ideologies, many of group's leaders were keenly aware of the dangers ideological intransigence posed for revolutionaries, as evidenced by resounding failures such as Guevara's botched Bolivian adventure. In the words of Luis Morantes (aka Jacobo Arenas), one of the FARC's chief ideologues during the group's early decades, doctrinal considerations came second to surviving in the uncertain context of the Colombian war.[35] Iván Ríos, another influential FARC commander, made a similar point while reflecting on the organization's pragmatism and autonomy, stating that "we cannot be bound by the ideas of anyone. We have our own process based on conditions in Colombia."[36]

Like many other insurgent groups of the time, the FARC professed admiration for the Cuban Revolution but underscored that it could not necessarily be replicated in Colombia. Over the years, the relationship between the FARC and the Communist leadership in Havana grew strained thanks to doctrinal differences and contradictory views on the best strategy for carrying out the revolutionary struggle. A major point of contention concerned whether revolution should be initiated by an urban vanguard, as Fidel Castro and Ernesto "Che" Guevara advocated, or whether it should emerge from a spontaneous social movement in the countryside, as the FARC argued.[37] These revolutionary differences were heightened by frictions deriving from the contrasting backgrounds and personalities of their members and leaders. Most of the first FARC commanders resented the fact that the Cuban leadership, which was urban and educated, belittled revolutionary spontaneity and was agnostic about the value of peasant and worker self-defense forces to the revolutionary cause.[38]

Conversely, many FARC leaders became true admirers of the Viet Cong, a Vietnamese guerrilla group that had similar peasant origins. In the view of most senior commanders at the time, some of whom traveled to Vietnam, the Viet Cong were a much more attractive model than the Cuban one. During their revolutionary exchange, FARC commanders were impressed by the Viet Cong's political consistency and military ingenuity. FARC commanders Iván Ríos and Fernando Caicedo noted in an interview that the Viet Cong's clever blending of ideology and pragmatism produced excellent results, while also praising the group for its humility, daringness, and revolutionary consistency.[39]

Some Central American second wave revolutionary groups also inspired FARC leadership, including the victorious Sandinistas in Nicaragua (1979) and the Salvadoran Farabundo Martí Liberation Front (Frente de Liberación Farabundo Martí, or FMLN).[40] Like many other leftist groups in the region, the FARC incorporated some of the successful strategies used by Central American revolutionaries—in particular the FMLN—such as creating a unified front among several guerrilla groups, a strategy that paid excellent dividends for the FMLN.[41] Drawing on this experience, the FARC participated in the 1985 Simón Bolívar National Guerrilla Coordination (Coordinadora Guerrillera Simón Bolívar), a short-lived, and ultimately unsuccessful, initiative (1987–1994) to unite guerrilla groups in a revolutionary confederation predicated on the Salvadoran example.

With the demise of the Soviet Union and the concomitant loss of revolutionary referents, the FARC shifted its allegiance from Marxism-Leninism to the more fashionable Bolivarianism.[42] Bolivarianism is a political movement based on certain ideas of Simón Bolívar, the iconic figure of Latin America's independence movement, including his views on social justice, anti-imperialism, and Latin American unity.[43] Overall, however, for many insurgent groups that took up arms during the polarized Soviet era, the end of the Cold War was a major challenge and often led to the relaxing of ideological views.[44] During this process, the FARC would flirt with and then gradually embrace criminal activities, making the drug trade an increasingly crucial part of its operations.[45] The relaxation of its revolutionary principles and the introduction of a criminal element affected the group's core identity. The changes were gradual but significant and manifested themselves more clearly following the FARC's demobilization in 2016, as discussed in the book's conclusion. Plentiful evidence of this trajectory can be found in the secret files of FARC commander Raúl Reyes, who died in a military raid in Ecuador in 2008.[46] Yet, in his sober assessment of the FARC's relationship with criminality, Francisco Gutiérrez-Sanín argues that despite these illicit activities, the group's ideological dimension remained a fundamental aspect of its identity.[47]

Leadership and Repertoires of Terrorism

It is not entirely clear exactly when the FARC began to incorporate terrorism. Locating evidence for when this tactical decision was made is especially difficult because, to the extent that organizations deny allegations that they engage in terrorism, they deliberately avoid discussing the issue or leaving a paper trail. This corresponds with the natural tendency of armed groups to conceal inhumane actions that seem inconsistent with their purported values, a phenomenon Albert Bandura calls moral disengagement.[48] The opacity of the decision-making notwithstanding, ample evidence underlines the importance of the FARC's leadership in developing repertoires of terrorism.

In the highly hierarchical structure of a revolutionary organization such as the FARC, the leadership—in this case the members of the powerful Central Command known as the Secretariat—played a critical role in the adoption of distinctive terrorist tactics.[49] After FARC commanders selected tactics that aligned with the group's revolutionary identity, they proceeded to socialize them through two main methods: political indoctrination and military training. FARC commanders were influenced by the transnational diffusion of knowledge common among revolutionary organizations in Latin America and beyond during those years. Such cooperation included training in urban warfare tactics, including the use of explosives, and in other sophisticated agitational techniques.

As indicated in chapter 2, FARC leadership was influenced by a new wave of urban insurrection groups popping up across Latin America, including the National Liberation Movement Tupamaros in Uruguay, the Revolutionary Leftist Movement in Venezuela and Chile, the Montoneros in Argentina, and the National Liberation Action (Ação Libertadora Nacional) in

Brazil. Between 1968 and 1972, a period during which many of these groups emerged, the FARC suffered several significant military defeats that led to an organizational crisis.[50] After stabilizing from these setbacks, FARC leaders began to incorporate some of the bolder tactics pioneered by Southern Cone radical groups around 1973 or 1974.

This revisionist second wave insurgency was encapsulated by M-19, a group modeled on urban guerrilla clans and led by Jaime Bateman Cayón—who had been expelled from the FARC—and other disillusioned members of the National Liberation Army, or Ejército de Liberación Nacional (ELN), affiliated with the National Popular Alliance (Alianza Nacional Popular), a centrist movement formed by General Gustavo Rojas Pinilla as a platform for his presidential run.[51] Mimicking the actions of Southern Cone groups, M-19 initially carried out a string of highly symbolic, nonviolent actions such as stealing Bolívar's sword from a well-guarded military base in central Bogotá.[52] These actions garnered public support and sympathy for the group, but, similar to the trajectory of other Southern Cone organizations, M-19 began embracing more violent tactics, including hostage taking seizing the Dominican Embassy in Bogotá, and, most dramatically, assaulting Colombia's Supreme Court building in 1985.[53]

As discussed in chapter 2, this new insurrectional wave resulted from writers and intellectuals such as Abraham Guillén critically rethinking the failed rural campaigns in Bolivia, Venezuela, and Peru. Guillén in particular concluded that in an epoch of developed urban centers, it was a mistake to restrict insurgent operations to isolated, sparsely populated areas without strategic relevance.[54] Regarding this point, Daniel Pécaut argues that the showy activities of the M-19 had a powerful demonstrative effect, socializing terrorism practices that would be later incorporated by Colombian guerrillas, including the FARC.[55] In this context, and pressured by the growing visibility of M-19, the FARC leadership would gradually embrace urban terrorism in a characteristically pragmatic shift. In accordance with Carlos Marighella's agitational playbook, the FARC exploited the propagandistic potential of carrying out destructive, high-profile attacks in semi-urban and urban settings, choosing easy targets requiring just a few well-trained operatives.

The FARC's use of abductions is illustrative of the worldwide diffusion of terrorist tactics among leftist armed groups in the late 1960s. In Latin America, one of the first groups to use highly visible kidnappings for agitational purposes was the Guatemalan Revolutionary Armed Forces, which kidnapped the U.S. ambassador to Guatemala in 1968.[56] This tactic rapidly spread to Argentina, Brazil, Uruguay, and Venezuela, where leftist organizations began to routinely abduct foreign dignitaries and executives, demanding exorbitant amounts for their release in cleverly staged publicity stunts that sought to increase the visibility of their plight. Many of these operations ended up with executions of the victims by their captors. As discussed in chapters 1 and 2, insurgent groups saw abductions as an effective agitational mechanism that weakened the foundations of ruling regimes and demoralized its forces.[57]

The use of abductions goes back to the mid-1960s but became more widespread in Colombia during the 1970s.[58] Despite its repeated denials to the contrary, the FARC officially incorporated abductions into its repertoire of action during its Sixth Conference in 1978. The move put an end to a traditional PCC policy of carrying out solely "political abductions" and avoiding the inhumane treatment of captives.[59] FARC leaders soon embraced the new tactic. While discussing the case of Richard Strauss, an American scientist kidnapped by the FARC, Jacobo Arenas candidly admitted that, like many other groups in the region, the FARC used this tool to further its revolutionary goals. Justifying this practice on ideological grounds, he described it as an inevitable part of revolutionary warfare.[60]

Abductions would eventually become a centerpiece of FARC strategy and its trademark. The group kidnapped high-value targets such as executives, landowners, diplomats, and other foreigners and wealthy individuals. Moreover, its growing military and tactical capacity in the 1990s allowed the FARC to extend this practice to major metropolitan areas such as Medellín, Cali, and the capital Bogotá. During the height of its power between 1998 and 2002, the FARC routinely kidnapped people, either selectively or through so-called miraculous fishing operations (in which people were randomly snatched at roadblocks). Abductions were facilitated by the FARC's control over a demilitarized zone in Caquetá, where many of the targets would be held.[61]

This push by FARC leaders to integrate insurgent forms of terrorism is widely supported by empirical evidence. Figure 3.3 presents the evolution of FARC abductions, showing how initially modest numbers rose sharply in the mid-1990s and then declined markedly especially after 2002 when FARC gradually began to lose military power.[62]

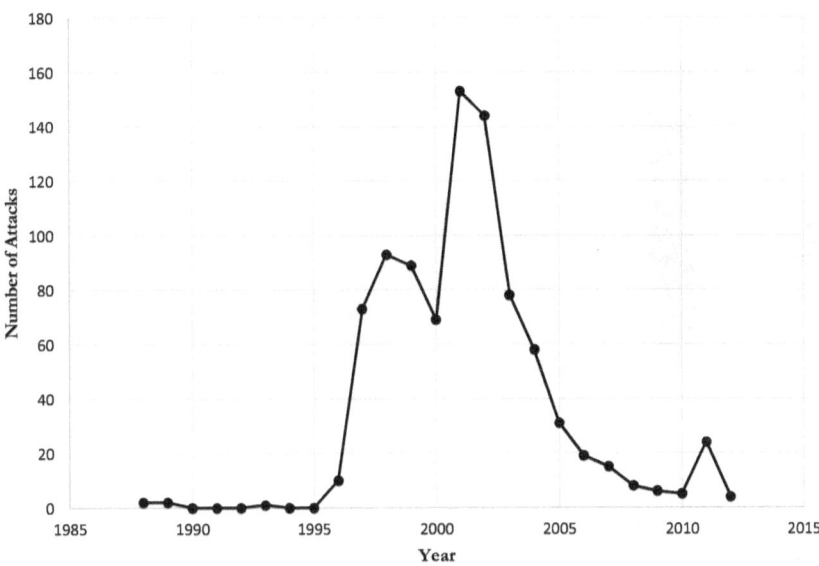

FIGURE 3.3 Evolution of FARC abductions, 1988–2012.

Source: Author's tabulation based on CINEP data.

Figure 3.4, in turn, shows the FARC's use of abductions relative to those of other Colombian armed parties. The FARC carried out the highest number of abductions: it is behind 884 cases, equivalent to 29 percent of the total in the sample.[63] Abductions account for a little more than a third (36 percent) of the FARC's total number of terrorist attacks, a smaller proportion than that of the ELN (52 percent) but significantly higher than that of paramilitary groups (12.3 percent) and the CSSF (12.2 percent) (see figure 3.5).[64] As to the identity of the abducted, 59 percent were armed forces members and public servants, 39 percent worked in agrobusiness (cattle ranchers, large and small landowners), and 33 percent were businesspeople.[65]

In line with the urban insurrectional playbook, FARC leadership also incorporated bombing attacks into its repertoire of terrorism. These indiscriminate attacks foster widespread commotion and, like abductions, dent the reputations of states by demonstrating their inability to protect citizens. Explosive devices have been used in resistance movements going back to World War I. Ernesto Guevara underlines their value in his *Guerra de Guerrillas*,[66] as does the Viet Cong, which relied on makeshift bombs while

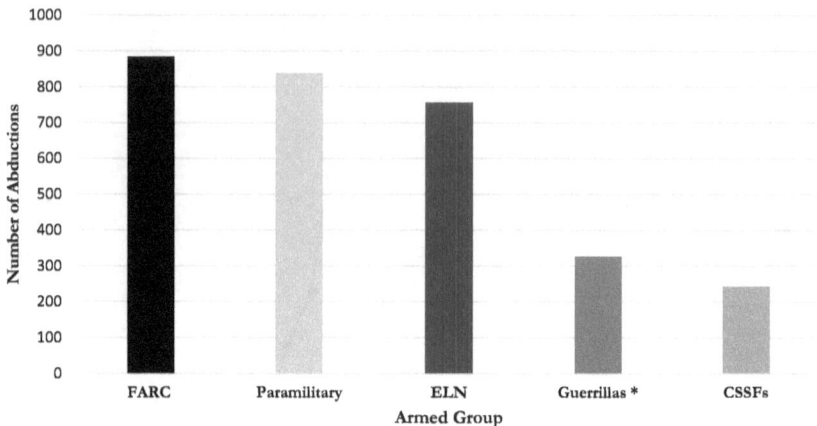

FIGURE 3.4 FARC abductions, 1988–2012.

Source: Author's tabulation based on CINEP data.

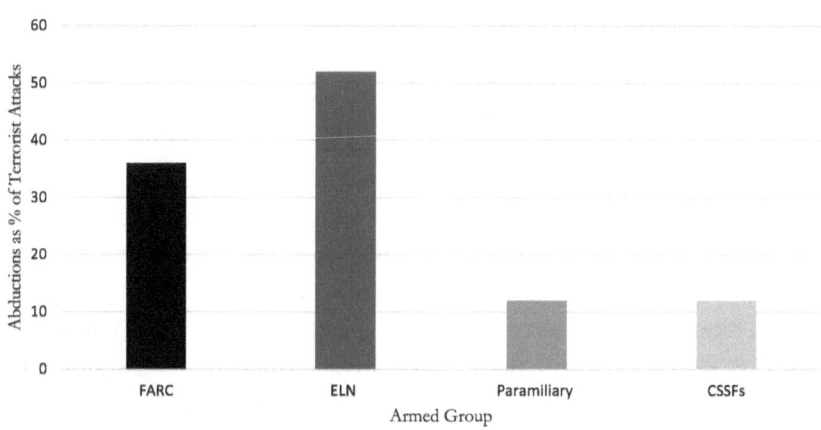

FIGURE 3.5 Abductions within FARC's repertoire of terrorism, 1988–2012.

Source: Author's tabulation based on CINEP data.

fighting French and American troops. In Colombia, bomb attacks were deployed during the chaotic days following the assassination of Jorge Eliécer Gaitán in 1948 and later by liberal guerrillas linked to Guadalupe Salcedo in Casanare in the 1950s. Influenced by the transnational diffusion of tactics among radical leftist groups, Colombian guerrillas, in particular the

ELN, incorporated this tactic into its repertoire in the mid-1970s.[67] M-19 and especially the FARC would follow suit; the FARC developed considerable know-how in explosives, expertise acquired in part through the revolutionary networks developed by the organization's leadership. Román Ortiz, a security expert, asserts that FARC leadership sought the assistance of revolutionary groups such as the Japanese Red Army, Basque Homeland and Liberty, and the Irish Republican Army to train FARC operatives in the use of such tactics.[68] Members of an Irish splinter group that would come to be known as the Provisional Irish Republican Army also traveled to the FARC's demilitarized zone and trained its operatives on urban terror.[69] This training helped FARC operatives perfect this insurrectional tactic and maximize its impact.[70]

The investigation of the notorious El Nogal attack provides a rare glance into the FARC's planning and execution of terrorist bombings. Forty-six days prior to the attack, the FARC posted a declaration on its official website indicating that the Colombian state was turning a blind eye to paramilitary activity: it stated that authorities were aware of several meetings between paramilitary operatives, politicians, and businesspersons at several of the most exclusive private clubs in Bogotá.[71] In an internal communication from two members of the FARC's Secretariat, Alfonso Cano and Iván Márques, to Fernando Arellán, the perpetrator of the attack, they wrote,

> Comrade Manuel. Our greetings. . . . The order we gave *The Paisa* was to blow up the car bomb in the El Nogal club when there were important people there such as generals, government ministers, etc. But lately, a real opportunity has arisen to carry it out [targeting] 150 industrialists and 10 diplomats, who meet there weekly. We agree, like el Mono, [to do it] before everything collapses, because in Bogotá there is a frightening witch hunt. Yesterday 11 helicopters passed over San Vicente. Greetings, Jorge, Joaco, Fabían, Martín.[72]

In terms of the use of this tactic, the number of FARC bombings remained relatively steady, though marked by noted increases in some years (1991, 1992, 1997, 2002, and 2012). In a comparative perspective, the FARC used bombings more than other groups both numerically and proportionally (see figures 3.6 and 3.7). The FARC carried out 43 percent of all bombing

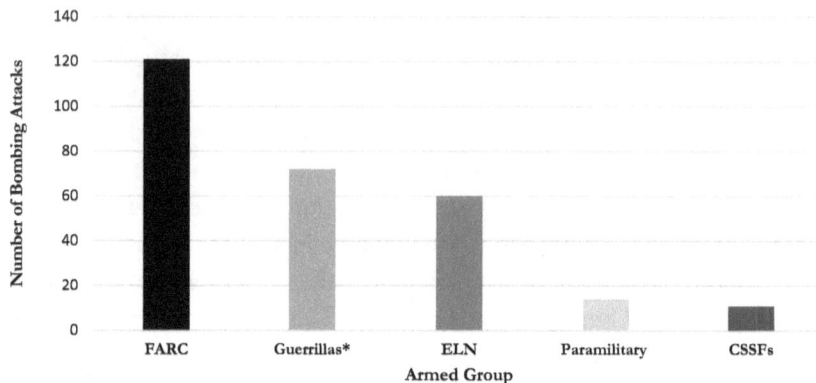

FIGURE 3.6 FARC bombings, 1988–2012.

Source: Author's tabulation based on CINEP data.

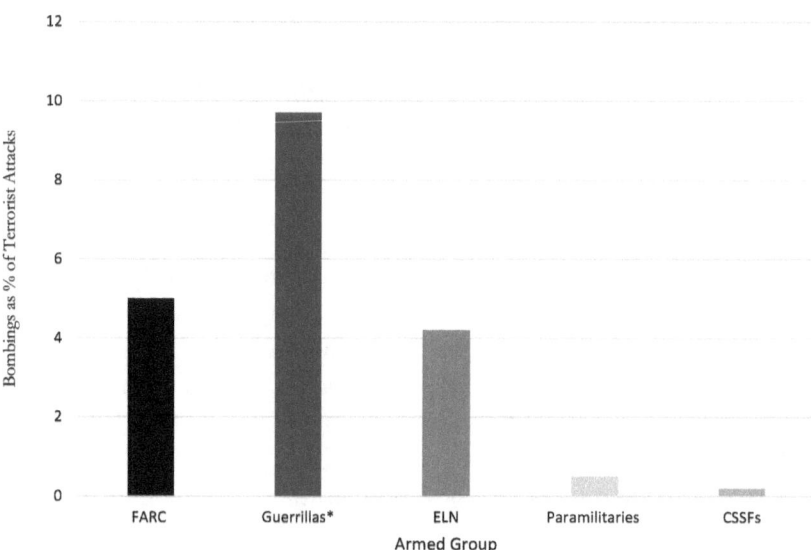

FIGURE 3.7 Bombings in FARC's repertoire of terrorism, 1988–2012.

Source: Author's tabulation based on CINEP data.

attacks registered in CINEP's database, almost equaling the percentage of such attacks by all other guerrilla groups combined. Interestingly, only 53 percent of the bombing attacks were carried out against targets in large and medium-size cities,[73] the rest (47 percent) affecting rural municipalities.[74] Although many of these attacks were carried out with rudimentary explosive devices such as gas cylinders, they often had devastating effects on civilians.

Apart from bombings, the FARC also incorporated torture into its repertoire of action, a tactic especially used with hostages and members of the armed forces captured during battle. The group also used disappearance, which was widespread across the country. The Colombian Truth Commission tallied 121,768 disappearances between 1985 and 2016.[75] Even though 54 percent of cases could not be traced to any armed actor, of the rest, 24 percent were attributed to the FARC. In the case of the FARC, this tactic was mostly used to dispose of the bodies of victims of abduction and forced recruitment.[76]

THE INCORPORATION OF TERRITORIAL TERRORISM

Major changes in the dynamics of the civil war prompted the FARC to incorporate the systematic use of territorial terrorism into its repertoire. The groundwork for this decision was laid during the FARC's Seventh National Conference, which took place in 1982 and was a watershed moment in the organization's history: it sanctioned the FARC's transformation from a traditional peasant guerrilla group into a highly militarized revolutionary army.[77] During the conference, top members engaged in lengthy talks over the best course of action for the organization. The discussion drew on a document presented by Victor Suárez Rojas (aka Alfredo Briceño, Mono Jojoy), a young commander and Marulanda protégé quickly rising up the organizational ranks; he advocated for a new strategy blending traditional agitation tactics with a more aggressive military stance.[78] The plan, called New Operational Form (Nueva Forma de Operar) was a variation of the Maoist strategy of popular warfare adopted by the Viet Cong known as *dau tranh* (struggle), an insurgency method that complemented insurrectionist military operations with political actions.[79] Suárez, who became the top military commander of the FARC and leader of the feared Eastern Bloc, promoted the creation of special schools to train operatives in Vietnam-style military and terrorist tactics.[80]

In the political realm, meanwhile, the FARC gradually shifted from its historically rural orientation and sought to penetrate popular neighborhoods and universities in order to build a network of sympathizers and informants. In a critical component of this strategy, the FARC created its own party, the Patriotic Union, in 1985 following the opening of peace negotiations with the administration of Conservative President Belisario Betancourt (1982–1986). The move backfired tragically, however, as Patriotic Union activists began to be systematically targeted by extremist right-wing groups.[81] Alluding to this violent repression, Jacobo Arenas asserted that Colombians, and the FARC, had to resist the state's terrorist actions by complementing the revolutionary armed struggle with other forms of (violent) popular resistance.[82]

In addition to nurturing an already strong sense of victimization, the FARC's failed electoral experiment reinforced the group's view that violence was the only way and that the state could never be trusted. It also inadvertently strengthened the position of the FARC's military leadership, including Briceño and even Marulanda, over that of more political commanders such as Raúl Reyes and Alfonso Cano. As a result, the group increasingly embraced dehumanizing practices, justifying them as an inevitable escalation in response to "reactionary forces." Deceased FARC leader Alfonso Cano, considered a moderate within the group, captures the organization's mindset during this time: "You can talk about terrorism when the assumption is that you are deliberately trying to instill panic in the population and when a concrete policy is put in place to carry out such a practice. But that is not [the] FARC's policy, and we are not doing it. What does happen is that war, when it becomes generalized, creates scenarios that not one of us desires."[83]

In the military domain, the FARC unveiled plans to escalate the conflict from conducting guerrilla warfare to confronting security forces in open battle.[84] The group thus gradually expanded its presence from its traditional strongholds in central Colombia, venturing into semi-urban and urban areas that the FARC sought to render ungovernable to force the Colombian security forces to overextend themselves. The FARC's overall strategy yielded excellent results, dramatically expanding the group's influence and military power. Between 1983 and 1991, the FARC more than tripled its number of fighters, from 1,500 to 5,800.[85]Meanwhile, the number of active fronts increased from eight to sixty-five between 1983 and 1995, the group operating across a substantial part of Colombia's territory.[86]

The FARC's gradual strengthening allowed the organization to openly challenge security forces on the battlefield, often inflicting humiliating defeats on them.[87] Around this time—and to finance its rapid growth—the FARC increased its use of abductions and began to charge drug traffickers a revolutionary tax for protection in a practice known as *gramaje*. In the municipalities where the group was able to establish its presence, FARC operatives sought to garner the support of local authorities and the civilian population.[88] When such measures failed, though, the FARC would turn to brutal methods. The group's decision to embrace territorial terrorism was also prompted by the irruption of paramilitary groups in the early 1980s. The rapid expansion of this new implacable enemy forced guerrilla groups, and in particular the FARC, to adapt its insurrectional strategy. As indicated in chapter 2, paramilitary groups rendered the war more complex and intractable and affected the methods of armed parties: localized forms of terrorism soon became central components of military strategy.[89]

Pressured by a relentless paramilitary enemy that made use of brutal tactics to obliterate its enemies' support bases, the FARC responded in kind by stepping up attacks against civilians and employing targeted assassinations. This move corresponded with the FARC's need to hold on to strategic territory, protect its economic interests, and secure indispensable civilian support.[90] Although the FARC had historically relied on summary executions to render revolutionary "justice" (*ajusticiamientos*), this practice became much more systematic and widespread as the group tried to "liberate" regions by following a strategy pioneered by the Viet Cong and later the Salvadoran FMLN.[91] Attacks rose markedly between 2001 and 2005, the most intense period of the war linked to intense territorial disputes among parties.

From a comparative perspective, as figure 3.8 shows, the FARC used this tactic more sporadically than other groups, carrying out 1,204 summary executions, far less than paramilitary groups and the CSSF and slightly more than the ELN. Proportionally, the group used the tactic less than its enemies but more than the ELN: summary executions account for

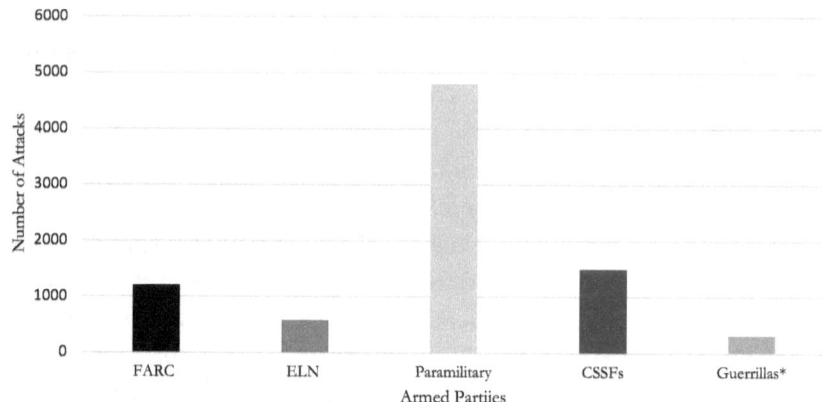

FIGURE 3.8 FARC summary executions, 1988–2012.

Source: Author's tabulation based on CINEP data.

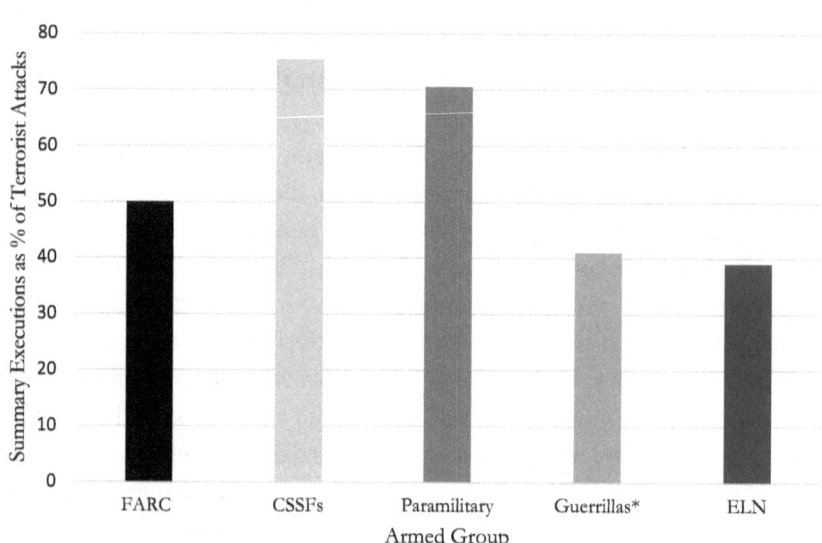

FIGURE 3.9 Summary executions within FARC's repertoire of terrorism, 1988–2012.

Source: Author's tabulation based on CINEP data.

50 percent of FARC terrorist attacks relative to 75 percent by the CSSF, 70 percent by paramilitaries, and 39 percent by the ELN (see figure 3.9).

Only a handful of summary executions by the FARC in CINEP's sample report the use of sacralized forms of violence known as *sevicia*, or overkill, in which the bodies of victims are displayed in gruesome ways to maximize population intimidation. FARC leadership rejected the use of graphic violence as it considered such acts degrading and a remnant of criminal codes of conduct (and therefore anti-revolutionary). Rhetorically at least, the group would always underscore its commitment to carry out military operations as opposed to acts of brutality, including overkill.[92] This is borne out by data from the Historic Center for National Memory, which reports that guerrillas were responsible for only 5.1 percent of the total cases in which parties employed extreme and graphic displays of cruelty on bodies to maximize fear.[93]

Massacres, the other main tactic associated with territorial terrorism, is less conspicuous within the FARC's repertoire but follows the same general pattern as summary executions: few of these attacks in the beginning of the conflict, rising numbers as territorial disputes intensified until 2002, after which attacks diminish steadily (with a brief exception in 2009). From a comparative perspective, the FARC was less likely than paramilitaries and the state to carry out these acts.

The FARC, as the data show, was behind two hundred massacres, only a fraction of that of paramilitary groups (1,156) and slightly less than the CSSF (232) (see figure 3.10). Among guerrilla organizations, however, the FARC carried out twice as many massacres as all other insurgent groups put together, and more than three times the number of ELN attacks (sixty). Proportionally, meanwhile, massacres account for 8.3 percent of FARC terrorist acts, relative to 17 percent by paramilitary groups, 11.6 percent by the CSSF, and 4.1 percent by the ELN (see figure 3.11).

Notably, none of the massacres by the FARC tracked in CINEP's sample involved the use of overkill, a finding that coincides with other accounts.[94] As to the logic informing massacres, the data show that a significant share of FARC massacres occurred after paramilitary groups penetrated FARC-controlled areas. In these contexts, it is possible to observe a clear pattern of attack and retaliation in which paramilitary massacres precede those of the FARC in disputed areas. Examples found in the sample include massacres in the municipalities of Apartadó, Medellín, San Carlos, Tame, Puerto

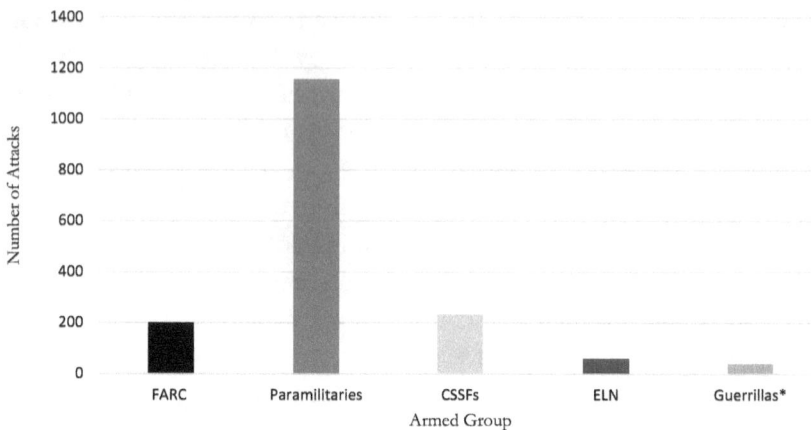

FIGURE 3.10 FARC massacres, 1988–2012.

Source: Author's tabulation based on CINEP data.

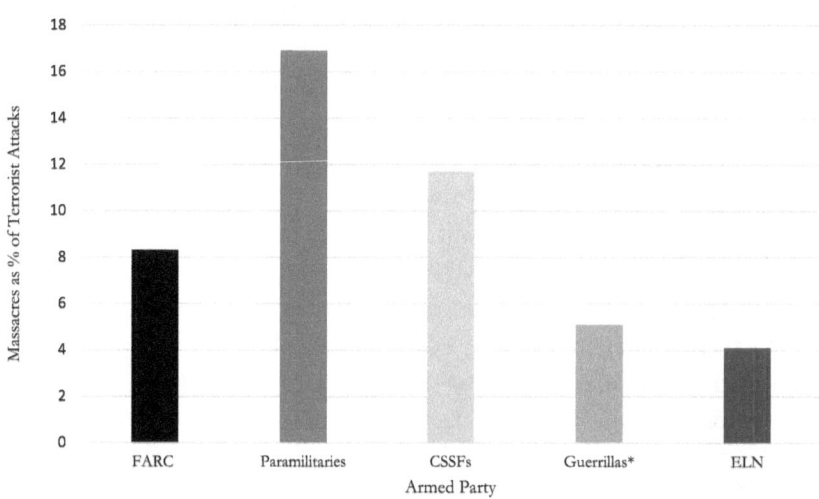

FIGURE 3.11 Massacres in FARC's repertoire of terrorism, 1988–2012.

Source: Author's tabulation based on CINEP data.

Libertador, Acevedo, Barbacoas, Tibú, and Buenaventura. The FARC has also used massacres extensively against so-called Peace Communities (communities that refrained to take sides in the conflict, such as the one in San José de Apartadó), as well as against indigenous communities that challenged their rule. Interestingly, and contrary to some accounts, the data show that massacres and executions were not used as complementary methods. These two practices were rarely combined, the exception being during attacks in the municipalities of El Carmen de Bolívar and San Pablo, both in the department of Bolívar.

To assess the dynamics of territorial terrorism, I plotted the FARC's use of this tactic geographically. In keeping with the literature, I assume that the group employed terrorist tactics such as summary executions and massacres in efforts either to control or dispute territory with its enemies.[95] I reviewed all municipalities in which the FARC perpetrated five or more summary executions or massacres in any given year. I assume that municipalities in which only the FARC used these tactics were controlled by that group, and, conversely, that those municipalities in which attacks by both the FARC and other armed parties occurred during the same year were contested areas. In other words, simultaneous terrorist attacks are used as a proxy for territorial contestation, whereas unilateral actions are seen as a sign of territorial control. As figure 3.12 illustrates, of 158 municipalities in which five or more terrorist acts were committed by the FARC, the FARC used terrorism while disputing territory with enemies and rivals in sixty-nine (44 percent) of them.[96] In another twenty-nine areas (18 percent), the FARC used terrorism unilaterally to control territory. In the remaining sixty-one municipalities (38 percent), a dual pattern is observable whereby the FARC controlled the municipality over a certain period but disputed the territory with enemies and rivals for other periods during the length of the conflict. Data thus show that most use of the group's massacres and summary executions are linked to strategic territorial disputes.

GEOGRAPHIC DIMENSIONS OF FARC TERRORISM

In closing, I expand the discussion on terrorist repertoires to offer an analysis of the geographical dimension of terrorism, which is critical to understanding the phenomenon's patterns. The FARC used this tactic across the country, but the data show that the bulk of its terrorist activity was concentrated in selected departments, and within them specific municipalities.

A compilation of FARC terrorist attacks broken down by municipality and their respective levels of economic activity and strategic value is presented in the appendix. It reveals how FARC terrorist attacks disproportionately affected municipalities with strategic value as drug producing

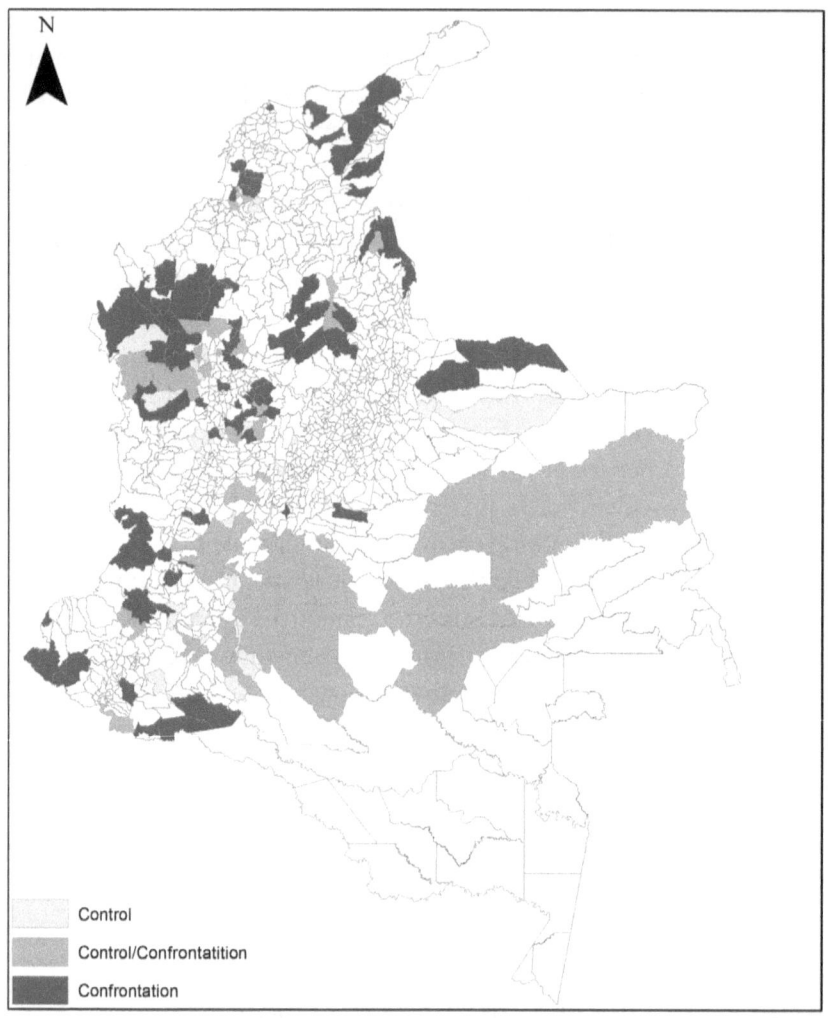

FIGURE 3.12 Dynamics of FARC's territorial terrorism, 1988–2012.

Source: Author's tabulation based on CINEP data.

and transshipment zones; as corridors connecting remote, difficult-to-access areas of the country; and as major poles of economic activity. Regarding the distribution of FARC terrorism at the municipal level, data show that even though rural communities were more afflicted by insurgent terrorism, urban municipalities such as Medellín, Cali, Neiva, Villavicencio,

TABLE 3.1 Distribution of FARC Terror Attacks by Fronts

Unit	Region	Number of attacks
Front 34	Antioquia/Chocó	68
Front 35	Antioquia/Sucre	55
Front 47	Antioquia/Caldas	46
Front 37	Bolívar/Sucre	40
Front 21	Tolima	28
Front 6	Cauca/Valle	28
Front 36	Antioquia	25
Front 9	Antioquia	23
Front 19	Magdalena	21
Front 33	Norte de Santander	19
Front 5	Antioquia	18
Mobile Column Teófilo Forero	Huila	17
Front 25	Tolima	16
Front 57	Chocó	15
Front 61	Huila	14
Front 59	La Guajira	14
Front 41	Cesar	14

Source: Author's tabulation based on CINEP data.

Buenaventura, Valledupar, and Cúcuta also endured significant terrorist incidents.

Finally, table 3.1 presents the use of terrorism by units (front and mobile columns). As the table makes clear, the distribution of terrorist acts varies considerably across FARC fronts. The intensity of attacks depends on geographical dimensions, territorial disputes, and the inclination of particular fronts and their top commanders to deploy this tactic.

Conclusions

This chapter examines the evolution, logic, and nature of the FARC's terrorist practices. The discussion shows that this group relied extensively on this strategy across Colombia for twenty-five years. The analysis reveals how the group's repertoire of terrorism is the product of the group's unique identity as an organization. Heavily influenced by the destruction of the Independent Peasant Republics, the FARC developed an identity as a highly independent peasant guerrilla group from its early, formative years and displayed a great deal of pragmatism despite its adherence to orthodox revolutionary thinking. FARC terrorist practices evolved over time, driven by a leadership that viewed terrorism as a legitimate tactic in its class warfare against the Colombian state.

The FARC used terrorism as an agitational strategy to advertise its revolutionary cause. Terrorist acts such as abductions and bombings were used to delegitimize the Colombian state by demonstrating its inability to protect ordinary citizens and, more broadly, to undermine the existing sociopolitical status quo. Over time, however, the FARC would incorporate territorial terrorism in land disputes with paramilitaries and the CSSF, particularly in municipalities with high strategic value. The use of terrorism, which ebbed and flowed in accordance with key events in the theater of war (i.e., military offensives, demobilizations, strategic defeats), was always conducted in ways that reflected the organization's revolutionary nature. Although the group relied on several forms of terrorism, insurgent acts of an agitational nature were the cornerstone of its repertoire.

4

The ELN

From *Foquismo* Warfare to Terrorism

On a Sunday morning in May 1999, members of the National Liberation Army (Ejército de Liberación Nacional, or ELN) front José María Becerra descended on La María church in southern Cali and kidnaped 198 people attending mass. Guerrillas arrived unexpectedly to the ceremony, posing as members of Grupo Gaula, a specialized anti-kidnapping unit of the Colombian Police, and after killing a bodyguard, proceeded to snatch all churchgoers, including dozens of children and the priest. ELN operatives forced the captives to board several minibuses and ferried them to Jamundí, a rural municipality. Eighty-six people were eventually rescued by the army, another fifteen managed to escape the day of the attack, and the rest were kept in extremely difficult conditions for various periods of time. The last hostage was released six and a half months later as part of a humanitarian exchange secured by the International Committee of the Red Cross. All hostages were unharmed. The attack, the largest collective abduction in the modern history of Colombia, was carefully planned by the ELN high command and followed a string of similar collective kidnappings, including that of an Avianca airliner.[1] This daring daytime attack in a posh Cali neighborhood had a clear agitational intent: to terrorize Colombians by demonstrating the state's inability to protect its citizens, even the most influential and powerful.

100 THE ELN

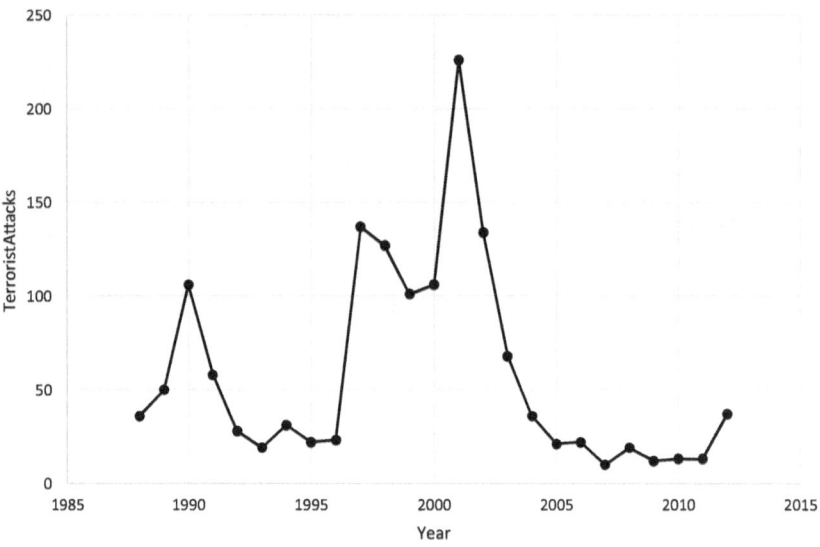

FIGURE 4.1 ELN's use of terrorism, 1988–2012.

Source: Author's tabulation based on CINEP data.

This chapter unpacks the methods and motives behind the ELN's repertoire of terrorism. It traces the historical development of the group, the role of its leadership, and its internal organizational practices. Figure 4.1 presents a chronological display of the terrorist attacks ascribed to the ELN in my database between 1988 and 2012. It shows that the group relied consistently on this strategy over the examined period, carrying out 1,455 terrorist acts, some 10.4 percent of the total recorded in the sample. ELN terrorist attacks show significant oscillation, with moderate to high levels between 1988 and 1991, a drop between 1992 and 1996, a later surge between 1997 and 2002, a gradual decline until 2012, and after that another modest increase.

Figure 4.2, in turn, illustrates the ELN's repertoire of terrorism: the group relied most heavily on abductions and summary executions and far less so on explosive attacks and massacres. Of all groups, it proportionally relied most on abductions. Its use of summary executions is also relevant though less pronounced than those of the other three groups. Its use of bombing attacks is significant relative to that of paramilitaries and Colombian state security forces (CSSF), but smaller relative to that of the Revolutionary

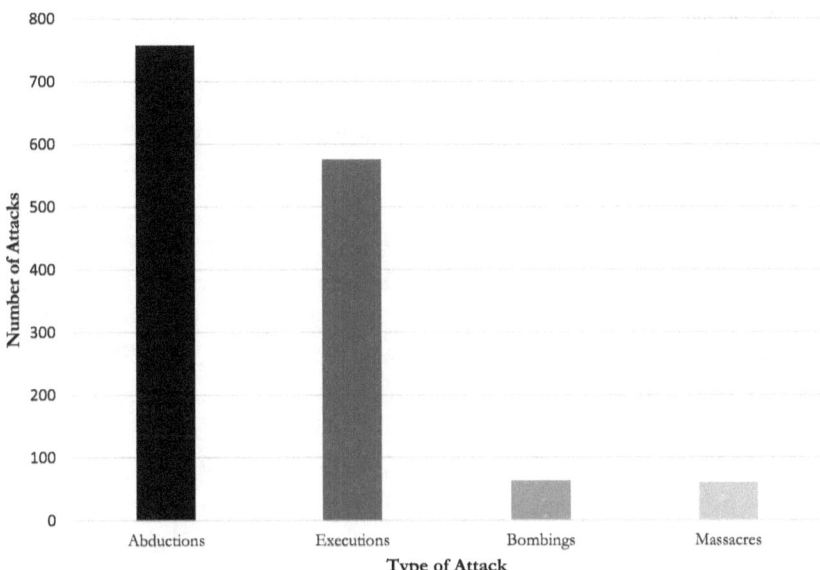

FIGURE 4.2 ELN's repertoires of terrorism, 1988–2012.

Source: Author's tabulation based on CINEP data.

Armed Forces of Colombia (FARC). Insofar as massacres are concerned, the ELN trails all others by a significant margin. This short account underlines the extent to which the ELN's terrorism blueprint differs substantially from both the FARC and opposing groups with antithetical goals.

The chapter argues that ELN's distinct repertoire of terrorism results from the group's unique organizational identity. The ELN was heavily influenced by the Cuban revolutionary doctrine fashionable during the early 1960s. Ideologically, the ELN embraced a complex mixture of Cuban Marxism á la Guevara; a nationalistic, anti-imperialist stance; and a Christian outlook vis-à-vis the poor predicated on liberation theology. The group's identity is encapsulated in the notion of Ser Eleno, which holds that members should commit themselves to bringing about social change and defending the oppressed—by force if necessary. Influenced by revolutionary maximalism and the fatality of class contradiction, the ELN, like the FARC and other leftist armed groups, rationalized civilian casualties as the inevitable result of class warfare.[2] Such views were promoted within the group through training and socialization.

The ELN's incorporation of terrorism was influenced by their leaders' decision to adhere to the revisionist urban guerrilla warfare thesis and, later, to the Vietnamese Prolonged Popular War (PPW) doctrine. ELN commanders embraced insurgent, agitational terrorist tactics such as abductions and bombing attacks. The systematic incorporation of terrorism was spearheaded by members of the Domingo Laín front, whose successful political-military strategy blending extortion, attacks against infrastructure, and agitational terrorism served as a blueprint for the ELN. In response to the irruption of paramilitary groups in the 1980s, the ELN also incorporated some forms of territorial terrorism as it sought to defend territory from its enemies. Overall, though, the ELN's repertoires of terrorism relied more on agitational terrorism and less on territorial forms.

This chapter proceeds as follows. I first provide a detailed overview of the creation and evolution of the ELN, underlining the importance of the Cuban revolutionary doctrine in shaping the organization's identity. I then detail how ideology evolved within the group and influenced commanders' views on their revolutionary endeavors. Relatedly, I look at institutional mechanisms such as training and indoctrination within the group, which promoted a singular terrorist repertoire. In conclusion, I reflect on how the group's unique character and organizational trajectory set it apart from other violent actors, including the FARC, that used terrorism in the Colombian civil war.

The Origins and Development of the ELN

The ELN was created in 1964, part of the first wave insurgent movement that sprang up across Latin American the 1959 Cuban Revolution. As such, it is a prime example of the *foquista* guerrilla model in vogue in Latin America in the 1960s. Developed during the uprising against the Batista regime, *foquismo* (focus) calls for a group of enlightened individuals, a vanguard of sorts, to begin an armed insurrection to awaken the peasantry's revolutionary consciousness and topple oppressive regimes.[3]

The ELN's origins can be traced to a heterogeneous group of leftist militants from two main sources.[4] The first was a dissident wing of the Liberal Revolutionary Movement associated with Alfonso López Michelsen that attracted scores of young students, who formed a broad, nationally relevant organization—the National University Federation. The second was Rafael Rangel's self-defense group, a peasant force associated with the Liberal Party that had been active in small municipalities in the Magdalena Medio (e.g., San Vicente del Chucurí, Simacota, and Barrancabermeja) during La Violencia. The ELN benefited from the experience of these militias during these tumultuous years.[5]

As true of many other leftist organizations of the time, the rise of the ELN was enabled by Cuba's new revolutionary regime, which offered both ideological guidance and material support. In this regard, the ELN owes much to a small group of leftist militants—the Antonio Galán Brigade—who traveled to Cuba to learn about its successful revolutionary tactics. Seven of them, including the ELN's first supreme commander, Fabio Vásquez Castaño, his brother Manuel, and Nicolás Rodríguez Bautista (aka Gabino)—the most important figure in the group and its chief commander for forty-five years (1974–2021)—received ideological and military training and later returned to Colombia to launch an armed insurrection.[6]

Drawing on the Cuban experience, the group carried out violent actions in the hopes of awakening the peasantry's revolutionary consciousness. The January 1965 assault against a police station in the town of Simacota, Santander, the ELN's first military operation, is indicative of the organization's early strategy. The group selected a military target (a small police station) with high symbolic value and perpetrated the attack in accordance with the principles of guerrilla warfare.[7] It also carried out several similar attacks and ambushes against the army and the National Police, as well as high-profile robberies of banks and weapons depots. These tactics were necessary because despite its close ties to the Cuban regime, the ELN received very modest external military and financial help from its revolutionary allies and thus had to scrape up resources (arms, money) largely on its own.[8]

Notwithstanding some successful operations, the group's beginnings were inauspicious. Facing challenging conditions during its early years (1965–1973), the ELN suffered several setbacks that threatened its existence. Several of its commanders were killed or captured, including Camilo Torres, the emblematic priest turned *guerrillero* who was gunned down in 1966. Torres's loss was a devastating blow for the organization because his presence was critical in the group's recruiting efforts among often apathetic, mistrustful peasants. In the following years, the group suffered other damaging defeats at the hands of security forces. In what is known as the Anorí assault of August 1973, the Colombian Army—under the leadership of veterans recently returned from the Korean War—struck the ELN, killing and capturing scores of militants. Fabio Vázquez barely escaped alongside a few other fighters. On hearing news of the assault, many members deserted.[9] The group was further weakened when the Colombian security services detained a group of urban militants in Bogotá in a raid known as the Febrerazo.[10] By the end of 1973, the ELN had shrunk to barely seventy fighters.[11] Amid a deep crisis characterized by mutual recrimination and increasing distrust within the organization, Fabio Vásquez resorted to brutal purges to maintain cohesion and curb defection. However, his reputation was dented by a string of poor operational results. Facing growing internal opposition, Vásquez traveled to Cuba in 1974, during which time he was removed as commander-in-chief by remaining ELN members in Colombia, who chose Gabino, Vásquez's twenty-four-year-old lieutenant, as their new leader.

The post-Anorí period saw the emergence of two groups within the organization. The first was a militaristic wing lead by Gabino, which advocated for persevering with the *foquista* strategy, with some necessary adjustments. This faction faced a rival, revisionist wing composed of urban theorists molded by liberation theology. Many had religious backgrounds like the Spanish priest Manuel Pérez (aka El Cura Pérez), who favored adopting complementary nonviolent strategies. Based on the successful model developed by the Salvadoran Farabundo Martí Liberation Front (FMLN)—and invoking the example of Camilo Torres— revisionists advocated undertaking an aggressive political campaign at the grassroots level to broaden the organization's social base.[12] This move was conceived in accordance with the Marxist principle of "combining all forms of struggle."

After a heated internal debate, Gabino's position prevailed. Under what was regarded as his pragmatic, conciliatory leadership, and with the support of Pérez and other influential commanders, the ELN embarked on a major organizational restructuring characterized by a much more democratic internal modus operandi designed to eradicate the intolerance and sectarianism that had almost destroyed it.[13] Following the celebration of the group's first National Reunion (1983), the ELN transitioned from a heavily centralized organization into a confederation of guerrilla groups in the Salvadoran model led by a central command, though various fronts maintained significant autonomy. In 1986, the ELN embraced the PPW doctrine based on the Viet Cong model. As explained in chapter 3, PPW was a broad strategy that combined executing military actions with cultivating so-called popular power.[14]

By most accounts, the ELN's survival and subsequent renaissance owed much to the Domingo Laín front.[15] This front was formed around 1979 by a small group of militants who struck out on their own after the Anorí debacle and moved into the Sarare jungle, a remote region linking the department of Santander with the eastern lowlands in the departments of Boyacá and Meta. Under the leadership of Gustavo Aníbal Giraldo (aka Pablito), who devised a clever strategy (discussed shortly) combining strategic violence and political actions to win the hearts and minds of the peasantry, the front began its remarkable ascent to becoming the most successful and powerful unit within the ELN.[16] Indeed, Domingo Laín would supply the template for restructuring the entire guerrilla group.[17] As this front and the ELN gained strength, the organization abandoned its formerly centralized structure, opting instead to create a Collegiate National Directorate composed of fifteen to twenty members. This move allowed the ELN to grow while maintaining the autonomy of its smaller regional fronts.[18]

This new strategic order paid huge dividends and initiated an important period of growth for the organization.[19] Before 1980, the group's force amounted to some 250 combatants, and its presence was limited to the departments of Santander, Antioquia, and southern Bolívar. From 1983 on, the ELN began a rapid expansion, growing to approximately 2,500 operatives by the early 1990s, divided up into five major war fronts and subdivided into thirty-five smaller units, each comprising seventy-five to eighty-five combatants on average. This astounding growth, particularly between 1986 and 1989, allowed the ELN to establish a footprint in most parts of central and northern Colombia.[20]

The ELN's growth was brought to an abrupt halt in the 1990s by the irruption of paramilitary groups and the increasing presence of army forces in areas where it operated. This buildup of paramilitary and state forces accelerated following the inception of Plan Colombia during the administration of President Andrés Pastrana (1998–2002). The ELN's decentralization, constant shuffling of resources (including experienced commanders), and inadequate military training structures undermined its capacity to respond to these new challenges, in particular to paramilitary encroachment on its territory.[21] Dramatically weakened, the group eventually yielded to the temptation of drug trafficking and other illicit activities to boost its depleted finances.[22] Against this backdrop, despite historical frictions and competition, it reached out to the FARC in search of a strategic alliance.[23] Both tactical shifts were crucial in allowing the group to continue fighting. By 2010, the ELN still had around 1,500 combatants supported by a larger number of militants—the so-called strategic reserve—who provided intelligence and logistical support in departments including Arauca, Santander, and Norte de Santander.[24]

Following the state's peace deal with the FARC and that group's subsequent demobilization, the ELN opened its own peace negotiations with the government. These talks, however, would be soon derailed by constant skirmishes with security forces and suspended during the administration of President Iván Duque. With the election of President Gustavo Petro, negotiations resumed in Mexico in early 2023. Meanwhile, the ELN began to take over FARC strongholds and recruited disgruntled FARC members opposed to their group's peace deal. Evidence of these moves can be seen in the growing ELN presence in departments including Valle del Cauca, Norte del Cauca, Chocó, and Nariño where the group had not previously operated. The ELN remains particularly strong in the eastern part of the country, even carrying out operations in Venezuela with the tacit approval of the Venezuelan government and its security forces.[25]

Currently, the ELN has seven main fronts and a fighting force of approximately 2,450 armed combatants, many of whom operate from Venezuela, where the Maduro regime has offered them sanctuary. Over the years, the group has evolved into an extremely decentralized organizational structure, where fronts enjoy almost total autonomy but remain unified under a central command that provides political guidance.[26] In 2021, chief commander Gabino resigned due to poor health and was replaced by Eliécer Erlinto Chamorro (aka Antonio García, or el Cura), Gabino's longtime lieutenant and the group's chief military commander.[27] Often referred to as the last group of the Latin American insurgency, the ELN has become the most powerful nonstate armed actor operating in Colombia, propelled by its growing and systematic involvement in criminal activities (drug and human trafficking, smuggling, illegal mining).[28] In March 2022, it carried out a nationwide armed strike that included blocking off major highways, detonating a series of explosives, burning vehicles, conducting summary executions, and even hanging its flag from public buildings. In a show of defiance to authorities and its rivals, the ELN ordered fighters to patrol the streets in towns and villages where the group has a strong presence.[29]

Ideology

The ELN's organizational identity largely stems from a hybrid worldview combining Marxism; a nationalistic, anti-imperialist discourse; and a Christian outlook toward the poor. Historically, the ELN adhered to a Marxist-Leninist view that views social reality through the lens of class struggle. As indicated earlier, the Cuban experience was extremely important in shaping the group's revolutionary views. In an interview, chief commander Gabino recalled how initially militants relied almost exclusively on two sources as guides for their struggle: Che Guevara's *Manual of Guerrilla Tactics* and Regis Debray's revisionist *Revolution Within the Revolution*.[30] Following precepts or ideas from these works, the ELN was conceived of as a strictly military organization. One of the early ideologues of the group, commander Jaime Arenas, explained that electoral strategies were discarded because they seemed futile and inadequate to bringing an end to what they regarded as an oligarchic rule in Colombia.[31]

In accordance with the Cuban foquista doctrine, the ELN strove to develop close links with the Colombian peasantry. The group's commanders were mindful that their success hinged on the support of the civilian population and, therefore, sought to avoid harming the peasantry. When discussing the nature of the ELN, Gabino explicitly underscores this point, as well as the group's efforts to curb banditry and abuse that plagued previous uprisings in Colombia.[32] Yet the influence of Guevarist thought on the ELN goes beyond military strategy. One of the group's most salient features is its cultivation of a strong group identity, one encapsulated in the previously mentioned notion of Ser Eleno, which entails a commitment to social change and defending the oppressed.[33] This view derives from the classical Marxist idea of the new man, a utopian concept essentially postulating that revolution would be brought about by strong, selfless individuals who had not been corrupted by capitalism's individualist ethos and were willing to sacrifice themselves for the collective.[34] The charismatic figure of commander Che Guevara, whose self-discipline, stamina, and willingness to endure exceptional hard conditions—in both wartime and peace—were legendary,[35] served as an inspiration for ELN members.[36] In sum, ELN members viewed themselves as integral and heroic social transformers ready to make the ultimate sacrifice for their revolutionary goals.

The ELN also distinguished itself from most other Colombian revolutionary organizations of the time by attracting progressive clergymen sympathetic to liberation theology doctrine.[37] This doctrine made notable inroads in Colombia following the 1968 Medellín Conference of the Latin American Episcopal Council, which debated the need to promote a preferential option for the poor and to create Christian communities in order to spread the gospel.[38] The ELN's links to this radical wing of the Church solidified when priest Camilo Torres decided to join the ELN in 1965 and became a tremendously influential figure within the group. Gabino indicates that even though Torres spent only five months with the organization—he was killed in his first battle, the Patio Cemento skirmish in February 1966—his impact on the ELN's doctrinal and political preferences were substantive. Several years later, the incorporation of three Spanish priests, Manuel Pérez, Domingo Laín, and Antonio Jiménez, into the leadership reinforced the group's religious component. Later, several other priests working in rural areas would also join, which allowed the ELN to deepen its bonds with the peasant population. Manuel Pérez underscored that clergy were in an ideal position to win the hearts and minds of peasants and, more important, recruit them.[39] The religious component of the ELN's strategy was further reinforced when, following the successful model of the Salvadoran FMLN, the ELN embarked on an aggressive campaign aimed at enhancing its popular bases in strategic urban areas.[40]

This religious element imbued the ELN with a sense of purpose and a distinct identity that inspired continued revolutionary struggle and buttressed internal cohesion. Commander Gabino noted how this aspect increased the group's resilience and helped it overcome difficult moments. Liberation theology also shaped the group's self-image as a righteous liberator, which influenced, in turn, its military strategy, including the use of terrorism, particularly its rejection of certain forms of violence deemed unworthy of the group. This self-image would also inform the ELN's early rejection of narcotrafficking as a financing method.[41]

In addition, the ELN articulated a strong nationalist discourse. Although leftist organizations at the time often adopted a harsh anti-imperialist stance, the ELN's embrace of Colombian national symbols contrasted with the more reserved nationalism of other insurgent groups such as the FARC, whose views followed the more conventional Marxist-Leninist transnational line.[42] From its early days, the ELN maintained a healthy distance from the Colombian Communist Party, which at the time was closely tied to the ruling Communist Party in the Soviet Union. In addition, despite its admiration for Cuban leadership, the group emphasized the importance of national self-determination, always striving for independence and reiterating the need to adapt revolutionary concepts to Colombia's unique conditions.[43] The ELN thus advocated for policies fostering economic sovereignty and emphasized that solutions to national problems ultimately had to come from within Colombia. In this vein, the centrality of its violent campaign against multinational corporations (see following) was clearly informed by a nationalistic view that rejected handing resources over to foreign entities.

The ELN developed a unique organizational identity, but, significantly, some of the group's doctrinal views were also imported from fellow revolutionary groups. Despite its cohesive nature and nationalistic discourse, the ELN forged meaningful links with other revolutionary organizations in the region and further afield, including the Guatemalan National Revolutionary Unity (Unidad Revolucionaria Nacional Guatemalteca), the Viet Cong, and, later, representatives of Latin America's second revolutionary wave such as the Salvadoran FMLN, the Nicaraguan Sandinistas, and the Tupac Amaru Revolutionary Movement (Movimiento Revolucionario Tupac Amaru) in Peru.[44] Although the ELN doctrinally rejected the practices of the revisionist second insurgency wave as conceived by the writers Abraham Guillén and Carlos Marighella—both vocal critiques of *foquismo* and the Cuban model—it incorporated some of the strategies developed by urban guerrillas, like many other groups in the region.[45] As alluded to in chapter 3, inspiration also flowed from the M-19, which followed the model of urban insurgency in the revisionist revolutionary tradition.[46]

Like the FARC's, the ELN's ideological stance informed the view that extreme violence, including terrorism, was not only an inevitable outcome of class struggle but also, and more fundamentally, a legitimate way to remedy injustice and reshape Colombian society.[47] In an interview, an anonymous ELN commander explained this tactical choice bluntly: "To the disgrace of the Colombian society, the governing class will only listen to the voice of dynamite and guns."[48] In this view, anyone opposing the revolutionary struggle could potentially become a legitimate target. The group was particularly adamant in going after "enemies of the people," a broad label including members of the oligarchy, foreign dignitaries and executives, and state officials. In a clear manifestation of categorical terrorism,[49] people accused of counterrevolutionary activities, in particular those from well-to-do backgrounds, could be targeted regardless of the evidence. Similarly, the group was merciless with those accused of being army informants (colloquially referred to as *sapos*). The group would also regularly hold so-called revolutionary trials against government representatives—mayors, judges, public administrators—who could be sentenced to death.[50]

In sync with such views, the ELN adopted a stance on international humanitarian law that allowed it to justify abuses against civilians. Unlike the FARC, the group does not proclaim that international humanitarian law is an instrument of the dominant bourgeois class and, therefore, an illegitimate means of ameliorating human suffering during war. However, it does hold that adhering to this body of law is contingent on certain conditions, including that the ELN be recognized as a legitimate fighting force; that its detained commanders receive special treatment; and, more outlandishly, that it receive assistance in procuring the resources necessary to continue its operations. A communique by the group articulates this position: "The ELN commits itself to suspending the detention or deprivation of liberty of persons for financial motives, provided that the problem of availability of sufficient resources for the ELN by other means is resolved and provided that . . . this will not result in a strategic weakening of the ELN."[51]

Leadership and Repertoires of Terrorism

It is not entirely clear when exactly the ELN incorporated terrorism into its modi operandi. As in the case of the FARC discussed in chapter 3, evidence is hard to find because of the opacity of such decision-making processes and the group's systematic denial that it engages in terrorism. Regardless, evidence gathered for this book shows how, once again, organizational leaders (chief commanders and members of the central command) played a critical role in developing repertoires of terrorism that accorded with the ELN's ethos and identity.[52] Once selected, repertoires were socialized through political indoctrination, military training, and the group's disciplinary regime.

Antecedents of the ELN's terrorist tactics can be traced back to the tenure of Fabio Vásquez, who significantly shaped the organization's early years with his larger-than-life personality. As stated earlier, the ELN essentially followed the Cuban model initially, fully adhering to a classical guerrilla warfare script. The group only attacked military targets and engaged in acts of sabotage. Mario Aguilera argues that during this period, the ELN operated as a rural police force of sorts in agricultural frontier areas with sparse state presence.[53] Rather than appropriating a portion of the people's production to feed its militants, as many groups had done in the past, the ELN paid peasants instead. Yet, because resources were scarce, and to the dismay of the peasants, it reimbursed them through so-called revolutionary bonds of hope, which were often nearly impossible to cash in. More generally, though, Vásquez instructed fighters to maintain friendly relations with the population, a cardinal element of the revolutionary strategy, and strictly prohibited abuses against civilians. So great was the concern about maintaining a positive relationship with civilians that militants were not allowed to socialize with them, especially women, to avoid potential conflicts with the population.[54] Respect for basic norms of humanity was also extended to adversaries. Despite his fame as a ruthless commander, Fabio Vásquez explicitly ordered that the lives of policemen and soldiers who surrendered be spared.[55] Those accused of collaborating with the enemy, however, would be shown no mercy.[56]

In interviews with historian Medina Gallego, ELN commanders Gabino and Poliarco conveyed that at its outset, the group was adamant about minimizing civilian suffering and respecting peasants' free will.[57] Such views were buttressed by Camilo Torres, whose charisma and intellect shaped the group's adherence to revolutionary ideals such as honesty, stoicism, sacrifice, and defending the oppressed. Torres, who traveled extensively, developed strong ties with revolutionaries across the region, including militants of guerrilla groups and priests such as Gustavo Gutiérrez, who advocated for peaceful change.[58]

Yet, over time, the group gradually began to relax these rules, adopting a more abrasive approach toward the civilian population.[59] The dogmatic Vásquez became hardened by the terrible war, and his idealistic respect for the civilian population weakened, opening the way for the group to incorporate terror tactics including targeted assassinations, often referred to as *ajusticiamientos* (rightful executions). Vásquez and his commanders justified such excesses against "enemies of the people" (oligarchs, the bourgeoisie, informants, and state agents opposing them) on ideological grounds.[60]

Following the Anorí attack that decimated the ELN, the increasingly embattled Vásquez relied on iron-fist measures, including brutal purges, against his own men to maintain cohesion and avoid desertions. Many detractors of the ELN leadership were accused of selling out and then executed in show trials.[61] This crisis, and the increasingly paranoid leadership's use of terror tactics against their own militants, are vividly described in the memoirs of Jaime Arenas, one of the group's founding commanders and principal ideologues, who gives a rare inside view into the world of insurgent groups.[62] Profoundly disappointed and disgusted by the arbitrariness and brutality exhibited by Vásquez and his followers, Arenas deserted in 1969. He would pay with his life two years later when an ELN urban commando gunned him down in Bogotá.

As noted, critical to the ELN's adoption of terrorist tactics was the ascendance of the Domingo Laín front within the organization. Gustavo Giraldo (aka Pablito), its leader, presided over a sweeping transformation of his front's modus operandi, shifting from a conventional rural guerrilla approach to a significantly more sophisticated model predicated on the Viet Cong's PPW formula. PPW combines political action with an insurrectionist strategy using a wide range of agitational tactics that include extortion, sabotage, and summary execution and abductions. The model secured the group vast sums of money and proved agitationally effective, disrupting the normal functioning of local economies.[63]

In this new phase, the ELN embarked on an aggressive path of agitational terrorism, carrying out a wave of abductions. In an interview, the ELN's supreme commander Gabino acknowledged that the group began to systematically abduct people in 1969.[64] In the early 1970s, the group perpetrated an average of three abductions per year. It generally targeted landowners, cattle ranchers, and, following the example of revolutionary groups in other countries, executives working for multinational companies.[65] In addition to generating vital revenue, these attacks had a clear subversive intent: kidnapping not only thwarted economic activities but also demoralized state agents by undermining state institutions, which seemed powerless to prevent these attacks. The ELN usually used victims as bargaining chips to secure the release of fighters captured by security forces, which further reinforced a sense of unease and insecurity among the population.[66] The group rejected accusations that these abductions constituted terrorism, claiming that they were legitimate acts against an oppressive regime with blood on in its hands. Commander Manuel Pérez, for example, insisted on a difference between kidnappings and the ELN's so-called retentions, in that the former were economically motivated criminal acts whereas the latter were political acts whose main objective was to further the organization's collective interest.[67]

The ELN leaders' adoption of insurgent forms of terrorism is amply supported by empirical evidence. Figure 4.3 presents the evolution of abductions by the group, with modest numbers rising sharply in the mid-1990s and then dropping markedly.

Data show the extent to which abductions constituted one of the cornerstones of the group's repertoire of terrorism. Figures 4.4 and 4.5

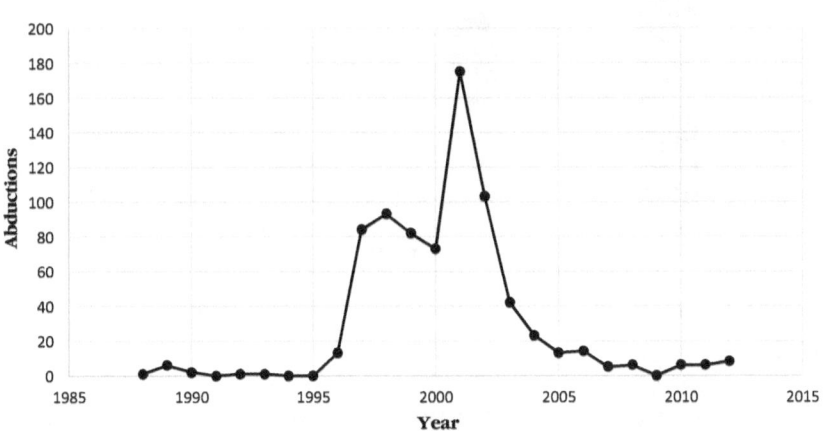

FIGURE 4.3 Evolution of ELN abductions, 1988–2012.

Source: Author's tabulation based on CINEP data.

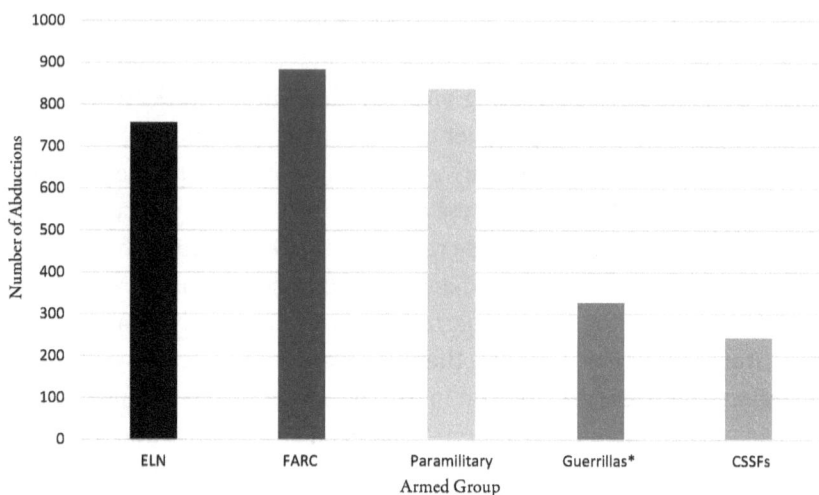

FIGURE 4.4 ELN abductions, 1988–2012.

Source: Author's tabulation based on CINEP data.
* Sum of guerrillas other than the FARC and ELN.

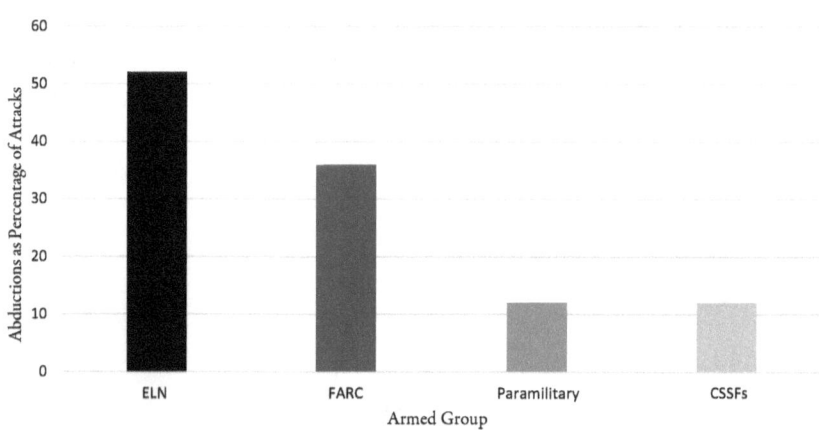

FIGURE 4.5 ELN abductions within repertoire of terrorism, 1988–2012.

Source: Author's tabulation based on CINEP data.

present the use of abductions from a comparative perspective among armed parties for the investigated period. As indicated, the ELN trails the FARC and paramilitary groups in the number of abductions, accounting for 24.8 percent of the total in the sample. Proportionally, though, the ELN relied most heavily on this tactic (52 percent) relative to the

FARC (36 percent), paramilitary groups (12.3 percent), and the CSSF (12.2 percent).[68]

In line with the urban insurrectional playbook, the ELN's leadership also incorporated bombing attacks into its repertoire of terrorism. Initially, the ELN used explosive attacks against military targets and, later, infrastructure; these acts of sabotage were in accordance with the main tenants of guerrilla warfare prescribed by Che Guevara and other thinkers. The ELN carried out its first explosive attack as early as 1964 when it bombed the Colombo American institute in Bucaramanga. Even though acts of sabotage do not constitute terrorism, the aggressive string of bombing attacks against infrastructure led to the ELN's depiction as a terrorist organization by the Colombian media.[69] Regardless of how one defines these actions, disrupting economic activity became one of the cornerstones of the ELN's military strategy. The group consistently bombed bridges, roads, the electric grid, and oil pipelines, among other targets, in an attempt to disrupt the provision of goods and services.[70] When vast oil reserves were discovered in the Magdalena Medio region, the group began a systematic onslaught against companies working in the production, refinement, and distribution of its oil, particularly those like the German company Mannesmann involved in developing the infrastructure for resource exploitation (e.g., the Caño Limón-Coveñas pipeline).[71]

In the early 1970s, the ELN turned to more aggressive bombing attacks that deliberately harmed civilians,[72] as evidenced by the data. Like the FARC, the group carried out attacks intermittently during the conflict, with peaks in 1992, 1997–1999, and 2012. Approximately half of the ELN's bombings were conducted in a major metropolis, though like the FARC, the group carried out several bombing attacks in rural municipalities as well (e.g., Agustín Codazzi in Cesar or San Vicente de Chucurí in Santander).

Comparative data show that bombings were also central to the group's modus operandi, although less so than abductions (see figure 4.6). The ELN committed sixty-three bombing attacks, overall, less than the FARC, but far more than those committed by paramilitaries (fourteen) and the state (eleven). The ELN accounts for 22.5 percent of the total. Proportionally, bombings represent 4.2 percent of the total terrorist attacks carried out by the ELN, less than the FARC (5 percent) but significantly more than the state (0.5 percent) and paramilitaries (0.2 percent) (see figure 4.7).

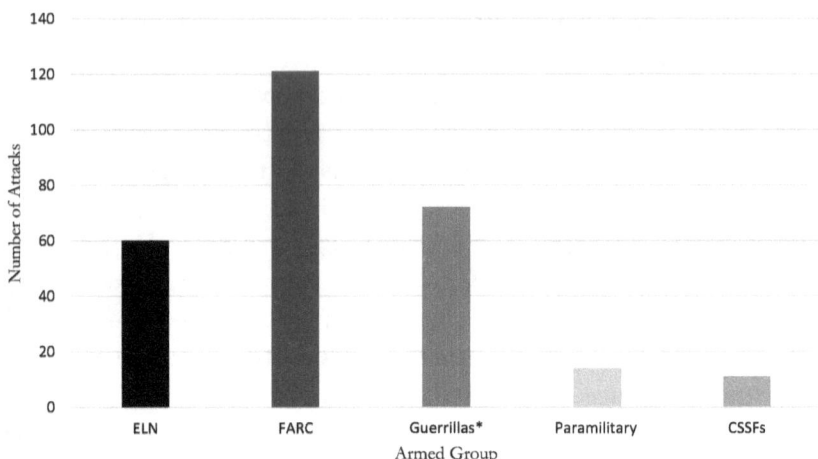

FIGURE 4.6 ELN bombings, 1988–2012.

Source: Author's tabulation based on CINEP data.
* Sum of guerrillas other than the FARC and ELN.

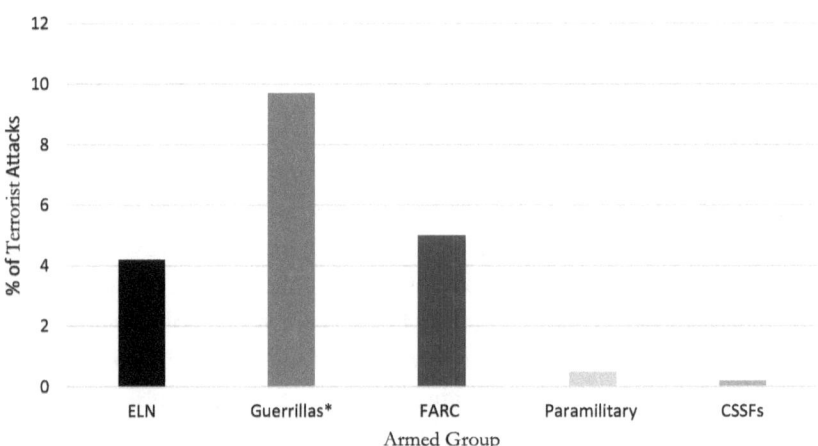

FIGURE 4.7 ELN bombing attacks within repertoire of terrorism, 1988–2012.

Source: Author's tabulation based on CINEP data.
* Sum of guerrillas other than the FARC and ELN.

From Agitational to Territorial Terrorism

As indicated earlier, the ELN grew significantly after 1983, thanks to the adoption of the Domingo Laín front's operational model. Expanding its operational range was pivotal for the organization, because if the ELN were to remain concentrated in a relatively small portion of territory, it would become more vulnerable to army raids. The group moved into strategic zones characterized by oil and mining activity (gold, silver, coal, nickel), agricultural zones producing bananas and African palms, and cattle ranching areas. It also made important inroads in many major cities (Barrancabermeja, Cúcuta, Valledupar, Medellín, Cali, and Santa Marta), where it built a vast network of non-armed members and sympathizers.[73]

In the zones it occupied, the ELN would rely on so-called armed proselytism, whereby it attempted to generate favorable conditions for the underprivileged groups it purported to represent. As part of this strategy, the ELN conducted extortion schemes in which it would demand money not only for its own operations but also to secure resources for the community. The ELN also monitored the social component of municipal plans at the local level (i.e., health, education, labor, and so forth) and the allocation and disbursement of resources.[74]

A critical part of the ELN's operational plan was to gain control of strategic municipalities by intervening in local elections and pressuring elected officials into implementing policies they supported. Important changes brought about by the Constituent Assembly (1991)—in particular decentralization, which granted municipal authorities more autonomy in budgetary matters[75]—provided incentives for the group to carry out violent attacks, including assassinations, to sway elected officials.[76] These activities were combined with extra-institutional operations, including civic strikes and land recovery schemes, aimed at creating a parallel regime, a strategy dubbed *armed clientelism*.[77] This doctrine entailed enlisting the masses at the grassroots level (e.g., through unions and peasant organizations) and using them to penetrate institutional channels and combat the state from within.[78]

Territorial expansion also meant increasing the use of violent tactics and adding territorial forms of terrorism such as massacres in response to the irruption of paramilitary groups and the increasing pressure of security forces. As in the FARC's case, the ELN's impressive growth and ambitious activities prompted a violent response from a vast network of regionally based paramilitary groups (see chapter 5). Paramilitary groups encroached on guerrilla-held territory and, relying on localized forms of terrorism, sought to destroy enemy bases of support.[79] The ELN would also be hit hard by the strategic overhaul of the Colombian armed forces initiated by Plan Colombia and Democratic Security Policy.

Given its structure, the ELN was particularly susceptible to the onslaught of paramilitaries. Many of the ELN's members were not full-time combatants, alternating their guerrilla activities with stints in civilian life. Paramilitaries shrewdly used this to their advantage by routinely attacking off-duty ELN militants. Alongside this cunning and savage paramilitary pressure, other elements further debilitated the group around 1992 or 1993. For example, chronic internal divisions within the ELN led the organization to splinter into several small (less powerful) groups, including the Guevarist Revolutionary Army and the People's Revolutionary Army. Furthermore, the ELN's shrinking territorial control curbed its recruiting capacity and finances.[80]

Faced with these military and organizational pressures, the ELN stepped up attacks against civilians. This move would allow the ELN to hold on to strategic territory, protect its economic interests, and secure the indispensable support of civilians. Summary executions in particular became more frequent in the group's attempt to confront the growing threat of paramilitary groups. The ELN historically used summary executions to render "revolutionary justice," but this practice became much more systematic and widespread as the group tried to "liberate" zones, following a strategy pioneered by the Viet Cong and later the Salvadoran FMLN.[81]

The analysis of the database shows that the ELN resorted extensively to summary executions throughout the conflict. Attacks ebbed and flowed, the highest numbers in 1990 and 1991 (during the paramilitary onslaught), 1997, and 2001; a hefty amount in the most acute phase of the war (1998–2003); and then declining numbers thereafter before picking up again in 2012. Figure 4.8 shows the ELN's use of summary execution relative to other armed parties. The ELN is behind 575, or 6.5 percent, of all targeted assassinations in the database. Even though the number of executions conducted by the ELN is significant in numerical terms, it is markedly lower than that of paramilitaries and the CSSF.

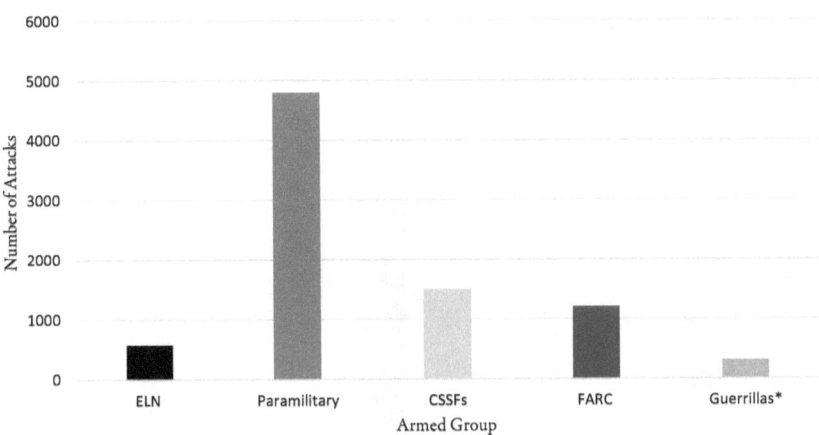

FIGURE 4.8 ELN summary executions, 1988–2012.

Source: Author's tabulation based on CINEP data.
* Sum of guerrillas other than the FARC and ELN.

When compared with other guerrilla groups, the ELN trails the FARC but conducted more executions than all the smaller guerrilla groups together. Proportionally, summary executions amount to 39 percent of the total terrorist attacks by the ELN, the lowest percentage of all examined parties (see figure 4.9).

None of the ELN summary executions in the Research Center for Investigation and Popular Education's (CINEP's) sample report overkill (*sevicia*). This evidence corroborates data from the Centro Nacional de Memoria Histórica reporting that guerrillas, and in particular the ELN, generally avoided mutilating and graphically exposing victims' bodies to maximize fear, something that the ELN leadership considered against the organization's revolutionary ethos.[82]

As for the ELN's use of massacres, the database ascribes sixty incidents to the group during the examined period, 3.5 percent of the total number of massacres in the sample (see figure 4.10). Interestingly, all of them took place in the group's traditional stronghold in the Magdalena Medio region. As with summary executions, the highest number of ELN massacres took place in the 1989 to 1991 period during the paramilitary offensive.

The ELN was less inclined to use massacres than other groups. From a numerical standpoint, the ELN relied the least on this practice (see figure 4.10), and proportionally, massacres account for only 4.1 percent of

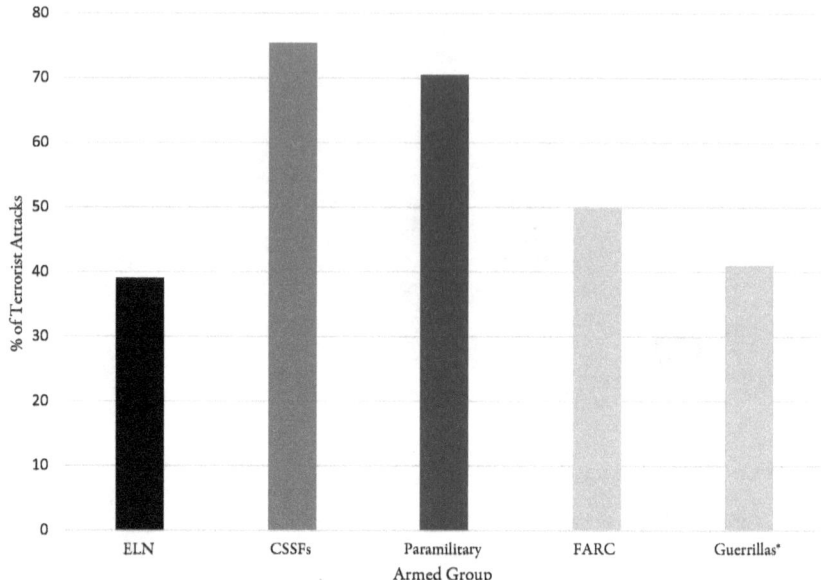

FIGURE 4.9 ELN summary executions within repertoire of terrorism, 1988–2012.

Source: Author's tabulation based on CINEP data.
* Sum of guerrillas other than the FARC and ELN.

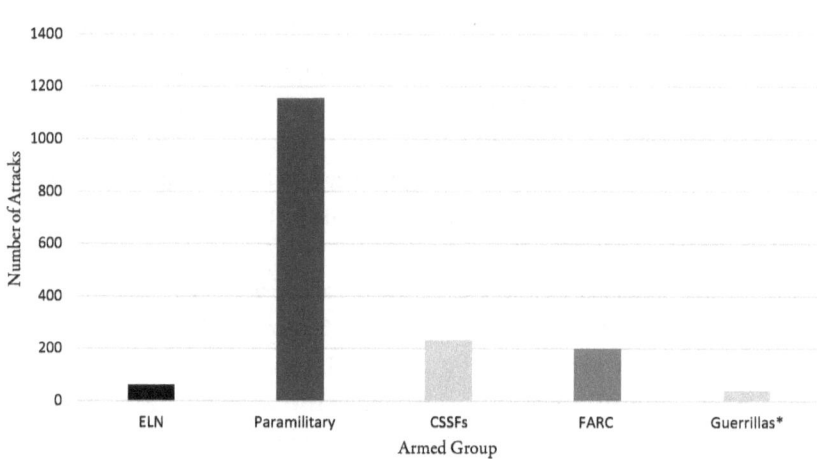

FIGURE 4.10 ELN massacres, 1988–2012.

Source: Author's tabulation based on CINEP data.
* Sum of guerrillas other than the FARC and ELN.

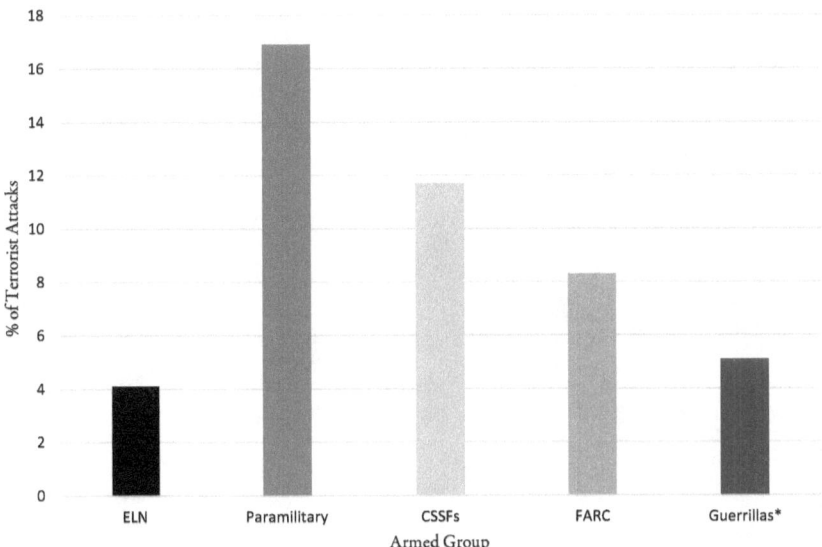

FIGURE 4.11 ELN massacres within repertoire of terrorism, 1988–2012.

Source: Author's tabulation based on CINEP data.
* Sum of guerrillas other than the FARC and ELN.

the total number of ELN terrorist attacks, roughly half the proportion for the FARC, a third for the CSSF, and less than a quarter for paramilitary groups (see figure 4.11). Again, none of the ELN massacres recorded in CINEP's sample reports *sevicia* (overkill), confirming similar findings from other studies.[83] The group also generally steered clear of disappearances, which ran counter to the group's revolutionary code of conduct.[84]

Although data confirm that the ELN relied far less on territorial terrorism than other actors, I also assessed the strategic dimension of this tactic for the group. Following the literature, I assume that the group used terrorist tactics such as summary executions and massacres either to control or dispute territory with its enemies. To measure the ELN's use of territorial forms of terrorism, I reviewed all municipalities in which the ELN perpetrated five or more summary executions or massacres in any given year. I also assume that when the ELN was the only group using these tactics in a municipality, that area was under their control; conversely, I assume that a municipality was contested when both the ELN and other armed parties carried out attacks during the same year. In other words,

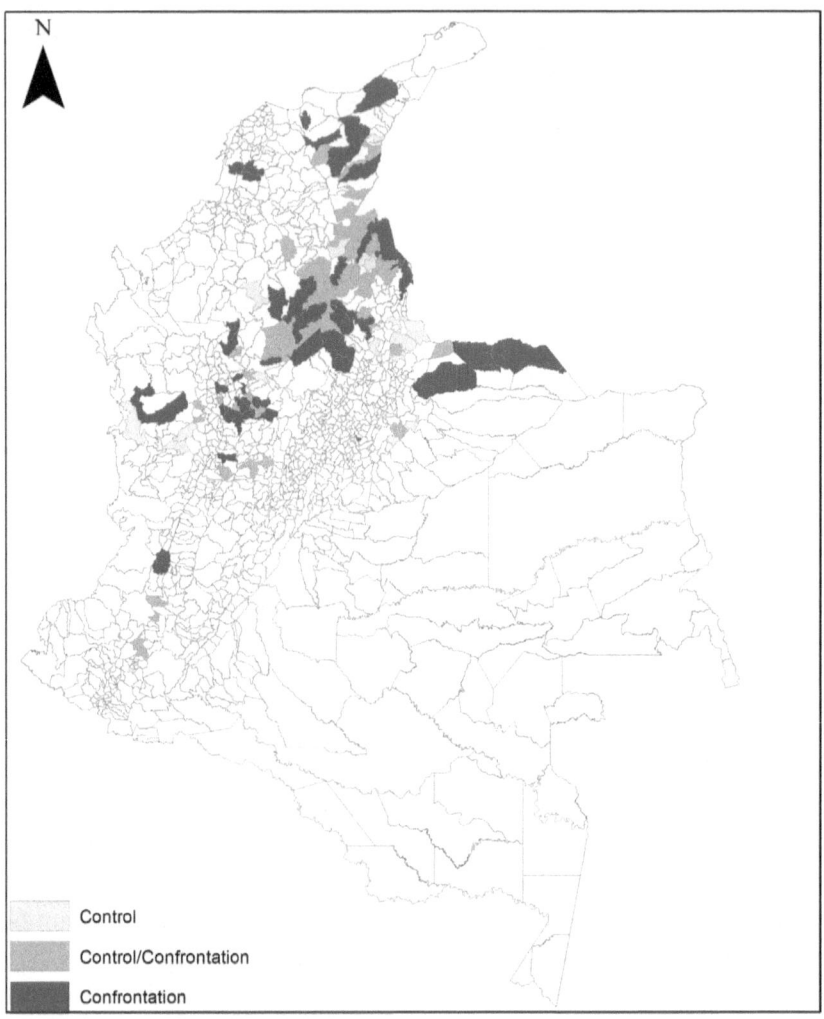

FIGURE 4.12 Dynamics of ELN territorial terrorism, 1988–2012.

Source: Author's tabulation based on CINEP data.

simultaneous terrorist attacks are used as a proxy for territorial contestation, whereas unilateral actions are seen as a territorial control mechanism.

As figure 4.12 shows, of the 104 municipalities in which the ELN perpetrated at least five acts of terrorism, it was disputing an area with hostile parties in forty-three of them (42 percent),[85] whereas in eighteen (16 percent), terrorism was used to control territory. In the other forty-three (42 percent), we observe a dual pattern in which terrorism was used both to control and dispute territory over the length of the conflict. Data thus confirm the extent to which ELN massacres and summary executions were linked to territorial disputes for the most part.

FARC AND ELN TERRORISM IN A COMPARATIVE PERSPECTIVE

Comparing the ways in which the FARC and the ELN used terrorist tactics reveals further evidence of the importance of organizational identity in developing repertoires of terrorism. According to conventional wisdom, we would expect guerrilla groups to emerge roughly at the same time, share ideological views and enemies, be organized in comparable structures, and develop similar repertoires of terrorism. This is hardly the case in the Colombian conflict, however. The FARC, as we have seen, was keener on using terrorism, perpetrating 40 percent more attacks than the ELN.[86] When looking at their respective terrorism repertoires, moreover, we can see other interesting differences between the two groups (see figure 4.13). The FARC used twice as many summary executions and bombings as the ELN, three times as many massacres, and 15 percent more abductions. Bombings, massacres, and summary executions are proportionally more important to the FARC's repertoire, though abductions are more important to the ELN's. The FARC was also more prone to disappear victims than the ELN. In sum, the data show that the two groups similarly embraced agitational terrorism, but that the FARC relied significantly more on territorial forms of terrorism.

GEOGRAPHIC DIMENSIONS OF ELN TERRORISM

Geography is one final important dimension of the analysis not strictly related to the types of terrorism waged. Even though the ELN used terrorism across the country, data show that the bulk of its activity was concentrated in selected departments—and within them, specific municipalities. An analysis reveals significant variation in the patterns of violence across the Colombian territory. The ELN's terrorist attacks disproportionately

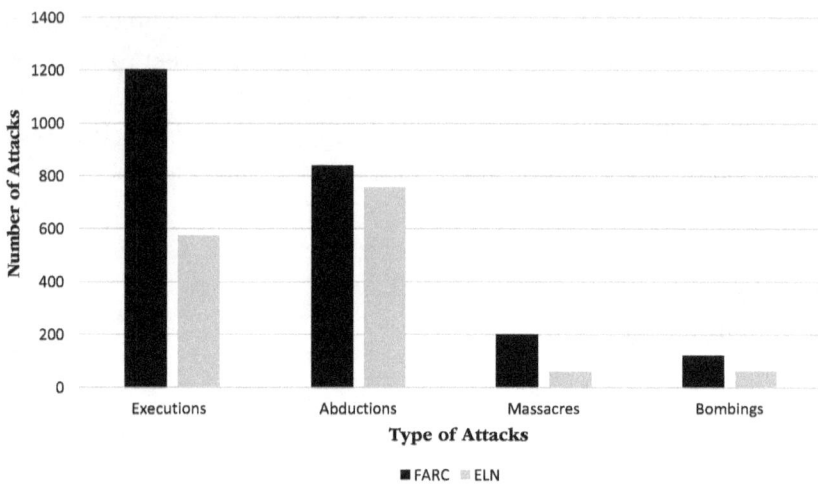

FIGURE 4.13 ELN and FARC repertoires of terrorism in comparative perspective, 1988–2012.

Source: Author's tabulation based on CINEP data.

affected certain departments and municipalities, mostly in Antioquia and in northeastern Colombia (Arauca, Cesar, Norte de Santander, and Santander). ELN terrorist attacks by municipality and information about the economic activity and strategic value of these areas is furnished in the appendix, which shows that the ELN's terrorist attacks took place in municipalities with strategic values as drug-producing and transshipment zones; as corridors connecting difficult-to-access areas of the country; and as major poles of economic activity.

Regarding the distribution of terrorism at the municipal level, the data show that though rural communities were more afflicted by insurgent terrorism, urban municipalities (Medellín, Cali, Neiva, Villavicencio, Buenaventura, Valledupar, and Cúcuta) also endured significant attacks. In short, the data illustrate that terrorism was unevenly distributed across the country and that it disproportionately affected certain municipalities characterized by military and economic strategic value. They also show how the ELN used this tactic to influence the population in territories they controlled as well as in areas they disputed with rival parties. Finally, data demonstrate how terrorism was more systematically used by certain ELN fronts, the most active being the Carlos Alirio Buitrago Front operating in Antioquia, the Camilo Torres front in Norte de Santander, and the Bolchevique Front in Tolima.

Conclusions

This chapter examines the evolution, logic, and nature of terrorism within the ELN. The discussion shows that this group relied extensively on this strategy across Colombia over twenty-five years. The analysis also reveals how the group's repertoire of terrorism was the product of the group's unique organizational identity. One of the first wave of insurgence groups inspired by the Cuban Revolution, the ELN embraced a complex mixture of Cuban Marxism á la Guevara; a nationalistic, anti-imperialist stance; and a Christian outlook toward the poor predicated on liberation theology. The ELN's terrorist practices evolved over time, driven by a leadership that viewed terrorism as a legitimate instrument in its class warfare against the Colombian state. The group underscored the righteousness of its actions and painted its enemies as legitimate targets. A pivotal development occurred when the group's Domingo Laín front developed a successful revolutionary model predicated on terrorist actions such as extortion and kidnapping imported from radical leftist groups in the Southern Cone and Vietnam.

The ELN used terrorism as an agitational strategy to advertise its revolutionary cause. Terrorist acts such as abductions and bombings were conducted to delegitimize the Colombian state by demonstrating its inability to protect ordinary citizens and, more broadly, to undermine the existing sociopolitical status quo. Over time, however, the ELN would incorporate territorial terrorism while disputing areas with paramilitaries and the CSSF, particularly in municipalities with high strategic value. Although the group relied on several forms of terrorism, insurgent forms of an agitational nature where the cornerstone of its repertoire, whereas territorial forms of terrorism were much more sporadic.

5

Paramilitary Terrorism
The Fusion of Counterinsurgency and Criminality

On a torrid January morning in 1989, a group of fighters dressed in combat gear intercepted a motor convoy and proceeded to indiscriminately fire on them, killing twelve people and injuring three others. The attack took place in broad daylight in the town of La Rochela, in the northeastern municipality of Simacota, Santander. The victims, members of a judicial commission (Unidad Móvil de Investigación) of the Colombian Attorney General's Office, had been dispatched to the area to investigate the massacre of nineteen traders and other violent events that had rocked the small rural community. After a lengthy investigation of the case, which was brought before the Inter-American Court of Human Rights, it was established that the attack had been perpetrated by a paramilitary group known as Los Masetos with the cooperation and acquiescence of drug traffickers and state agents. Henry Pérez, the powerful commander of the self-defense forces of the Middle Magdalena, ordered the attack to deter any potential investigation into these groups' illicit activities as they sought to control the strategic municipality.[1]

This brazen attack is illustrative of paramilitaries' systematic use of terrorism. As discussed in previous chapters, the advent of paramilitary groups marked an inflection point in the Colombian civil war by rendering the conflict more complex, intractable, and violent; it also ushered in

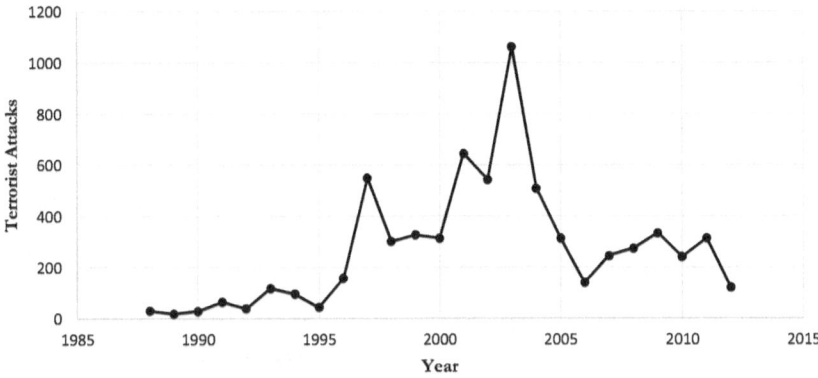

FIGURE 5.1 Paramilitaries' use of terrorism, 1988–2012.

Source: Author's tabulation based on CINEP data.

the widespread use of terrorism. Figure 5.1 presents a chronological display of paramilitary terrorism, showing that the group relied consistently on this strategy over the examined period.

All told, paramilitaries carried out 6,805 terrorist acts, corresponding to 50.2 percent of the total in the sample. Other forms of terrorism systematically used by these groups include disappearances and torture. On average, paramilitaries carried out 272 attacks each year. A chronological analysis of paramilitary terrorism illustrates how this practice correlates with dynamics in the theater of the war. Paramilitaries perpetrated an average of fifty-three strikes per year between 1988 and 1995. The number surged to 156 as the war escalated in 1996. As I will show, the upward trend coincides with the paramilitary leadership's decision to target the support system of guerrilla groups. This trend accelerated in 1997, the year the United Self-Defense Forces of Colombia (Autodefensas Unidas de Colombia, or AUC) was created. Paramilitary groups systematically applied terrorism during phases of expansion as they sought to take over strategic zones controlled by guerrilla groups. Paramilitary groups' reliance on terrorism increased once more between 2001 and 2003, with 643, 542, and 1,061 attacks per year, respectively. After 2003, terrorist attacks began to decline but remained considerable—an average of 237 per year between 2006 and 2012—evidence that paramilitary groups continued the practice even after their demobilization in 2005.

As indicated in the introduction, paramilitaries are by a wide margin the party with the greater propensity to employ terrorism in the Colombian civil war. Paramilitaries conducted more terrorist attacks than all guerrilla groups combined, and more than three times as many as the Colombian state security forces. These data illustrate that terrorism represented a critical part of their repertoire of violence. Moreover, their specific repertoire of terrorism contrasts markedly with that of other groups: as seen in figure 5.2, the bulk of paramilitary terrorism involved targeted assassinations (4,797). Though numerous, massacres (1,156) and abductions (838) were less represented, whereas explosive strikes—only fourteen cases—account for a miniscule share of the total.

This chapter traces the evolution of terrorist practices by paramilitary groups during the Colombian civil war. The examination unpacks the nature and logic of these groups' repertoires of terrorism. I argue that these repertoires reflect the groups' unique identity as hybrid organizations composed of markedly different adherents—landowners, criminals, former members of security forces—who coalesced around a radical anti-insurgency project. Influenced by a fervent anticommunist zeal, paramilitary leaders embraced counterinsurgency practices promoted by the Colombian Army based on military doctrines that were disseminated transnationally and in vogue during the Cold War. These doctrines were predicated on a military logic that sought to reclaim rural and urban areas

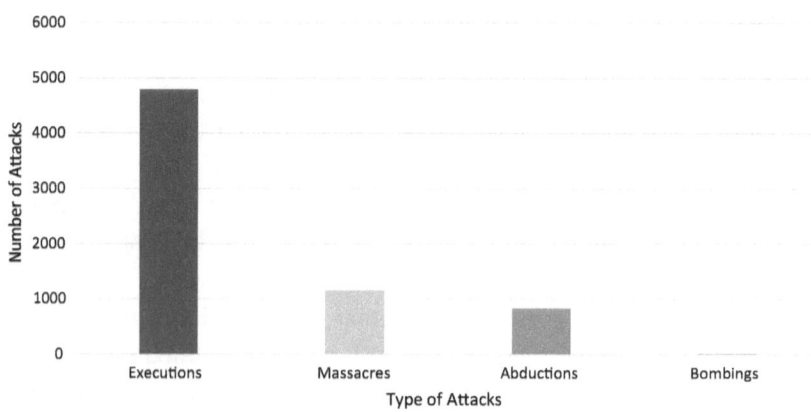

FIGURE 5.2 Paramilitaries' repertoires of terrorism, 1988–2012.

Source: Author's tabulation based on CINEP data.

under guerrilla control or influence by decimating the civilian support system of insurgent groups. Paramilitaries justified terrorism as a legitimate way of averting the collapse of the Colombian state, an inevitable outcome of counterinsurgency warfare. Targets included people considered "enemies of the state" who aided and abetted guerrillas (sympathizers, informants, so-called useful fools) and those voicing progressive political views (leftist organizers, union and grassroots leaders, intellectuals). The forms of terrorism deployed were also informed by a criminal ethos valorizing performative, reputational forms of violence such as overkill (*sevicia*) that sought to maximize fear among rivals and punish those who stood in their way.

The chapter proceeds as follows. The first section briefly discusses the nature of paramilitary groups. Subsequently, I offer a detailed analysis of the creation and evolution of these groups, underlining their hybrid nature. The third section examines the ideological traits and criminal ethos within the group, exploring how these ideas shaped the character and identity of paramilitary armed organizations. Relatedly, the discussion explores how such views influenced commanders' decisions to employ terrorist practices and briefly touches on institutional mechanisms such as training and indoctrination. I conclude with broader reflections on paramilitary terrorism.

What Is Paramilitarism?

The term *paramilitarism* is often used as a diffuse, catchall category describing groups of a markedly different nature that go by various names (militias, self-defense forces, death squads, vigilantes, and so forth). Conceptual ambivalence over the nature of paramilitarism stems from several factors. First is a certain tendency to use this category for instrumental or discursive motives: supporters describe these groups in lofty, eulogistic terms as focused on self-defense to broaden their appeal and legitimacy; detractors use derogatory terms—such as death squads—to delegitimize them. Second is the inherent difficulty in defining groups like paramilitary organizations that display diverse natures and attributes. Third, paramilitary groups often develop fuzzy links with the state, and the ambiguous nature of this relationship makes defining them more difficult.[2]

Julie Mazzei conceptualizes paramilitary groups as armed entities with political goals that are not organically linked to the state but operate with its support, including from factions within the state. She emphasizes that one of the main paradoxes of paramilitarism is that although these groups are on the margins of the law, they benefit from the "resources, access and status exclusive to the state."[3] This observation reflects an emerging consensus in the literature that paramilitary groups, despite their state connections, are essentially autonomous.[4]

Ana Arjona and Stathis Kalyvas offer a particularly useful typology of paramilitary organizations. They differentiate among four categories in accordance with two broad criteria: size and territorial dimension. The four categories are vigilantes, death squads, home guards, and militias and paramilitaries. The last refers to large, mobile organizations with a unified command, formal structures, full-time members, and the capability of conducting complex military operations over a prolonged period. These groups resemble small armies and exhibit a higher level of sophistication and durability.[5] They are, however, only able to wage nonconventional warfare, for example, the Janjaweed in Sudan or the Indian Border Security Force in Kashmir.[6]

In his comprehensive discussion of the Colombian case, Francisco Guitiérrez-Sanín defines paramilitaries as armed structures autonomous of the state's security apparatus and without access to its sophisticated weaponry.[7] These groups, he explains, have a wide variety of objectives but a common interest in eradicating insurgencies and communism. Another scholar in the field, Fernando Cubides, views Colombian paramilitary groups as irregular state entities of an extralegal nature that have taken the law into their own hands and that, in their struggle against guerrillas, replicate guerrilla methods step for step.[8] These groups, he states, have a centralized command and clearly defined functions, although these features vary among them.

To the extent that paramilitarism operated in sync with the central state's anti-insurgent political project and, more critically, was fostered by the Colombian state itself, debates emerged concerning these groups' actual degree of agency. Interpretations vary among authors. Some postulate that the state was in full control of these groups and could activate and deactivate them at will. According to this view, paramilitarism was simply an unofficial part of the state's counterinsurgency efforts.[9] A second, slightly different account points out that the relationship was collaborative, and that although the Colombian state exercised influence, it did not control these groups.[10] Human rights cases brought before the Inter-American Commission on Human Rights established that although paramilitaries perpetrated certain crimes, the state aided and abetted them by providing cover and logistical support.[11] Such support (financial, logistical, and military) varied during certain periods of the war. The state, however, did not always speak with one unified voice: state agencies would often compete with one another, supporting their preferred paramilitary faction depending on organizational preferences conditions in the theater of war, and political considerations.[12] Finally, a third interpretation argues that paramilitaries displayed significant autonomy and operated beyond the purview of the state, notwithstanding some degree of collusion.[13]

In short, although paramilitarism is a complex phenomenon, the consensus in the literature is that these groups are independent actors seeking their own political goals and that, despite their connections to the state, they are not organically linked to it. This conceptualization accurately captures the paramilitary phenomenon in the Colombian setting.

Emergence and Evolution of Colombian Paramilitary Groups

Analyzing the genesis and evolution of paramilitary groups is critical to understanding their repertoires of terrorism. These groups arose in an extraordinarily complex process marked by periods of expansion and contraction and a fair degree of mutation over time. Behind their emergence were three diverse sets of actors—provincial elites, criminals, and members of the security forces—whose interests coalesced at one point in time and who collaborated to create an armed force characterized by a hybrid identity. Paramilitaries are best described as a federation of regionally based armed groups adhering to a common cause whose composition and leadership are neither congruent nor uniform. Yet, as this chapter shows, despite the diversity and complexity of paramilitary groups, their modus operandi are consistent, underlining the extent to which they shared an overarching identity and goals.

Drawing on a comprehensive report produced by the Centro Nacional de Memoria Histórica, I trace the creation and development of paramilitarism, distinguishing among three main periods: paramilitary precursors, in particular the influential Puerto Boyacá model in the Magdalena Medio region; the apogee of paramilitary power, with the rise of Castaño Clan and the so-called Urabá model behind the AUC; and the decline of such groups following demobilization and peace negotiations (2004–2005).[14]

The emergence of contemporary paramilitary organizations dates to the mid-1960s and stems from the efforts of economic elites, in particular, regional bosses, landowners, and cattle ranchers in the southern Magdalena Medio region around the municipality of Puerto Boyacá. Concerned about rising peasant unrest linked to unresolved agrarian demands, these elites recruited local ruffians and organized them into lightly armed groups that stymied peasant mobilization. One of their main goals was to deter the forceful occupation of their properties by rural workers.[15] They were aided by the Colombian central state, which, concerned about the emergence of revolutionary groups, viewed them as a welcome partner in its counterinsurgency efforts. Against this backdrop, the state promoted legislation and a string of executive decrees authorizing the creation of self-defense groups during the Conservative administration of Guillermo León Valencia (1962–1966) and the Liberal administration of Carlos Lleras Restrepo (1966–1970).[16]

These self-defense groups responded to the need for private security in regions with scant or nonexistent state presence.[17] Demand for private security increased significantly with the rising power of guerrilla groups during the mid-1970s.[18] Mauricio Romero argues that this context created the conditions for the emergence of so-called coercion entrepreneurs, who through extortion and other pressures threatened private economic interests.[19] Moreover, the unexpected and sudden opening of peace negotiations between the administration of Belisario Betancur and the Revolutionary Armed Forces of Colombia (FARC) and M-19 in 1982 deepened concern among regional elites about their vulnerability vis-à-vis guerrillas. Preoccupation about guerillas' rapid expansion also mobilized some members of the security forces. Many of them, including high-ranking officers, felt betrayed by Betancur's decision to negotiate with guerrillas and thus threw their support behind the new civilian armed groups, believing that extraordinary measures were needed to stop the rise of insurgent groups.[20]

Most accounts highlight that the Colombian state played a pivotal role in the emergence and development of these groups. Some members of the armed forces not only turned a blind eye to paramilitaries' illegal operations but also actively endorsed their activities by providing weapons, training, logistical support, offering intelligence sharing, and, from time to time, conducting covert joint operations.[21] Given these informal links, paramilitaries often operated with impunity in areas of high military presence.[22] Other bureaucracies within the state, especially those at the provincial level, where regional elites wielded great influence, also played a critical role in the rise of paramilitary groups.[23]

Criminals, including emerald smugglers and especially narcotraffickers, constitute the third critical component of paramilitary groups. Around the 1980s, drug traffickers bought large swaths of land throughout rural Colombia to launder their vast illegal earnings. As noted, drug barons were exploiting a business opportunity, as many landowners, tired of guerrilla kidnappings and extortion, decided to sell their properties at a fraction of market price.[24] When these new criminal landowners were harassed by guerillas, they used their vast resources and expertise to protect themselves and their properties. Facing a common enemy, drug barons soon realized the strategic expediency of joining forces with traditional landowners, regional political elites, and members of the security forces.[25]

Paramilitary ruthlessness increased after these connections with the drug world were established. An often overlooked but important factor behind the emergence of these groups was the Death to Kidnappers (Muerte a Secuestradores, or MAS). This clandestine task force was set up by Medellín operatives following the botched attempt to abduct Carlos Lehder and the kidnapping of Martha Nieves Ochoa, the sister of Jorge Ochoa, one of Pablo Escobar's partners, by an M-19 commando in 1981.[26] MAS reacted with unusual virulence, killing relatives of M-19 members, and relentlessly hunting down those involved in the attacks. Its actions presaged the zeal and cruelty with which paramilitaries would act against leftist sympathizers and displayed clear trademarks of mafia-like retribution.[27]

The emblematic case of the Peasant Association of Cattle Ranchers and Agriculturalists of Magdalena Medio (Asociación de Campesinos y Ganaderos del Magdalena Medio, or ACDEGAM) exemplifies the first crop of paramilitary groups and illustrates the way in which legal and criminal entrepreneurs coalesced around their objective to root out insurgencies. Ramón Isaza, a landowner of rather humble origin who later became a major paramilitary commander, formed ACDEGAM in the early 1980s. The association grew out of the Escopeteros, a small, lightly armed, and amateurish self-defense group created by Isaza to fight the FARC's 4th Front around Puerto Boyacá in the mid-1960s. A natural organizer, Isaza reached out to fellow landowners and convinced them of the need to pool their resources and create a stronger, more professional force capable of eradicating the guerrilla presence. Isaza also enlisted drug traffickers from the Medellín Cartel, including Pablo Escobar, who had acquired land in the area, even though their relationship was often tense. ACDEGAM also recruited local army officers (active and retired) with whom Isaza had built personal connections over the years and who, in their private capacity, helped organize the group's newly formed armed structure.[28] These officers, along with international mercenaries, trained the group and helped gradually transform this relatively small and inexperienced militia into a force with a clear command structure and a formal payroll.[29]

ACDEGAM would become much more than an armed group, however, and develop an ambitious political platform characterized by strident anticommunist rhetoric. It began to compete with leftist organizations in the political arena by delivering social services to the public to enhance its legitimacy and strengthen its popular appeal. Despite its rapid and impressive ascendance, it would eventually succumb to internecine fighting. The group's demise followed Pablo Escobar's decision to initiate an open war against the Colombian state in his attempt to fight his extradition to the United States. Many of the association's original creators did not agree with this strategy, leading to a violent confrontation that fatally splintered the group.[30]

After the collapse of the ACDEGAM and the demise of the Medellín Cartel following the death of its leader, paramilitarism entered a new phase, one inextricably linked to the shadowy organization Perseguidos por Pablo Escobar (PEPES). This alliance, comprising the long list of Escobar's enemies who brought the powerful kingpin down,[31] became a powerful group and embraced a more lethal brand of paramilitarism that would catch on with other groups. Members of a modest property-owning family from Amalfi, Antioquia, the Castaño brothers Fidel, Vicente, and Carlos played a pivotal role in this process after their father was kidnapped and executed by the FARC in 1981. Fidel joined the ranks of the Medellín Cartel and, after overseeing its Bolivia drug-running operation, became a prominent cartel figure. Reacting virulently to the FARC's attack on his family, he set up a small militia, Los Tangueros, to target guerrillas and their sympathizers in the area around the Castaño family estate.[32] Later, though, Fidel would turn on his boss after Escobar attempted to have him killed. Following Escobar's death, Fidel seized part of the now-defunct Medellín Cartel operation and used its resources to build a powerful army alongside his two brothers. This organization, though short lived, was extremely significant because the links it developed between drug criminals and the Colombian security forces enhanced the paramilitary group's intelligence and military capabilities and conferred on it a significant degree of impunity.[33]

In 1993, the Castaño brothers founded yet another group, the Peasant Self-Defense Forces of Córdoba and Urabá (ACCU), which played a seminal role in articulating a national paramilitary project and answered a growing clamor for security by cattle ranchers and banana growers exasperated by EPL and FARC activity. Urabá—and Córdoba—would become the epicenter of paramilitarism in this phase, a transformation spurred partly by strategic considerations: the ACCU sought to create a corridor to expedite the transshipment of drugs to the United States via the strategic Gulf of Urabá.[34] The Castaño paramilitary experiment in northwestern Colombia would soon be replicated in various regions of the country (Cauca, Santander Boyacá).[35]

Gustavo Duncan asserts that the rise of the ACCU marked a qualitative change in paramilitary groups, which morphed from informal militias into much larger, well-organized private armies characterized by a clear command structure, distinctive group iconographies, a clearly articulated doctrine, and the capability to dispute territorial control with guerrillas. Small paramilitary groups were incorporated into the ACCU's project, sometimes by force.[36] This expansion led to the emergence of the AUC, an umbrella organization of national reach created by Carlos Castaño, Fidel's younger brother, who took over the ACCU following Fidel's disappearance in 1994. At its zenith, the AUC comprised approximately thirty-one thousand armed combatants serving in scores of fronts.[37]

One of the most formidable and long-lasting effects of paramilitarism's second phase was the reconfiguration of power in rural Colombia. To achieve their goals within zones under their control, paramilitaries began to regulate the activities of the population, repressing any attempts to defy their authority. They threatened or bought off elected local authorities and infiltrated state institutions such as the police, military, and the judiciary. Duncan argues that paramilitaries became the new dominant actor in many rural areas across the country, replacing traditional elites, who would eventually serve as links between their new patrons and the central state. As their grip over these zones strengthened, paramilitaries reshaped existing regional orders and instituted unaccountable and violent enforcement regimes. Moreover, these new armies discovered that along with controlling large areas of the country, they could leverage their military might to become important political players in Colombian politics.[38]

Paramilitarism's third and final phase, which continues to the present, was inaugurated after the partial demobilization of these armed groups following lengthy negotiations with the administration of President Álvaro Uribe (2003–2005). Under the Santa Fe de Ralito Peace Accord of 2006, 30,915 combatants formally demobilized. In accordance with the terms of the agreement, top commanders and mid-ranking officers agreed to lay down their arms in exchange for lighter sentences. Rank-and-file combatants, for their part, entered reintegration programs that would provide them with vocational training, financial assistance, and psychological support to ease their transition back to civilian life.[39]

Problems with the design and execution of the peace agreement ended up perpetuating paramilitarism, however. Many former paramilitary organizations refused to participate in the process, either because they feared retaliation or were unwilling to relinquish their power.[40] And as this demobilization was playing out, the Organization of American States Mission to Support the Peace Process, which oversaw the verifying the process, voiced its concerns about infringements: armed units were holding out or rearming.[41] Half of all paramilitary groups remilitarized within five years of the signing of the peace accord.[42]

The nature of these post-treaty groups has been debated, including their links with previous paramilitary organizations, their relationship with the Colombian state, and whether they are political or merely criminal entities. Some have labeled the successor groups *neo-paramilitaries*, emphasizing their connections with former paramilitaries, and underscoring that their existence is the inevitable consequence of a faulty and disingenuous peace process.[43] Others, in particular Colombian law enforcement agencies, refer to them as criminal gangs (*bandas criminales*, or Bacrim) deemphasizing their political nature and underlining their distinct genealogies from former groups.

The AUC's demobilization, even if partial, left an important power vacuum across vast territories and triggered a frantic struggle among successor groups to seize strategic areas for the development of legal businesses (cattle ranching, mining) as well as illegal ones (drugs, extortion). This dynamic also led to fierce competition to control populations formerly under paramilitary rule and to influence rural elites serving as intermediaries with the Colombian central state. Successor groups have also taken over particular zones of coca cultivation, drug production, and transshipment routes along border areas.[44] Massive abuses against the population, including terrorist tactics, have continued, as detailed in the conclusion. These groups stand accused of the forced recruitment of children and adolescents, targeted assassinations, disappearances, kidnappings, and other indiscriminate attacks. Indigenous and Afro Colombian communities inhabiting strategic areas have been particularly hard hit. Finally, paramilitary groups have also systematically targeted beneficiaries of the Victims and Land Restitution Law (2012).[45]

Ideology

The relevance of ideology in Colombian paramilitary groups is often downplayed. This book shows its defining role in shaping their organizational identity and repertoires of action. Before embarking on the analysis, though, two important caveats are in order. First (and as noted), these organizations are often examined as a unitary actor but are more accurately described as a loose confederation of regional groups with diverse trajectories, interests, leadership, and characteristics; they are united by their shared opposition to revolutionary ideas and their support for the central state's effort to eradicate guerrillas, whom they regard as an existential threat.[46] Second, from an ideological standpoint, these groups are not characterized by a profound normative commitment, or, to paraphrase Francisco Gutiérrez-Sanín and Elisabeth Wood, their program is ideologically weak.[47] Their pro-status quo inclinations are not dogmatic and are often characterized by a significant degree of pragmatism. Indeed, Duncan maintains that an element of posturing existed in the way paramilitary groups exaggerated their ideological commitments to justify their violent acts or clientelistic practices.[48] This pragmatic approach contrasts with the more dogmatic ideological views of guerrillas and security forces.

Ideologically, paramilitary groups are characterized by a conservative, pro-status quo vision of society predicated on a staunchly anti-revolutionary stance.[49] Eduardo Pizarro characterizes paramilitary ideology as right-wing populism.[50] Carlos Medina Gallego views it as pro-market in its defense of private property and libertarian in its commitment to self-defense rights.[51] These principles have deep roots in Colombian rural society among elites, who saw guerrilla incursions as a violent assault on their way of life. The sentiment also became widespread among peasants and small merchants, many of whom also held conservative views and became hardened from suffering guerrilla abuses.[52] A sense of humiliation at the treatment received from guerrillas also inspired deep-seated resentment in the population.[53]

Paramilitaries came from different backgrounds, and this diversity impacted their ideological stances. An anticommunism ideology, for example, was strongest among paramilitaries with links to the armed forces, as they were heavily influenced by the prevalent doctrine of national security (DNS)—a theme developed more fully in chapter 6. Such a view saw guerrillas as not only a danger to the sitting government but also as an existential threat to the nation. "Progressive" actors sympathizing with insurgent causes were often regarded as "useful fools" and even dire threats themselves.[54] The Colombian Armed Forces used DNS to build a powerful narrative that justified paramilitarism in terms of encouraging self-defense and boosting nationalism.[55] Colombian Army generals such as Rito Alejo del Río and Fernando Landazábal, who helped found paramilitary groups in Magdalena Medio in the 1980s, were among the most vocal supporters of this view within the armed forces.[56]

Anticommunism was also prevalent among landowners and cattle ranchers, though in their case, their zeal stemmed more from their fear that guerrillas were transforming social norms and structures in their communities. Pablo Guarín, a landowner who was elected to the lower chamber of

Congress for the Liberal Party in Puerto Boyacá and became an influential intellectual figure for these landowners, articulated the need to liberate communities from the threat posed by guerrillas and to defend their way of life in the absence of a functional state.[57]

Iván Duque Escobar (aka Ernesto Báez), a small landowner who would become political commander of the Bloque Central Bolívar, a powerful group within the AUC, expressed a similar position.[58] One of the group's chief ideologues, he defined paramilitaries as antisubversive, anticommunist military political organizations. In his view, paramilitarism was an economic, political, and social phenomenon that arose to defend people's liberty, honor, property, and way of life.[59] Carlos Castaño provides a similar description of the paramilitary aim: "In this country, authority is designed to protect the rich, the upper class; guerillas protect modest people, those from humble backgrounds, and we, the *paras*, protect the middle class."[60] Another important paramilitary figure, Salvatore Mancuso, the commander of several AUC *bloques* (Norte, Catatumbo) who came from a landed family in Montería, Córdoba, articulated similar views. In an official address delivered during peace talks in Santa Fe de Ralito, he underscored how Colombia could rely on paramilitarism to confront "threats and terrorist violence, which could forever defuse the real risk of a totalitarian leftist dictatorship" and how a Christian humanist spirit inspired paramilitary actions.[61]

These views expressed by provincial landowners are remarkably like those voiced by powerful members of the Colombian elite. Take, for example, a column written by an influential politician from a patrician Bogotá family, Fernando Londoño, following the assassination of Carlos Castaño in 2006: "Self-defense forces exist because there is a Marxist guerrilla. . . . . there are two intertwined elements in their origin: the opprobrious abuse suffered by Colombian peasants and the ineptitude of the Colombian state to guarantee their life, honor, wellbeing, and possessions, which is exactly the state's raison d'être."[62]

As for drug traffickers-turned-paramilitaries, they did not necessarily hold such strong ideological views for the most part. To a significant degree, anti-leftist views were alien to them because most came from modest backgrounds and therefore resented Colombian elites. Pablo Escobar, for example, demonstrated a commitment to helping marginalized sectors along with a manifest antipathy toward the Colombian upper class, which, in his view, disdained and excluded people like him.[63] In Colombia, well-to-do sectors referred to drug traffickers as *clase emergente*, a derogatory, class-based term connoting humble backgrounds, lack of sophistication and taste, and dreams of upward mobility.[64]

Yet, in becoming landowners, drug dealers eventually came to share the interests and ultimately the predicament of landed elites vis-à-vis guerrillas, leading to the gradual hardening of their position toward left-leaning groups. Consider the case of Diego Murillo (aka Don Berna), Pablo Escobar's former driver and bodyguard who broke ties with the kingpin and then rose within the ranks of Los PEPES to become one of its most feared and powerful commanders—leader of the Bloque Cacique Nutibará. While participating in the Santa Fe de Ralito talks, he underscored that he and his men never wanted to take up arms, but that they had to do so to defend Medellín from the twin menace of Escobar and the guerrillas. Explaining his purported acceptance of demobilization, Murillo said, "Now that the state demands we demobilize and society trusts the state, we could not continue waging war. We never wanted to confront the state."[65] Despite arguable elements of cynicism and posturing in Murillo's claims, his actions lend credence to his claim that his deeds were in part driven by anticommunist (or at least pro-state) motives.

Criminal Ethos

In addition to the described ideological views, the identity of paramilitary groups was also influenced by an unconventional factor: a criminal ethos or *esprit mafioso*.[66] This ethos is critical to understanding the nature of paramilitary groups and their behavior. Several studies have established that the leaders and rank-and-file members of paramilitary groups often had criminal backgrounds.[67] Drug traffickers' astronomical revenues allowed them to develop significant clout within the paramilitary project because they could fund these private armies. Their resources proved critical to accruing high-tech arsenal, recruiting mercenaries, establishing training camps, and financing operations and payrolls.[68] Many large landowners who supported these groups were themselves wealthy, but their resources were insignificant relative to those of drug traffickers. Drug traffickers' military and intelligence skills, as well as their incredibly brazen methods, further cemented their influence within paramilitarism.[69]

Drug lords can be seen, Vadim Volkov asserts, as violent entrepreneurs who acquire valuable organizational capabilities in the course of their criminal activities.[70] Duncan posits that the coercive wings of drug trafficking organizations were initially relatively limited and designed to serve specific functions such as protection, collection, intimidation, and, when needed, the elimination of rivals.[71] But eventually, and thanks to their unmatched resources, they amassed a large, sophisticated arsenal: Rafael Pardo relates how members of the Medellín Cartel wielded Colt AR-15 and Galil rifles, powerful Mini Uzi and Ingram machine pistols, and Steyr and Glock handguns.[72] Cartel bodyguards and contract killers, however, lacked sophisticated military skills. This would change after they joined self-defense groups and began receiving military training in battle tactics, explosives, telecommunications, and surveillance techniques. Their arms and newly acquired skills allowed them to subjugate adversaries such as the M-19 as well as challengers within their ranks.[73]

The *esprit mafioso* also manifested in paramilitary groups' increasingly predatory behavior. Originally created to protect estates and other properties, paramilitary groups gradually mutated into offensive organizations seeking to secure control over vast zones.[74] Reflecting their criminal approach, they boosted their revenues through the illegal appropriation of land and extortion. This expansion strategy was implemented to maintain strategic parity with hostile guerrilla groups, but also reflected the mindset of criminal organizations, which constantly seek new sources of revenue.

The criminal ethos also led to violent disputes and vendettas, which gave rise to significant instability within paramilitarism.[75] The presence of drug dealers within the ranks created repeated boom-and-bust cycles. Infighting between paramilitary groups vying for power and influence were common given that parties disagreed over contentious issues such as how to undertake operations, which methods to employ, how to resolve commercial disputes, and how to manage relations with the Colombian state. One particularly contentious issue was whether to participate in the peace negotiations and, if so, under what terms.[76]

Another major point of disagreement concerned the role of narcotics in the paramilitary project, which some leaders were apprehensive about.

Carlos Castaño, who participated in and benefited from the drug business but thought of himself as primarily an estate owner, wanted to focus on a political agenda. He thus created a major rift by calling on paramilitary groups to sever ties with drug traffickers. In the negotiations leading to the peace treaty with the government, he denounced narcotrafficking as a practice that was damaging paramilitary groups, eroding their legitimacy, and would ultimately destroy them. In a clear demonstration of the extent to which this criminal ethos had penetrated paramilitarism, he ended up caught up in a family vendetta and killed on the orders of his older brother Vicente.[77]

In sum, the identity of Colombian paramilitary groups evolved over time. The more ideological landowners and cattle ranchers relaxed their dogmatic views and became more pragmatic, welcoming the resources brought in by drug trafficking, even as drug traffickers adopted and articulated more political views.

Leadership, Socialization, and the Selection of Terrorist Tactics

Soon after the inception of paramilitary groups, their leaders adopted terrorism tactics. To compensate for their military and logistical inferiority vis-à-vis guerrilla groups, commanders began a furious onslaught against the support networks of insurgent groups.[78] Targets included people deemed guerrilla sympathizers, including leftist politicians, journalists, human rights activists, community organizers, and the state agents and authorities standing in their way.[79] Paramilitary leadership opted for highly visible violence, seeking to swiftly and decisively strike at the heart of guerrilla groups to wipe out their members, destroy their support system, and expel them from territory under their control or influence. Fear was key to such a strategy, and acts of violence were designed to guarantee the loyalty or submission of the civilian population.[80]

Paramilitary commanders opted for repertoires of terrorism that reflected and reinforced their organizational priorities, identity, and overall cosmovision of society. Hence tactics were calibrated with a clear pro-regime bent that would set paramilitaries apart from the agitational practices promoted by insurgent groups. Fueled by antipathy and distrust of socialist ideas, many paramilitary commanders embraced a view that dehumanized entire groups regarded as posing an existential danger to society—reflecting the DNS mentality dominant in those days.[81]

Although paramilitary groups were initially created as more informal self-defense organizations, commanders would soon set up training schools known as Escuelas de Formación that sought to train and socialize members. The first ones, such as Cero Uno and El Cincuenta, popped up around Puerto Boyacá in 1988 and were associated with the leadership of Peasant Association of Cattle Ranchers and Agriculturalists of Magdalena Medio, or Asociación de Campesinos y Ganaderos del Magdalena Medio. Ramón Isaza and Henry Pérez, among other commanders, hired British, American, and Israeli mercenaries—including retired Israel Defence Forces Colonel Yair Klein—to lead the courses, which normally lasted three weeks.[82] However, this short-lived program was marked by endemic disciplinary problems and fizzled out when internecine fighting broke out. With the revival of paramilitarism in Córdoba and Urabá a few years later, new schools were created under the leadership of Carlos Castaño and Salvatore Mancusso, among many others. Training was overseen by members of the Colombian armed forces and former Popular Liberation Army (Ejército Popular de Liberación, or EPL), commanders who had deserted and joined the ranks of paramilitary groups.[83]

Paramilitary commanders developed a model that blended military and political training. Ernesto Báez, one of the chief ideologues of the new breed of paramilitary groups, presided over the creation of new, more professionalized schools in which fighters learned a broad range of military tactics including open combat strategies, scorched earth policies, urban counterinsurgency tactics, enhanced interrogation techniques (torture), and other terror methods.[84] During his trial deposition, Salvatore Mancuso admitted that new recruits received training in torture and dismembering techniques.[85] Trainees also received instruction on political thought, including communism, ecclesiastical doctrine, and conservatism.[86] This curriculum was important to socialize group members to the view that violence was a legitimate means of maintaining social order and averting the collapse of Colombia's existing socioeconomic and political structure.[87]

The number of training schools would increase in the mid-1990s after the AUC formed. José Efraín Pérez Cardona (aka Eduardo 400), a former Colombian soldier-turned-paramilitary commander of the Bloque Centauro, played an important role in developing these schools, among which was La 35—which trained approximately two thousand fighters from paramilitary groups across the country—and Acuarela, a more exclusive training site for mid- and high-level commanders.[88] Again, these programs zealously incorporated pro-regime and territorial forms of terrorism such as disappearance, torture, summary executions, and massacres against guerrillas and their civilian supporters.

Summary executions and massacres became paramount within paramilitary groups' repertoire of terrorism. Paramilitaries consistently relied on summary executions throughout the period, a highly effective method that sowed fear in the wider population.[89] Although use of this tactic was relatively limited until 1994, it follows a sharp, nonlinear uptick—except for a brief decrease between 1998 and 2000—before reaching a zenith in 2003. Targeted assassinations dropped markedly around 2004 during AUC's demobilization. Successor groups have continued this practice but at significantly lower rates: groups carried out an average of 204 summary executions in the 2006 to 2012 period. This trend can be attributed to the fact that the number and strength of paramilitary groups diminished sharply after 2005.

When looking at the use of this strategy from a comparative perspective, paramilitary groups perpetrated the highest number of summary executions (4,797) (see figure 5.3). These groups are responsible for 57 percent of the total number of targeted assassinations in the sample. Proportionally, the use of this practice by paramilitaries far exceeds that of guerrilla groups but trails that of security forces: summary executions account for 70 percent of the group's total number of terrorist attacks relative to 75 percent of the state's (see figure 5.4).

Although the bulk of these actions took place in urban areas such as Barrancabermeja, Medellín, and Cúcuta, they also affected rural areas. Elaborating on the modus operandi of paramilitary groups, Duncan explains that paramilitary groups used summary executions when attempting to seize control of an area.[90] Their operatives would enter small villages (*veredas*) and rural areas, and execute community leaders and those providing services and employment to the community (small shops owners, those buying the harvest from peasants) to convey to everyone that they were in charge.[91] At times, they would arrive in hamlets with a list in hand, executing those on it, often publicly. On several occasions, former guerrilla deserters who switched sides and became paramilitary operatives would identify guerrilla supporters to be executed.[92]

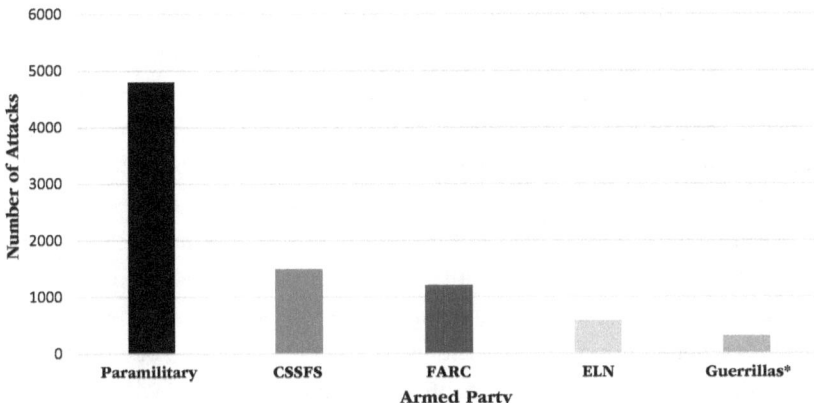

FIGURE 5.3 Paramilitary summary executions, 1988–2012.

Source: Author's tabulation based on CINEP data.
* Sum of guerrillas other than the FARC and ELN.

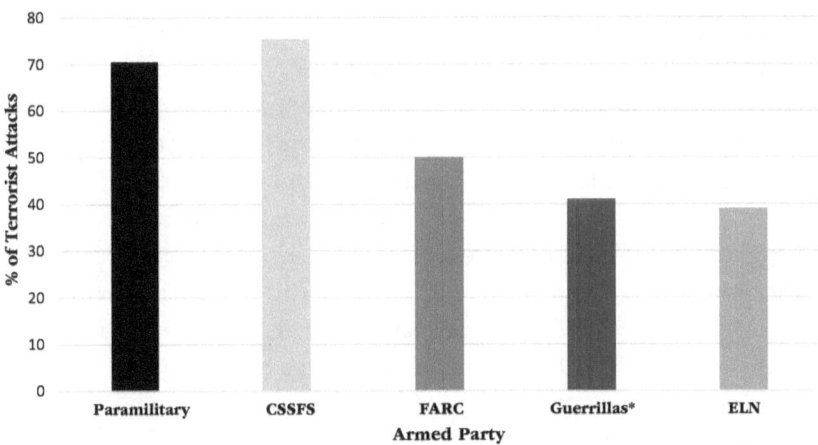

FIGURE 5.4 Paramilitary summary executions within repertoire of terrorism, 1988–2012.

Source: Author's tabulation based on CINEP data.
* Sum of guerrillas other than the FARC and ELN.

In his trial deposition, Freddy Rendón Herrera (aka El Alemán), commander of the Bloque Elmer Cárdenas, asserted that paramilitary groups used summary executions as a form of punishment against individuals who were accused of collaborating with guerrillas, perceived as suspicious, failed to comply with the commands given by paramilitary groups, openly antagonized them, or committed common crimes. In their investigation, prosecutors of the Office of the Attorney General of Colombia (Fiscalía General de la Nación) established that summary executions depended on several clearly defined criteria for the victims: those with purported links with enemy groups; those who had committed a crime, collaborated with authorities, or disobeyed rules; and those who were in a position of power.[93]

Although this motive was not explicitly stated, summary executions were also clearly meant to frighten the population. Some commanders revealed that in areas of high guerrilla presence, people could be "preventively" targeted if they were considered suspect, a logic that obviously created widespread fear.[94] Brazen public executions in broad daylight magnified such fears and mirrored the modus operandi of criminal groups using similar methods to settle accounts or punish those defying them. Moreover, the regular use of overkill against victims of summary executions also reflects a clear intention to maximize fear.

Massacres were the most distinct terrorism trademark of paramilitary groups,[95] as shown by this study's robust evidence: paramilitary groups perpetrated 1,156 massacres, which account for 70 percent of the sample.[96] Many of the victims were elderly people, women, and children.[97] Paramilitary massacres were concentrated during periods following their incursion into areas controlled by the FARC and the National Liberation Army (ELN). A pattern of attack and retaliation in which paramilitary massacres precede guerrilla violence in fiercely disputed territories is clear. Massacres were also used as a mechanism to control territory and keep civilians in line.[98] Following this trend, massacres rose during the paramilitary expansion phase (1997–2003)—coinciding with the creation of the AUC project—and diminished precipitously following the demobilization of these groups in 2005.

Paramilitaries carried out five times more massacres than the Colombian security forces and the FARC and almost twenty times more than the ELN (see figure 5.5). Among the examined groups, massacres proportionally play the largest role in its repertoire, accounting for 17 percent of paramilitary attacks relative to 11 percent by state security forces, 8 percent among the FARC, and 4 percent among the ELN (see figure 5.6).

From a communicational standpoint, paramilitaries used massacres to warn the population about the risks of helping guerrillas and to undermine the idea that guerrillas could offer sufficient protection to civilians living in areas under their control.[99] The testimony of one victim recalls

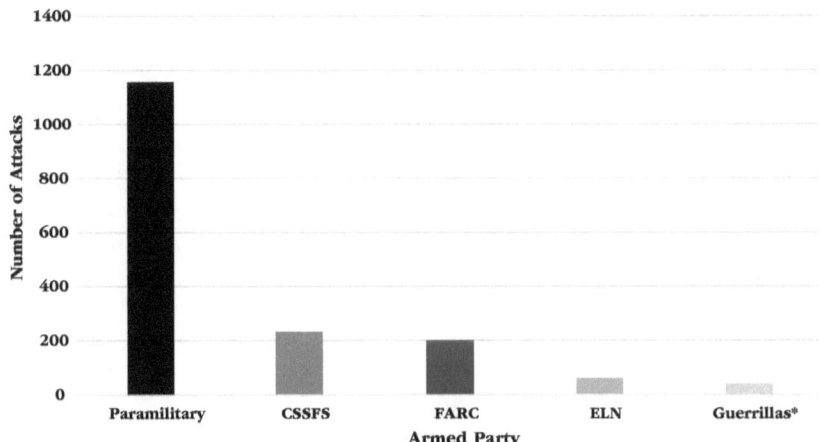

FIGURE 5.5 Paramilitary massacres, 1988–2012.

Source: Author's tabulation based on CINEP data.
* Sum of guerrillas other than the FARC and ELN.

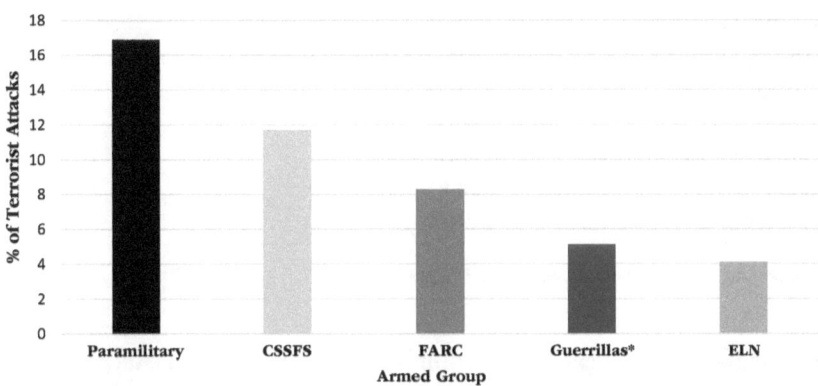

FIGURE 5.6 Paramilitary massacres within repertoire of terrorism, 1988–2012.

Source: Author's tabulation based on CINEP data.
* Sum of guerrillas other than the FARC and ELN.

how, after carrying out a massacre, paramilitaries assembled the community and mockingly told them, "Call guerrilleros to defend you now!" (¡llamen a los guerrilleros para que los defiendan ahora!).[100] As indicated earlier, paramilitary massacres were concentrated in areas where these groups attempted to dislodge guerrillas, including major urban centers and municipalities with strategic military or economic value. Table 5.1 shows the

TABLE 5.1 Paramilitary Massacres by Municipality

Massacre	Municipality	Number of victims
Medellín	Antioquia	44
Ciénaga	Magdalena	29
Apartadó	Antioquia	23
San Carlos	Antioquia	22
Buenaventura	Valle	21
Cúcuta	Norte de Santander	16
Carmen de Bolívar	Bolívar	14
Valledupar	Cesar	14
Tibú	Norte de Santander	13
Agustín Codazzi	Cesar	11
Santa Marta	Magdalena	11
Tuluá	Valle	10
Fundación	Magdalena	10
Bello	Antioquia	10
Peñol	Antioquia	10
San Pablo	Bolívar	9
Puerto Libertador	Chocó	9
San Diego	Cesar	8
Dabeiba	Antioquia	8
Guane	Antioquia	8
Riosucio	Chocó	8
Santander del Quilichao	Cauca	7
Tame	Arauca	7
Tumaco	Nariño	7

Source: Author's tabulation based on CINEP data.

municipalities with the highest number of paramilitary massacres in the 1988 to 2012 period.

Following widespread condemnation of massacres, paramilitaries sought to diminish their use, opting for so-called massacres "in slow motion," whereby they would carry out a series of single executions over a longer time.[101] Indeed, the database shows how between 2001 and 2003, paramilitary groups drastically reduced massacres (from 222 to 89) but committed notably more summary executions (from 366 to 794).[102] The drop in the number of massacres committed by these groups since 2003 is notable. This trend corresponds to a deliberate strategy by paramilitary groups to curb the political damage to their image that massacres were causing. Paramilitaries thus modified their strategy, opting for less visible targeted assassinations to avoid undermining their efforts to open peace negotiations with the Colombian government.[103]

As discussed earlier, paramilitary groups used terrorism following a strategic logic: to erode guerrillas' support system, dislodge them from strategic areas, and—once this goal was accomplished—exert control over them.[104] To assess how this logic aligns with the record of attacks, I plotted paramilitary groups' reliance on territorial forms of terrorism. Once more, I assume with the literature that the group used summary executions and massacres while disputing or seeking to control territory. I reviewed all municipalities in which paramilitaries perpetrated five or more summary executions or massacres in any given year. Simultaneous terrorist attacks are used as a proxy for territorial contestation, whereas unilateral actions are seen as a territorial control mechanism. Figure 5.7 presents the results. Paramilitary groups perpetrated five or more massacres and summary executions per year in 161 municipalities between 1988 and 2012. In 108 municipalities (66 percent), a dual pattern of confrontation and control

FIGURE 5.7 Dynamics of paramilitary territorial terrorism.

Source: Author's tabulation based on CINEP data.

emerges, whereby groups entered a territory, disputed it with guerrillas, and later achieved control. In fifteen (9 percent) attacks, the group used terror while disputing territory with enemies,[105] whereas in another thirty-eight (23 percent), terror was used unilaterally to control the area. The data underline how paramilitary groups deployed terrorist tactics principally while disputing territory with guerrilla groups and, to a much lesser extent, as a mechanism to control the population.

PERFORMATIVE FORMS OF TERRORISM: THE USE OF OVERKILL

Targeted assassinations and massacres carried out by paramilitary groups were often accompanied by overkill (*sevicia*), which (as noted) entail gruesome acts of cruelty and sacralized forms of violence perpetrated against the bodies of victims, which are later displayed in public to maximize fear in the population. The most common practices include slitting the victim's throat, beheading, burning, castration, evisceration, dismemberment, or impalement. As indicated in previous chapters, although information about these dehumanizing practices tends to be quite hazy, existing accounts concur that among armed groups, paramilitaries were significantly more prone to using overkill.

In one of the most detailed accounts of this practice, the National Commission of Historic Memory found 588 violent incidents in which overkill was employed and bodies were exhibited. These included 433 summary executions and 155 massacres and a total of 1,520 victims. As figure 5.8 shows, the majority (63 percent) are attributable to paramilitary groups.[106]

Similarly, Andrés Suárez reports that in the case of Urabá, between 1988 and 2002, about 10 percent of paramilitary massacres included excessive acts of cruelty, and that paramilitary groups were three times more likely than the FARC to rely on these methods.[107] A report of the Colombian Commission of Jurists for the 1997 to 2001 period offers similar findings.[108] The National Commission of Historic Memory finds that overkill was more common in massacres involving a smaller number of victims, speculating that paramilitary groups strategically used *sevicia* in targeted assassinations and smaller massacres to match the widespread levels of terror generated by large massacres.[109]

Controversy surrounds this interpretation: in line with arguments in the literature of civil war attributing brutality to lack of discipline within

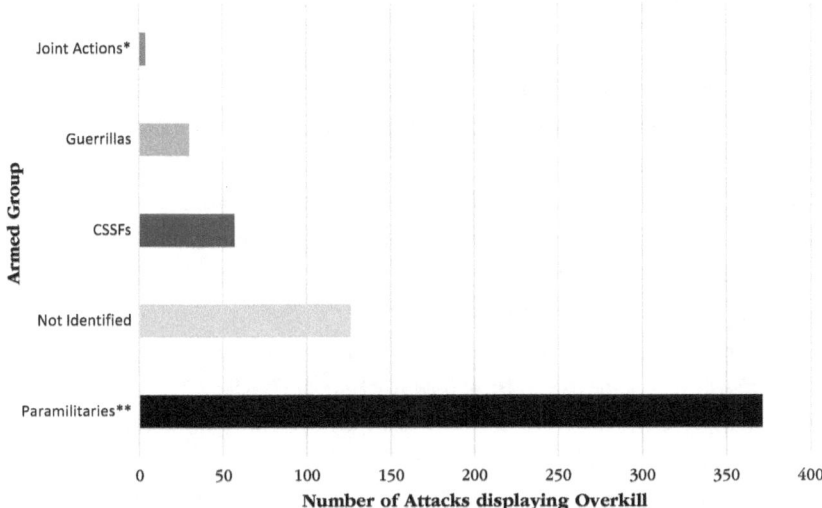

FIGURE 5.8 Paramilitary use of overkill in comparative perspective.

Source: Author's tabulation based on CINEP data.
* Between CSSFs and paramilitaries.
** Sum of guerrillas other than the FARC and ELN.

armed parties, some studies emphasize that overkill does not seem to correspond to a deliberate, systematic policy promoted by a central command.[110] Alternative accounts argue these excesses were acts of revenge.[111] Paramilitary leaders deny their use altogether. Carlos Castaño, for example, vehemently denied ever perpetrating acts of extreme cruelty, such as the use of electric chainsaws.[112] Similarly, Freddy Rendón Herrera (aka El Alemán), commander of the Bloque Elmer Cárdenas, testified in his trial deposition that the group never ordered members to decapitate or torture victims.[113] Members of the Bloque Calima in Valle del Cauca, by contrast, explained that they did dismember several bodies, including some victims who were still alive, and that they threw their remains into a mass grave. They explained that such acts of cruelty were not AUC policy but were nonetheless widespread and directed by commanders on the ground.[114]

Yet the systematic use of this practice over the years, as well as the copious evidence that combatants were trained in overkill, provides evidence that these actions were calibrated and purposefully incorporated into these groups' repertoires of terrorism. During his trial deposition, Salvatore Mancuso testified under oath that new recruits received training in military tactics, including torture and dismembering techniques.[115]

This account is corroborated by several other paramilitary commanders, who acknowledge that these techniques were taught in what were colloquially referred to as "dismembering and death schools" such as El Tomate and La 35.[116] Overkill also reflects a mafia-like uses of violence, which, as noted, is commonly used by members of the underworld to convey messages to enemies and authorities. Many of the paramilitary practices described by victims, prosecutors, and former group members have all the hallmarks of criminal modus operandi.[117] These include extreme forms of violence—both symbolic and performative elements—used to bolster reputations, maximize fear, constrain and paralyze enemies, and deter those who seeking to interfere in their activities.[118] In other words, the use of overkill seems to stem from a murky synergy between extreme counterinsurgency techniques and criminal forms of communication.[119]

In an especially interesting finding, data reveal that paramilitaries regularly used abductions as well: 838 cases during the examined period. This tactic was seldom used until 1996, reaching its peak in 2003, and finally decreasing markedly. From a comparative perspective, as figure 5.9 shows, paramilitary groups account for 27.5 percent of all cases in the sample, trailing the FARC but exceeding the number committed by the ELN, the state, and smaller guerrilla groups. Although the number of paramilitary abductions is high, the tactic's proportional use within the group's repertoire of terrorism is much lower. Abductions account for only 12 percent of the total number of paramilitary terrorist events, the same as security forces but significantly lower than the ELN (52 percent) and the FARC (37 percent) (see figure 5.10).

Although paramilitary groups relied on abductions extensively, their use of this tactic qualitatively differs from that of guerrillas. Paramilitary abductions were specifically targeted at their enemies, and unlike in the guerrilla case, not designed to threaten a wider population of people considered class enemies. In addition, they were conducted discreetly to avoid attracting publicity and seldom for extortive, financial purposes.[120] Instead, attacks targeted the families of guerrilla members as retaliation, a practice also common among members of organized crime.[121] Abductions would at times also be used as leverage to secure the liberation of hostages held by guerrillas.[122] In other words, paramilitary leaders adapted this practice to their organizational preferences and identity and deliberately avoided using it with an agitational intent.

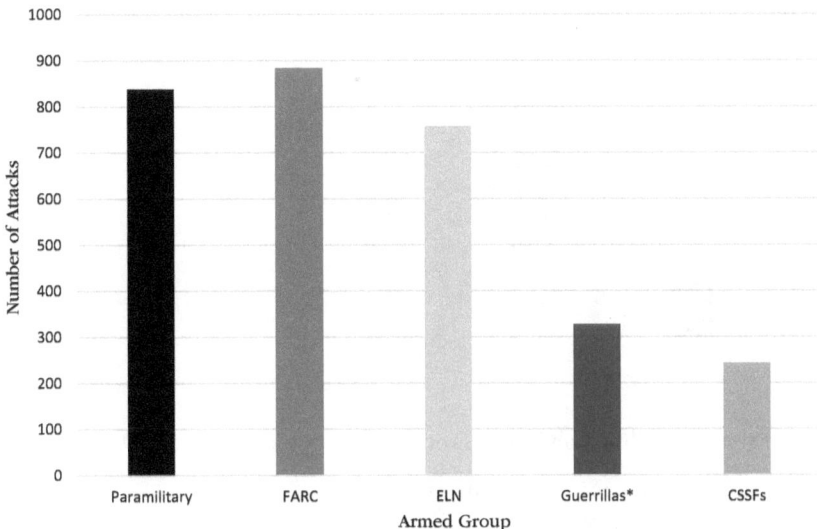

FIGURE 5.9 Paramilitary abductions, 1988–2012.

Source: Author's tabulation based on CINEP data.
* Sum of guerrillas other than the FARC and ELN.

Some paramilitary groups, such as MAS, emerged precisely to combat the practice of guerrilla kidnapping.[123] As a result, the subsequent use of abductions was controversial within these groups. Commenting on this practice, Carlos Castaño explained, "I never ordered a kidnapping for economic reasons, only for political ones."[124] Under his orders, relatives of Alfono Cano, a member of the FARC's secretariat, were kidnapped and later released in exchange for prisoners held by the FARC.[125] At one point, the AUC, also under Castaño's orders, kidnapped seven members of Congress to pressure the government to open a channel of communication with the group.[126] The Bloque Norte, under the leadership of Rodrigo Tovar Pupo (aka Jorge 40), also relied extensively on abductions.[127]

Paramilitary groups also incorporated forced disappearance into their repertoire of terrorism. Enforced disappearance refers to a victim's abduction, imprisonment, killing, and later concealment of the body.[128] As discussed in the introduction, although this practice has historically been associated with state terror—and in the Latin American context with repressive right-wing dictatorships—it has become more generalized over

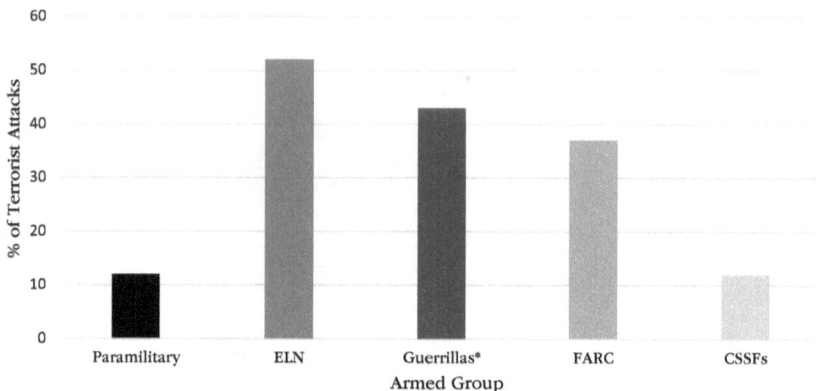

FIGURE 5.10 Paramilitary abductions within repertoire of terrorism, 1988–2012.

Source: Author's tabulation based on CINEP data.
* Sum of guerrillas other than the FARC and ELN.

time as nonstate actors began to embrace it.[129] Although Colombian parties have systematically practiced disappearances,[130] it is difficult to compile an accurate picture because available information is incomplete and problematic. Given that parties deliberately conceal the victims' bodies and their relatives and loved ones are understandably reluctant to come forward, fearing retaliation, producing an accurate estimate about the use of this practice poses a major challenge.[131] Given these factors, the database of the Research Center for Investigation and Popular Education, or Centro de Investigación y Educación Popular (CINEP), captures only a small fraction of these events under the category of abductions (i.e., civilians retrieved by force whose whereabouts remained unknown at the time of CINEP's reporting).

These problems notwithstanding, the Colombian Truth Commission provides partial data that allow us to infer patterns in the use of this terrorist tactic. It acknowledges 121,768 disappearances in the 1985 to 2016 period. Up to 54 percent of the cases could not be traced to any armed actor. Of the rest, the report attributes 52 percent to paramilitaries, more than all other actors combined. The report also indicates that paramilitary forces used this tactic more frequently after 1982, often with the tacit support of security forces, and attributes 9 percent of the cases to multiple actors, presumably meaning agents of the state operating in coordination with paramilitary groups.[132]

Geographic Dimensions of Paramilitary Terrorism

As in previous chapters, I conclude with a geographical discussion concerning the use of terrorism. Although paramilitary groups practiced terrorism across the country, data show that the bulk of such activity is clustered around selected departments, and within them specific municipalities.

Attacks are concentrated in the northwest (Antioquia, Cesar, Magdalena, Chocó, Córdoba), the eastern region bordering Venezuela (Santander and Norte de Santander), and to a lesser degree in the southwest (Valle, Cauca, and Nariño) and eastern lowlands (Meta). Paramilitary terrorist attacks disproportionately affected municipalities with strategic value as drug producing and transshipment zones, corridors connecting difficult-to-access areas of the country, and major poles of economic activity (see appendix). Regarding the distribution of terrorism at the municipal level, the data show that urban communities bore the brunt of paramilitary attacks, in particular large metropolitan areas where guerillas had developed an important network of sympathizers and which paramilitary groups targeted with special zeal: Barrancabermeja, Cúcuta, Buenaventura, Santa Marta, Medellín, Cali, Bucaramanga, Bogotá, and Cartagena. Paramilitary terrorism also hit smaller towns hard, especially those strategically located for the transshipment of drugs, among them Turbó, Quibdó, Valledupar, Apartadó, and Tumaco (see appendix). Rural communities with strategic importance linking different zones or departments of the country—important locations for agriculture, cattle ranching, mining, and other relevant economic activities—were also epicenters of paramilitary terrorist attacks as these groups sought to defend and, later, appropriate these areas.

Conclusion

This chapter shows that paramilitary groups resorted systematically to terrorism as part of their unique repertoire of violence. Of all groups participating in the war, paramilitaries used this tactic most extensively and consistently to advance their military and political objectives in their quest to root out Colombia's guerrilla presence. Their use of terrorism reflects their unique identity as hybrid organizations composed of markedly different patrons—landowners, criminals, former members of security forces—who coalesced around a radical anti-insurgency project concerned about an "internal enemy." These groups combined a strong counterinsurgency, anticommunist bent with a criminal ethos and military indoctrination.

Paramilitary leaders opted for terrorist tactics that matched this stance, including pro-regime and territorial forms of terrorism, such as summary executions and massacres, while avoiding agitational forms associated with guerrillas such as bombing attacks. At times, paramilitaries used graphic forms of violence as a kind of gruesome communication method that sought to paralyze rivals and enemies and terrorize communities into submission. Paramilitary abductions differed in nature from those carried out by guerrillas. Lacking economic motivations, paramilitary abductions were almost always used to neutralize or bargain with their enemies, again reflecting how paramilitary leaders adapted terrorist practices to their ideational preferences and distinguished themselves from their enemies.

6

State Terror in the Colombian Civil War

In a hearing held at the main theater in Ocaña, a small town in Norte de Santander, former members of the Colombian Army met with relatives of the so-called *falsos positivos* (false positives) scandal. The meeting, one of several formal symbolic hearings (Audiencias de Reconocimiento) organized by the Special Jurisdiction of Peace (Jurisdicción Especial para la Paz) to shed light on human rights violations perpetrated during the civil war, dealt with this clandestine operation in which members of the Colombian Army abducted and killed youth from humble origins and staged them to look like enemy casualties (as if they were guerrillas or criminals). Military personnel were offered monetary compensation, promotions, and holidays—incentives implemented by the institution's High Command and tacitly supported by the Ministry of Defense—in exchange for increasing enemy casualties. As part of this operation, the Colombian Army summarily executed 6,402 civilians. The number could be much higher.[1]

The families attending the hearing, mostly peasants, expressed their dismay and rage, underscoring that their sorrow was worsened by a profound sense of betrayal. The mother of one of the victims rhetorically asked the former members of the military in attendance, "When did the armed forces decide to relinquish their duty to protect ordinary Colombians? Were the lives of our sons, husbands, and grandchildren worth the perks?"

Visibly shaken, a former army corporal of the 95th regiment, Néstor Guillermo Gutiérrez, who confessed to participating in several illegal killings, conveyed what transpired in detailed fashion, explaining that although it did not excuse his deeds, he and his men were acting under specific orders. Minutes later, Paulino Coronado Gámez, a retired army general also found responsible for the murders, stated, "I offer you my condolences for not having acted more diligently and pledge to try and restore the damage and the pain caused. I would like to convey my deep remorse, one that shreds my soul. I know we affected entire families, fathers, mothers, sons, grandchildren. We left an enormous vacuum."[2]

The scandal, which rattled the foundations of the Colombian Army and tarnished its reputation, exemplifies the grievous excesses perpetrated by this force during the country's civil war. The Colombian state security forces (CSSF) are arguably the most consequential actor in the long conflict: state forces have been battling guerrilla groups since the latter rose up in arms in the mid-1960s and have played a critical role in the emergence and development of paramilitary forces, a major party in the conflict. During the war, the CSSF—in particular the military—committed serious crimes during counterinsurgency and counternarcotics operations, and many of these abuses amounted to terrorism. Based on data from the Research Center for Investigation and Popular Education (Centro de Investigación y Educación Popular, or CINEP) extracted for this work, figure 6.1 shows how CSSF use of terrorism ebbs and flows, reflecting different phases of the civil war: it remains low from 1988 to 1992, picks up significantly in 1993 and 1994, drops between 1995 and 2000, and rises again between 2001 and 2008, diminishing thereafter. The CSSF account for 1,982 terrorist incidents, or 16 percent of the total. This amounts to fewer than 33 percent of acts committed by paramilitary groups and 82 percent of those by the Revolutionary Armed Forces of Colombia (FARC) but is higher than the number of National Liberation Army (Ejército de Liberación Nacional, or ELN) attacks.

As to the CSSF's repertoire of terrorism, their blueprint differs from that of nonstate actors participating in the conflict (see figure 6.2) in that they specialized mostly in targeted assassinations and, to a lesser extent, massacres, and abductions, whereas bombings were carried out on a very limited basis. Although these acts are not recorded in the sample, the CSSF also used torture and disappearance extensively.

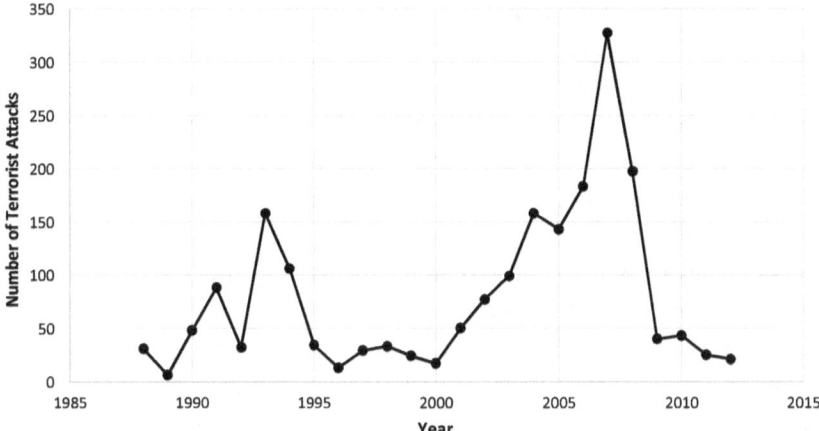

FIGURE 6.1 CSSF use of terrorism, 1988–2012.

Source: Author's tabulation based on CINEP data.

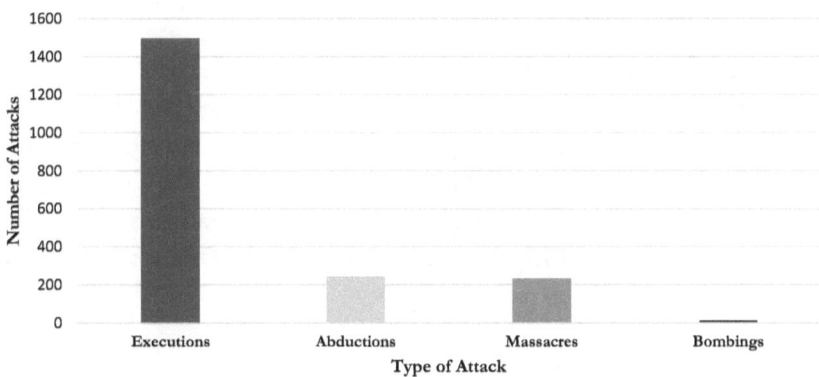

FIGURE 6.2 CSSF repertoires of terrorism, 1988–2012.

Source: Author's tabulation based on CINEP data.

This chapter traces the evolution of the CSSF's terrorism practices, unpacking what factors inform its repertoire of terrorism. It argues that the CSSF resorted to terrorism as part of an aggressive state security policy. Terrorism surfaced in stages, first during a repressive wave reminiscent of state terror campaigns in the Southern Cone and later as part of a counterinsurgency strategy seeking to deprive guerrillas of civilian support. These terrorist tactics evolved with changing conditions in the theater of war (i.e., guerrilla offensives, truces, and tactical retreats). State terrorism was directed most prominently against guerrillas' civilian support structure and people associated with these groups. I also maintain that the democratic nature of Colombia's regime partially constrained CSSF actions, preventing more widespread use of terrorism and creating incentives to contract out part of the counterinsurgency effort to paramilitary allies. As I demonstrate, state terrorism displays a clear pro-status quo logic inspired by a harsh ideological view that regarded insurgency—and the socialist ideas inspiring it—as an existential threat to the country. The CSSF saw themselves as the nation's protectors, a view heavily influenced by the Cold War-era doctrine of national security (DNS) and its internal enemy thesis. State forces, which enjoyed significant autonomy, justified terrorism as a legitimate way of averting a national tragedy, rationalizing it as a necessary yet inevitable outcome of counterinsurgency warfare.

The chapter proceeds as follows. It begins with a conceptual discussion of state terror and its relationship to civil war, before presenting a brief historical account of the nature and evolution of the CSSF since 1945. In the third section, it details how ideational aspects such as DNS and foreign transnational counterinsurgency doctrines shaped the CSSF's identity. In the fourth section, it details how military leadership adopted and promulgated these views through institutional mechanisms, primarily training. It concludes with brief reflections on the role of the security forces in the development of terrorism.

State Terrorism in Civil War

An important notion informing this work is that state and nonstate terrorism occur simultaneously during armed conflicts. Christopher Mitchell and his colleagues explain that state terror is usually associated with the illegal use of force by states to curb dissent and inhibit collective action. They define it as purposeful coercion through violence (or the threat of violence) to induce extreme fear in observers identifying with the targets of violence such that they perceive themselves as potential future victims. Fear, they explain, compels viewers to consider changing their behavior according to the wishes of the perpetrator.[3] Michael Walzer, similarly, views state terror as acts perpetrated by state agents or by private groups acting on the orders of or on behalf of a state to propagate anxiety among citizens with the goal of curbing political opposition.[4]

Some authors consider state terror to be a problematic, fuzzy category better captured under the general rubric of state repression, contending that the label does not contribute much to our theoretical understanding of the phenomenon.[5] They argue that one of the main weaknesses of state terror as a concept is that by nature, states utilize coercion to pursue their objectives (i.e., to ensure their survival, maintain order). As a result, discerning whether fear in the population stems from legitimate state actions or from state terrorism is not necessarily straightforward.[6] The point is well taken because states may use violence in accordance with certain principles (legality, proportionality, expedience, transparency) and still generate fear in the population. Alternatively, states may resort to violence in illegitimate ways to maintain order but not necessarily to spread fear.[7] Furthermore, though it might seem counterintuitive, states can also rely on terrorism to shore up their legitimacy. In such cases, terrorist acts are used to signal their determination and capacity to root out challenges to their power.

Another complicating factor is the difficulty of distinguishing state from nonstate terrorism, given the propensity of states to support the actions of nonstate groups relying on terrorism.[8] As discussed in the introduction, some authors distinguish between state terror, understood as violence and intimidation by states against their own population, and terrorism, understood as terrorist actions by nonstate groups.[9] In state-sponsored terrorism, relatedly, a state relies on proxy actors to carry out illicit and clandestine terrorist actions to undermine both domestic and external enemies[10]—a dynamic that renders the lines between state and nonstate terrorism difficult to discern.[11]

Conversely, scholars defending state terrorism as a category, including members of the Critical Terrorism Studies School, claim that ignoring the specific role of states glosses over the phenomenon's complexity. To avoid what they regard as a misguided conceptual differentiation, they advocate for an act-based approach capable of incorporating both categories, that is, state and nonstate terror.[12] This book advocates using state terror as a distinct category. State terrorism is conceptualized as the unlawful use of direct, lethal physical force against civilians—in violation of cardinal international humanitarian law principles such as distinction and proportionality—perpetrated by state agents seeking to induce fear in victims to influence their future behavior in the context of a civil war.

Regarding Colombia, state terrorism has some particularities that set it apart from other cases, at least in the Latin American setting. As Tim Wilson reminds us, states use terror differently depending on considerations such as regime type and context.[13] In the Latin American setting, state violence and terrorism—including torture, disappearances, and widespread incarceration—were prevalent during the height of the Cold War in most dictatorships: Argentina, Brazil, Chile, El Salvador, Guatemala, Nicaragua, and Uruguay.[14] Recent studies have also revealed that this strategy was more widespread than originally thought in Mexico.[15] Terrorism in Latin America manifested under what Ruth Blakeley refers to as national security state.[16] It was often inscribed in the context of so-called dirty wars, which featured clandestine operations in which state agencies overtly killed unarmed civilians as part of broad repressive campaigns.[17] Colombia and Peru were regional outliers in that state terrorism surfaced there during democratic administrations confronting civil wars.[18] In Colombia, as will be shown, the state engaged in the systematic and widespread use of terrorism, first during a brief repressive period under President Turbay Ayala (1978–1982) and later, more extensively, as part of counterinsurgency operations conducted despite the country being under democratic rule.

Historical Evolution of the Colombian Security Forces

This section succinctly discusses the evolution of the Colombian state security apparatus. It is beyond the scope of the chapter to furnish a detailed account of the CSSF's history, a task that has been undertaken elsewhere.[19] Instead, this discussion traces how the CSSF's institutional trajectory shaped their identity and informed their repertoires of terrorism. The analysis looks at three main phases: La Violencia and the National Front (NF) years (1948–1974), guerrilla expansion and paramilitary emergence (1975–1997), and guerrilla retreat and state strengthening during the implementation of the Democratic Security Policy (DSP) (1998–2012).

THE DEVELOPMENT OF MILITARY AUTONOMY (1948-1974)

The Colombian National Army was created in 1819 during the war for independence from Spain. However, despite undergoing significant reform in 1907 and its triumph in the Peruvian-Colombian war (1932-1933), the army did not really become a modern military until the early 1960s. Similarly, the Colombian National Police, founded in 1890, remained a relatively small, poorly trained force with limited capacity beyond the capital and some provincial metropolitan areas until the National Front years.[20] Scholars have argued that the Colombian state struggled to develop its coercive capacity, which they attribute to a difficult state-building process marked by constant disputes and major pushback from regional elites, who resisted state efforts to centralize and consolidate power.[21]

The period between the beginning of La Violencia and the end of the National Front (1948-1974) was critical in shaping the CSSF's modern identity and characteristics. It was during these years that coercive state institutions, in particular the military, developed a fierce sense of autonomy from civilian administrations, an attitude that had a considerable impact on their overall approach to security. Civil-military relations in Colombia have historically been fraught. The military strived to remain neutral against the backdrop of the country's acutely partisan political life.[22] Doing so, however, was often thorny given that many members of the military—officers and rank-and-file soldiers—belonged to families with deep ties to the two dominant parties (Liberals and Conservative), and also because ruling administrations often pressured the army to intervene on their behalf during repeated and violent disputes with their political rivals. Following the election of Conservative Laureano Gómez in 1949, for example, the army, and particularly the national police, were used as "partisan political instruments by Conservative administrations and were increasingly involved politically as repressive instruments of the central government."[23]

Civil-military relations changed drastically when partisan violence during La Violencia became so ferocious that it prompted General Gustavo Rojas Pinilla to seize power. One of Rojas Pinilla's first and most consequential measures was to place the national police under army command.[24] The decision, though it helped reduce violence at the time, essentially militarized the police.[25] Even though Rojas Pinilla's brief rule (1953-1957) was an exception to Colombia's established constitutional order and its long tradition of military subordination to civilian rule, the power acquired by the military during his rule—and more generally during La Violencia—elevated it to become an important player in Colombian politics. Worried about the army's rising power, the subsequent administration of President Lleras Camargo (1958–1962) adopted a series of measures and institutional reforms aimed at extricating the military from politics.[26] Around this time, an arrangement emerged that would prove consequential in the Colombian military's trajectory. In exchange for the army's commitment to stay away from politics, politicians granted the military considerable autonomy in matters related to defense and security. A military officer would be appointed as defense minister, the army would have total latitude in the disbursement and allocation of defense budgets, and, most critically, military leadership would design and execute internal and external national security policies.[27]

THE EXPANSION OF COUNTERINSURGENCY (1975–1997)

The end of the NF years coincided with a severe worsening of security conditions linked to growing guerrilla strength and the emergence of powerful drug cartels. The difficulties plaguing the CSSF in this period were exacerbated by the military's new autonomy, which inadvertently contributed to organizational complacency; relatively insulated, the army failed to aggressively pursue a sustainable, long-term military strategy against guerrillas. As discussed in chapters 3 and 4, although the FARC and the ELN took up arms in the mid-1960s, they initially did not pose a real threat to the Colombian state. In this context, the Colombian Army opted for a low-intensity strategy that sought to contain guerrillas and restrict their presence to remote, unpopulated zones.[28] During this period, counterinsurgency initiatives were characterized by their reactive, short-sighted nature, a dynamic that Nazih Richani describes as a "comfortable impasse."[29]

The military's attempts to control the Independent Peasant Republics (described in more detail in chapter 3) illustrates its zigzagging, ad hoc strategy. Following years of detachment and inaction, in 1965 President Guillermo León Valencia finally ordered the army to destroy these enclaves, which were perceived in military and political circles to be dangerous. The operation, known as Plan Lazo (1962), was conceived by General Alberto

Ruiz Novoa, a veteran of the Colombian Battalion (Batallón Colombia), a special force of the Colombian Army dispatched in 1951 to fight alongside U.S. and allied forces in the Korean War. Plan Lazo is considered the first comprehensive long-term security policy in Colombia.[30] Predicated on the Latin American security operations model developed by the United States, it involved a two-pronged approach: reorganizing military structures into special brigades to enhance operational efficacy and staging campaigns to win peasant hearts and minds.[31] Significantly, Plan Lazo was defined by a developmental vision that, in accordance with the conventional wisdom of the time, sought to combat insurgency by integrating the military more deeply into society through an aggressive array of civic-military actions aimed at limiting the appeal of insurgent groups.[32] Its achievements notwithstanding, Plan Lazo would be discontinued when a rival faction within the military opposed to Ruiz's developmental approach took control of the army.[33]

With the end of Plan Lazo, the state strategy shifted from a strategy of confrontation back to one of containment. As discussed in chapters 3 and 4, many have argued that with this decision, the CSSF wasted a precious opportunity to defeat guerrillas during their embryonic years when they were weak and vulnerable.[34] Indeed, the strengthening of guerrilla groups toward the end of NF laid bare the limitations of the CSSF's containment strategy.[35] Eventually, hard pressed to confront raging violence and impunity they could no longer disregard—kidnapping and extortion were becoming a common occurrence in rural areas—but constrained by its own institutional limitations, the state chose to entrust its counterinsurgency operations to paramilitary organizations.[36]

The strengthening of the FARC and the ELN also coincided with the emergence of several second-generation revolutionary groups such as the Armed Movement Quintín Lamé (Movimiento Armado Quintín Lamé) and the April 19 Movement (Movimiento 19 de Abril, or M-19), which worsened an already delicate security context. These developments prompted civilian governments to enhance the CSSF's role in internal security, a move predicated on a novel and more expansive interpretation that included domestic threats. Given the limitations placed on the military's role in domestic affairs in the constitution of 1886, this new plan was enacted through a series of executive orders invoking a state of exception.[37] As would be the case throughout Latin America, in Colombia these provisions provided cover for serious human rights abuses perpetrated in the name of security.[38]

It was against this backdrop that the Liberal administration of Julio César Turbay Ayala (1978–1982) implemented stringent security measures, honoring a campaign promise to "wage war against crime and subversion."[39] Marco Palacio reports that up to sixty thousand people were detained in the first year of Turbay Ayala's government and that the state resorted to widespread, systematic torture.[40] Targets included leftist militant intellectuals, labor unionists, and members of armed groups. Complementing these measures, within a month of Turbay Ayala's inauguration, General Luis Carlos Camacho Leyva, the newly appointed defense minister, announced an "unrestrained offensive against guerilla activities."[41] The move was carried out under the auspices of Legislative Decree 1923 (Estatuto de Seguridad), which granted the military robust judicial powers, notably jurisdiction over many "political crimes" and the authority to try those cases in their own courts. In 1979, the Turbay Ayala administration embarked on a massive campaign that resulted in some one thousand arrests—including of numerous artists and intellectuals—and produced many reports of torture. Two years later, the government launched a search-and-destroy policy undertaken by the army in the department of Caquetá that resulted in widespread abuses and significant population displacement.[42]

During the administration of Belisario Betancur (1982–1986), massive repression intended to intimidate opposition forces would gradually give way to more isolated abuses, mostly confined to counterinsurgency operations in rural zones and peripheral urban areas.[43] More critically, the administration also restricted the purview of CSSF operations and opened peace negotiations with the FARC. These actions placed tremendous strain on the civilian-military relationship, as sectors within the military began to feel their independence was threatened by an overreaching civilian administration.[44] As noted, the CSSF based their self-perception partly on the notion that security was their exclusive purview and thus firmly objected to any form of civilian interference.

The military's stance was apparent during the famous M-19 assault on the Palacio de Justicia in 1985. After guerillas laid siege to the country's Supreme Court, the army stormed the building without the government's authorization in a defiant and destructive show of force. The move caused concern among politicians and the public that the army had become a rogue, unconstrained force.[45] Such a view was buttressed by the fact that the CSSF would often undercut peace efforts undertaken by civilian administrations.[46] Although the CSSF's skepticism toward peace negotiations was at times based on legitimate objections (the army believed that the guerrillas were not negotiating in good faith and simply using talks to strengthen their position), it also arose from self-serving interests such as protecting military budgets, salaries, and benefits (notably pensions).[47] Military autonomy also weakened civilian oversight and contributed to a series of negative phenomena, ranging from corruption and massive human rights abuses to complicity in creating shadowy paramilitary organizations.

The country's security crisis worsened with the meteoric rise of the Medellín Cartel. The assassination of Defense Minister Rodrigo Lara Bonilla by cartel operatives in 1984 convinced the Betancur administration to allow the extradition of its leaders to the United States. It also resulted in the expansion of the range of military operations into antinarcotics, which would continue during the presidency of Virgilio Barco (1986–1990).[48] With a decimated national police force struggling to contain cartel violence, which included widespread terrorist campaigns, a desperate Barco enlisted the army and the Administrative Security Department (Departamento Administrativo de Seguridad, or DAS) to help confront the so-called extraditables (leaders of the powerful drug cartels).[49] However, stretched thin by the growing power of guerrillas, the Colombian Army was reluctant to become involved in narcotics operations because most high-ranking officers believed that criminal activities fell under the purview of the National Police and thought drug cartels did not pose a threat to national security and the social order.[50]

As violence raged across the country, Colombia approved a new constitution in 1991, the product of a diverse National Constituent Assembly that brought together various sectors of society—political parties, civil society, and several insurgent groups.[51] The new constitution created several institutions to buttress democratic procedures and the rule of law.[52] It did not, however, substantively alter the constitutional provisions concerning military autonomy.[53] A thorny issue arose over whether to allow military tribunals (as opposed to civilian bodies) to continue to investigate military abuses, as such a system perpetuated conditions of impunity.⁵⁴ Nonetheless, the administration of César Gaviria (1990–1994), which was in power during the negotiations over and implementation of the new constitution, did create several mechanisms to increase civilian oversight over military affairs and civilian involvement in designing and executing security policies.⁵⁵ Rafael Pardo, who was appointed by Gaviria as defense minister, became the first civilian in the post since 1953, and another civilian became the head of DAS. In a significant move, Defense Minister Pardo streamlined and strengthened reporting mechanisms, increased the number of professional officers and soldiers, and created new units such as the Special Army Counterinsurgent Mobile and Intelligence Brigades. These measures notwithstanding, the military retained significant autonomy.⁵⁶

DSP AND PEACE AGREEMENT (1998–2016)

In the mid-1990s, the CSSF, in particular the army, suffered a string of humiliating defeats at the hands of the FARC. Then came 1998, which was a particularly adverse year: in March, the FARC attacked Battalion 52 in El Billar, Caquetá, killing sixty-four soldiers and taking forty-three prisoners.⁵⁷ Three months later, the insurgent group took over Colombia's main antinarcotics army base in José de Miraflores, Guaviare, killing sixty-four people and taking 129 members of the armed forces and police hostage.⁵⁸ In a watershed moment in the war, the FARC seized Mitú, the capital of the department of Vaupés, even as it was finalizing details for participating in a new round of peace negotiations with the newly inaugurated Conservative administration of Andrés Pastrana (1998–2002). The town, which is surrounded by thick jungle and has no road access, could only be reached with the cooperation of Brazilian authorities, who granted the Colombian Army permission to use a nearby military base from which they organized an assault. The army retook the city after three days of intense fighting.⁵⁹

It was against this backdrop—and despite the objections of the Colombian military—that the Pastrana administration granted the FARC a demilitarized zone in Caquetá as a goodwill gesture to start peace negotiations. As detailed in chapter 3, the FARC used the area to aggressively recruit and train new operatives, stage attacks, consolidate its finances, and—critically—develop military and terrorism expertise.⁶⁰ This expertise allowed the FARC to bring the fight to major metropolitan areas including Medellín, Cali, and the capital Bogotá. All the while, the ELN was stepping up its attacks against infrastructure and expanding its influence in the country's northeast.

Fearing that the FARC had attained strategic parity with the Colombian Army,[61] the Pastrana administration began to work on a plan to modernize and strengthen the CSSF. The military overhaul, entrusted to Defense Minister Rodrigo Lloreda and Generals Fernando Tapias and Enrique Mora, introduced important changes in matters such as training, recruitment, equipment, and operation.[62] Measures included increasing the number of troops; revising deployment processes to avoid overstretching forces; improving training with a view to advancing professionalization; inverting the ratio of combatants to logistical support personnel, which at the time was heavily tilted toward the latter; investing in modernizing military and telecommunications equipment, especially for the Colombian Air Force; increasing military intelligence capacities to disrupt guerrilla operations; and strengthening coordination between the different branches of the military, the DAS, and the national police.[63]

Pastrana's reforms were buttressed by military aid furnished by Plan Colombia, a multipronged initiative promoted by the U.S. government to help the Colombian state confront the threat posed by nonstate armed groups like guerrillas and drug cartels. Under the initiative, Colombia received approximately $7.5 billion in military assistance, including helicopters, air troop transports, and telecommunications and surveillance equipment. This infusion made Colombia into the largest recipient of U.S. military aid outside the Middle East and Afghanistan. U.S. military assistance furnished through Plan Colombia was enormously critical to boosting the capacity of the CSSF, in particular that of the military, to wage war against guerrillas.[64]

Although the decision to overhaul Colombia's security apparatus was taken under President Pastrana, as discussed in chapter 3, it was President Álvaro Uribe (2002–2010) who implemented a comprehensive security policy characterized by a massive military buildup. Once in power, Uribe decided to implement the so-called Democratic Security Policy, an aggressive and controversial plan that sought to address problematic conditions by boosting the state's coercive and infrastructural capacity.[65] DSP presided over the militarization of vast zones of Colombian territory and, as will be shown, coincided with a drastic worsening of the CSSF's human rights record, which came to include systematic use torture, enforced disappearance, massacres, and summary executions.[66] The administration justified the policy by claiming that militarization was the only response to the nation's insecurity, and that the military buildup was crucial not only to buttressing the rule of law but also to promoting economic and social development. Uribe effectively deployed a hawkish rhetoric that portrayed the FARC as a narcoterrorist organization, underscoring the idea that the state could only meet the dangers posed by the group through successful military actions.[67]

A major element of DSP was the so-called Plan Patriota (2002–2007), a comprehensive military program launched in 2002. Plan Patriota, which expanded on the changes introduced during the Pastrana years, increased the number of professional soldiers and police officers, and concentrated their deployment across strategically valuable areas; created anti-insurgent helicopter air battalions that gave Colombian security forces more mobility to strike guerrillas in remote areas; and ramped up intelligence by investing in cutting-edge surveillance technology that would help them intercept enemy communications. Plan Patriota attacked guerrillas head on, disrupting their sources of financing (drug trafficking, extortion, and kidnapping), dislodging them from strategic territory, interrupting their logistical operations, and targeting their high-ranking commanders.[68]

Plan Patriota achieved significant results. It derailed the FARC's plan to encircle Bogotá, relying on its fronts in Cundinamarca, Boyacá, and Meta. Following its successful disruption of guerrilla positions, the army pressed on, seeking to penetrate the FARC's strategic rearguard in southern Colombia in departments including Guaviare, Meta, Caquetá, and Putumayo. The army's seizure of the municipality of La Macarena, Meta, a FARC strategic hub, forced the guerilla group to withdraw further into the remote jungle areas and dented its operational capacity.[69] Plan Patriota would be followed by other strategic operations such as Plan Consolidación in 2007 and Plan Espada de Honor (Sword of Honor) in 2011. Doctrina de Acción Integral, a wide-ranging plan seeking to neutralize insurgent groups by integrating civilian-military, further consolidated military gains.[70]

Changes in the CSSF's strategy, coupled with the irruption of paramilitary groups, helped Colombian security forces regain strategic superiority over the FARC following the killing and capture of several important commanders and the massive desertion of lower-ranking fighters.[71] Weakened and without any viable alternatives, the FARC's leadership agreed to begin formal negotiations with the administration of President Juan Manuel Santos in 2012, reaching a final peace deal in 2016. As the next section relates, however, the state's military offensive coincided with an increase of terrorism attacks on the part of the CSSF, in particular, after the demobilization of the United Self-Defense Forces of Colombia (Autodefensas Unidas de Colombia) in 2005.

Guardians of Social Order

This historical account allows us to better understand the trajectory and development of the CSSF as an institution. This section complements that analysis by looking at how ideational preferences shaped the CSSF's self-image, identity, and how this in turn informed the development of distinct repertoires of terrorism. Over the years, the CSSF developed a distinctive Weltanschauung based on their self-perception as the ultimate guardians of Colombian social order. Such a perception, built on an ultramontane view of society, displayed a preference for traditional practices and values, which they vowed to preserve, for example, Catholicism and private property.[72]

To a significant degree, this trend is common in the political and social evolution of Latin American societies. Historically, the military (alongside the Church) has been one of if not the most influential societal institutions in almost every country in the region, carving out a special status for itself.[73] Throughout the region, various armies have acquired critical influence over the social, economic, and political life of their respective countries.[74] This dynamic can be traced to a mix of institutional and organizational determinants, as argued in the classic work by Guillermo O'Donnell on bureaucratic authoritarianism and Alfred Stepan's studies on military politics and corporativism.[75] To understand the army's role in Colombia and beyond, it is critical to note that military leaders were influenced by European geopolitical theories in vogue in the nineteenth century that found their way to Latin America. These theories incorporated Darwinian ideas of natural life into social thinking, advancing the view that states were organic entities struggling for survival. They underscored the strategic nature of natural resources and borders and, in sync with realist approaches to international relations, considered foreign relations a perpetual fight over preservation and preeminence in which states competed for limited resources and space.[76] This ideology was aligned with conservative political views, which explains why in Colombia (and Latin America), the military has historically been closely tied to conservative elites, even though most officers and rank-and-file soldiers are from rural, middle-class, or humble origins.[77]

Even though the emergence of fervent anticommunism within the military can be traced to the 1920s, the CSSF began to fashion themselves as traditionalist protectors of a desirable social order in the post–World War II era.[78] Colombian security forces, in particular the army, embraced what Francisco Gutiérrez-Sanín and Elisabeth Wood describe as a strong ideological program in line with the doctrine of national security.[79] First articulated in the 1940s, DNS is best described as a collection of views on domestic security and national interest developed by the Latin American military.[80] These interrelated sets of principles and ideas on how to preserve the national well-being integrated general notions of the state, development, counterinsurgency warfare, and, most critical, security into a single doctrine. DNS viewed the military as an elite institution within society that, apart from its security responsibilities, was more fundamentally the "depository of the interests and values of the nation."[81] The military thus claimed the right to do whatever necessary to protect the nation from external and internal foes, particularly if civilian governments were deemed incapable of fulfilling their duty.[82]

An erroneous yet widely held assumption is that the United States, eager to contain the Soviet Union, created and then propagated DNS in Latin America. Such a view rather uncritically links DNS to U.S. counterinsurgency programs (e.g., training by the U.S. National War College), and more broadly, the Kennedy administration's Alliance for Progress.[83] In reality, DNS's roots lie in classical European geopolitical thinking, which spread among Latin America militaries due to their close connections with European military leadership. The rise of the Soviet Union as a global power—and the spread of its ideology and worldview—merely cemented the idea among conservative sectors in Latin America that communism posed grave risks. In these sectors and against the backdrop of ideological rivalry, Soviet communism came to be portrayed as a nihilistic, atheistic ideology that threatened widely held customs and traditional institutions.[84] Subtler accounts, by contrast, view DNS as a Latin American adaptation of the anticommunist military doctrine developed in Washington and Paris, tracing its origins to military theories cultivated in Brazil's War College (Escola Superior de Guerra) and Peru's Center for Higher Military Studies (Centro de Altos Estudios Militares).[85] U.S. geostrategic thinking undoubtedly contributed to the articulation and later development of DNS, but other sources also played an important role, including the influential antirevolutionary warfare doctrine developed by the French military (*guerre revolutionnaire* theory) during colonial wars in Algeria and Indochina.[86]

One aspect of DNS critical to analysis of the CSSF's behavior is the internal enemy thesis, the idea that external aggression often materialized domestically through the actions of revolutionary groups supported by communist regimes. It is no coincidence that DNS gained considerable ground in the early 1960s after the new Cuban regime presided over by Fidel Castro began to export its revolutionary model throughout Latin America. Predicated on DNS, the CSSF and many Conservative-minded sectors openly called for repressive measures, including curtailing basic freedoms and rights, expanding intelligence services, and developing brutal counterinsurgency operations to supposedly protect society from the dangers posed by subversion.[87]

Rather than being a monolithic doctrine, however, DNS was heterogeneous and surfaced in different forms across Latin America. David Pion-Berlin makes an important distinction between soft-line and hard-line versions of DNS, which offered contrasting views of the state, the military's role, and strategies for containing insurrection. Hard-liners espoused a more extreme version of DNS based on an organic conception of the state that considered those opposing it (e.g., guerrillas, leftist activists, and intellectuals) as malign, akin to cancerous cells that needed to be excised to preserve the life of the entire organism. They therefore viewed extreme forms of repression as totally justified. For their part, soft-line proponents also regarded the state as an organism, yet they articulated a more measured view of societal discord based on Catholic social doctrine. Although they would not shy away from enacting repressive measures, they thought it was critical to address the root sources of inequality and grievances afflicting societies and were therefore firm proponents of development programs.[88]

Within Colombia's military establishment, various factions espoused harder or softer versions of DNS. Most authors distinguish between a militaristic wing adhering fervently to DNS and a more developmentalist one associated with officers who served in the Korean War.[89] As noted earlier, the Turbay Ayala administration, with the support of high-ranking officers, promoted the most extreme version, as encapsulated by General Alberto Rueda's proclamation that "domestic security represents the principal concern of the Colombian military against the backdrop of a climate of subversion dominated by Marxist ideologies at odds with western civilization."[90]

Overall, however, DNS's softer version would end up having a greater influence, which explains why Colombia has relatively lower levels of state repression than Brazil and Southern Cone countries despite being in a state of internal conflict.[91] This outcome is generally attributed to the existence of a democratic regime that, though unable to fully subordinate the military, was at least able to erect some institutional guardrails. Colombia's milder version of DNS was characterized by an integrated strategy based on combining counterinsurgency measures and development initiatives, as illustrated by Plan Lazo and later security programs such as Plans Andes, Guerra Perla, Desarrollo, and Consolidación.[92]

Although the idea of the domestic enemy is associated with Cold War dynamics, it has survived that period and shaped the thinking of security forces even as they have had to adapt to new threats. In the 1980s—and due to the rise of the Medellín Cartel—the idea that narcotrafficking posed a threat to national security emerged among members of the military establishment. Later, the attacks of September 11, 2001, would further reorient the national security apparatus and spur security forces to commit excesses, including acts of terrorism,[93] a phenomenon discussed later in the chapter.

U.S. INFLUENCE

Given the close military cooperation between Colombia and the United States, it is important to consider how the United States influenced the CSSF's worldview. The robust partnership between Washington and Bogotá dates to the creation of the Hemispheric Security Regime in the 1940s. Following the United States' victory in World War II, Colombia and several other Latin American countries joined this newly created, U.S.-centric regional regime, which became solidified through several treaties[94] and the 1948 creation of the Organization of American States.[95] Purportedly intended to promote hemispheric peace and security, the regime institutionalized U.S. dominance in the Western Hemisphere and therefore would be highly influenced by Cold War containment dynamics, particularly forestalling Soviet encroachment in the region.[96]

The United States' involvement in Colombia had historically been relatively benevolent, with the exception of Washington's role in supporting Panama's independence from Colombia in 1903.[97] Despite some reservations, therefore, Colombia joined the security regime and eventually became one of its most active supporters, paving the way for close military cooperation between it and the United States.[98] As alluded to earlier, the administration of Laureano Gómez, seeking closer ties with Washington, agreed to dispatch a battalion to Korea to fight alongside U.S. forces.[99] A year later, the United States and Colombia signed a military assistance agreement.[100] The training received from American advisors and, more critically, the combat experience acquired from fighting alongside Allied troops proved to be transformative for the Colombian officers and troops who served in the Korean War.[101] According to General Ruiz Novoa, the experience was invaluable to strengthening and modernizing the Colombian Army.[102]

The United States sent its first military training delegation to Colombia in 1961, and soon thereafter Colombian officers visited the United States to receive instruction.[103] Military cooperation during the Cold War went beyond training exercises, however, because military assistance programs sponsored by the United States incorporated a broad range of issues from sanitation to new counterinsurgency techniques and psychological warfare.[104] Most consequentially for understanding the evolution of the CSSF's worldview, U.S. military instruction reinforced the intellectual justifications for holding anticommunist views and introduced Colombian officials to questionable counterinsurgency methods (torture, scorched earth tactics, psychological warfare) that were later incorporated into their operations.[105]

As the Cold War wound down, the highly ideologized components of U.S. military assistance programs to Colombia (and elsewhere) were phased out. A reconfigured, more modern security agenda arose that incorporated nontraditional sources of insecurity such as drug trafficking.[106] However, Washington never fully abandoned its view of leftist-inspired guerillas, and its strategic thinking synthesized old and new threats into a modern security agenda that would simultaneously address insurgency and narcotrafficking, as illustrated by the vision behind Plan Colombia.[107] That a Cold War imaginary still influenced U.S. assistance was also apparent in the invocation of the vague category *narcoterrorism* by American diplomats and members of the Pentagon involved in Colombian operations, particularly following the September 11 attacks.[108] In sum, a certain Cold War spirit lingered, Washington continuing to provide substantial military aid and training to the CSSF while disregarding egregious human rights abuses, notwithstanding some efforts to enhance accountability for human rights violations.[109]

Leadership, Socialization, and Selection of Repertoires of Terrorism

In the highly hierarchical structure of the Colombian Armed Forces, the leadership played a critical role in selecting and developing repertoires of violence and terrorism. Chief commanding officers of the distinct branches of the armed forces (Army, Navy, Air Force) and police presided over complex operations in their purported mission of maintaining general conditions of peace and stability in the country.[110] In this respect, terrorism was one element of a multipronged strategy to neutralize domestic threats conceived by military leadership as a complement to conventional, legal efforts to defeat guerrillas through military means.[111]

Of particular importance in the analysis of terrorist repertoires are counterinsurgency strategies, which provided the intellectual and technical justification for the tactics used. CSSF leadership adapted specific repertoires of violence to ideational views and preferences that reflected and reaffirmed the institution's singular identity and goals. Many commanders voiced their profound concern over the state of Colombian society and the threat posed by guerrillas and leftist organizations more generally. Harold Bedoya, former chief commander of the Colombian Armed Forces, once said, "Terrorist subversion has infiltrated the state in some of the most sensitive areas: justice, education, many labor unions, Congress ... all this has rendered the country ungovernable."[112] Military commanders selected tactics that best reflected the CSSF's views and proceeded to socialize these practices through military and political training. According to investigations, most of the CSSF's illicit use of force—including many terrorist attacks—cataloged in this work were conducted by special units within antiguerrilla battalions and mobile brigades of the Colombian Army, intelligence units, the antiterrorist units of the National Police, and elite anti-kidnapping units (Personal Liberty Unified Action Groups, Grupos de Acción Unificada por la Libertad Personal, or GAULA).[113] Terrorist attacks including disappearances, massacres, and summary executions were carried out by these groups under the cover of broader military and security operations.[114] Because these were largely illegal policies, however, no record was left of their development, planning, and execution. Yet, as is common with such programs, we can find evidence when looking at military training activities, domestic and international judicial cases (such as before the Inter-American Human Rights System), and documents such as the Truth Commission's final report.

Transnational factors also played an important role in shaping the views of military leaders, particularly the diffusion of ideas and military know-how through formal military assistance aid programs from the United States. In this regard, the Colombia Battalion played a crucial role. On returning from the Korean War, this unit helped create a special school in counterinsurgency known as Lanzeros, which trained Colombian operatives in irregular warfare.[115] Such programs were later buttressed during the administration of President Lleras Camargo, who pleaded with the Eisenhower administration for more military aid following uprisings in Cuba and throughout the region in the early 1960s.[116] In his detailed study on U.S. counterinsurgency assistance to Colombia, Dennis Rempe details how in the early 1960s, U.S. military advisors began training Colombian officers in a host of counterinsurgency special operations at the Special Warfare School at Fort Bragg (now Fort Liberty), North Carolina, and later in Panama and Fort Benning (now Fort Moore), Georgia; these programs would come to be known as the School of the Americas. As indicated, Colombian officers learned about psychological warfare, interrogation, and intelligence gathering.[117] Forrest Hylton finds similar evidence in a report by a high-ranking U.S. officer who was dispatched to Bogotá[118] to organize teams of irregulars (*localizadores*) to infiltrate and neutralize suspect revolutionary civilian structures. These groups, according to the report, engaged in "counter-agent and counter-propaganda functions, sabotage, and/or terrorist activities against known communist proponents."[119]

These activities would continue in the following decades, as amply reported by human rights watchdogs both local and foreign. Human Rights Watch, for example, details how U.S. Army Special Forces personnel continued training Colombian Army personnel in joint counterinsurgency tactics through the mid-1990s, with many of the Colombian officers eventually implicated in unlawful counterinsurgency operations.[120] Locally, work by the Colombian Commission of Jurists, De Justicia, CINEP, and other Colombian NGOs also unearthed and denounced still-operating secret training schools and clandestine links with paramilitary groups. The National Center for Historical Memory reports that more than four thousand Colombian officers received some form of special military training in counterinsurgency special operations from the United States, either in Colombia or abroad.[121] This training is an important element of the CSSF's terrorism repertoire, one clearly marked by a pro–status quo logic predicated on a "total war" counterinsurgency strategy.

CSSF tactics are best described as a combination of pro-regime and territorial forms of terrorism seeking to obliterate guerrillas' logistical and support systems and inhibit civil society's capacity to challenge the state's power. Summary executions are the most common form of state terrorism. This practice has lasted throughout the war, with peaks in the 1993–1994 and 2003–2008 periods. Attacks correlate with theater-of-war developments such as the military offensive that ensued after peace talks collapsed in 2002 and, later, the implementation of the DSP. During this period, units within the CSSF engaged in unlawful killings of unarmed civilians (such as the false positives scandal) described at the beginning of the chapter.[122]

The CSSF made widespread use of summary executions (see figure 6.3). Of all armed parties, the CSSF proportionately relied most on this form of terrorism (see figure 6.4). The 1,492 targeted assassinations attributed to the CSSF account for 75 percent of its total terrorist attacks, slightly higher than with paramilitary groups (70 percent) and significantly more than guerrillas, 50 percent and 39 percent for the FARC and the ELN, respectively. As suggested in previous chapters, this practice was consistently used because it was seen as a very efficient and cost-effective way to target guerrillas' support system.

Looking at the CSSF's use of summary executions reveals an inverse correlation with paramilitary usage: periods of high paramilitary attacks coincide with low levels of state terrorism (1997–2003) and vice versa (2005–2008). Data also provide evidence of coordination among the state and

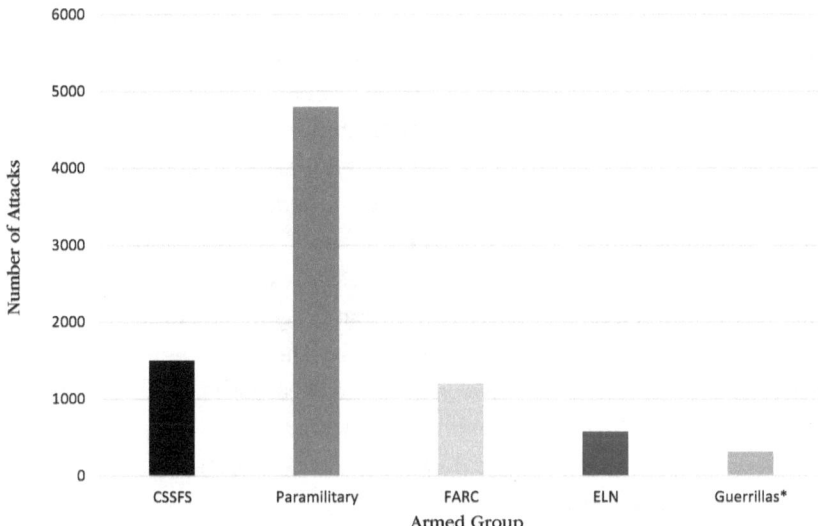

FIGURE 6.3 CSSF summary executions, 1988–2012.

Source: Author's tabulation based on CINEP data.
* Sum of guerrillas other than the FARC and ELN.

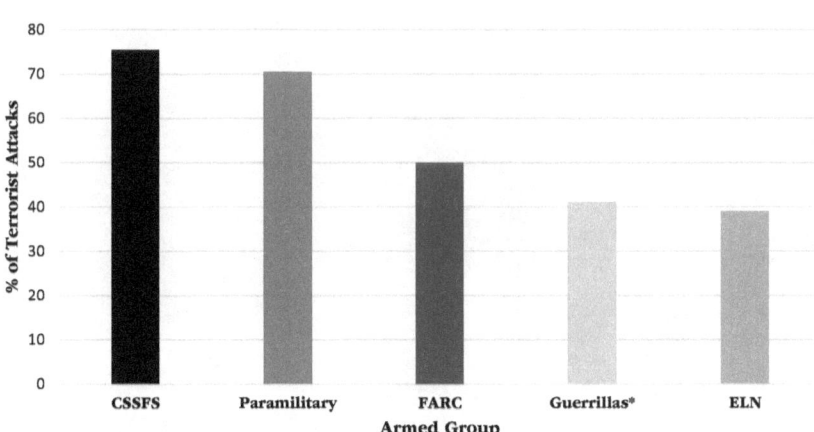

FIGURE 6.4 CSSF summary executions within repertoire of terrorism, 1988–2012.

Source: Author's tabulation based on CINEP data.
* Sum of guerrillas other than the FARC and ELN.

paramilitary groups: several years (1993, 1994, 2004) saw military offensives with high levels of targeted assassinations committed by both actors (a similar pattern can be observed in the use of massacres). The CSSF followed a strategic logic akin to that of paramilitaries in that the tactic was deployed to obliterate guerrillas' support system and dislodge them from strategic areas. Once this goal was accomplished, attacks were then perpetrated to maintain control over these areas.[123]

The CSSF also conducted numerous massacres, 232 in total. Although they did so throughout the period, these attacks again tend to correlate with specific developments in the theater of war. The most were perpetrated between 1993 and 1994 and between 2004 and 2008, both periods of military expansion when the CSSF were advancing toward areas controlled by the FARC and the ELN. A chronological examination of the data reveals that CSSF massacres generally preceded guerrilla terrorist attacks. From a comparative perspective (see figure 6.5), the use of massacres by the CSSF is high. The CSSF perpetrated slightly more massacres than the FARC and almost four times more than the ELN, but only one-fifth that of paramilitary groups.

A significant number of paramilitary massacres had the active or tacit support of the CSSF, in particular the army, as discussed in chapter 5. For

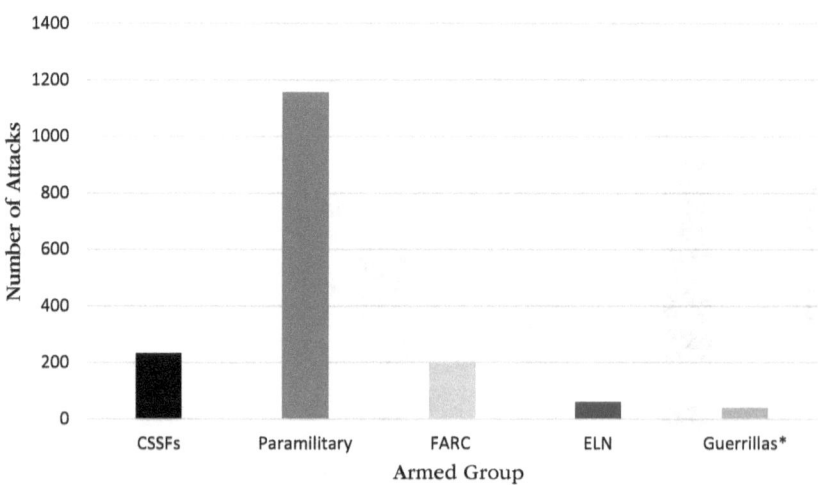

FIGURE 6.5 CSSF massacres, 1988–2012.

Source: Author's tabulation based on CINEP data.
* Sum of guerrillas other than the FARC and ELN.

example, former General Rito Alejo del Rio, commander in chief of Brigade XVII in Urabá, was tried, found guilty, and condemned to twenty-five years in prison for homicide by a Colombian tribunal for ordering such attacks.[124] Proportionally, state massacres account for 11.7 percent of the total number of terrorist attacks perpetrated by the CSSF in the sample, relative to 16.9 by paramilitary groups, 8 percent by the FARC, and 4 percent by the ELN (see figure 6.6).

Even though the CSSF and paramilitary groups used this tactic in similar ways, the CSSF incorporated overkill only rarely. Under a much higher level of scrutiny from civilian authorities, the CSSF presumably sought to avoid the unnecessary exposure that gruesome acts of cruelty and sacralized forms of terrorism normally brought.

To further assess the dynamics of territorial forms of terrorism, I plotted the CSSF's reliance on massacres and targeted assassinations. I assume with the literature that the group perpetrated these attacks while disputing or seeking to control territory. I reviewed all municipalities in which the CSSF perpetrated five or more summary executions or massacres in any given year. I assume that when only the CSSF used these tactics in a given municipality, that area was under their control; conversely, I assume that places where attacks were perpetrated by both the CSSF and other armed parties

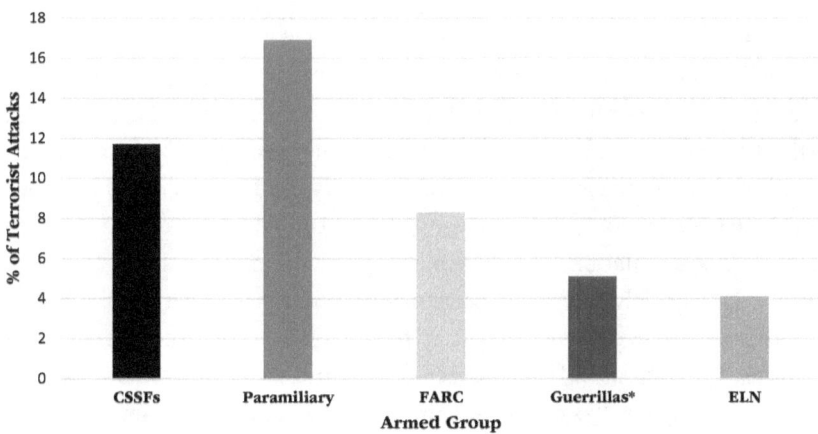

FIGURE 6.6 CSSF massacres within repertoire of terrorism, 1988–2012.

Source: Author's tabulation based on CINEP data.
* Sum of guerrillas other than the FARC and ELN.

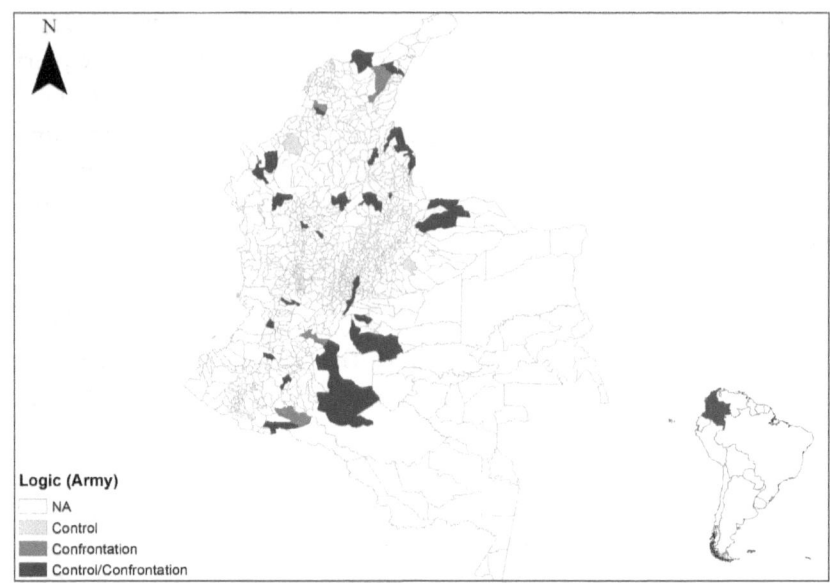

FIGURE 6.7 Dynamics of CSSF territorial terrorism.

Source: Author's tabulation based on CINEP data.

during the same year were contested areas. In other words, simultaneous terrorist attacks are used as a proxy for territorial contestation, whereas unilateral actions are seen as a territorial control mechanism.

As figure 6.7 shows, of the forty-four municipalities experiencing five or more CSSF terrorist incidents of a territorial nature between 1988 and 2012, a dual pattern of confrontation and control emerges in thirty-three (75 percent) of them. In these cases, the CSSF initially used massacres to push out guerrillas but, after achieving their goal, continued to rely on the tactic to control the population. Of the remaining eleven municipalities, the CSSF used attacks solely to dispute territory in four cases (9 percent),[125] but in another seven (16 percent), they used terror unilaterally to control municipalities. The data show that massacres and summary executions were usually to drive guerrillas out of certain territories and, to a lesser extent, to control the population in so-called red zones, that is, contested areas.

The CSSF also relied extensively on enforced disappearances, although as discussed in previous chapters, existing data are not reliable. The Colombian Truth Commission, however, provides partial data that allows us to infer patterns. It attributes 8 percent of the cases to the CSSF, relative to 52 percent to paramilitaries and 24 percent to the FARC. The report indicates that state security forces used this strategy throughout the conflict, particularly between 1970 and 1982, when disappearance was incorporated into the repertoires of violence during so-called states of exception, though the authors note that information about this period was impossible to find. The report attributes most disappearances after 1982 to paramilitary groups, which, as in the case of massacres, had the tacit support of security forces. Indeed, the report attributes 9 percent of the cases to multiple actors, presumably agents of the state and paramilitary groups.[126]

The CSSF used abductions more rarely, carrying out 243 and accounting for 12.2 percent of its terror attacks.[127] Abductions, for the most part, were carried out by elite GAULA units within specific army battalions who would infiltrate guerrilla kidnapping cells and proceed to abduct their relatives and sequester them in safe houses. They would then torture them to get information about the whereabouts of people abducted by guerrillas or use them as bargaining chips to secure the liberation of hostages. This modus operandi was systematic between 1995 and 2004, and investigators identify GAULA as behind many of these disappearances.[128] From a comparative perspective, the CSSF account for 9 percent of the abductions in the sample. They carried out abductions sporadically during the sample's time frame, except for two periods, from 1991 to 1993 and from 2002 to 2008, when cases become much more prevalent. Abductions carried out by state agents were much less systematic but also qualitatively different from those carried out by guerrillas, which, as extensively discussed, had agitational and pecuniary motives. CSSF abductions were used sporadically and in a targeted way against selected individuals who state agents wanted to intimidate or extract information from. They were also discreetly conducted, given that state agents deliberately sought to minimize publicity, and were never for extortive, financial purposes.

Finally, like their paramilitary allies, the CSSF almost completely refrained from explosive attacks against civilian targets, a common guerrilla tactic that, as explained in earlier chapters, has overt agitational connotations. Bombing attacks account for only 0.5 percent of terrorist acts perpetrated by the CSSF during this twenty-five-year period and 5 percent of the explosive attacks in the sample.

Geographic Dimensions of State Terrorism

In closing, I offer a brief geographical analysis of state terrorist patterns. Although the CSSF used this tactic across Colombia, data show that the bulk of their terrorist activity was concentrated in selected departments including the south (Huila, Valle), the eastern region bordering Venezuela (Norte de Santander and Santander), the northwest (Antioquia and Bolívar), and the eastern lowlands (Meta). State terrorist attacks disproportionately affected municipalities with strategic value in which there were open confrontations with guerrillas (see appendix 1).

Because military forces are deployed in specific areas, a geographic analysis reveals crucial information about which units within the Colombian Army were most likely to use terrorist tactics. These include the Seventh Division covering the Department of Antioquia, especially Brigades 4 and 14 operating in Medellín, central, and eastern Antioquia; the Fourth Division, Department of Meta, in particular Brigade 7 operating in western and central Meta, including Villavicencio; the Second Division, the Department of Norte de Santander, especially Brigade 5, covering Cúcuta and the eastern part of the department bordering Venezuela; the Second Division, Department of Santander, with Brigades 10 and 13 operating in central, southern Santander, and in and around Bucaramanga; the Third Division, Department of Valle, with Brigades 3 and 19 covering Cali and the southern part of the department, including Popayán; and finally the Fifth Division, the Department of Huila, with Brigade 9. This finding supports the thesis that state terrorism was not used uniformly by the CSSF. Many areas characterized by significant military disputes with guerrillas do not show the same frequency of state terrorism, given that some CSSF units were much more willing to use this tactic than others.

Another striking finding concerns the geographical overlap between state and paramilitary terrorist attacks: 60 percent of the municipalities with the highest incidence of state terrorism also saw high levels of paramilitary terrorism. All were municipalities with strategic value that guerrillas were eager to control, including coca-producing areas, corridors linking bordering departments, economic hubs, or areas with access to important highways and fluvial connecting routes such as rivers or coasts (see appendix). Regarding the distribution of attacks at the municipal level, data show that urban communities bore the brunt of state terror, including large metropolitan areas where guerillas had built an important network of sympathizers and informers (e.g., Bogotá, Medellín, Cali, Barrancabermeja, Cúcuta, Popayán, Bucaramanga, and Valledupar). Rural areas with strategic value controlled by guerrillas were also epicenters of CSSF terrorism.

Conclusions

The chapter provides an extensive analysis of the use of terrorism tactics on the part of the CSSF. It illustrates how a long, complex institutional process marked by problematic state-building and repeated cycles of internal violence deeply influenced the trajectory and identity of the CSSF. This process led the Colombian Armed Forces to perceive themselves as the ultimate defenders of the social order and the national spirit. The advent of the Cold War, and in particular the development of DNS—a macro theory of state and society depicting complex societal problems and potential solutions from a strictly military viewpoint—reinforced intolerant views and justified the use of repressive ways to neutralize sectors demanding social change, particularly those that take up arms. Intransigent views within the CSSF were buttressed by U.S. foreign cooperation security schemes, in particular training in counterintelligence and counterinsurgency tactics strongly influenced by Cold War dynamics. These views permeated the mindset of CSSF leadership, which in the name of a greater good—the preservation of the existing order—introduced counterinsurgency policies that employed, and justified, extreme measures including terrorism.

Regarding repertoires of terrorism, the CSSF's strategic blueprint is markedly different from that of guerrilla and paramilitary groups. The CSSF relied on pro-regime forms of terrorism, in particular massacres and to a lesser extent abductions. Their use of targeted assassinations, torture, and enforced disappearances was extensive as well, though the CSSF generally avoided publicity claiming responsibility and carried out attacks discreetly. State forces did not use overkill and avoided bombing attacks altogether. At the same time, their use of terrorism was uneven, some branches or units displaying a higher propensity to rely on terrorism than others.

7

Terrorism in Criminal Wars

In November 2016, the administration of President Juan Manuel Santos and the Revolutionary Armed Forces of Colombia (FARC) signed a peace accord that purportedly put an end to decades of deadly conflict. Following a lengthy and tortuous process that included a referendum to approve the agreement, the accord was finally reached to the satisfaction of both parties. In exchange for promises over rural land reform, special political representation, the creation of transition cantonments, and the establishment of a special transitional justice tribunal—the Jurisdicción Especial para la Paz—the FARC agreed to cease fighting and become a political party. Subsequently, as many as seven thousand combatants handed over their weapons in a process verified by the United Nations and the Organization of American States.[1]

Although the accord created enormous expectations that the country would achieve lasting peace, violence has raged on. Early signs seemed auspicious: in 2016, the country's homicide rate dropped by twelve thousand annually (to 24.4 per 100,000 inhabitants), the lowest rate since 1974.[2] Despite some zigzagging, it remained relatively stable.[3] However, a new round of violence broke after confrontations arose between nonstate armed parties, including regionally based paramilitary successor groups;[4] the National Liberation Army (Ejército de Liberación Nacional, or ELN), which, according to most accounts, has become the most powerful nonstate armed party in Colombia;[5] and renegade members of the FARC, including fighters who, disillusioned with the peace process, returned to fighting.[6] Recent reports estimate that FARC dissident groups have between three and a half thousand and five thousand active combatants.[7] These groups have been violently clashing over strategic areas for the transshipment and production of drugs and over sites rich in natural resources (mining, timber) previously controlled by the FARC. Meanwhile, landholding elites, many with ties to paramilitary groups, have contributed to the violence in their attempts to block land distribution reforms.[8]

This rather bleak security context shows that Colombia is entering a new phase of the conflict, one Francisco Gutiérrez-Sanín describes as the third cycle of violence.[9] In the view of most experts, Colombia is transitioning from a conventional civil war to a conflict in which the warring armed parties are motivated strictly by economic gain and deeply involved in a vast array of illicit activities.[10] The latest phase of the Colombian conflict resembles conditions elsewhere in Latin America (Mexico, El Salvador, Honduras, Ecuador, Brazil) and beyond (Nigeria, Libya), where the boundaries between war and criminality are fluid and hard to discern. Such conditions amount to what the specialized literature describes as criminal wars.

As chapter 5 underlined, criminality was certainly present in the previous phases of the Colombian war, but its weight and influence seem to have grown significantly. Several factors explain this change. First, as discussed in chapter 5, following the demobilization of the United Self-Defense Forces of Colombia, or AUC, in 2005, the political dimension of paramilitarism faded, giving rise to a third paramilitary generation driven predominantly by a criminal agenda.[11] Second, even the more ideologically minded guerrillas still fighting have also drifted into criminality and abandoned almost any pretense that theirs is a revolutionary struggle seeking to improve the conditions of ordinary Colombians, notwithstanding some rhetorical vestiges. In the case of the FARC, most of the former cadre and leadership abandoned the fighting, were arrested, or killed. Remaining members, in particular combatants, are for the most part recent recruits who have not gone through the traditional training process described in chapter 3. Luciano Marín Arango (aka Iván Márquez), a former member of the FARC secretariat who demobilized but returned to lead a successor group known as Segunda Marquetalia, has attempted to reanimate the group's insurgent ideology and enhance operational coordination, though without great success.[12]

The ELN has retained a higher degree of unity and purportedly clings to its original ideological motivations but also become involved in mounting criminal endeavors. Over the years, its modus operandi has evolved and its structure has splintered into increasingly atomized units. These units are decoupled from the group's leadership, operate at the regional level, and focus on controlling illicit activities in those areas. The ELN, which as discussed in chapter 4 historically rejected illegal activities it considered decadent and contrary to its revolutionary principles—in particular drug trafficking—has relaxed its standards and embraced a plethora of illegal activities from drug trafficking and gasoline smuggling to illegal mining and extortion.[13] An even more extreme case is that of the EPL, a former Maoist group that, after demobilizing in 1993, splintered into various factions embracing criminality—especially its main dissident group, the Libardo Mora Toro Front, which relocated to the Catatumbo region.[14]

Third, state security forces have not consistently moved into areas vacated by the FARC, creating a major power vacuum that nonstate parties have stepped in to fill. To a significant degree, this dynamic is also related to shortcomings in the implementation of the peace accord.[15] Domestic and international actors, including facilitators and brokers of the peace deal, have expressed their frustration at the difficulties experienced throughout the implementation phase.[16] A recent report underscores that "the territorial vacuum left by the old insurgency, and the absence of many promised government reforms, has unleashed a criminal morass as new groups form, and old groups mutate, in a battle to control flourishing illicit economies."[17]

Despite changes in the composition and goals of armed groups, the post-conflict context has preserved some of the conditions characterizing the ex ante period, including massive human rights violations and the widespread use of terrorism. Attacks of a terrorist nature such as abductions, executions, bombing attacks, and massacres have continued. According to human rights organizations, between November 2016 and December 2020, 972 social leaders have been assassinated in Colombia.[18] Colombia's ombudsperson emphasizes that armed groups attack community leaders to paralyze communities and neutralize potential challenges to their power.[19]

This drift toward criminality and the concomitant evolution of the conflict has to some extent affected the identities of armed parties. This chapter assesses whether and how such transformations have influenced armed parties' terrorist repertoires. The examination reveals a fair degree of tactical continuity in the current phase of the war, and, moreover, that groups continue to display different repertoires of terrorism. Such differences, however, seem less pronounced than in previous phases. I argue that changes in parties' repertoires of terrorism derive from the relaxation of ideological views. Notwithstanding a degree of convergence in the use of this tactic, discernable differences remain among the repertoires of various groups, and these differences reveal organizational stickiness (i.e., parties are clinging to their core identities) and a fair degree of inertia.

The chapter is organized as follows. The first section briefly discusses the concept of criminal wars, comparing it with civil war. The chapter then examines the use of terrorism by nonstate armed groups in Colombia in the post–peace accord period and discusses changes and continuities in the use of this tactic. It then broadens the discussion by examining the use of terrorism in Mexico's criminal war, a shadow case that complements my analysis of conditions in Colombia and sharpens our understanding of existing terrorist dynamics. The conclusion offers some reflections.

Criminal Wars

Recent developments in Colombia exemplify a growing global trend in which high levels of violence, often surpassing the threshold of conventional wars (more than one thousand battle-related deaths per year) are traceable to criminal disputes or state capture (i.e., when criminals take over state functions and replace the state partially or totally).[20] In many of these conflicts, parties have systematically used terrorism as part of their repertoires of violence. Although not exclusive to Latin America, this trend is particularly conspicuous in this region, where armed conflicts stemming from a problematic socioeconomic mix (authoritarianism, high levels of discrimination, inequality, and endemic institutional fragility) have morphed into large-scale criminal violence.[21] Two excellent examples are Brazil, where powerful criminal syndicates such as Primeiro Comando da Capital and Comando Vermelho are fighting each other and security forces for control over illicit businesses in favelas, prisons, and at the borders,[22] and Venezuela, where a plethora of armed groups, including criminal organizations, pro-state militias (Colectivos), and Colombian armed parties violently clash.[23] Arguably, the most emblematic case is Mexico, where an explosion of violence is linked to criminal violence and a powerful repressive response on the part of the Mexican state and self-defense forces to protect communities from criminality.[24]

Against this backdrop, a fascinating debate has emerged over how to characterize these situations. Some authors reject the idea that the conflagrations amount to civil wars, notwithstanding their high levels of violence, because no political motivation behind the violence is discernable.[25] One important aspect of this debate concerns whether civil war or organized crime can both be understood as forms of state-making. To the extent that the ultimate objective of rebel groups is to topple and replace formal rulers, some authors view civil wars as competitive state-building processes.[26] Given this logic, the same could be said of criminal syndicates that have stepped in and assumed many state functions, including the provision and distribution of public goods (i.e., security, justice).[27] Although some see clear boundaries between the two, others advocate for a holistic view that considers criminal and rebel governance as intertwined.[28]

Two works have considered this intriguing phenomenon with notable conceptual clarity. Benjamin Lessing, who should be credited for coining the concept, affirms that these conflicts amount to criminal wars, or situations in which criminal syndicates use violence to inhibit state action.[29] Rather than seeking to topple or replace the state, criminal organizations simply wish to constrain state action and impede any interference in their activities. In the pursuit of these goals, Lessing observes, criminals have different options, including bribes and violence— "silver or lead" in Pablo Escobar's famous maxim. In this view, criminal groups typically seek territorial and population control only if it furthers their interests and goals.[30]

Guillermo Trejo and Sandra Ley, for their part, conceptualize criminal wars as "militarized conflicts over the control of illicit markets and subnational territories in which Organized Criminal Groups (OCGs) and their private militias fight criminal groups and/or the state."[31] Challenging the conventional wisdom, they postulate that criminal groups might use violence for political purposes if doing so helps them achieve their objectives. Their reasoning is simple: although seeking to control a territory and its population may not be essential or even desirable, criminal groups have discovered that embracing such governance can be good for business. This is exactly what has happened in Mexico, where OCGs are increasingly seeking effective control over territory, populations, and the government to increase their revenues.[32]

The criminal war contexts mentioned feature the regular use of terrorism on the part of armed groups. Beyond targeting the families of their rivals and enemies—a common practice—criminal syndicates have begun to use terrorism in similar ways to groups with more overtly political motivations. Therefore, as discussed in chapter 5, the boundaries between the criminal and the political are becoming more blurred, resulting in the cross-fertilization of tactics among armed parties. Several examples illustrate this point. The Brazilian Comando Vermelho and Primeiro Comando da Capital, as well as Salvadoran gangs, have deliberately attacked civilian targets by torching passenger-filled buses to pressure the government to cease military operations or to negotiate truces.[33] In Mexico, terrorist attacks by criminal groups have also become frequent in the last ten years.

Armed Groups' Repertoires of Terrorism in Colombia's Post-Conflict Context

The new post-conflict phase in Colombia displays the stubborn persistence of terrorism and human rights violations. A cursory analysis of terrorist patterns based on the Research Center for Investigation and Popular Education (CINEP) database across four selected indicators for the 2017 to 2019 period reveals several interesting findings. Data show that terrorism has continued, though with less intensity. Attacks during this period numbered 1,385: of these, 979 are unidentified and 406 could be attributed to a perpetrator; 2017 and 2018 show almost the same number of identified incidents, with attacks declining sharply in 2019 (see figure 7.1). The average yearly number of identified terrorist attacks (121) in the post–peace agreement period is more than four times lower than the average for the 1988 to 2012 period.

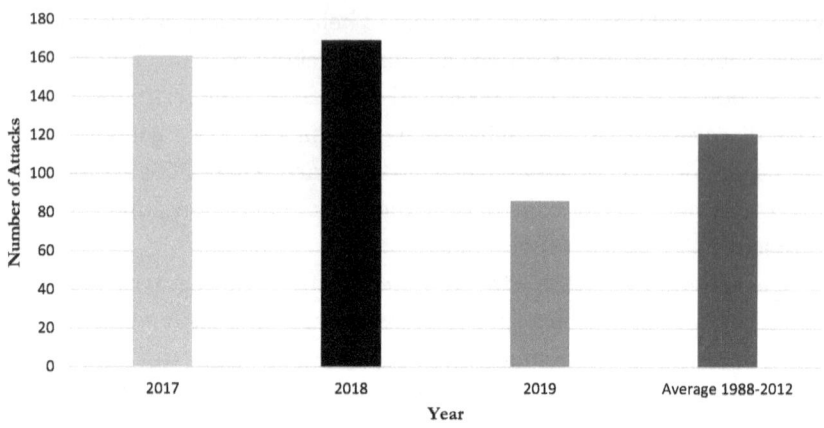

FIGURE 7.1 Terrorist attacks in Colombia, 2017–2019.

Source: Author's tabulation based on CINEP data.

As to the geographical distribution of terrorist attacks, they have become even more concentrated in certain departments and municipalities than during the civil war period. Terrorism seems to be heavily concentrated in four departments bitterly disputed by armed parties: the epicenter of violence has shifted toward the west to the departments of Nariño, Bolívar, Chocó, and Cauca, and toward the northeast in Norte de Santander. Antioquia, which endured the bulk of terrorist attacks during the previous phase, has seen a sharp decline in terrorism levels (see figure 7.2).

Breaking down terrorist attacks by actor also furnishes interesting results (see figure 7.3). Paramilitaries continue to carry out the highest number of terrorist attacks, followed in descending order by the state, the ELN, and FARC dissidents. Among paramilitary groups, the Auto-Defensas Gaitanistas perpetrated the most.

Analysis of armed parties' reliance on terrorism in this period offers some revealing trends. The differences are less marked than in the previous period, when paramilitary terrorism exceeded the number of attacks by all other groups combined. The proportion of terrorist attacks perpetrated by the state is also significantly higher (24 percent versus 15 percent). Among guerrilla groups, the ELN now accounts for a slightly higher number of attacks than the FARC, whereas in the previous phase, the ELN carried out two-thirds fewer.

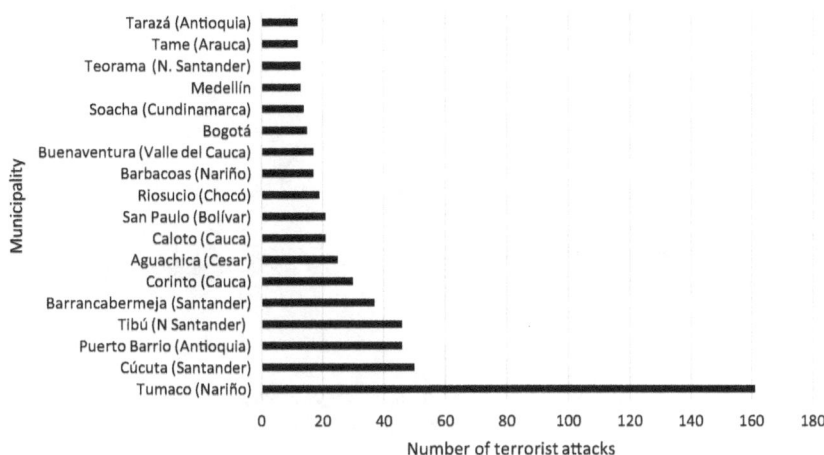

FIGURE 7.2 Terrorist attacks by municipality, 2017–2019.

Source: Author's tabulation based on CINEP data.

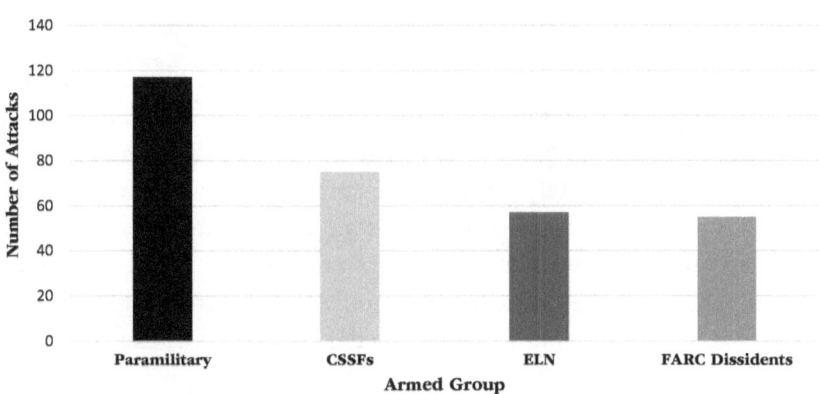

FIGURE 7.3 Terrorist attacks by group, 2017–2019.

Source: Author's tabulation based on CINEP data.

Concerning armed parties' repertoires of terrorism, a fair degree of continuity with the previous period is evident (see figure 7.4). Summary executions continue to be the most prevalent form of terrorism among all groups. Bombings, which guerilla groups perpetrated, especially the FARC, during the civil war period, continue, although only sporadically. The

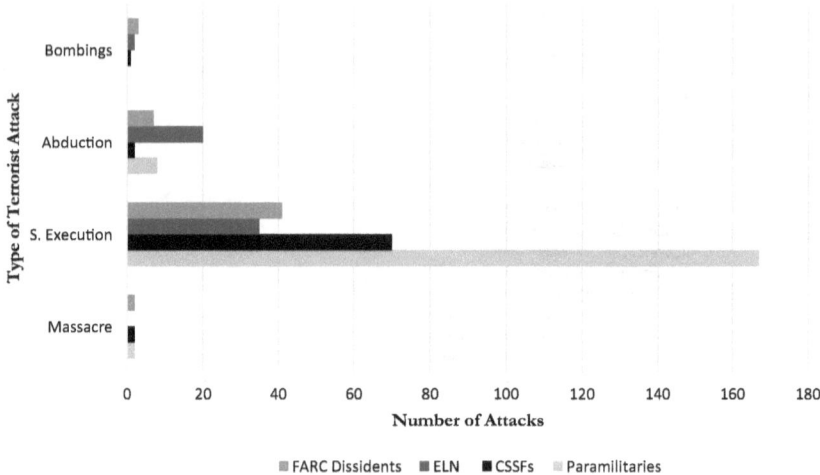

FIGURE 7.4 Colombian armed groups' repertoires of terrorism, 2017–2019.

Source: Author's tabulation based on CINEP data.

Colombian state security forces (CSSF) and paramilitary groups continue to avoid employing bombing attacks. Abductions are still a significant trademark of guerrilla groups, especially the ELN, but also among paramilitary groups. The only significant change from the previous period relates to massacres, a common type of attack during some phases that has declined substantially across armed groups. Findings should be treated carefully because the data account for only three years of fighting, but seem to indicate that groups have retained their terrorism blueprints only slightly altering their repertoires.

There are at least three potential explanations for the persistence of similar repertoires of terrorism among armed parties in this new phase of the war. First, it could be argued that armed groups retained their core identity. Consequently, observing important degrees of continuity in their use of terrorism would not be surprising. This thesis is compelling in the case of the CSSF, which have retained their essential, traditional identity. The explanation, however, seems weaker for the rest of the groups, which have essentially changed their leaderships and structures. As indicated, the FARC renegade groups and successor paramilitary organizations experienced significant upheaval, as did the ELN following the resignation of

Commander Gabino, its long-term leader, and the absorption of many former FARC fighters.[34]

A second explanation is that despite changes in their identity—for example, embracing criminality and abandoning ideological goals—armed parties preserved their repertoires of violence because of organizational inertia. New leaders were therefore reluctant or unable to modify core tactics deeply embedded in their groups. Relatedly, groups leaders might have clung to old tactics in attempts to distinguish themselves from rivals and enemies in the uncertain and fluid context of a criminal war.

Third, it could be argued that it will take time for the changes in the identity of Colombian armed groups to manifest in their repertoires of terrorism, especially given that this transitional period of the conflict is only the beginning of a new phase. If this is the case, then because the *esprit mafioso* thoroughly permeates all these groups, one would expect to observe greater degrees of convergence in their repertoires of terrorism in the future. Turning to the Mexican case offers interesting insights into these hypotheses.

A Brief Detour: Repertoires of Terrorism in Mexico's Criminal War

To deepen our understanding of repertoires of terrorism in criminal wars, I compare the latest phase of the Colombian conflict with arguably one of the most emblematic contemporary cases of the phenomenon: Mexico.[35] Over the last two decades, Mexico has witnessed a steady deterioration of security conditions linked to clashes between security forces, OCGs, and self-defense forces. Violence in the country has reached unprecedented levels, comparable only to the worst moments of the Mexican Revolution (1910–1917). Conservative estimates cite approximately 150,000 crime-related casualties since the so-called war on drugs began in 2006.[36] Also, an estimated 90,000 to 150,000 people have disappeared.[37] An additional 357,000 have been internally displaced, and many more have fled to the United States as refugees.[38] In explaining this crisis, most authors concur that Mexico's democratization process, which was marred by endemic corruption inherited from the country's authoritarian period, set the stage for violence to flourish.[39]

An examination of the Mexican case sheds light on the use of terrorism in criminal wars and validates my findings on Colombia. As John Gerring explains, incorporating a peripheral study allows researchers to shift their focus from an individual case to "to a sample of cases."[40] Although the Colombia-Mexico comparison is not exhaustive, it is helpful in determining possible consistencies in armed parties' repertoires of terrorism across the two cases.

Notwithstanding the historical, political, and geographic differences, the two cases have significant similarities. For one, the countries' contemporary conflicts are similarly configured, in that in both at least three sets of actors—the state, criminal groups, and self-defense forces—are active participants. In both cases, moreover, drug trafficking is a major driver of violence, although other illicit industries also play a role.[41] Furthermore, terrorism has been widely used by armed parties in both instances. The two cases have some differences as well, however. Unlike in Colombia, guerrillas are not a relevant party in Mexico. Perhaps the most important difference, though, is that Colombia has a centralized, unitary administrative state system, and Mexico boasts a federal system characterized by several superimposed governance layers (federal, state, municipal).

Any understanding of the violent conditions (including the use of terrorism) in Mexico requires a basic understanding of its complex security context. First, Mexico is an enormous country with vast regional variation in which localized forms of violence are the norm.[42] Second, and relatedly, the clandestine nature of OCGs and their constant evolution has created a fragmented, ever-changing criminal landscape. An investigation by the International Crisis Group found 198 active criminal groups in 2019.[43] Violence is heightened by the predatory nature of these groups and their tendency to encroach on their rivals' territory as they vie for control over so-called *plazas*: strategic locations for the transshipment of drugs into the United States, including corridors, ports, and border cities. Third, an unconstrained and unaccountable state apparatus has contributed to massive levels of violence. Mexican security forces are organized into a gargantuan, multilayered apparatus whose siloed segments rarely cooperate with one another. Endemic corruption, regional differences, and mutual distrust in a context characterized by the criminal infiltration of state security agencies—especially at the state level—further exacerbate this fragmentation.[44]

Last, Mexico has also seen a rapid expansion of self-defense groups (commonly known as *auto-defensas*) that have popped up in several states (Nuevo León, Coahuila, Tabasco, Guerrero, and Michoacán), clashing with criminal groups and at times seizing entire municipalities. These militia groups have often refused to obey orders to disarm and have even confronted state forces. Although purportedly created to combat criminal groups, many self-defense groups have, as in Colombia, turned predatory and committed serious excesses.[45]

Against this backdrop, daily violence is all too common across the country and includes massacres, abductions, bombings, summary executions, population displacement, torture, sexual violence, arson, forced recruitment, human trafficking, and enforced disappearances.[46] A significant number of these involve the graphic display of violence (e.g., mutilating, disfiguring, and displaying corpses).[47] In sync with recent work on violence and terrorism in Mexico, this book argues that a subset of the violent acts plaguing the country clearly correspond to terrorism in that they often deliberately target civilians as part of a communicative logic seeking to instill fear in the wider community.[48]

In the following section, I present a succinct analysis of Mexican armed parties' repertoires of terrorism. Although preliminary and based mostly on secondary sources and interviews with scholars and security and human rights experts, the analysis reveals clear evidence of different repertoires of terrorism on the part of armed groups.

MEXICAN SECURITY FORCES

Mexican security force units have been responsible for widespread, egregious, and massive human rights violations in the name of combating crime.[49] Civilians, particularly those from humble backgrounds, are regularly victimized during searches and raids, at checkpoints, and during large-scale counternarcotics operations. Abuses include disproportionate uses of force or the systematic violation of due process guarantees against purported members of criminal organizations.[50]

The modi operandi of Mexican security forces clearly resemble pro-regime forms of terrorism used by their Colombian counterparts. The repertoire includes three main types of attacks: torture, enforced disappearance, and summary executions. Even though massacres and bombing attacks have been carried out by Mexican security forces, they are far less widespread. State agents regularly target civilians suspected of cooperating or sympathizing with criminal groups, capturing them during routine controls at checkpoints, on the street, or based on anonymous tip-offs. These actions seek to cripple criminal groups by going after their members and wider support system.[51] As Alejandro Anaya Muñoz and Barbara Frey emphasize, "behind the smokescreen of criminal violence, state actors are engaging or acquiescing in human rights violations with almost total impunity."[52]

These tactics harken back to those employed by Mexican security forces during the nation's "dirty war" period, when state agents used torture, enforced disappearance, and extrajudicial execution (1960–1980) against people suspected of belonging to opposition groups. Although in the past, forces deployed terrorism in the name of fighting communism, the tactical goal of these acts remains unchanged: to inhibit civil society's collective action.[53] In other words, a certain degree of inertia seems to be fueling state violence in that security forces have simply transferred the repertoire of action developed during their fight against communism to their current crusade against criminality.

SELF-DEFENSE GROUPS

The emergence of *auto-defensas* is a negative externality of the violence affecting Mexico. As in Colombia, these militias are diverse in origin and scale. Some groups were set up by powerful local elites (avocado and lime growers, cattle ranchers, mine owners) to defend their interests from extortion and sabotage on the part of criminal groups.[54] Others correspond to traditional community policing forces known in Mexico as Policía Comunitaria, which are formed by groups of citizens, including middle-class professionals, peasants, and indigenous communities seeking to protect their land and forests from criminals and the venal authorities colluding with outlaws. What unites these groups are their common objective—to protect themselves from the violence and abuses committed by OCGs—and their frustration at the utter incapacity or unwillingness of the state to protect them.[55]

Mexican *auto-defensas* have surfaced across Mexico, a recent account identifying thirty-one in the country.[56] Although most have emerged in states displaying high levels of criminal activity (Chihuahua, Guanajuato, Guerrero, Michoacán, México, Morelos, Tabasco, Tamaulipas, and Veracruz), they have also formed in states with relatively lower levels of violence, such as Campeche and Quintana Roo. The spread has been especially robust in Guerrero and Michoacán, where strong business interests, a scattered state presence, and a history of insurgency[57] created an ideal context for the rise of these increasingly powerful organizations.[58]

Although purportedly created to protect citizens from generalized conditions of violence, most *auto-defensas* stand accused of committing a series of abuses themselves. A significant share of these groups ultimately went rogue and turned into abusive, destructive forces. In what has become a prevalent problem, many were ultimately subverted by organized crime structures or corrupt state forces seeking to neutralize their power.[59]

Self-defense groups' repertoires of violence have included a variety of tactics, some of which amount to terrorism. However, given the sketchy information available, the large number of groups, their scattered presence in different parts of the country, and that many have been infiltrated by OCGs, it is hard to establish a clearly delineated modus operandi. A study by the Mexican National Human Rights Commission on *auto-defensas* in the state of Michoacán provides at least some hints about their violent repertoires. It found that between 2006 and 2014, these groups perpetrated 13,964 violent acts: of these, 52 percent were homicides, 27 percent extortions, 23 percent rapes, and 8 percent kidnappings.[60] Other fine-grained, qualitative descriptions provide further evidence that terrorism per se is not widespread among these groups. This is particularly so of peasant and indigenous *auto-defensas*, whose violent methods have generally entailed using harsh, illegal surveillance methods (roadblocks, raids, searches, detention) and targeting corrupt authorities and OCG members.[61]

Self-defense groups that would later emerge in towns such as La Ruana and Tepaltepec in an area known as Tierra Caliente (the Hotlands)—and associated with the charismatic leadership of figures such as José Manuel Mireles, Estanislao Beltrán (aka Papa Smurf), and Hipólito Mora—used more abrasive methods including torture, summary executions, and abductions.[62] Some of these attacks match the definition of terrorism used in this work in that they purposefully targeted civilians with the intention of crushing resistance and sending a message to the wider community.[63] In his remarkably rich account of violence in Guerrero, Chris Kyle describes how in their attempt to thwart OCGs, communitarian security forces across the state have also carried out attacks amounting to terrorism, such as abducting, torturing, or killing civilians accused of having links with organized crime.[64]

ORGANIZED CRIME GROUPS

Mexico has also seen a meteoric rise of OCGs.[65] These violent organizations have amassed enormous fortunes and considerable military capacity and staff, including security specialists (i.e., former members of the Mexican security forces).[66] Most OCGs have gained control of slices of territory and become the de facto authorities there. Mexican OCGs have also relied systematically on terrorism to advance their objectives, routinely resorting to summary executions, bombings, massacres, abductions, forced disappearances, forced recruitment, and sexual violence.[67] Some of these acts have incorporated the graphic display of victims' bodies (mutilation, dismembering, decapitation), which are paraded publicly, often accompanied with sinister statements known as *narcomantas* meant to maximize fear in the population.[68] Over the years, Mexicans have grown accustomed to the widespread use of these displays, which Ana Villarreal dubs "spectacular violence."[69] For example, during the height of the violence in Monterrey, Nuevo León, Los Zetas hanged bodies with visible signs of torture from bridges and overpasses in the early hours of the morning to frighten commuters. In Urapán, Michoacán, an armed commando of the Familia Michoacana stormed a disco and threw five severed heads on the dance floor, then displayed signs claiming credit for the action and warning rival cartels of the consequences of encroaching on the group's turf.[70] Moreover, OCGs would upload videos of graphic violence (torture, executions, rape) to internet sites such as YouTube and use these scenes for propagandistic purposes.[71]

Arguably, the litany of atrocities unleashed by OCGs is a complex and multifaceted phenomenon. In one of the most compelling accounts to date on the matter, Phil Williams notes that the increase of gratuitous, anomic violence defies conventional interpretations, making it "more complex and intractable than terrorism and insurgent violence."[72] He posits that violence in Mexico is best characterized as a series of layers superimposed on each other and informed by diverse logics (i.e., competition, outsourcing, and factionalism) and thus takes issue with accounts depicting violence as terrorism. Agreeing with Williams' general thesis, I argue that only a subset of OCG violence corresponds to terrorism, notwithstanding the frightening nature of other forms of violence and their traumatizing effect on Mexican society.

In accordance with the definition used in this book, only actions that deliberately target civilians with the intention of producing bodily harm and whose ultimate goal is generating fear in the wider public amount to terrorism. Following this conceptualization, the killing of OCG operatives by rival criminal groups—however violent or numerous—should not be considered terrorism. This evaluation is based on the fact that, under the international humanitarian law (IHL) rubric, drug trafficking organizations (DTO) operatives can be considered (unlawful) combatants (i.e., they are under a responsible command and openly carry weapons).[73] Although purportedly civilians, these individuals often actively take part in hostilities and thus contribute to their parties' military efforts. Their violent deaths—and particularly the display of their bodies—might create a public commotion, but such actions nonetheless can be classified as acts of war covered by IHL regulations. Of course, many of the actions against OCGs operatives constitute serious IHL breaches and amount to war crimes, and probably crimes against humanity given their systematic nature.[74] However, organized crime violence should be considered as terrorism only when the victims are not part of criminal organizations or are not directly contributing to militarily efforts.

As indicated, Mexican OCGs often target civilians who refuse to comply with their orders, resist them, are witnesses to crimes, fail to pay extortion fees, or are more generally perceived as a threat. In addition to regular citizens, these victims can include journalists, human rights activists, and governmental and state officials (politicians, judges) and members of their families. DTO's family members are also considered civilian targets.[75] Following this theoretical distinction, this works posits that OCG's tactics mutated from a conventional use of mafia-like repertoires of violence—targeting rivals in traditional turf wars and informed by an underworld logic in which extreme violence is used for reputational purposes—into outright terrorism practices as these organizations began to purposefully attack civilians according to what resembles a civil war logic of controlling population and territory.

The use of terrorism by criminal syndicates adheres to three complementary logics. First, as Trejo and Ley show, criminal organizations often use terrorism to control territory and populations and buttress their operational capacity.[76] As indicated, OCGs are particularly interested in gaining control of strategic plazas (e.g., border cities, ports, production enclaves) and corridors to move their product. Second and relatedly, as explained earlier in this chapter, these organizations use violence to prevent the state from interfering in their business.[77] Third, OCGs have often resorted to terrorism in areas controlled by rival groups. While conducting these attacks, OGGs conceal their identity, seeking to place the blame on their enemies in order to trigger a repressive response by federal government—a method colloquially known as *calentar la plaza* (heat up the square).[78]

OCGs began to incorporate terrorist practices during the escalation of turf wars following the gradual breakdown of the state protection racket.[79] The uncertainty created by these changes prompted DTOs to form paramilitary wings to prevent rival organizations from entering their territory and to expand their presence in rivals' territory. The creation of La Línea by the Juárez Cartel, Los Negros by the Sinaloa Cartel, the Fuerzas Especiales de Arturo by the Beltrán Leyva DTO, and, most consequentially, Los Zetas by the Gulf Cartel are cases in point.[80] Most of these groups were composed of former members of state security forces who defected to DTOs.[81] In a significant deterioration of the conflict, clandestine techniques of repression linked to counterinsurgency operations developed by Mexican security forces during the Cold War (i.e., torture, execution, forced disappearance, massacres) were transferred to OCG repertoires by these rogue state officials.[82] These tactics included direct attacks on civilians unrelated to the drug business in what clearly amounted to terrorism, adding another layer of complexity to the country's ultraviolent security outlook.[83]

Although seemingly similar, different OCGs developed their own repertoires of terrorism, some cartels more prone to using certain attacks than others. What follows is a succinct description of the modi operandi of four groups: the Gulf Cartel, Los Zetas, the Knights Templar, and the Cartel Jalisco Nueva Generación (Jalisco Cartel New Generation, or CJNG). The Gulf Cartel has an interesting trajectory that sets it apart from many other OCGs. Originally, it was a relatively nonviolent organization that resolved most conflicts through bribery and corruption.[84] Yet, over time, and as the drug war progressed, it created its own paramilitary wing, Los Zetas, to which it outsourced violent enforcement and turf protection. When Los Zetas went out on its own, the Gulf Cartel began to resort to more violent methods to regain its control over contested plazas and match the growing influence of their former armed wing.[85] To accomplish this goal, the cartel carried out high-profile violent acts designed to inspire fear in rival cartels, potential enemies, and the public, such as visible executions and abductions. One notable example was the assassination of Juan Jesús Guerrero Chapa, the former lawyer of Gulf Cartel leader Osiel Cárdenas, and his wife in broad daylight outside of the Dallas Fort Worth International Airport after it was revealed that Chapa was a government informant.[86] The Gulf Cartel also became notorious for systematic kidnappings that, though incredibly prolific, were nonetheless highly selective in their targeting.[87] According to military sources, these kidnappings primarily targeted potential recruits or relatives of rival gangs with the intent of spreading fear in the population.[88]

As for Los Zetas, they intensified their attacks soon after splintering from the Gulf Cartel and came to be considered the most violent OCG in the country. Los Zetas have relied on a diverse set of terrorist tactics. Early on, they incorporated acts such as massacres to tighten their grip on certain territories, such as the notorious Allende massacre in 2011.[89] In this case, after police officers on the Los Zetas payroll were suspected of cooperating with the U.S. Drug Enforcement Agency, the group responded brutally to such disloyalty. They invaded the town, sacking and burning as many as forty houses and seven ranches as well as abducting hundreds of people in a rampage that lasted three days. Once it was over, three hundred civilians were dead.[90] Terrorism was also used by the group to further expand its business portfolio. The attack on Casino Royale in the city of Monterrey in 2011 is a prime example. Zeta operatives stormed the building and set fire to it, killing fifty-seven civilians inside. The attack served as a punishment against the owner for refusing to pay extortion fees. The group has also been reported to use explosives, including grenade attacks and car bombings, on civilian targets to solidify their control over certain *plazas*.[91]

Another group, the Knights Templar, which operates mostly in the western states of Michoacán and Guerrero, displays unique traits including religious posturing—fashioning themselves as modern-day versions of the

Crusaders.[92] Like other groups, it initially used money rather than violence to solve its problems, but as its control started to wane, it became increasingly predatory and violent. This shift began with the fracturing of its alliance with *Los Zetas*, prompting an acute wave of spectacular violence.[93] Afterward, the cartel began to apply harsh methods such as executing alleged criminals accused of kidnapping, rape, or murder in town squares. They also began murdering rivals and suspected informants and some members of their families, cutting off their heads and tossing them into town squares. As time went on, they targeted civilians with several terrorist tactics, including forced recruitment, targeted assassination, abductions, and detonating explosive devices in public places.[94] Overall, the Knights Templar seemed keen to avoid the large-scale violence of other cartels but wanted to spread the message that they were in control and that they would kill anyone who opposed their power in an area.[95]

Finally, CJNG arose from the successive fragmentation of the powerful Sinaloa Cartel. Previously known as the Milenio Cartel, CJNG emerged as a splinter group in the Jalisco region and was formed by Ignacio Coronel (aka Nacho), the Sinaloa Cartel's representative in Jalisco until his death in July 2010. A power struggle between Coronel's lieutenants divided the group further. The winning faction, known as the Torcidos (the Crooked), would later become the CJNG and dominate Jalisco under the leadership of Nemesio Osegura Cervantes (aka El Mencho). CJNG made it their mission to battle Los Zetas, adopting the name of Matazetas, or Zetas Killers. Their rise to power began in 2011; since then, they have been involved in a series of deadly attacks against rival cartels, security forces, and civilians. Despite this propensity for terror, they have also been highly active in distributing altruistic propaganda. During the COVID-19 pandemic, they handed out toys to children and supplies to various parts of the country with few resources. The group has expanded its presence in most of the country, with the exception of Sinaloa and the Golden Triangle. Their fiercest enemies are Sinaloa, Santa Rosa de Lima Cartel, Old School Zetas, Knights Templar, and state security forces.[96]

CJNG's repertoire of terrorism resembles that of the Zetas. Both groups practice a vast array of terrorist tactics (bombings, targeted assassinations, disappearances, massacres), often using graphic displays of violence to maximize fear. Indeed, CNJG's tactics are even more daring as the group has sought to overtake their feared Zeta rivals in ever bolder ways. CJNG has bombed U.S. consulate offices and attempted assassinations in broad daylight in major urban centers, including Guadalajara, Guanajuato, and even Mexico City. The group has also honed its digital communications, making YouTube videos and social media posts to advertise its presence. CJNG has also developed a website that spreads propaganda and documents its violent achievements. It has relied on drones and implemented complex financial schemes to cement its technological advantage further. Finally, it has adopted some of the Knights Templar Cartel's philanthropic messaging approach, claiming to be combating the truly "dangerous" cartels as a justification for their violence.[97]

Mexican armed parties' use of terrorist tactics is shown in table 7.1. As the table makes clear, although all groups perpetrate terrorism, each displays a particular repertoire of action in accordance with preferences linked to its organizational identity. Distinctions exist both among categories as well as within group types, OCGs in particular. As for commonalities regarding specific forms of terrorism, all groups use targeted assassinations and torture. As for differences, several trends stand out: barring state security forces, all parties use abductions; only Los Zetas and the Knights Templar use bombings; self-defense forces and the Gulf Cartel have avoided massacres; and only OGCs use overkill.

Findings in the Mexican case reinforce the argument that groups develop different repertoires of terrorism over time, and that such differences correspond to organizational identities. The analysis reveals commonalities and differences with some of the Colombia findings. For example, the modus operandi of Mexican state security forces resembles the pro-regime repertoire of terrorism used by the CSSF, as seen by their propensity to use torture and disappearances and by their reluctance to engage in abduction and overkill. With respect to self-defense forces and OCGs, variation is greater. Mexican OCGs' repertoire of terrorism bears a certain resemblance to the playbook of Colombian paramilitary groups, particularly their propensity to maximize fear using sacralized forms of violence. Differences arise, however, in the willingness of Mexican criminal groups to use abductions and bombing attacks (except for the Gulf Cartel). This indicates that Mexican OCGs are willing to expand their repertoires and embrace insurgent terrorism tactics that in Colombia are typically associated with guerrillas. The absence of guerrilla groups in the Mexican setting (other than in isolated pockets such as Guerrero and Chiapas) facilitates this repertoire

TABLE 7.1 Mexican Armed Parties' Repertoires of Terrorism

	Torture	Abduction	Massacres	Targeted assassinations	Overkill	Bombings
Self-Defense	Yes	Yes	No	Yes	No	No
State Security	Yes	No	Yes	Yes	No	No
Gulf Cartel	Yes	Yes	No	Yes	Yes	No
Los Zetas	Yes	Yes	Yes	Yes	Yes	Yes
Knights Templar Cartel	Yes	Yes	No	Yes	Yes	Yes
Jalisco Cartel New Generation	Yes	Yes	Yes	Yes	Yes	Yes

Source: Author's tabulation.

expansion given that groups do not feel the need to differentiate their tactics, as they clearly do in Colombia. Mexican self-defense forces, for their part, seem to show greater restraint than Colombian paramilitary groups, given their avoidance of massacres and overkill. These patterns, I speculate, may indicate that criminal elements have a thinner presence or less influence among self-defense groups in Mexico than among paramilitary groups in Colombia.

Conclusions

This chapter offers a reflection on the use of terrorism during criminal wars by examining the post–peace agreement period in Colombia, which began in 2016 and is ongoing. I inquire whether armed parties' repertoires of terrorism in Colombia changed in this new phase of the conflict and whether some distinct patterns emerged. Evidence shows that armed parties' tactics have remained stable, notwithstanding a significant drop in the intensity of violence. This finding shows that in the face of internal turmoil, shifting goals, and leadership changes, organizational identity is sticky, and significant levels of organizational inertia persist. The examination also underlines that although differences in parties' repertoires of terrorism remain, they seem less pronounced than in previous phases of the war. This change is attributed to a diminishing role of ideology within armed parties in this new context of violence.

The examination is complemented with a detailed examination of the Mexican case to probe whether differences also exist among armed groups' repertoires of terrorism in other criminal war contexts. The analysis supports the claim that armed parties display differences in their repertoires of terrorism, reflecting distinct organizational identities. It reveals a significant degree of inertia in the modus operandi of Mexican security forces, which stem from a counterinsurgency logic dating back to the country's dirty war period. Mexican self-defense groups have developed their own specific repertoires that have deliberately avoided some of the hallmarks of OCGs, in particular, shying away from massacres and graphic displays of violence. In the case of criminal groups, repertoires of terrorism are broad because they stem from a criminal ethos and actors have no need to differentiate their repertoires from insurgent groups. Reinforcing the main argument of the book, findings show that OCGs themselves develop different terrorist blueprints, with some groups adopting a broader portfolio of terrorist tactics than others.

Conclusion

This book offers an extensive analysis of the use of terrorism in civil war. Terrorism is a depressingly familiar feature in civil wars: armed parties regularly perpetrate it to advance their strategic objectives. A puzzling aspect of these contexts—and one this book tries to unpack—is that though armed groups in civil wars rely extensively on terrorism, they specialize in certain types of attacks and avoid others. Moreover, they often use the same tactics in markedly different ways: some groups seek to attract as much publicity as possible, whereas others attempt to maintain plausible deniability. On occasion, groups determined to maximize fear use macabre techniques (i.e., graphically marking victims' bodies); others reject going to such lengths. This book seeks to explain this intriguing variation with a view to enhancing our understanding of how this singular form of violence is deployed in these contexts.

To approach this topic, the book examines the dynamics of violence through a comprehensive investigation of the Colombian civil war. Colombia represents a rich laboratory in that the country's long and bloody civil war has been defined by the extensive use of terrorism by a host of warring factions including guerrilla groups, paramilitary organizations, and state security forces. Complementing existing conceptualizations on the use of violence against protected persons during civil war, this book argues that terrorism constitutes a subset of civilian targeting characterized by a strategic logic: armed groups rely on terrorism to frighten—and ultimately cow—civilians and adversaries. Ample evidence furnished in this book illustrates that armed parties develop singular repertoires of terrorism over time. These repertoires, or blueprints, of terrorism constitute a form of communication that distinguishes them from their enemies and rivals. The analysis shows how organizations' repertoires are the product of a unique organizational identity, which blends ideology, group features, and leadership preferences. Rather than monolithic, these identities tend to be hybrid and multifaceted, often combining multiple, and at times seemingly incompatible, worldviews (ideological, criminal, religious).

Although parties deploy terrorism to attain their strategic goals, they do so in accordance with their preferred repertoires of action, which in essence become signals or calling cards of their presence in a given space. Such identity markers are nurtured over the lifetime of an organization as behaviors are shaped by leaders and socialized via training and disciplinary processes. Repertoires of terrorism reveal institutional and ideological preferences and character, but groups often also adapt their methods in accordance with evolving conditions on the ground or borrow enemy tactics. In doing so, however, they still attempt to fit their actions into their ideological framework to maintain internal consistency and group identity.

These findings have important implications in at least three main areas: conceptualizing terrorism as a distinctive form of violence during civil war; grasping the mechanisms informing armed parties' violent strategies, and in particular the link between armed parties' organizational attributes and their repertoires of violence, including terrorism; and refining our grasp of the intrinsic complexity of armed parties, including an increasing hybrid nature in which political and criminal motivations are intertwined. In the following pages, I discuss the theoretical relevance of these three dimensions.

The Nature of Terrorism During Civil War

As discussed in chapter 1, and following recent work on political violence, this study assumes that despite their manifest linkage and overlap, terrorism and civil war constitute two manifestations of violence.[1] To the extent that armed conflicts are ideal microcosms for terrorism to emerge, they are best conceptualized as adjacent phenomena.[2] Yet important elements distinguish these forms of violence. Civil wars are theoretically governed by basic principles codified under international humanitarian law (IHL) designed to alleviate the most cruel and inhumane effects of violence, for example, prohibitions against the targeting of civilians (i.e., distinction). Most civil wars are characterized by IHL breaches, yet rules governing conduct do exist, and the expectation is that parties will abide by them.[3] Terrorism, conversely, negates humanitarian principles and regulations because its prevailing logic entails deliberately infringing on civilian immunity to disseminate fear.[4]

Relatedly, the logic and purpose of violence differ in civil war and in terrorism. In the former, parties use military tactics against their enemies to defeat them. Thus the nature of violence tends to be direct in that parties attempt to overwhelm their adversaries militarily and impose their will on them.[5] Terrorism is characterized by a manifestly different logic. Conceptually, it is not a military strategy, but instead a tactic characterized by a communicational rationale.[6] In other words, even though violence against civilians regularly occurs during civil war, it is not a constitutive element in that these wars are defined by sustained operations (battles) among militarily organized parties. In terrorism, conversely, deliberately targeting civilians is a conditio sine qua non.

Another relevant point concerning the nature of violence is that terrorism and civilian targeting, though related, are in essence analytically different. Developed by cross-fertilizing elements of the terrorism and civil war literatures—and in sync with recent studies advocating for disaggregating the category of civilian targeting[7]—this book posits that terrorism constitutes a particular form of violence best conceptualized as a subcategory of civilian targeting. The key element that distinguishes terrorism from other types of civilian attacks is the act's purpose: terrorism seeks to deliberately target civilians because its blatant disregard for the basic principles of humanity maximizes fear (i.e., if innocent people, including children, the elderly, and so forth can be targets, then everyone is at risk). The targets may be deliberately or randomly selected if they are civilian. Crucially, however, terrorist violence is conducted in pursuit of an ulterior motive (i.e., promoting a cause) that is not encapsulated in the act itself.[8] Conversely, many other forms of intentional civilian violence during civil wars entail concrete goals. Parties often attack civilians with the tangible objective of dispossessing them for economic gain or exterminating them for a variety of reasons (religious, ethnic, cultural, social, economic, political).[9] In other words, terrorism can be conceptualized as a subset of violence perpetrated during civil war. Terrorism, though, differs from other forms of violence perpetrated in civil war, including conventional warfare, guerrilla warfare, ethnic cleansing, and genocide, in that it deliberately violates cardinal IHL principles with the clear intent to spread fear beyond the target of violence.

Identity and the Production of Terrorism

A second critical insight of the book concerns the role of identity in the production of violence, in particular terrorism, during civil war. Evidence regarding the modi operandi of Colombian armed parties illustrates how these groups' unique blend of ideology, organizational features, and leadership preferences shaped their repertoires or blueprints of terrorism. Beyond acknowledging the role of identity, the book's findings underscore the need for a more nuanced interpretation of the nature of armed parties, one that captures their unique features and particularities.

As indicated, rather than being uniform, the identities of armed groups are often multifaceted and characterized by diverse and occasionally incompatible features. This book therefore conceptualizes identity as the product of an intersubjective construction predicated on superimposed doctrines and ideas influenced by a group's unique history, leadership, and transnational forces. Such unique identities were critical in the development of terrorist repertoires and explain the significant variation not only among organizations with polar opposite worldviews but also among groups espousing similar views.

The book offers ample empirical evidence of this point. For example, even though inspired by Marxist doctrine, the Revolutionary Armed Forces of Colombia (FARC) was more prone to employing territorial terrorism (e.g., massacres) than other insurgent groups because of its view of the war and its origin as a self-defense force. In comparison, the identity of the National Liberation Army, or Ejército de Liberación Nacional (ELN), which combined Cuban-inspired Castroite thought, nationalism, and liberation theology, explains why this group showed more restraint than the FARC, limiting massacres and bombings and for the most part avoiding overkill. Furthermore, paramilitary and Colombian state security forces (CSSF) repertoires of terrorism display important differences with guerrilla groups. The nature of their attacks reflects a clear preference for pro-status quo actions seeking to control the population, such as massacres and summary executions, and shore up the state's legitimacy. Interestingly, however, as in the case of guerrilla groups, CSSF and paramilitary repertoires of terrorism reveal critical differences, despite their significant institutional overlap and the fact that they often acted with significant coordination. Paramilitaries perpetrated massacres more regularly, often staging graphic displays of violence against victims to maximize fear. The CSSF rarely did so. Paramilitary groups were also more inclined to use abductions, which were openly claimed and often followed a retaliatory logic. CSSF abductions were more isolated, conducted surreptitiously to punish kidnappers, and never involved monetary rewards. In the case of paramilitaries, terrorism was also informed by a criminal ethos in which predatory behavior and ruthless displays of violence (common in the underworld) were employed to punish those who stood in their way.

Last, as pointed out earlier, tactics evolve over time. In the case of guerrillas, terrorism practices followed a clear sequence: influenced by revolutionary ideologies in vogue in the 1970s such as urban guerrilla warfare, the FARC and ELN incorporated agitational terrorism, particularly abductions and bombing attacks. As time went on, their repertoires began to incorporate summary executions and explosive attacks. With the irruption of paramilitary groups and their subsequent strengthening in the mid-1990s, both groups—but especially the FARC—borrowed and adapted tactics from their rivals, in particular massacres. Massacres followed a strategic logic informed by military necessity as parties sought to control territory and the population in highly disputed strategic areas. Paramilitaries followed an inverse route: their original repertoires, informed by counterinsurgency doctrine, began to incorporate some adaptations of traditional insurgent tactics, in particular abductions. Paramilitary abductions, however, were qualitatively different from those carried out by guerrillas: they were much more targeted at their specific enemies rather than a wider population of people considered class enemies. Also, for the most part, these abductions were discreetly conducted and never for extortive financial purposes. The CSSF displayed a more consistent terrorism repertoire over time, one strongly influenced by their counterinsurgency training. These findings underscore that even though strategic considerations matter, they are not capable on their own of fully capturing the nature and forms of terrorism in the context of civil war. Ideational aspects must be considered as well. This approach also allows for the cross-fertilization of important strands within the civil war and terrorism literatures.

Criminal Wars and Terrorism

A third relevant theoretical implication concerns the role of a criminal ethos or *mafioso spirit* as a factor influencing armed parties' repertoires of violence, including terrorism. This book provides concrete evidence for the theoretical insights developed by the civil war and the crime-terror nexus literatures on the link between criminality and the production of violence. As discussed, a criminal ethos shaped Colombian paramilitary groups, the actor that most extensively relied on this practice—paramilitary use of terrorism exceeded that of the other three main civil war protagonists combined. Once again, this finding highlights the importance of developing a nuanced understanding of the nature of armed parties and their repertoires of violence, one that avoids caricaturizing groups as either fully ideological or criminal. In particular, the evidence reinforces an important finding of the criminal terrorism nexus literature: namely, the fluid boundary between the political and criminal within armed parties. As this book makes abundantly clear, armed parties' repertoires of violence stem from unique processes linked to organizational preferences that often blend ideological and criminal codes of conduct. The gradual drift of Colombian armed parties toward criminality and the changing conditions in the contemporary phase of the conflict allows us to measure the extent to which changes in identity affect repertoires of terrorism. A cursory analysis reveals that despite their evolution, armed parties' repertoires of terrorism retained a fair degree of continuity. Although preliminary, this finding underlines the permanence (i.e., stickiness) of parties' core identities and demonstrates how this dynamic informs organizational inertia.

The book's main insights and findings acquire even more relevance when considering the evolving landscape in Latin America and beyond, where criminal violence is increasing. Since the end of the Cold War, traditional civil wars linked to political grievances have morphed into large-scale conflicts marked by criminal violence.[10] Some controversy as to the true nature of these conflagrations aside, what is beyond dispute is that they are becoming more and more prevalent throughout the region and the world. In a great many cases, violence levels in criminal wars have exceeded those in conventional civil wars (more than one thousand battle deaths per year). The use of terrorism in many of these conflicts has become common, as shown in the discussions of the post-peace era in Colombia and the emblematic case of Mexico. Moreover, in one of this book's interesting preliminary findings, organizational identity also plays a role in the production of terrorism in criminal war settings and accounts for differences in how various parties use this tactic.

Policy Implications

The book's main findings have a series of relevant policy implications for societies undergoing civil or criminal wars where terrorism is systematically employed. Specifically, this research may inform public policy in two main areas: humanitarian considerations for civilians living in contexts of civil and criminal wars; and measures that could diminish overall levels of insecurity and violence. This section succinctly touches on these two points.

First, in contexts of civil and criminal wars, protecting civilians and, more generally, implementing measures to ameliorate violence and shield society from the ominous consequences of dehumanizing practices such as terrorism are vital goals. In this vein, the book reminds us of the need to pay close attention to how armed parties' unique historical trajectories shape their behavior and repertoires of violence. Any measures seeking to discourage armed parties from perpetrating terrorism as a tactic requires a historically grounded account that takes into consideration their motivations, fears, and biases. Also relevant is the awareness that practices often evolve over time in accordance with identity-based logics. Consequently, it is imperative to avoid the common mistake of assigning armed parties prepackaged, broad labels (Marxist, Criminal, Conservative) that overlook their hybrid identity and, ultimately, oversimplify their true nature and stances.[11]

A more nuanced understanding of armed parties may also help us devise better targeted measures to engage with belligerents and persuade them to modify their behavior. Such dialogues may be critical to broadening humanitarian spaces to better assist and protect civilians, a point underscored repeatedly by humanitarian organizations such as the International Committee of the Red Cross, Médecins Sans Frontières, and several UN agencies working in conflict areas. In private conversations conducted for this research, humanitarian workers emphasized time and again the need to find common ground with armed parties, regardless of their nature. The case of the ELN is very revealing in this respect. A superficial reading of the organization's identity and goals that ignores the religious component nurturing its organizational culture potentially misses a critical insight that could be useful in establishing a humanitarian dialogue. Similarly, in the case of paramilitaries, acknowledging (and adapting negotiations to) their pro-status quo, conservative views helped open up a humanitarian dialogue that saved many lives.[12] And in the case of state security forces, a more nuanced understanding of the ideational underpinning of their training may be critical to modifying their behavior and making interventions to improve their human rights practices.

Another critical finding of this monograph regards the role of criminally affiliated nonstate actors and their influence on the production of violence in both civil and criminal wars. As indicated, any measure to address the challenges posed by these parties and diminish overall violence, including terrorism, requires developing a granular understanding of their nature and actions to productively engage with them. Although this book underlines how a criminal ethos shaped the identity and behavior of many armed parties (e.g., Colombian paramilitaries), it also posits that criminal motives and logics often dovetail with considerations of a more ideological and political nature. A common view is to assume, prima facie, that most of these groups are simply criminal organizations with no political motivations and that therefore any potential humanitarian engagement would be difficult, if not impossible. However, even though negotiating with criminal groups is inherently a process full of "flaws, contradictions and challenges,"[13] it is certainly not impossible, particularly if humanitarian organizations embark on a long-term strategic commitment to identify potential issues these organizations are ready to discuss.[14] Though controversial, negotiations with gangs in Central America and current negotiations in Colombia furnish valuable insights regarding how to possibly open humanitarian space to assist and protect vulnerable populations and, concomitantly, how to diminish the violence raging in the region.[15]

As extensively discussed in this book, most armed parties do indeed have preferences of a political nature, weak ideological programs of sorts.[16] Because criminal groups are motivated by greed, they often view politics to achieve their goals, as described in the analysis of Mexican drug trafficking organizations. Hence, rather than conceptualizing criminal and political organizations that use terrorism as antithetical groups, we should instead examine the intersections and intensities of criminal and political dimensions within each organization, as underlined in Tamara Makarenko's seminal work.[17] Moreover, the increasing growth and salience of zones characterized by criminal governance (i.e., "the imposition of rules or restrictions on behavior by a criminal organization") requires us to move away from rigid and ultimately unhelpful preconceptions about criminality and the state.[18] Instead, we should adopt pragmatic strategies of engagement that take into consideration the complex dynamics of contemporary zones of conflict. Of particular importance is opening a serious dialogue with states and civil society and devising ways to overcome the stigma associated with negotiating with armed parties engaged in criminal activities.[19] As Marco Sassòli points out, the best chance of creating a meaningfully protective umbrella for civilians in situations of armed conflict or generalized situations of violence is to establish a dialogue with all kinds of nonstate parties.[20]

With respect to the second theme—how to diminish overall conditions of violence—this book's findings could inform measures in the realm of security. For starters, assessing different uses of terrorism might help authorities differentiate the degree of danger posed by the various armed parties. Recent literature underscores the usefulness of calibrating repressive mechanisms as a way to diminish levels of violence, either by withholding coercive efforts and maintaining the threat of coercion as a deterrent,[21] centering attacks on the most violent groups,[22] or rethinking the strategy of decapitating the leadership of violent groups.[23] Beyond these considerations, however, the use of terrorism can have particularly nefarious impacts on the social fabric given that it inhibits collective action and undermines the legitimacy of the state and its institutions. Having a clear idea of groups' repertoires of violence including terrorist practices may inform the allocation of public resources (physical and human) that could lessen the impact of these organizations' misdeeds.

A deeper understanding of armed parties' repertoires may also help in developing effective strategies for pressuring groups to modify their behavior. Despite obvious limits to naming and shaming recalcitrant parties intent on using terrorism, a correct reading of their standing, motivations, and tactics that is attentive to their identity as organizations could inform multifaceted communicational campaigns and identify pressure points. In the Colombian case, as chapter 5 discusses, mounting pressure on paramilitary groups made them rethink the utility of carrying out massacres versus the reputational costs of this practice; in the end, they decided to limit these acts. Similarly, kidnapping, a guerrilla trademark in the Colombian setting, was also targeted for an aggressive communicational campaign that ultimately contributed to reducing its prevalence.

Ultimately, developing a sounder and more nuanced understanding of armed parties' repertoires of terrorism may inform concrete policies that governments and humanitarian actors can implement to modify the behavior of belligerents. Such policies could enhance protections for communities affected by civil and criminal wars, and more generally, help humanize violent contexts like those afflicting societies in Latin America and beyond.

Appendix 1

The Use of Terrorism by Colombian Armed Parties

TABLE A.1 FARC

Municipality	Department	Number of terror attacks	Strategic relevance	Economic base
Dabeiba	Antioquia	39	Connects interior with the Urabá Gulf	Cattle ranching and agriculture
San José del Guaviare	Guaviare	36	Connects Guaviare and Meta	Cattle ranching and agriculture
Carmen de Bolívar	Bolívar	32	Connects Bolívar and Sucre	Agriculture (tobacco)
Tibú	N Santander	31	Border with Venezuela	Oil and gas-producing area
Tame	Arauca	30	Connects Arauca and Casanare	Cattle ranching, agriculture, timber
Apartadó	Antioquia	25	Controls passage to the Urabá Gulf	Agriculture (banana)
Ciénaga	Magdalena	25	Port for transshipment of drugs	Agriculture (banana), coal
Neiva	Huila	24	Corridor connects Huila, Caquetá, and Tolima	Cattle ranching and agriculture
Ovejas	Sucre	24	Connects Sucre and Bolívar	Cattle ranching and agriculture

(continued)

TABLE A.1 (Continued)

Municipality	Department	Number of terror attacks	Strategic relevance	Economic base
Mutatá	Antioquia	23	Connects Córdoba, Antioquia, and Urabá; accesses Atlantic	Agriculture, timber, mining
Medio Atrato	Chocó	23	Connects Antioquia and Chocó	Timber and agriculture
San Carlos	Antioquia	23	Critical center for electricity production	Cattle ranching and agriculture
Tumaco	Nariño	22	Strategic outlet Pacific	Palm oil and fishery
Valledupar	Cesar	22	Connects with La Guajira and Magdalena	Cattle ranching and agriculture
Vista Hermosa	Meta	21	Connects Meta and Guaviare	Cattle ranching and agriculture
Yarumal	Antioquia	20	Connects Medellín and Montería	Agriculture and cattle
Medellín	Antioquia	20	Capital of Antioquia	Industrial hub
Urrao	Antioquia	20	Connects Antioquia with Chocó	Cattle ranching and agriculture
Planadas	Tolima	20	Connects Tolima and Huila	Agriculture (coffee)
Samaná	Caldas	20	Connects Caldas and Antioquia	Agriculture (coffee)
Tierralta	Córdoba	20	Connects Córdoba and Antioquia	Agriculture
Algeciras	Huila	20	Connects Huila and Tolima	Agriculture, cattle ranching, mining

Source: Author's tabulation based on data from Justicia y Paz and Noche y Niebla.

TABLE A.2 ELN

Municipality	Department	Number of terror attacks	Strategic relevance	Economic base
Cocorná	Antioquia	60	Corridor connecting Antioquia with Caldas	Agriculture (sugar), cattle ranching
San Luis	Antioquia	37	Corridor connecting Antioquia with Caldas and Boyacá	Agriculture (sugar, coffee)
Valledupar	Cesar	36	Capital of Cesar	Cattle ranching and agriculture
Saravena	Arauca	33	Connects Boyacá, Arauca, and Venezuela	Commerce, agriculture, and cattle
Aguachica	Cesar	33	Gateway to Catatumbo region	Cattle ranching
Barrancabermeja	Santander	27	Major port Magdalena River	Oil industry
Ocaña	N. Santander	23	Center of Catatumbo	Coca producing area, mining, and agriculture
Cúcuta	N. Santander	21	Capital of department/border with Venezuela	Commerce
Curumaní	Cesar	19	Corridor connecting Huila, Caquetá, and Tolima	Cattle ranching and agriculture
Ciénaga	Magdalena	18	Port for Transshipment of Drugs	Agriculture (banana), coal
Tibú	N. Santander	17	Border with Venezuela	Oil and gas-producing area
Pelaya	Cesar	15	Corridor connecting Cesar and Norte de Santander and Venezuelan border	Agriculture (maize)
Barbosa	Antioquia	15	Suburb of Medellín	Major metropolitan area

(continued)

TABLE A.2 (Continued)

Municipality	Department	Number of terror attacks	Strategic relevance	Economic base
Arauquita	Arauca	14	Border with Venezuela	Commerce, agriculture, and cattle
S. Vicente Chucurí	Santander	15	Links corridor connecting Santander and Antioquia	Agriculture (cacao, coffee)
Quibdó	Chocó	13	Port for transshipment of drugs	Fishing and agriculture
Ábrego	N. Santander	12	Connects Norte de Santander and Cesar	Agriculture and cattle
Bucaramanga	Santander	12	Capital of department	Cattle
Simití	Bolívar	11	Connects Bolívar and Cesar	Agriculture and cattle

Source: Author's tabulation.

TABLE A.3 CSSF

Municipality	Department	Number of terror attacks	Strategic importance	Economic base
Bogotá	Bogota City	65	Capital	Industry, service, bureaucracy
Medellín	Antioquia	55	Capital of Antioquia	Industrial, trade, and service hub
Barrancabermeja	Santander	50	Major port	Oil industry hub
Vista Hermosa	Meta	45	Connects Meta and Guaviare	Cattle ranching and agriculture
Cali	Valle del Cauca	37	Departmental capital	Service and commerce hub
Soacha	Cundinamarca	31	Capital satellite city	Service

TABLE A.3 (Continued)

Municipality	Department	Number of terror attacks	Strategic importance	Economic base
Apartadó	Antioquia	26	Controls passage to the Urabá Gulf	Agriculture (banana)
Tame	Arauca	26	Connects Arauca and Casanare	Cattle, agriculture, timber
Granada	Antioquia	25	Access highway to Bogotá and Medellín, guerrilla stronghold	Cattle ranching and agriculture
Saravena	Arauca	23	Connects Boyacá, Arauca, and Venezuela	Commerce, agriculture, and cattle
Popayán	Cauca	21	Departmental capital	Services, tourism
Bucaramanga	Santander	19	Capital of Santander	Cattle
Remedios	Antioquia	19	Connects Antioquia and Bolívar	Mining and cattle
Cúcuta	N. Santander	18	Bordertown with Venezuela	Commerce
Cartagena del Chairá	Caquetá	18	Coca leaf production	Agriculture
Aguazul	Casanare	17	Oil fields	Oil, industry hub/ agriculture
Ciénaga	Magdalena	16	Port for transshipment of drugs	Agriculture (banana), coal
San Juan de Cesar	La Guajira	16	Connects La Guajira with Cesar and Venezuela	Cattle
Valledupar	Cesar	16	Capital of Cesar	Cattle ranching and agriculture
Santa Marta	Magdalena	15	Capital of Magdalena	Tourism and services

Source: Author's tabulation.

TABLE A.4 Paramilitarities

Municipality	Department	Number of terror attacks	Strategic importance	Economic base	Units involved
Barrancabermeja	Santander	415	Major port	Oil industry hub	Autodefensas Campesinas del Magdalena Medio Autodefensas Campesinas del Magdalena Medio Bloque Central Bolívar
Cúcuta	Norte de Santander	312	Border town with Venezuela	Commerce	Bloque Catatumbo
Medellín	Antioquia	204	Capital of Antioquia	Industrial hub	Autodefensas Campesinas de Córdoba y Urabá Bloque Mineros Bloque Metro Bloque Cacique Nutibara
Ciénaga	Magdalena	154	Port for transshipment of drugs	Agriculture (banana), coal	Bloque Norte
Aguachica	Cesar	104	ELN stronghold		Autodefensas Campesinas de Santander y Sur del Cesar Bloque Norte
Valledupar	Cesar	97	Capital of Cesar	Cattle ranching and agriculture	Bloque Norte
El Castillo	Meta	97	Foothills, eastern Cordillera	Cattle ranching and agriculture	Bloque Centauros
Dabeiba	Antioquia	85	Connects interior with the Urabá Gulf	Cattle ranching and agriculture	Autodefensas Campesinas de Córdoba y Urabá Bloque Elmer Cárdenas

Apartadó	Antioquia	80	Controls passage to the Urabá Gulf	Agriculture (banana)	Bloque Bananero
Buenaventura	Valle	76	Major port for transshipment of commerce and drugs	Commerce, transport	Bloque Calima
Santa Marta	Magdalena	77	Transshipment of drugs; main access to the Atlantic Ocean	Agriculture (banana, coffee) and tourism	Bloque Resistencia Tayrona Bloque Norte
Quibdó	Chocó	69	Major port for transshipment of commerce and drugs	Commerce, transport, fishing	Bloque Elmer Cárdenas
Villa del Rosario	Norte de Santander	69	Controls access to Cúcuta and borders Venezuela	Agriculture, cattle, and mining	Bloque Catatumbo
San José del Guaviare	Guaviare	65	Connects Guaviare and Meta	Cattle ranching and agriculture	Bloque Centauros Autodefensas Campesinas de Meta y Vichada
Vista Hermosa	Meta	65	Connects Meta and Guaviare	Cattle ranching and agriculture	Bloque Centauros
San Pablo	Bolívar	62	Connects Antioquia and Santander via Bolívar	Agriculture, cattle, and mining	Bloque Central Bolívar
Bogotá	Bogotá	59	Capital	Commerce, finance, government	Bloque Capital Autodefensas Campesinas de Córdoba y Urabá Bloque Cundinamarca Autodefensas Campesinas del Casanare
Tame	Arauca	59	Connects Arauca and Casanare	Cattle, agriculture, timber	Bloque Vencedores de Arauca

(continued)

TABLE A.4 (Continued)

Municipality	Department	Number of terror attacks	Strategic importance	Economic base	Units involved
Yondó	Antioquia	58	Connects Bolívar and Santander		Autodefensas Campesinas del Magdalena Medio Autodefensas de Puerto Boyacá Bloque Central Bolívar
Tumaco	Nariño	54	Strategic outlet to Pacific Ocean	Palm oil, fishery	Bloque Libertadores del Sur
Carmen de Bolívar	Bolívar	51	Connects Bolívar and Sucre	Agriculture (tobacco)	Bloque Héroes de Los Montes de María
Montería	Córdoba	51	Capital of Córdoba	Cattle ranching and agriculture	Autodefensas Campesinas de Córdoba y Urabá Bloque Córdoba
San Carlos	Antioquia	50	Critical center for electricity production	Cattle ranching and agriculture	Bloque Metro
Barranquilla	Atlántico	44	Port for transshipment of drugs	Commerce transport	Bloque Norte
Riosucio	Chocó	41	Transshipment of drugs, access to Panama and Atlantic Ocean	Cattle and agriculture (palm oil)	Autodefensas Campesinas de Córdoba y Urabá Bloque Elmer Cárdenas
Fundación	Magdalena	41	Connects Magdalena and Cesar	Cattle ranching and agriculture	Bloque Norte
Zona Bananera	Magdalena	41	Transshipment of drugs, access to Atlantic Ocean	Agriculture (banana, palm oil)	Bloque Norte
Tuluá	Valle	41	Connects Valle del Cauca and	Agriculture and cattle	Bloque Calima

Cartagena	Bolívar	38	Transshipment of drugs, access Atlantic Ocean	Tourism, commerce, transport	Bloque Héroes de Los Montes de María
Montelíbano	Córdoba	37	Connects Antioquia and Bolívar	Mining	Autodefensas Campesinas de Córdoba y Urabá Bloque Mineros
Bucaramanga	Santander	36	Capital of Santander	Cattle	Bloque Central Bolívar Autodefensas de Puerto Boyacá Autodefensas de Santander y Sur del Cesar
Turbó	Antioquia	35	Transshipment of drugs, access to Panama and Atlantic Ocean	Commerce, transport, fishing	Autodefensas Campesinas de Córdoba y Urabá Bloque Bananero Bloque Elmer Cárdenas
Granada	Meta	35	Location of army base	Cattle and agriculture	Bloque Centauros
Tibú	Norte de Santander	34	Bordertown with Venezuela	Oil and gas-producing area	Bloque Catatumbo
Saravena	Arauca	33	Connects Boyacá, Arauca, and Venezuela	Commerce, agriculture, and cattle	Bloque Vencedores de Arauca
Aracataca	Magdalena	33	Connects Magdalena and Cesar	Agriculture and cattle	Autodefensas Campesinas de Córdoba y Urabá Bloque Norte
Sabana de Torres	Santander	33	Connects Bolívar and Cesar	Agriculture, cattle, timber	Autodefensas Campesinas de Santander y Sur del Cesar Bloque Central Bolívar
Puerto Berrío	Antioquia	31	Connects Antioquia and Santander	Agriculture, cattle, mining	Bloque Central Bolívar

Source: Author's tabulation based on Noche y Niebla data.

Appendix 2
Interviewees

Humanitarian and Human Rights Officers

Sibylla Brodzinsky, UN High Commissioner for Refugees
Adriana Buchelli, UN High Commissioner for Refugees
Thomas Ess, International Committee of the Red Cross
Gustavo Gallón, Comisión Colombiana de Juristas
Juanita Gobertus, Office of the High Commissioner for Peace, Colombia
Diana Guiza, De Justicia
Christoph Kleber, International Committee of the Red Cross
Christoph Harnisch, International Committee of the Red Cross
Daniel Helle, International Committee of the Red Cross
Todd Howland, UN Office High Commissioner for Human Rights
Karl Matli, International Committee of the Red Cross
Reto Meister, International Committee of the Red Cross
Carlos Negret, Ombudsman (Defensor del Pueblo) Colombia
Fabio Varoli, United Nations High Commissioner for Refugees

Academics

Sergio Aguayo, Colegio de México
Alejandro Anaya-Muñoz, CIDE

Fernando Cubides, Universidad Nacional de Colombia
Gustavo Duncan, Universidad EAFIT, Medellín.
Jorge Durand, Universidad de Guadalajara
Camilo Echandía, Universidad del Externado
Eric Lair, Universidad del Rosario
Francisco Leal Buitrago, Universidad Nacional
Iván Orozco, Universidad de los Andes
Roman D. Ortiz, director of the Defense and Security Observatory of Latin America
Angelika Rettberg, Universidad de los Andes

Public Servants

Fernando Cepeda, former Colombian ambassador to the United Nations
Juan Carlos Fernández, first secretary, Chilean Embassy Colombia
Pilar Gaitán de Pombo, director of international affairs, General Prosecutors Office, Colombia
Otto Granados, former Mexican ambassador to Chile and governor of the state of Aguascalientes
Gustavo Mohar, director for international affairs, Center for Investigation and National Security
Alejandro Poiré, former secretary of interior, Mexico
Johan Vibe, Norwegian ambassador to Colombia

For security reasons, several sources who requested anonymity are not listed.

Notes

Introduction

1. Juan E. Ugarriza and Nathalie Pabón, *Militares y Guerrillas: La memoria histórica del conflicto armado en Colombia desde los archivos militares 1958-2016*, 2nd ed. (Bogotá: Universidad del Rosario, 2018), 285.
2. Interamerican Court on Human Rights, "Masacre Mapiripán v/s Colombia: Sentencia," September 15, 2005, https://www.corteidh.or.cr/docs/casos/articulos/seriec_134_esp.pdf.
3. *El Tiempo*, "En combates murió autor intelectual de secuestro de avión de Avianca," February 16, 2015, https://www.eltiempo.com/archivo/documento/CMS-15259155.
4. Juan Forero, "Blast at Social Club Struck at Colombia's Elite," *New York Times*, February 9, 2003, https://www.nytimes.com/2003/02/09/world/blast-at-social-club-struck-at-colombia-s-elite.html.
5. By CSSF, this book refers to the ensemble of state entities with responsibilities in the realm of security, including the military—Army, Navy, Air Force—the National Police, and the Intelligence Services. Hereafter, I use the term generically unless concrete reference is made to a specific entity.
6. Terrorism therefore refers to physical attacks. For this book, and in accordance with this definition, violent actions that produce deadly results but offer no proof that armed parties deliberately sought to kill civilians are not considered terrorism. Some examples include attacks against infrastructure, aerial fumigation, and bombardments by the Colombian Armed Force (FAC), shelling with gas pipes (*pipetas*) by the FARC, and the ELN's explosive attacks against oil refineries.
7. Within the sample of 29,672 incidents, 16,912 could not be traced to a clearly identifiable perpetrator. Details on the data set are provided in the methodology section.

8. All parties have used other forms of terrorism not included in the sample, such as torture and disappearance.
9. Concerned about its image, the AUC at one point sought to diminish the number of massacres it perpetrated, opting instead for targeted assassinations, which people in rural areas sarcastically referred to as *massacres in slow motion*. Gustavo Gallón, director, Colombian Commission for Jurists, interview by the author, Bogotá, May 2018.
10. Humanitarian worker, interview and translation by the author, Villavicencio, July 2011.
11. Mauricio Aranguren, *Mi confesión: Carlos Castaño revela sus secretos* (Bogotá: Oveja Negra, 2001), 208.
12. Toward the end of the AUC's existence, paramilitaries briefly engaged in economically motivated kidnappings, a sign of their degradation given that these groups were originally created to combat kidnappers, see Francisco Gutiérrez-Sanín, *Clientelistic Warfare: Paramilitaries and the State in Colombia (1982-2007)* (Oxford: Peter Lang, 2019), 157.
13. See Charles Tilly, "Contentious Repertoires in Great Britain, 1758-1834," *Social Science History* 17, no. 2 (1993): 253-80. For a broader conceptualization, patterns of violence defined as the "relatively stable and recognizable configuration of violence" an armed organization develops over time, see Francisco Gutiérrez-Sanín and Elizabeth Jean Wood, "What Should We Mean by 'Pattern of Political Violence?' Repertoire, Targeting, Frequency, and Technique," *Perspectives on Politics* 15, no. 1 (2017): 21. See also Amalia Hoover Green, *The Commander's Dilemma: Violence and Restraint in Wartime* (Ithaca, NY: Cornell University Press, 2018), 6-9.
14. Benjamin Lessing, "Logic of Violence in Criminal War," *Journal of Conflict Resolution* 59, no. 8 (2015): 486-516.
15. Thérése Pettersson, Shawn Davies, Amber Deniz, Garoun Engström, Nanar Hawach, Stina Högbladh, and Margareta Sollenberg Magnus Öberg, "Organized Violence 1989-2020, with a Special Emphasis on Syria," *Journal of Peace Research* 58, no. 4 (2021): 809-25.
16. Donatella Della Porta, *Social Movements, Political Violence, and the State: A Comparative Analysis of Italy and Germany* (Cambridge: Cambridge University Press, 2006); Walter Laqueur, *The Age of Terrorism* (Boston: Little Brown, 1987); Charles Tilly, "Terror, Terrorism, Terrorists," *Sociological Theory* 22, no. 1 (2004): 5-13.
17. Andreas E. Feldmann and Victor J. Hinojosa, "Terrorism in Colombia: Logic and Sources of a Multidimensional and Ubiquitous Phenomenon," *Terrorism and Political Violence* 21, no. 1 (2009): 42-61; Susanne Martin and Leonard Weinberg. *The Role of Terrorism in Twenty-First-Century Warfare* (Manchester, UK: Manchester University Press, 2017).
18. Stathis N. Kalyvas, *The Logic of Violence in Civil War* (Cambridge: Cambridge University Press, 2006). For an overview of this literature, see Lisa Hultman, "Violence Against Civilians," in *Routledge Handbook of Civil Wars*, ed. Edward Newman, and Karl DeRouen Jr. (London: Routledge, 2014), 289-99.

19. For a detailed discussion of this literature, see chapter 2. See also Leonard Weinberg, Ami Pedahzur, and Sivan Hirsch-Hoeffler, "The Challenges of Conceptualizing Terrorism," *Terrorism and Political Violence* 16, no. 4 (2004): 777–94.
20. Charity Butcher, "Civil War and Terrorism: A Call for Further Theory Building," *Oxford Research Encyclopedia Politics* August (2017): 1–24.
21. On conceptual understanding, see Nicholas Sambanis, "Terrorism and Civil War," in *Terrorism, Economic Development, and Political Openness*, ed. Philip Keefer, and Norman Loyza (Cambridge: Cambridge University Press, 2008), 174–206; Jessica A. Stanton, "Terrorism, Civil War and Insurgency," in *The Oxford Handbook of Terrorism*, ed. Erica Chenoweth, Richard English, Andreas Gofas, Stathis N. Kalyvas (Oxford: Oxford University Press, 2019), 348–65. On strategic uses, see Sara M. T. Polo and Kristian Skrede Gleditsch, "Twisting Arms and Sending Messages: Terrorist Tactics in Civil War," *Journal of Peace Research* 53, no. 6 (2016): 815–29; David Fielding and Anja Shortland, "The Dynamics of Terror During the Peruvian Civil War," *Journal of Peace Research* 49, no. 6 (2012): 847–62; Susanne Martin and Leonard Weinberg, "Terrorism in an Era of Unconventional Warfare," *Terrorism and Political Violence* 28, no. 2 (2016): 236–53.
22. Rawi Abdelal, Yoshiko M. Herrera, Alastair Iain Johnston, and Rose McDermott, "Identity as a Variable," *Perspectives on Politics* 4, no. 4 (2006): 696.
23. Rogers M. Smith, "Identities, Interests, and the Future of Political Science," Perspectives on Politics 2, no. 2 (2004): 301–12.
24. On this general point, see James Fearon, "What Is Identity? (As We Now Use the Word)" (unpublished paper, Department of Political Science Stanford University, 1999), https://web.stanford.edu/group/fearon-research/cgi-bin/wordpress/wp-content/uploads/2013/10/What-is-Identity-as-we-now-use-the-word-.pdf. The use of identity as an explanatory variable in political science has increased significantly over the last decade despite criticism on its purported lack of a commonly accepted definition and difficulties in its operationalization. On criticism about the use of this concept, see Rogers Brubaker and Frederick Cooper, "Beyond 'Identity,'" *Theory and Society* 29, no. 1 (2000): 1–47.
25. Nicholas Greenwood Onuf, *World of Our Making: Rules and Rule in Social Theory and International Relations* (London: Routledge, 2012); Alexander Wendt, "Anarchy Is What States Make of It: The Social Construction of Power Politics," *International Organization* 46, no. 2 (1992): 391–425.
26. Martha Finnemore, *National Interests in International Society* (Ithaca, NY: Cornell University Press, 1996).
27. Emmanuel Adler, "Seizing the Middle Ground: Constructivism in World Politics," *European Journal of International Relations* 3, no. 3 (2015): 319–63; Richard Price and Christian Reus-Smit, "Dangerous Liaisons? Critical International Theory and Constructivism," *European Journal of International Relations* 4, no. 3 (1998): 259–94.
28. See Bernd Bucher and Ursula Jasper, "Revisiting 'Identity' in International Relations: From Identity as Substance to Identifications in Action," *European Journal of International Relations* 23, no. 2 (2016): 391–415; Ted Hopf, "The Promise of

Constructivism in International Relations Theory," *International Security* 23, no. 1 (1998): 171–200. For a critical view rejecting the use of identity as a variable, see Felix Berenskoetter, "Identity in International Relations," in *The International Studies Encyclopedia*, ed. Robert A. Denmark, and Renée Marlin-Bennett (Oxford University Press, 2017), 3594–611.

29. Francesco N. Moro, "Organizing Emotions and Ideology in Collective Armed Mobilization," *PS: Political Science & Politics* 50, no. 4 (2017): 944–47.
30. Francisco Gutiérrez-Sanín and Elisabeth Jean Wood, "Ideology in Civil War: Instrumental Adoption and Beyond," *Journal of Peace Research* 51, no. 2 (2014): 214.
31. Ricardo Vargas, "State and *Espirit* Mafioso and Armed Conflict in Colombia," in *Politics in the Andes: Identity, Politics, Reform*, ed. Jo Marie Burt, and Phillip Mauceri (Pittsburgh, PA: University of Pittsburgh Press, 2004), 107–25.
32. Vadim Volkov, *Violent Entrepreneurs: The Use of Force in the Making of Russian Capitalism* (Ithaca, NY: Cornell University Press, 2002); Federico Varese, "What Is Organized Crime," in *Redefining Organised Crime: A Challenge for the European Union*, ed. Stefania Carnevale, Serena Forlati, and Orsetta Giolo (Oxford: Hart Publishing, 2017), 27–53; Feldmann and Lopez, *Repertoires of Terrorism*; Williams, *Terrorism Debate*.
33. Klaus Schlichte, *In the Shadow of Violence: The Politics of Armed Groups* (Frankfurt-am-Main: Campus Verlag, 2009).
34. Peter G. Thompson, *Armed Groups The 21st Century Threat* (Boulder, CO: Rowman Littlefield, 2014).
35. Jeffrey T. Checkel, "Socialization and Violence: Introduction and Framework," *Journal of Peace Research* 54, no. 5 (2017): 592.
36. Elisabeth Jean Wood, "The Social Processes of Civil War: The Wartime Transformation of Social Networks," *Annual Review of Political Science* 11, no. 1 (2008): 546.
37. Green, *Commanders Dilemma*.
38. On breakdowns in discipline, Macartan N. Humphreys and Jeremy M. Weinstein, "Handling and Manhandling Civilians in Civil War," *American Political Science Review* 100, no. 3 (2006): 429–47; on irrationality, Kieran Mitton, "Irrational Actors and the Process of Brutalisation: Understanding Atrocity in the Sierra Leonean Conflict (1991–2002)," *Civil Wars* 14, no. 1 (2012): 104–22.
39. Kalliopi Koufa, *Terrorism and Human Rights: Progress Report*, E/CN.4/Sub.2/2001/31 (UN Commission on Human Rights, Economic and Social Council, June 27, 2001), 8.
40. Michael Stohl, *The Politics of Terrorism* (New York: Marcel Dekker, 1988).
41. Attacks on military targets can also harm civilians, who are often euphemistically referred as collateral damage. Although reprehensible, these actions do not amount to terrorism because no deliberate intent to harm civilians is present.
42. See Weinberg, Pedahzur, and Hirsch-Hoeffler, "Challenges of Conceptualizing Terrorism."
43. Walter Laqueur, "Interpretations of Terror: Facts, Fiction and Political Science," *Journal of Contemporary History* 12, no. 1 (1977): 1–42.

44. George Lopez, "Terrorism in Latin America," in *The Politics of Terrorism*, ed. Michael Stohl (New York: Marcel Dekker, 1988), 497–524.
45. Alex P. Schmid, Albert Jongman, and Michael Stohl, eds., *Political Terrorism: A New Guide to Actors, Authors, Concepts, Data Bases, Theories, and Literature* (New Brunswick, NJ: Transaction Publishers, 1988), 28. For an excellent account on definitional debates of terrorism, see Alex P. Schmid, "The Definition of Terrorism," in *The Routledge Handbook of Terrorism Research*, ed. Alex P. Schmid (London: Routledge, 2011), 39–98.
46. Bruce Hoffman, *Inside Terrorism* (New York: Columbia University Press, 2006).
47. Bradley McAllister and Alex Schmid, "Theories of Terrorism," in *The Routledge Handbook of Terrorism Research*, ed. Alex P. Schmid (London: Routledge, 2011), 203. For a discussion on state terror as a concept see Michael Stohl, "The State as Terrorist: Insights and Implications," *Democracy and Security* 2, no. 1 (2006): 1–25; David Claridge, "State Terrorism? Applying a Definitional Model," *Terrorism and Political Violence* 8, no. 3 (1996): 47–63.
48. Christopher Mitchell, George Lopez, David Carleton, and Michael Stohl, "State Terrorism: Issues of Concept and Measurement," in *Government Violence and Repression: An Agenda for Research*, ed. Michael Stohl and George Lopez (New York: Greenwood Press, 1986), 5.
49. Michael Walzer, "Five Questions About Terrorism," *Dissent* 49, no. 1 (2002): 5.
50. Hoffman, *Inside Terrorism*, 253–58.
51. Erica Chenoweth, "Terrorism and Democracy," *Annual Review of Political Science* 16, no. 1 (2013): 355–78.
52. Charles Tilly, "State Incited Violence, 1900–1999," in *Political Power and Social Theory*, ed. Diane E. Davis and Howard Kimeldorf (Greenwich, CT: JAI Press, 1995), 164.
53. Hoffman, *Inside Terrorism*, 16.
54. I thank an anonymous reviewer for calling my attention to this important theoretical point.
55. Jessica A. Stanton, "Terrorism in the Context of Civil War," *Journal of Politics* 75, no. 4 (2013): 1009–22.
56. See Sarah V. Mardsen and Alex P. Schmid, "Typologies of Terrorism and Political Violence," in *The Routledge Handbook of Terrorism Research*, ed. Alex P. Schmid (London: Routledge, 2011), 158–200.
57. Gregory Raymond, "The Evolving Strategies of Political Terrorism," in *The New Global Terrorism: Characteristics, Causes and Control*, ed. Charles W. Kegley Jr. (Upper Saddle River, NJ: Prentice Hall, 2003), 71–83.
58. Thomas Thornton, "Terror as a Weapon of Political Agitation," in *Internal War*, ed. Harry Eckstein (New York: Free Press, 1964), 71–99.
59. Martha Crenshaw, "The Causes of Terrorism." *Comparative Politics* 13, no. 4 (1981): 379–99; Robert Pape, "The Strategic Logic of Suicide Terrorism," *American Political Science Review* 97, no. 3 (2003): 343–61.

60. Groups also pursue strategies seeking to guarantee the organization's survival (e.g., obtaining resources, preserving cohesion, and developing a recruitment and support system). See Raymond, "Evolving Strategies."
61. For an interesting account on the logic behind bombings, see Michael J. Boyle, "Weapon of Choice: Terrorist Bombings in Armed Conflict," *Studies in Conflict & Terrorism* 45, no. 9 (2022): 778–98. The author asserts that groups that resort to this tactic are those that transitioned into capable fighting armies but lacked popular support.
62. Ariel Merari, "Terrorism as a Strategy of Insurgency," *Terrorism and Political Violence* 5, no. 4 (1993): 213–51.
63. Carlos Marighella, *Minimanual of Urban Guerrilla* (Chapel Hill: North Carolina University Press Documentary Publications, 1985).
64. Timothy Wickham-Crowley, "Terror and Guerrilla Warfare in Latin America 1956–1970," *Comparative Studies in Society and History* 32, no. 2 (1990): 201–37; Andreas E. Feldmann, "A Shift in the Paradigm of Violence: Non-Governmental Terrorism in Latin America Since the End of the Cold War," *Revista de Ciencia Política* 25, no. 2 (2005): 3–35.
65. Walzer, "Five Questions," 5.
66. See, for example, Patricia Weiss Fagen, "Repression and State Security," in *Fear at the Edge: State Terror and Resistance in Latin America*, ed. Juan Corradi, Patricia Weiss Fagen, and Manuel Antonio Garretón (Berkeley: University of California Press, 1992), 39–89.
67. On dirty wars, see David Pion Berlin, *The Ideology of State Terror: Economic Doctrine and Political Repression in Argentina and Peru* (Boulder, CO: Lynne Rienner, 1989); on civil wars and India's counterinsurgency campaign against the Naxalites as a case in point, see Prem Mahadevan, "The Maoist Insurgency in India: Between Crime and Revolution," *Small Wars & Insurgencies* 23, no. 2 (2012): 203–20; on monopoly of force, see Bruce B. Campbell, "Death Squads: Definition, Problems and Historical Context," in *Death Squads in Global Perspective: Murder with Deniability*, ed. Bruce B. Campbell and Arthur D. Brenner (New York: St Martin Press, 2000), 1–26.
68. Kalyvas, *The Logic*.
69. Stathis N. Kalyvas and Matthew Kocher, "How Free Is Free Riding in Civil Wars? Violence, Insurgency, and the Collection Action Problem," *World Politics* 59, no. 2 (2007): 177–216. For an excellent account of this logic in the case of urban warfare in Colombia, see Gonzalo Vargas, "Urban Irregular Warfare and Violence Against Civilians: Evidence from a Colombian City," *Terrorism and Political Violence* 21, no. 1 (2009): 110–32.
70. For an alternative explanation for parties' use of territorial forms of terrorism, arguing that in addition to controlling logistics and the flow of information, territorial terrorism facilitates extortion, see Gustavo Duncan, Santiago Sosa, and José Antonio Fortou, "Terrorism and Organized Crime in Colombia," in *The Nexus Between Organized Crime and Terrorism*, ed. Letizia Paoli, Cyrille Fijnaut, and Jan Wouters (Cheltenham, UK: Edward Elgar, 2022), 412–32.

71. Stathis N. Kalyvas, "Wanton and Senseless: The Logic of Massacres in Algeria," *Rationality and Society* 11, no. 3 (1999): 243–85; Martha Crenshaw, *Revolutionary Terrorism: The FLN in Algeria 1954-1962* (Stanford, CA: Hoover Institution Press, 1978); Alex Bellamy, *Massacres and Morality: Mass Atrocities in an Age of Civilian Immunity* (Oxford: Oxford University Press, 2012).
72. I thank Angélica Durán-Martínez for raising this distinction.
73. Danielle Gilbert argues that the ELN and the FARC use kidnappings for ransom to enforce protection rackets that serve as their main source of funding. See Gilbert, "The Logic of Kidnapping in Civil War: Evidence from Colombia," *American Political Science Review* 116, no. 4 (2022): 1226–41. As the empirical chapters on Colombian guerrillas show, although abductions were a critical source of revenue, they were also a signature tactic of revolutionary groups' attempts to destabilize and undermine the state's legitimacy through fear.
74. Summary executions, the most efficient and operationally simple terrorist practice, defies easy categorization (falling under insurgent, territorial, and pro-regime terrorism). It accounts for 63 percent (8,071 acts) of terrorist attacks in this sample and was used extensively by all groups; the state and paramilitaries were more prone to execution than the ELN and the FARC, but both guerrilla groups systematically practiced it as well.
75. Francisco Gutiérrez-Sanín, "Telling the Difference: Guerrillas and Paramilitaries in the Colombian War," *Politics & Society* 36, no. 1 (2008): 3–34; Jenny Pearce, *Colombia Inside the Labyrinth* (Nottingham, UK: Russell Press, 1990).
76. Mario Aguilera, "ELN: Entre las armas y la política." in *Nuestra guerra sin nombre: Transformaciones del Conflicto en Colombia*, ed. Francisco Gutiérrez-Sanín, María Emma Willis, and Gonzalo Sánchez (Bogotá: IEPRI/Norma, 2006), 222.
77. Gustavo Duncan, *Los señores de la guerra: De paramilitares, mafiosos y autodefensas en Colombia* (Bogotá: Planeta, 2006).
78. In Colombia, this tradition is known as *violentología*.
79. Eric Lair, "El terror, recurso estratégico de los actores armados: Reflexiones en torno al conflicto colombiano," *Análisis Político* 37 (May/August 1999): 60–72; Román D. Ortiz, "Insurgent Strategies in the Post-Cold War: The Case of the Revolutionary Armed Forces of Colombia," *Studies in Conflict & Terrorism* 25, no. 2 (2002): 127–43; Francisco Gutiérrez-Sanín, "Internal Conflict, Terrorism and Crime in Colombia," *Journal of International Development* 18, no. 1 (2006): 137–50; Andreas E. Feldmann, "Revolutionary Terror in the Colombian Civil War," *Studies in Conflict & Terrorism* 41, no. 10 (2018): 35–52.
80. A case study is defined as "a detailed examination of an aspect of a historical episode to develop or test historical explanations that may be generalizable to other events." Alexander George and Andrew Bennett, *Case Studies, and Theory Development in the Social Sciences* (Cambridge, MA: MIT Press, 2005), 5.
81. Commission for the Clarification of Truth, Coexistance and Non-Repetition, 2022, https://www.comisiondelaverdad.co.

82. The Global Terrorism Data Base (GTD) reports 9,045 terrorist incidents for Colombia (1970–2020), the fourth highest in the world for that period behind Afghanistan, India, and Iraq. See National Consortium for the Study of Terrorism and Responses to Terrorism Global Terrorism, "Colombia," May 18, 2023, https://www.start.umd.edu/gtd/search/Results.aspx?chart=overtime&search=Colombia

83. The importance of chronicling human rights abuses, even in the darkest moments of violence and repression, is powerfully articulated by Chilean human rights lawyer José Zalaquett. See Comisión Nacional de Verdad y Reconciliación, "Informe Final," tomo 1, 1991," 1–10, https://bibliotecadigital.indh.cl/bitstream/handle/123456789/170/tomo1.pdf.

84. Database created arguable represents an undercount linked to difficulties of registering the enormous number of incidents in the vast Colombian territory with a limited budget and due to the fear of reporting on the part of victims and witnesses.

85. On this point, see Alex P. Schmid and Neil G. Bowie, "Data Bases on Terrorism," in *The Routledge Handbook of Terrorism Research*, ed. Alex P. Schmid (London: Routledge, 2011), 295–340.

86. Comisión para el Esclarecimiento, "Hallazgos y Recomendaciones."

87. Andreas E. Feldmann, "Colombia's Polarization Peace Efforts," in *Divided Democracy: The Global Challenge of Political Polarizations*, ed. Tom Carothers and Andrew O'Donohue (Washington, DC: Brookings Institution Press, 2019), 153–74.

88. Jack Levy, "Case Studies: Types, Designs, and Logics of Inference," *Conflict Management and Peace Studies*, 25, no. 1 (2008): 1–18.

89. On the methodological difficulties of studying the use of violence by criminal organizations, see Angélica Durán-Martínez, *The Politics of Drug Violence: Criminals, Cops and Politicians in Colombia and Mexico* (Oxford: Oxford University Press, 2018), 24–26; Rebecca V. Bell-Martin and Jerome F. Marston Jr., "Confronting Selection Bias: The Normative and Empirical Risks of Data Collection in Violent Contexts," *Geopolitics* 26, no. 1 (2019): 159–92.

90. Three fabulous examples are Durán-Martínez, *The Politics*; Ana Arjona, *Rebelocracy: Social Order in the Colombian Civil War* (New York: Cambridge University Press, 2016); and Sarah Z. Daly, *Organized Violence After Civil War: The Geography of Recruitment in Latin America* (Cambridge: Cambridge University Press, 2016).

91. Sources are incorporated in the text and identified whenever possible. A list of the interviewees is provided in the appendix.

92. On this process, see Centro Nacional, "Iniciativas de Memoria," 2021, https://centrodememoriahistorica.gov.co/iniciativas-de-memoria.

93. This material might have some shortcomings, as in exchange for confessing to their acts, perpetrators would receive lighter sentences from the tribunal, which could have influenced their accounts. See Gutiérrez-Sanín, *Clientelistic*, 2–5.

94. A massacre is defined as a face-to-face killing of at least four civilians in a single incident (Kalyvas "Wanton and Senseless," 247). Summary executions refer to a face-to-face encounter in which fewer than four civilians are killed. Abductions

are defined as any incident where someone is taken without consent. These include people abducted and held for ransom or used as bargaining chips for prisoner exchanges. Victims are considered abducted whether they are released or perish in custody. Cases in which victims are presumed dead—forcefully taken and never heard from again—are not included. Illicit bombings are defined as incidents where parties deliberately use explosives devices that cause civilian casualties.
95. Noche y Niebla is the most comprehensive, rigorous, and evenhanded database on political violence in Colombia. Organizations including the UN High Commissioner on Human Rights, Human Rights Watch, Amnesty International, and the Inter-American Commission and Court on Human Rights have relied extensively on it over the years.
96. Political violence is defined as "violence exercised as a means of political-social struggle aimed at maintaining, modifying, substituting, or destroying a particular model of state or society, or to destroy or repress a human group, organized or not, with a defined identity within society as a result of its social, political, labor, ethnic, racial, religious or ideological allegiance" (translation by the author). Noche y Niebla classifies political violence according to four criteria: human rights violations (life, integrity, liberty); violations of international humanitarian law; political violence of a more general nature (i.e., political persecution, social intolerance); and hostilities among the warring parties. See CINEP, "Banco de Datos," May 18, 2023, https://www.nocheyniebla.org.
97. In 1995 and 1996, the groups briefly merged operations, and CINEP and Justicia y Paz jointly published Noche y Niebla. CINEP has continued to publish Noche y Niebla since that time. The author thanks William Rosso Alvarez and the staff at CINEP for generously granting access to their archives and allowing us to use the Justicia y Paz data.
98. John Gerring, *Case Study Research Principles and Practices* (Cambridge: Cambridge University Press, 2007).

1. Theorizing Armed Parties' Repertoires of Terrorism During Civil Wars

1. Jessica A. Stanton, "Terrorism, Civil War and Insurgency," in *The Oxford Handbook of Terrorism*, ed. Erica Chenoweth, Richard English, Andreas Gofas, and Stathis N. Kalyvas (Oxford: Oxford University Press, 2019), 348–65.
2. This important research area investigates several aspects of this phenomenon, including the civil war's onset, duration, termination, and civilian targeting.
3. Exceptions include the classic analysis of terrorism in the Algerian War, see Martha Crenshaw, *Revolutionary Terrorism: The FLN in Algeria 1954-1962* (Stanford, CA: Hoover Institution, 1978). See also Andreas E. Feldmann and Victor J. Hinojosa, "Terrorism in Colombia: Logic and Sources of a Multidimensional and Ubiquitous

Phenomenon," *Terrorism and Political Violence* 21, no. 1 (2009): 42–61; Susanne Martin and Leonard Weinberg, "Terrorism in an Era of Unconventional Warfare," *Terrorism and Political Violence* 28, no. 2 (2016): 236–53.
4. Nicholas Sambanis, "Terrorism and Civil War," in *Terrorism, Economic Development, and Political Openness*, ed. Philip Keefer and Norman Loyza (Cambridge: Cambridge University Press, 2008), 174–206.
5. David Fielding and Anja Shortland, "The Dynamics of Terror During the Peruvian Civil War," *Journal of Peace Research* 49, no. 6 (2012): 847–62.
6. Stathis N. Kalyvas, "The Landscape of Political Violence," in Chenoweth et al., *The Oxford Handbook of Terrorism*, 11–33.
7. Carl Von Clausewitz, *On War* (Princeton, NJ: Princeton University Press, 1976).
8. Lotta Themnér and Peter Wallensteen, "Armed Conflict 1946–2012," *Journal of Peace Research* 50, no. 4 (2013): 509–21.
9. Conceptualizations of terrorism vary as to whether the crucial attribute is audience, target, frequency, or purpose. Jeff Goodwin, "A Theory of Categorical Terrorism," *Social Forces* 84, no. 4 (2006): 2027–46.
10. Eugen Victor Walter, *Terror and Resistance* (Oxford: Oxford University Press, 1969).
11. Hedley Bull, *The Anarchical Society* (New York: Columbia University Press, 1984).
12. Ana Arjona explains that various types of orders emerge in the context of civil war because of two factors: armed groups' time horizon and the quality and density of preexisting local institutions. Ana Arjona, *Rebelocracy: Social Order in the Colombian Civil War* (New York: Cambridge University Press, 2016), 2.
13. Paul Staniland, *Networks of Rebellion: Explaining Insurgent Cohesion and Collapse* (Ithaca, NY: Cornell University Press, 2013).
14. Adam Roberts, "The Civilian in Modern War," in *The Changing Character of War*, ed. Hew Strachan and Sibylle Scheipers (Oxford: Oxford University Press, 2011), 357–81.
15. François Bugnion, *The International Committee of the Red Cross, and the Protection of War Victims* (Oxford: MacMillan for the International Committee of the Red Cross, 2003).
16. Marco Sassòli, *International Humanitarian Law: Rules, Controversies, and Solutions to Problems Arising in Warfare* (Cheltenham, UK: Edward Elgar, 2019).
17. Theodor Meron, *The Humanization of International Law* (Leiden: Brill Nihjoff, 2006).
18. Although IHL does not provide a specific definition of terrorism, it clearly delineates (and prohibits) acts or threats aimed at spreading fear in the civilian population in the context of armed conflicts. These acts include collective penalties, indiscriminate attacks, attacks on civilians and civilian objects, attacks on works and installations containing dangerous forces, taking hostages, and the murder of persons who are not (or are no longer) taking part in hostilities, see Sassòli, *International Humanitarian Law*.
19. Ian Beckett, *Encyclopedia of Guerrilla Warfare* (Santa Barbara, CA: ABC-CLIO, 1999).
20. Nicholas Sambanis, "What Is Civil War? Conceptual and Empirical Complexities of an Operational Definition," *Journal of Conflict Resolution* 48, no. 6 (2004): 814–58.
21. Clausewitz, *On War*.

22. Jeff Goodwin, "The Causes of Terrorism," in Chenoweth et al., *The Oxford Handbook of Terrorism*, 253–67.
23. Alex P. Schmid and Janny de Graaf, *Violence as Communication: Insurgent Terrorism and the Western News Media* (London: Sage, 1982).
24. Charles Tilly, "Terror, Terrorism, Terrorists," *Sociological Theory* 22, no. 1 (2004): 5–13.
25. Richard Clutterback, *Terrorism and Guerrilla Warfare* (London: Routledge, 1990).
26. Stathis N. Kalyvas, "The Landscape of Political Violence," in Chenoweth et al., *The Oxford Handbook of Terrorism*, 24.
27. On this point see, Charity Butcher, "Civil War and Terrorism: A Call for Further Theory Building," *Oxford Research Encyclopedia Politics*, August 22, 2017, https://doi.org/10.1093/acrefore/9780190228637.013.520.
28. Luis de la Calle and Ignacio Sánchez-Cuenca, "What We Talk About When We Talk About Terrorism," *Politics & Society* 39, no. 3 (2011): 451–72. For criticism of this view, see Erica Chenoweth and Pauline E. Moore, *The Politics of Terror* (Oxford: Oxford University Press, 2018), 30.
29. Jessica A. Stanton, *Violence and Restraint in Civil War: Civilian Targeting in the Shadow of International Law* (Cambridge: Cambridge University Press, 2016); Sara M. T. Polo and Kristian Skrede Gleditsch, "Twisting Arms and Sending Messages: Terrorist Tactics in Civil War," *Journal of Peace Research* 53, no. 6 (2016): 815–29.
30. Erica Chenoweth, "Democratic Competition and Terrorist Activity," *Journal of Politics* 71, no. 1 (2010), 16n1.
31. For an alternative view looking at the rhetorical use and genealogy of the term terrorism, see Mathias Thaler, *Naming Violence: A Critical Theory of Genocide, Torture, and Terrorism* (New York: Columbia University Press, 2018). His examination reveals how existing notions of terrorism are influenced by what he calls liberal moralism, which, he states, too often fail to acknowledge how the semantics of the term are imbued in power-based political considerations. Such notions, he asserts, permeate our perceptions of what does or does not constitute an act of terrorism.
32. Eugen Victor Walter, *Terror and Resistance* (Oxford: Oxford University Press, 1969).
33. Jessica A. Stanton, "Terrorism in the Context of Civil War," *Journal of Politics* 75, no. 4 (2013): 1009–22.
34. See also Luis de la Calle and Ignacio Sánchez-Cuenca, "Rebels Without a Territory: An Analysis of Nonterritorial Conflicts in the World, 1970–1997," *Journal of Conflict Resolution* 56, no. 4 (2012): 580–603.
35. David Keen, *The Economic Functions of Violence in Civil Wars*, Adelphi Paper 38 no. 320 (Oxford: Oxford University Press for the International Institute for Strategic Studies, 1996).
36. Benjamin Valentino, *Final Solutions, Mass Killings and Genocide in the Twentieth Century* (Ithaca, NY: Cornell University Press, 2004).
37. Hugo Slim, "Why Protect Civilians? Innocence, Immunity and Enmity in War," *International Affairs* 79, no. 3 (2003): 481–503.

1. THEORIZING REPERTOIRES OF TERRORISM DURING CIVIL WARS

38. A potential critique to the argument about a difference between terrorism and other types of civilian targeting is that it amounts to *conceptual stretching* (i.e., a distortion that occurs when a concept does not match a new case). See Giovanni Sartori, "Concept Misformation in Comparative Politics," *American Political Science Review* 64, no. 4 (1970): 1033–53. To the extent that the purpose and logic of violence is different in various cases, the distinction is not artificial. I thank Ana Arjona for challenging me on this matter.
39. Francisco Gutiérrez-Sanín and Elisabeth Jean Wood, "What Should We Mean by 'Pattern of Political Violence?' Repertoire, Targeting, Frequency, and Technique," *Perspectives on Politics* 15, no. 1 (2017): 20–41.
40. For an overview of this vast literature, see Laia Balcells and Jessica A. Stanton, "Violence Against Civilians During Armed Conflict: Moving Beyond the Macro- and Micro-Level Divide," *Annual Review of Political Science* 24, no. 1 (2021): 45–69.
41. Stathis N. Kalyvas, *"The Logic of Violence in Civil War* (Cambridge: Cambridge University Press, 2006). On ethnic conflict, see Ted Robert Gurr, *Minorities at Risk: A Global View of Ethnopolitical Conflicts* (Washington, DC: United States Institute of Peace Press, 2003). Mary Kaldor argues that civilian targeting stems from changes in armed parties' behavior (i.e., recruitment, financing, and war methods) following the end of the Cold War, which led to a decline in ideological motivations and a rise in criminal behavior. Mary Kaldor, *New and Old Wars* (Stanford, CA: Stanford University Press, 2001).
42. Other arguments regarding civilian targeting based on a military logic include the following seven contentions. First, weaker parties compensate military weakness. See Kristine Eck and Lisa Hultman, "One-Sided Violence Against Civilians in War: Insights from New Fatality Data," *Journal of Peace Research* 44, no. 2 (2007): 233–46. Second, parties seek to extract resources in areas where they dispute control over civilians. See Claire Metelits, *Inside Insurgency: Violence, Civilians and Revolutionary Group Behavior* (New York: New York University Press, 2010). Third, states use the tactic as a coercive mechanism to weaken insurgencies. See Christopher M. Sullivan, "Undermining Resistance: Mobilization, Repression, and the Enforcement of Political Order," *Journal of Conflict Resolution* 60, no. 7 (2015): 1163–90. Fourth, parties use it to induce policy changes by targeting a rival's constituency. See Hanne Fjelde and Lisa Hultman, "Weakening the Enemy: A Disaggregated Study of Violence Against Civilians in Africa," *Journal of Conflict Resolution* 58, no. 7 (2013): 230–57. Fifth, parties use it to improve their standing in a potential peace negotiation. See Reed M. Wood and Jacob D. Kathman, "Too Much of a Bad Thing? Civilian Victimization and Intrastate Conflicts," *British Journal of Political Science* 44, no. 3 (2014): 685–706. Sixth, it decreases the cost of the conflict. See Michael Weintraub, Juan F. Vargas, and Thomas E. Flores, "Vote Choice and Legacies of Violence: Evidence from the 2014 Colombian Presidential Elections," *Research and Politics* 2, no. 2 (2015): 1–8. Seventh, it amounts to tit-for-tat dynamics among warring parties. See David Fielding and Anja Shortland, "The Dynamics of Terror During the Peruvian Civil War," *Journal of Peace Research* 49, no. 6 (2012): 847–62.

43. On this criticism, see Daniel Bultmann, "The Social Structure of Armed Groups. Reproduction and Change During and After Conflict," *Small Wars & Insurgencies* 29, no. 4 (2018): 607–28.
44. Comisión de la Verdad y Reconciliación, "Reporte Final," 2004, https://www.cverdad.org.pe/ifinal.
45. Benjamin Lessing, "Logic of Violence in Criminal War," *Journal of Conflict Resolution* 59, no. 8 (2015): 486–516.
46. Andreas E. Feldmann and Marc Lopez, "Repertoires of Terrorism in Mexico's Criminal War," *Perspectives on Terrorism* 16, no. 2 (2022): 4–13.
47. On enforcement mechanisms, Idean Salehyan, David Siroky, and Reed M. Wood, "External Rebel Sponsorship and Civilian Abuse: A Principal-Agent Analysis of Wartime Atrocities," *International Organization* 68, no. 3 (2014): 633–61; on recruitment mechanisms, Daly, *Organized Violence*; on personal gain or revenge, Devorah Manekin, "Violence Against Civilians in the Second Intifada: The Moderating Effect of Armed Group Structure on Opportunistic Violence," *Comparative Political Studies* 46, no. 10 (2013): 1273–300.
48. On this criticism, see Francisco Gutiérrez-Sanín and Elisabeth Jean Wood, "Ideology in Civil War: Instrumental Adoption and Beyond," *Journal of Peace Research* 51, no. 2 (2014): 213–26.
49. Jeremy M. Weinstein, *Inside Rebellion: The Politics of Insurgent Violence* (Cambridge: Cambridge University Press, 2007).
50. Arjona, *Rebelocracy*.
51. Laia Balcells, "Rivalry and Revenge: Violence Against Civilians in Civil War," *International Studies Quarterly* 54 no. 2 (2010): 291–313.
52. Jessica A. Stanton, *Violence and Restraint in Civil War: Civilian Targeting in the Shadow of International Law* (Cambridge: Cambridge University Press, 2016).
53. Hyeran Jo, *Compliant Rebels: Rebel Groups and International Law in World Politics* (Cambridge: Cambridge University Press, 2015)
54. Amalia Hoover Green, *The Commander's Dilemma: Violence and Restraint in Wartime* (Ithaca, NY: Cornell University Press, 2018).
55. C. J. M. Drake, "The Role of Ideology in Terrorists' Target Selection," *Terrorism and Political Violence* 10, no. 2 (1998): 53–85.
56. Donatella Della Porta, *Social Movements, Political Violence, and the State: A Comparative Analysis of Italy and Germany* (Cambridge: Cambridge University Press, 2006).
57. Ehud Sprinzak, "Right-wing Terrorism in a Comparative Perspective: The Case of Split Delegitimization," *Terrorism and Political Violence* 7, no. 1 (1995): 17–43.
58. George Lopez, "National Security Ideology as an Impetus to State Violence and State Terror," in *Government Violence and Repression: An Agenda for Research*, ed. Michael Stohl and George Lopez (Westport, CT: Praeger, 1986), 73–95.
59. David C. Rapoport, *Waves of Global Terrorism: From 1879 to the Present* (New York: Columbia University Press).
60. Timothy Wickham-Crowley, "Terror and Guerrilla Warfare in Latin America 1956–1970," *Comparative Studies in Society and History* 32, no. 2 (1990): 201–37;

Andreas E. Feldmann, "A Shift in the Paradigm of Violence: Non-Governmental Terrorism in Latin America Since the End of the Cold War," *Revista de Ciencia Política* 25, no. 2 (2005): 3–35.

61. David A. Lake, "Rational Extremism: Understanding Terrorism in the Twenty-First Century," *Dialogue IO* 1, no. 1 (2002): 15–28; Walter Enders and Todd Sandler, *The Political Economy of Terrorism* (Cambridge: Cambridge University Press, 2006).

62. As a strategy, Schmid and De Graff, *Violence as Communication*; Andrew Kydd, and Barbara Walter, "The Strategies of Terrorism," *International Security* 31, no. 1 (2006): 49–80. On the state's energy, Ekaterina Stepanova, *Terrorism in Asymmetrical Conflict: Ideological and Structural Aspects* (Oxford: Oxford University Press, 2008). On compensating, Ethan Bueno de Mesquita, "Conciliation, Counterterrorism, and Patterns of Terrorist Violence," *International Organization* 59, no. 1 (2005): 145–76.

63. Charles Tilly, "Terror, Terrorism, Terrorists," *Sociological Theory* 22, no. 1 (2004): 5–13.

64. Crenshaw, *Revolutionary Terrorism*.

65. Robert Pape, "The Strategic Logic of Suicide Terrorism," *American Political Science Review* 97, no. 3 (2003): 343–46; Mia Bloom, *Bombshell: Women and Terrorism* (Philadelphia: University of Pennsylvania Press, 2011).

66. This definition is an adaptation of the one found in the literature on organizational behavior. See David Whetten, "Albert and Whetten Revisited Strengthening the Concept of Organizational Identity," *Journal of Management Inquiry* 15, no. 3 (2006): 220.

67. David A. Snow and Scott Byrd, "Identities, Interests, and the Future of Political Science," *Perspectives on Politics* 2, no. 2 (2004): 301–12.

68. Rawi Abdelal, Yoshiko M. Herrera, Alastair Iain Johnston, and Rose McDermott, "Identity as a Variable," *Perspectives on Politics* 4, no. 4 (2006): 695–711.

69. Abdelal et al., "Identity," 695–96.

70. On this point see, Roger M. Smith, "Identities, Interests, and the Future of Political Science," *Perspectives on Politics* 2, no. 2 (2004): 301–12.

71. James Fearon, "What Is Identity? (As We Now Use the Word)" (unpublished paper, Stanford University, 1999), 26, https://web.stanford.edu/group/fearon-research/cgi-bin/wordpress/wp-content/uploads/2013/10/What-is-Identity-as-we-now-use-the-word-.pdf. The use of identity as an explanatory variable in political science has gained significant ground in the last decade despite criticism around its purported lack of a commonly accepted definition and difficulties in its operationalization, see Rogers Brubaker and Frederick Cooper, "Beyond 'Identity,'" *Theory and Society* 29, no. 1 (2000): 1–47.

72. John Ruggie, "What Makes the World Hang Together? Neo-utiliarianism and the Social Constructivist Challenge," *International Organization* 54, no. 4 (1998): 855–85.

73. Martha Finnemore, *National Interests in International Society* (Ithaca, NY: Cornell University Press, 1996).

74. Emmanuel Adler, "Seizing the Middle Ground: Constructivism in World Politics," *European Journal of International Relations* 3, no. 3 (2015): 319–63.

75. Richard Price and Christian Reus-Smit, "Dangerous Liaisons? Critical International Theory and Constructivism," *European Journal of International Relations* 4, no. 3 (1998): 259–94.
76. Bernd Bucher and Ursula Jasper, "Revisiting 'Identity' in International Relations: From Identity as Substance to Identifications in Action," *European Journal of International Relations* 23, no. 2 (2016): 392. For a critical view rejecting the use of identity as a variable, see Felix Berenskoetter, "Identity in International Relations," in *The International Studies Encyclopedia*, ed. Robert A. Denmark and Renée Marlin-Bennett (Oxford: Oxford University Press, 2017), 3594–611.
77. See Donald Horowitz, *Ethnic Groups in Conflict* (Los Angeles: University of California Press, 2000).
78. Elisabeth Jean Wood, *Insurgent Collective Action, and Civil War in El Salvador* (Cambridge: Cambridge University Press, 2003).
79. Elisabeth Jean Wood, "The Social Processes of Civil War: The Wartime Transformation of Social Networks," *Annual Review of Political Science* 11, no. 1 (2008): 539–61.
80. Ann Fujii Lee, *Killing Neighbors: Webs of Violence in Rwanda* (Ithaca, NY: Cornell University Press, 2009), 104.
81. Anastasia Shesterinina, *Mobilizing in Uncertainty: Collective Identities and War in Abkhazia* (Ithaca, NY: Cornell University Press, 2021).
82. Work on organizational behavior in business also discusses corporate identity. For a good overview, see Anna Blombäck and Olof Brunninge, "Corporate Identity Manifested Through Historical References," *Corporate Communications: An International Journal* 14, no. 4 (2009): 404–19.
83. On identity formation, see Alexander Wendt, "Collective Identity Formation and the International State," *American Political Science Review* 88, no. 2 (1994): 384–96.
84. Klaus Schlichte, "With the State Against the State. The Formation of Armed Groups," *Contemporary Security Policy* 30, no. 2 (2009): 246–64.
85. Paul Staniland, *Networks of Rebellion: Explaining Insurgent Cohesion and Collapse* (Ithaca, NY: Cornell University Press, 2013).
86. For a seminal constructivist articulation of how this process works in the international system, see Alexander Wendt's treatment of the agent-structure problem in which he compellingly argues that agents and structure are mutually implicated and interrelated. Alexander Wendt, "The Agent-Structure in International Relations Theory," *International Organization* 41, no. 3 (1987): 335–70.
87. For a treatment of the importance of emerging conditions in organizational behavior theory, see Phillipe Selznick, *Leadership in Administration: A Sociological Interpretation* (Evanston, IL: Row Peterson, 1957).
88. Francesco N. Moro, "Organizing Emotions and Ideology in Collective Armed Mobilization," *PS: Political Science & Politics* 50, no. 4 (2017): 944.
89. Jason Seawright, "Review of *Measuring Identity: A Guide for Social Scientists* by Abdelal et al.," *Perspectives on Politics* 9, no. 2 (2011): 455.
90. This trajectory accords with explanations linking group creation to moral outrage felt over experiencing severe violence. See Wood, "Social Processes," 548.

91. Timothy Wickham-Crowley, "Two Waves of Guerrilla Movement Organizing in Latin America, 1956–1990," *Comparative Studies in Society and History* 56, no. 1 (2014): 215–42; Thomas Wright, *Latin America in the Era of the Cuban Revolution* (New York: Praeger, 1991).
92. Gutiérrez-Sanín and Wood, *Ideology in Civil War*, 215.
93. Jonathan Leader Maynard, "Ideology and Armed Conflict," *Journal of Peace Research* 56, no. 5 (2019): 635–49.
94. Gutiérrez-Sanín and Wood, *Ideology in Civil War*, 214–17.
95. Jonathan Maynard disagrees with this point and posits that the sharp distinction between the weak and strong programs presents a false dichotomy, as groups normally do not divorce ideological concerns from strategic ones: "Ideologies are not simply idealistic political programs pursued with blind disregard for strategic interests, but shapes actors' understanding of security, strategy and power politics." Maynard, "Ideology and Armed Conflict," 637.
96. Hoffman, *Inside Terrorism*; Laqueur, *The Age*.
97. Chenoweth and More, *Politics of Terror*, 126.
98. Konstantinos Kavrakis, "Identity and Ideology Through the Frames of Al-Qaeda and Islamic State," *Terrorism and Political Violence*, 2022, https://doi.org/10.1080/09546553.2022.2035366.
99. Albert Bandura, "Moral Disengagement in the Perpetration of Inhumanities," *Personality and Social Psychology Review* 3, no. 3 (1999): 193–209.
100. Ehud Sprinzak, "The Psychopolitical Formation of Extreme Left Terrorism in a Democracy: The Case of the Weathermen," in *Origins of Terrorism: Psychologies, Ideologies, Theologies, States of Mind*, 2nd ed., ed. Walter Reich (Washington, DC: Woodrow Wilson Center Press, 1998), 65–85. See also Rebecca Littman and Elizabeth Levy Paluck, "The Cycle of Violence: Understanding Individual Participation in Collective Violence," *Political Psychology* 36, no. 1 (2015): 79–99; Dara Kay Cohen, "The Ties That Bind: How Armed Groups Use Violence to Socialize Fighters," *Journal of Peace Research* 54, no. 5 (2017): 701–14.
101. Goodwin, "The Causes."
102. He distinguishes among four distinct mechanisms: commitment, adoption, conformity, and instrumentalization. Maynard, "Ideology and Armed Conflict," 639.
103. Rapoport, *Waves of Global Terrorism*.
104. Ami Pedahzur and Leonard Weinberg, "Modern European Democracy and Its Enemies: The Threat of the Extreme Right," *Totalitarian Movements and Political Religions* 2, no. 1 (2001): 52–72; Vincent Auger, "Right-Wing Terror," *Perspectives on Terrorism* 14, no. 3 (2020): 87–97.
105. Adam Scharpf, "Ideology and State Terror: How Officers Beliefs Shaped Repression During Argentina's 'Dirty War,'" *Journal of Peace Research* 55, no. 2 (2018): 206–21. Benjamin Valentino makes a similar point, although his explanation of terrorism is based on rationalist arguments linked to military counterinsurgency strategies. See Benjamin Valentino, *Final Solutions, Mass Killings, and Genocide in the Twentieth Century* (Ithaca, NY: Cornell University Press, 2004).

106. Jerrold M. Post, "Terrorist Psycho-Logic: Terrorist Behavior as Product of Psychological Forces," in *Origins of Terrorism: Psychologies, Ideologies, Theologies, States of Mind*, 2nd ed., ed. Walter Reich (Washington, DC: Woodrow Wilson Center Press, 1988), 34.
107. Hugo Slim, *Killing Civilians: Method, Madness, and Morality in War* (New York: Columbia University Press, 2008).
108. United States Congress, "The 9/11 Commission Report: Final Report of the National Commission on Terrorist Attacks upon the United States," Y3.2:27/2/FINAL, July 22, 2004, https://www.govinfo.gov/app/details/GPO-911REPORT.
109. Ted Robert Gurr, "Terrorism in Democracies: Its Social and Political Basis," in Reich, *Origins of Terrorism*, 87–88.
110. Austin C. Doctor, "Rebel Leadership and the Specialization of Rebel Operations," *Civil Wars*, April (2021): 1–32.
111. Peter G. Thompson, *Armed Groups: The 21st Century Threat* (Boulder, CO: Rowman Littlefield, 2014).
112. Green, *Commander's Dilemma*.
113. Jeffrey T. Checkel, "Socialization and Violence: Introduction and Framework," *Journal of Peace Research* 54, no. 5 (2017): 594.
114. Wood, "Social Processes," 548.
115. David R. Segal and James Burk, eds., *Military Sociology* (Thousand Oaks, CA: Sage, 2011).
116. Della Porta, *Social Movements*.
117. Wolfgang Kraushaar, *Die RAF und der Linke Terrorismus* (Hamburg: HIS Verlag, 2006).
118. Green, *Commander's Dilemma*.
119. Dennis Rodgers, "Bróders in Arms: Gangs and the Socialization of Violence in Nicaragua," *Journal of Peace Research* 54, no. 5 (2017): 648–60.
120. Green, *Commander's Dilemma*, 29.
121. See Weinstein, *Inside Rebellion*. For an insightful, critical discussion of these line of argumentation, see Kalyvas, *Logic of Violence*, 55–58.
122. Elisabeth Jean Wood, "Variation in Sexual Violence During War," *Politics & Society* 34, no. 3 (2006): 307–42.
123. For an excellent account of the varieties of terrorism tactics from a historical perspective, see Laqueur, *Age of Terrorism*, 112–16.
124. Timothy Wickham-Crowley, "Terror and Guerrilla Warfare in Latin America 1956–1970," *Comparative Studies in Society and History* 32, no. 2 (1990): 202.
125. Carlos Marighella, *Minimanual of Urban Guerrilla* (Chapel Hill: North Carolina University Press Documentary Publications, 1985).
126. Andreas E. Feldmann and Maiju Perälä, "Reassessing the Causes of Nongovernmental Terrorism in Latin America," *Latin American Politics and Society* 46, no. 2 (2004): 101–32.
127. David Pion-Berlin, "The National Security Doctrine: Military Threat Perception and the Dirty War in Argentina," *Comparative Political Studies* 21, no. 3 (1988): 382–407.

128. Stathis N. Kalyvas and Laia Balcells, "International System Technologies of Rebellion: How the End of the Cold War Shaped Internal Conflict," *American Political Science Review* 104, no. 3 (2010): 415–29.
129. James J. F. Forest, ed., *Teaching Terror: Strategic and Tactical Learning in the Terrorist World* (Lanham, MD: Rowman Littlefield, 2006).
130. Michael C. Horowitz, "Nonstate Actors and the Diffusion of Innovations: The Case of Suicide Terrorism," *International Organization* 64, no. 1 (2010): 33–64.
131. Wickham-Crowley, "Terror and Guerrilla Warfare"; Laqueur, *Age of Terrorism*, 245–65.
132. Román D. Ortiz, "Insurgent Strategies in the Post-Cold War: The Case of the Revolutionary Armed Forces of Colombia," *Studies in Conflict & Terrorism* 25, no. 2 (2002): 127–43.
133. Daniel Pécaut, "From Banality of Violence to Real Terror: The Case of Colombia," in *Societies in Fear: The Legacy of Civil War, Violence and Terror in Latin America*, ed. Kees Kooning and Dirk Kruijt, 141–68 (London: Zed Books, 1999).
134. An important dynamic related to the transmission if ideas, at least in the Colombian case, was party switching. Such shifts affected the groups' use of violence. As the empirical cases show, guerrilla members of the Popular Liberation Army would often switch sides and join paramilitary groups, incorporated their expertise into their new groups. The same holds true for former CSSF members who joined paramilitary groups. This dynamic has accelerated in recent years.
135. The literature uses the term *terrorist organizations* to describe groups with political goals that rely on terrorism. To the extent that terrorism is a tactic, I avoid this parlance that conflates organizations' motives with their modi operandi.
136. Walter Laqueur, *New Terrorism: Fanaticism and the Arms of Mass Destruction* (New York: Oxford University Press, 2000), 199.
137. Peter Grabosky and Michael Stohl, *Crime and Terrorism* (London: Sage, 2010).
138. Louise Shelley, *Dirty Entanglements: Corruption, Crime and Terrorism* (Cambridge: Cambridge University Press, 2014).
139. Chris Dishman, "Terrorism, Crime and Transformation," *Studies in Conflict & Terrorism* 24, no. 1 (2001): 43–58.
140. See Thomas M. Sanderon, "Transnational Terror and Organized Crime. Blurring the Lines," *SAIS Review* 24, no. 1 (2004): 49–61.
141. Louise Shelley, and John Picarelli, "The Diversity of Crime Terror Interaction," *International Annals of Criminology* 43 (2005): 51–81.
142. Some terrorism studies scholars, however, believe that given the markedly different motivations of criminals and political groups, full convergence is simply not possible. See Steven Hutchinson and Pat O'Malley, "A Crime-Terror Nexus? Thinking on Some of the Links Between Terrorism and Criminality," *Studies in Conflict and Terrorism* 30, no. 12 (2007): 1095–107; A. P. Schmid, "Links Between Transnational Organized Crime and Terrorist Crimes," *Transnational Organized Crime* 2, no. 4 (1996): 40–82.

143. Tamara Makarenko, "The Crime-Terror Continuum: Tracing the Interplay Between Transnational Organised Crime and Terrorism," *Global Crime* 6, no. 1 (2004): 135.
144. International Institute for Strategic Studies, *The FARC Files: Venezuela, Ecuador, and the Secret Archive of Raúl Reyes* (London: International Institute for Strategic Studies, 2011).
145. Barnett R. Rubin, *Afghanistan from the Cold War Through the War on Terror* (Oxford: Oxford University Press, 2013).
146. Makarenko, "The Crime Terror."
147. Kaldor, *New and Old Wars*.
148. Stathis N. Kalyvas, "'New' and 'Old' Civil Wars: Valid Distinctions?," *World Politics* 54, no. 1 (2001): 99–118.
149. This analysis uses organized crime and mafia interchangeably. See Diego Gambetta, *The Sicilian Mafia: The Business of Private Protection* (Cambridge, MA: Harvard University Press, 1996). Other authors make a distinction, arguing that organized criminal groups engage in the production and distribution of a broader array goods and services, which clearly go beyond protection; these scholars therefore consider mafia practices to be a specific repertoire of action within the general rubric of organized crime. See Anna Sergi, *From Mafia to Organised Crime. Critical Criminological Perspectives* (New York: Palgrave, 2017).
150. Gambetta, *The Sicilian Mafia*.
151. Marie Anne Matard-Bonucci, *Histoire de La Mafia* (Brussels: Editones Complexe, 1994).
152. Federico Varese, "What Is Organized Crime," in *Redefining Organised Crime: A Challenge for the European Union*, ed. Stefania Carnevale, Serena Forlati, and Orsetta Giolo (Oxford: Hart Publishing, 2017), 27–53.
153. Leopoldo Franchetti, *Condizioni Politiche E Amministrative Della Sicilia* (Rome: Donzelli Editore, 1993), 71.
154. See Diego Gambetta, *Codes of the Underworld: How Criminals Communicate* (Princeton, NJ: Princeton University Press, 2009).
155. Varese, "What Is Organized Crime," 235.
156. Gambetta, *Codes of the Underworld*. Of course, not all criminal group rely on or use these methods. In Colombia, the Cali Cartel generally steered clear of violence, seeking to avoid unnecessary attention. When it did use violence, however, it was lethal and often gruesome.
157. Courtis Milhaupt and Mark D. West, "The Dark Side of Private Ordering: An Institutional and Empirical Analysis of Organized Crime," *University of Chicago Law Review* 67, no. 1 (2000): 41–98.
158. Roberto Saviano, *Zero, Zero, Zero* (New York: Penguin Books, 2015).
159. Ricardo Vargas, "State and *Espirit* Mafioso and Armed Conflict in Colombia," in *Politics in the Andes: Identity, Politics, Reform*, ed. Jo Marie Burt and Phillip Mauceri (Pittsburgh, PA: University of Pittsburgh Press, 2004), 107–25.
160. Elijah Anderson, *Code of the Street: Decency, Violence, and the Moral Life of the Inner City* (New York: Norton, 1999).

161. See, for example, Rodgers, *Bróders in Arms*.
162. Benjamin Lessing, *Making Peace in Drug Wars: Crackdowns and Cartels in Latin America* (Cambridge: Cambridge University Press, 2017), 64–65.
163. Angélica Durán-Martínez, *The Politics of Drug Violence: Criminals, Cops and Politicians in Colombia and Mexico* (Oxford: Oxford University Press, 2018), 13.

2. The Evolution of the Colombian Civil War: From Conventional to Criminal Warfare

1. One of the best historical accounts of the Colombian conflict include Rafael Pardo's encyclopedic *History of Wars in Colombia* (Bogotá: Vergara, 2004). French political scientist Daniel Pécaut also provides a detailed treatment of the matter throughout his profuse work, see Daniel Pécaut, *Guerra contra la sociedad* (Bogotá: ESPASA, 2012). For a superb, overall account of Colombian history, see David Bushnell, *The Making of Modern Colombia: A Nation in Spite of Itself* (Berkeley: University of California Press, 1993).
2. Regarding the general argument on the link between geographical conditions and rebellion, see James Fearon and David Laitin, "Ethnicity, Insurgency and Civil War," *American Political Science Review* 97, no. 1 (2003): 75–90.
3. Eduardo Pizarro, *Las FARC 1949-2011: De guerrilla campesina a máquina de guerra* (Bogotá: Norma, 2012).
4. Nicholas Sambanis, "Terrorism and Civil War," in *Terrorism, Economic Development, and Political Openness*, ed. Philip Keefer and Norman Loyza (Cambridge: Cambridge University Press, 2008), 174–206.
5. Francisco Leal Buitrago, "La crisis del régimen bipartidista," in *El Estado en Colombia*, ed. Luis Javier Orjuela, 67–111 (Bogotá: Universidad de Los Andes, 2010).
6. Hillel Soifer, *State Building in Latin America* (Cambridge: Cambridge University Press, 2015), 41–45.
7. The strength or weakness of a state can be conceptualized as a continuum with ideal types at its extremes. Strength results from two main dimensions. One is what Michael Mann conceives of as infrastructural power: the capacity of the state to effectively exercise authority and implement public policies across its (entire sovereign) space. See Michael Mann, *The Sources of Social Power: A History of Power from the Beginning to AD 1760* (Cambridge: Cambridge University Press, 1986). The other is legitimacy, an abstract but critical component of statehood related to the *idea* of the state or its sense of purpose stemming from two fundamental elements: rightfulness and efficacy. See Kalevi Holsti, *State War and the State of War* (Cambridge: Cambridge University Press), chap. 5.
8. Jennifer Holmes and Sheila Amin-Gutiérrez de Piñares, "Violence and the State: Lessons from Colombia," *Small Wars and Insurgencies* 25, no. 2 (2014): 372–403; Andreas E. Feldmann, "Measuring the Colombian Success Story," *Revista de Ciencia Política* 32, no. 3 (2012): 739–52.

9. Alejandro Reyes and Liliana Duica, *Guerreros y campesinos: El despojo de la tierra en Colombia* (Buenos Aires: Norma, 2009). On the relationship between land distribution, reform, and violence in Colombia, see Michael Albertus and Oliver Kaplan, "Land Reform as a Counterinsurgency Policy: Evidence from Colombia," *Journal of Conflict Resolution* 57, no. 2 (2013): 198–231.
10. One of the best and most accurate treatments of this period asserts that up to two hundred thousand people perished. See Paul Oquist, *Violence Conflict and Politics in Colombia* (New York: Academia, 1980).
11. Jonathan Hartlyn, *The Politics of Coalition Rule in Colombia* (Cambridge: Cambridge University Press, 1988).
12. Alfredo Rangel makes an interesting point when asserting that Colombian guerrillas had an uncharacteristically long gestation period. See Alfredo Rangel, *Guerra insurgente: Conflictos en Malasia, Perú, Filipinas, El Salvador y Colombia* (Bogotá: Intermedio, 2001).
13. Richard Gott, *Guerrilla Movements in Latin America* (New York: Doubleday, 1971).
14. Gonzalo Sánchez and Donny Meertens. *Bandoleros, gamonales y campesinos: El caso de La Violencia en Colombia* (Bogotá: IEPRI Universidad Nacional de Colombia, 1983).
15. Eric Hobsbawn, "The Revolutionary Situation in Colombia," *The World Today* 19, no. 6 (1963): 248–58.
16. Román D. Ortiz, "La Guerrilla Mutante," in *La Encrucijada: Colombia en el siglo XXI*, ed. Francisco Leal Buitrago (Bogotá: Norma, 2006), 325.
17. On the different revolutionary models of the time see Jorge Giraldo, *Las ideas en la guerra: Justificación y crítica en la Colombia contemporánea* (Bogotá: Debate, 2015), chap. 1.
18. Carlos Medina Gallego, *ELN: Una historia contada dos veces* (Bogotá: Rodríguez Quito Editores, 1996), 46–48.
19. On the emergence of these groups, Juan E. Ugarriza and Nathalie Pabón, *Militares y guerrillas: La memoria histórica del conflicto armado en Colombia desde los archivos militares 1958-2016*, 2nd ed. (Bogotá: Universidad del Rosario, 2018), 55. On magnified fears, William Ratliff, "Revolutionary Warfare" in *Violence and Latin American Revolutionaries*, ed. Michael Radu (New Brunswick, NJ: Transaction, 1988), 15–36.
20. Nazih Richani, *Systems of Violence: The Political Economy of War and Peace in Colombia*, 2nd ed. (Albany: State University of New York Press, 2013), 45.
21. Eduardo Pizarro, *De la guerra a la paz: Las fuerzas militares entre 1996 y 2018* (Bogotá: Planeta, 2019), 58–59.
22. Camilo Echandía, *Dos décadas de escalamiento del conflicto armado en Colombia 1986-2006* (Bogotá: Universidad del Externado, 2006).
23. Claire Metelits, *Inside Insurgency: Violence, Civilians and Revolutionary Group Behavior* (New York: New York University Press, 2010).
24. Ana Arjona, *Rebelocracy: Social Order in the Colombian Civil War* (New York: Cambridge University Press, 2016), 138–39.

25. One author traces the beginning of these groups to the late 1960s, see Francisco Gutiérrez-Sanín, *Clientelistic Warfare: Paramilitaries and the State in Colombia (1982-2007)* (Oxford: Peter Lang, 2019), 69–71.
26. Centro Nacional "Paramilitarismo," 2018, 140, https://centrodememoriahistorica.gov.co/wp-content/uploads/2020/01/Paramilitarismo.pdf.
27. On the relationship between number of parties and complexity in a civil war, see Corinna Jentzsch, Stathis N. Kalyvas, and Livia Isabella Schubinger, "Militias in Civil Wars," *Journal of Conflict Resolution* 59, no. 5 (2015): 755–69. On influence, Andreas E. Feldmann and Victor J. Hinojosa, "Terrorism in Colombia: Logic and Sources of a Multidimensional and Ubiquitous Phenomenon," *Terrorism and Political Violence* 21, no. 1 (2009): 47.
28. I thank Gustavo Duncan for raising this important point.
29. Gutiérrez-Sanín, *Clientelistic Warfare*, 71.
30. These include Decreto 3398 (1965), Ley 48 (1968). See Centro Nacional, "Basta Ya! Colombia: Memorias de guerra y dignidad," 2013, 158, https://www.centrodememoriahistorica.gov.co/descargas/informes2013/bastaYa/resumen-ejecutivo-basta-ya.pdf.
31. Gustavo Duncan, *Los señores de la guerra: De paramilitares, mafiosos y autodefensas en Colombia* (Bogotá: Planeta, 2006).
32. Alejandro Reyes, "Compra de tierras por narcotraficantes," in *Drogas ilícitas en Colombia: Su impacto político, económico y social*, ed. Francisco Thoumi (Bogotá: Ariel, 1997), 279–346.
33. Duncan, *Los Señores*.
34. Feldmann and Hinojosa, "Terrorism;" Eric Lair, "El terror, recurso estratégico de los actores armados: Reflexiones en torno al conflicto colombiano," *Análisis Político* 37 (May/August 1999): 60–72.
35. Human Rights Watch, "Colombia's Killer Networks: The Military Partnership and the United States," November 1996, https://www.hrw.org/reports/1996/killer2.htm.
36. Andrés Suárez, "La sevicia en las masacres de la guerra colombiana," *Análisis Político* 63 (May/August 2008): 59–77.
37. Arjona, *Rebelocracy*, 253–55.
38. Gutiérrez-Sanín, *Clientelistic Warfare*, chap. 8.
39. International Institute for Strategic Studies, *The FARC Files: Venezuela, Ecuador, and the Secret Archive of Raúl Reyes* (London: International Institute for Strategic Studies, 2011), 26.
40. Pizarro, *Las FARC 1949-2011*.
41. Gary Leech, *The FARC: The Longest Insurgency* (London: ZED Books, 2011).
42. Daniel Pécaut, *Las FARC ¿Una Guerrilla Sin Fin o Sin Fines?* (Bogotá: Norma, 2008).
43. Pizarro, *Las FARC 1949-2011*.
44. Daniel Pécaut, "From Banality of Violence to Real Terror: The Case of Colombia," in *Societies in Fear: The Legacy of Civil War, Violence and Terror in Latin America*, ed. Kees

Kooning and Dirk Kruijt (London: Zed Books, 1999), 153; Steven Dudley, *Armas y urnas: Historia de un genocidio político* (Bogotá: Planeta, 2008), chap. 6.

45. Andrés Peñate, "El sendero estratégico del ELN: Del idealismo guevarista al clientelismo Armado," in *Reconocer la guerra para construir La paz*, ed. Malcolm Deas and María Victoria Llorente (Bogotá: Uniandes-Cerc-Norma, 1999), 94–96.
46. Mario Aguilera, "ELN: Entre las armas y la política," in *Nuestra guerra sin nombre: Transformaciones del Conflicto en Colombia*, ed. Francisco Gutiérrez-Sanín, María Emma Willis, and Gonzalo Sánchez (Bogotá: IEPRI/Norma, 2006), 222.
47. Andreas E. Feldmann, "Revolutionary Terror in the Colombian Civil War," *Studies in Conflict & Terrorism* 41, no. 10 (2018): 832.
48. Echandía, *Dos Décadas*, 110–18.
49. Feldmann, "Revolutionary Terror."
50. Timothy Wickham-Crowley, *Guerrillas and Revolution in Latin America: A Comparative Study of Insurgents and Regimes Since 1956* (Princeton, NJ: Princeton University Press, 1992).
51. Several other revolutionary groups emerged around this time including the Quintín Lamé Revolutionary Movement, a self-defense movement formed by indigenous communities in the Cauca Valley, the Revolutionary Worker's Party (which split from the Communist Party in 1982), the Jaime Bateman Cayón Group, the Latin American Patriotic Army, the People's Revolutionary Army, and the Guevarist Revolutionary Army, a splinter of the EPL.
52. Francisco Leal Buitrago, *El oficio de la guerra: Seguridad nacional en Colombia* (Bogotá: Tercer Mundo Editores-IEPRI, 1994).
53. Marco Palacio, *Violencia pública en Colombia 1958-2010* (Ciudad de México: Fondo de Cultura Económica, 2012), 269.
54. For an analysis of these attacks' logic, see Benjamin Lessing, *Making Peace in Drug Wars: Crackdowns and Cartels in Latin America* (Cambridge: Cambridge University Press, 2017), 150–53. He asserts these attacks amounted to violent lobbying tactic, that is, an attempt to compel a government to alter a given public policy (e.g., extradition) by using terrorist campaigns.
55. Attacks also included military targets, such as the bombing against the Colombian Intelligence Service (Dirección Administrativa de Seguridad) headquarters in December 1989. The Medellín Cartel also killed more than five hundred police officers—its leaders offered $2,000 for each killed police. See Pardo, *History*, 580–82.
56. Gustavo Duncan, Santiago Sosa, and José Antonio Fortou, "Terrorism and organized crime in Colombia," in *The Nexus Between Organized Crime and Terrorism*, ed. Letizia Paoli, Cyrille Fijnaut, and Jan Wouters (Cheltenham, UK: Edward Elgar, 2022), 412–32.
57. Pécaut, "Banality," 153.
58. Marc Bowden, *Killing Pablo: The Hunt for the World's Greatest Outlaw* (New York: Grove Press, 2001).
59. Centro Nacional, "Paramilitarismo," 62–65.

60. Gutiérrez-Sanín, *Clientelistic Warfare*, 81.
61. Nazih Richani, "Caudillos and the Crisis of the Colombian State: Fragmented Sovereignty, the War System and the Privatization of Counterinsurgency in Colombia," *Third World Quarterly* 28, no. 2 (2007): 403.
62. See Gutiérrez-Sanín, *Clientelistic Warfare*, 83–88. In 1999, a ruling of Colombia's Constitutional Court declared the CONVIVIR unconstitutional, and President Pastrana ordered their dismantlement.
63. Pizarro, *De la guerra*, 173–82.
64. Román D. Ortiz, "Insurgent Strategies in the Post-Cold War: The Case of the Revolutionary Armed Forces of Colombia," *Studies in Conflict & Terrorism* 25, no. 2 (2002): 127–43.
65. International Institute, *The Farc Files*, 31.
66. Duncan, *Los Señores*, 277.
67. "From Private to Public Violence: The Paramilitaries" in *Violence in Colombia: Waging War and Negotiating Peace*, ed. Charles Bergquist, Ricardo Peñaranda, and Gonzalo G. Sánchez (Wilmington, DE: SR Books, 2001), 127–50.
68. Dudley, *Armas y urnas*, 113.
69. Gustavo Duncan, *Más plata que plomo: El poder político del narcotráfico en Colombia y México* (Bogotá: Debate, 2015).
70. Independent sources indicate that in early 2000s, some twenty-one thousand armed guerrillas and twelve thousand unarmed security support structures known as *milicianos* existed. Juan E. Ugarriza and Nathalie Pabón, *Militares y guerrillas: La memoria histórica del conflicto armado en Colombia desde los archivos militares 1958-2016*, 2nd ed. (Bogotá: Universidad del Rosario, 2018), 310.
71. Although Plan Colombia began during the administration of Andrés Pastrana, the initiative was fully implemented under President Uribe, see Jonathan D. Rosen, *The Losing War: Plan Colombia and Beyond* (Albany: State University of New York Press, 2014).
72. Presidencia de la República Colombia, "Política de Defensa y Seguridad Democrática," June 16, 2003, https://www.oas.org/csh/spanish/documentos/colombia.pdf.
73. Richani, "Caudillos and the Crisis," 407.
74. Enzo Nussio, "Learning from Shortcomings: The Demobilisation of Paramilitaries in Colombia," *Journal of Peacebuilding & Development* 6, no. 2 (2011): 89–90.
75. The law became known as Peace and Justice. For an assessment see María José Guembe and Helena Olea, "No Justice, No Peace: Discussion of the Legal Framework Regarding Demobilization of Non-State Groups in Colombia," in *Transitional Justice in the New Millennium: Beyond Truth and Reconciliation*, ed. Naomi Roth-Arriaza and Javier Mariezcurrena (Cambridge: Cambridge University Press, 2006), 120–42.
76. Sarah Z. Daly, *Organized Violence After Civil War: The Geography of Recruitment in Latin America* (Cambridge: Cambridge University Press, 2016), 4.
77. Nussio, "Learning from Shortcomings," 89–90.
78. Pécaut, *Las Farc*, 67.

79. Camilo Echandía, "Auge y declive del Ejército de Liberación Nacional: Análisis de la evolución militar y territorial de cara a la negociación," *Fundación Ideas para la Paz*, Informe 21, November 2013, https://www.files.ethz.ch/isn/175224/529debc8a48fa.pdf.
80. United Nations Office of Drugs and Crime, "Colombia Coca Cultivation Survey 2013," June, 2014, https://www.unodc.org/documents/crop-monitoring/Colombia/Colombia_coca_cultivation_survey_2013.pdf.
81. See United Nations Human Rights Council, "Report of the Special Rapporteur on Extrajudicial, Summary or Arbitrary Executions: Mission to Colombia," A/HRC/14/24/Add 2, March 31, 2010, 3, https://www.refworld.org/docid/4c0763db2.html; on infiltration, BBC Mundo, "De qué se acusa Álvaro Uribe y por qué su arresto domiciliario es histórico en Colombia," August 4, 2020, https://www.bbc.com/mundo/noticias-america-latina-53658947.
82. The agreement included provisions for a transitory period in which the FARC would be allocated five seats in the 172-seat lower house and five of 108 seats in the Senate.
83. Renata Segura, and Delphine Mechoulan, "Made in Havana: How Colombia and the FARC Decided to End the War." *International Peace Institute*, February 27, 2017, https://www.ipinst.org/2017/02/how-colombia-and-the-farc-ended-the-war.
84. Francisco Gutiérrez-Sanín, *¿Un Nuevo Ciclo de La Guerra En Colombia?* (Bogotá: Debate, 2020), chap. 8.
85. Benjamin Lessing, "Logic of Violence in Criminal War," *Journal of Conflict Resolution* 59, no. 8 (2015): 486–516.
86. International Crisis Group, "Tackling Colombia's Next Generation in Arms," January 27, 2022, https://www.crisisgroup.org/latin-america-caribbean/andes/colombia/tackling-colombias-next-generation-arms.
87. Angelika Rettberg, "From Old Battles to New Challenges in Colombia," in *Divisive Politics and Democratic Dangers in Latin America*, ed. Tom Carothers and Andreas E. Feldmann (Washington, DC: Carnegie Endowment for International Peace Press, 2020), 18–23.
88. Viviana García Pinzón and Jorge Mantilla, "Contested Borders: Organized Crime, Governance, and Bordering Practices in Colombia-Venezuela Borderlands," *Trends in Organized Crime* 24 (2021): 265–81.
89. Natalio Cosoy, "Why Has Colombia Seen an Increase in Activist Murders," BBC World, May 19, 2017, https://www.bbc.com/news/world-latin-america-39717336.
90. Carlo Nasi and Angelika Rettberg, "Colombia's Farewell to Civil War," in *How Negotiations End*, ed. William Zartman, 62–82 (Cambridge: Cambridge University Press, 2019).
91. Johan Vibe, Norwegian ambassador to Colombia, interview by the author, Bogotá, April 2018.
92. Antje Dieterich, "Are FARC Militias a Wild Card in Colombia Peace Process?" InSight Crime, September 15, 2016, https://insightcrime.org/news/brief/are-farc-militias-a-wild-card-in-colombia-peace-process.

256   2. THE EVOLUTION OF THE COLOMBIAN CIVIL WAR

93. International Crisis Group, "Tackling Colombia's Next Generation."
94. Julie Turkewitz, "Deep in Colombia, Rebels and Soldiers Fight for the Same Prize: Drugs," *New York Times*, April 20, 2022, para. 10, https://www.nytimes.com/2022/04/20/world/americas/colombia-comandos-armed-groups.html.
95. Instituto de Estudios para el Desarrollo y la Paz, "El primer asesinato de un líder social en Colombia ocurrió al mediodía del 1 de enero de 2021," January 2, 2021, https://www.infobae.com/america/colombia/2021/01/02/el-primer-asesinato-de-un-lider-social-en-colombia-ocurrio-al-mediodia-del-1-de-enero-de-2021/#.
96. Carlos Negret, ombudsman, interview by the author, Bogotá, May 2018.
97. International Crisis Group, "Protecting Colombia's Most Vulnerable on the Road to Total Peace," Latin America Report no. 38, February 24, 2023, https://www.crisisgroup.org/latin-america-caribbean/andes/colombia/98-protecting-colombias-most-vulnerable-road-total-peace.

3. The Mighty FARC and the Use of Terrorism

1. *El Tiempo*, "Se cumplen 18 años del atentado del Nogal," February 7, 2021, https://www.eltiempo.com/justicia/jep-colombia/atentado-al-club-el-nogal-se-cumplen-18-anos-del-carro-bomba-en-que-va-el-proceso-judicial-565243. Brothers Hemínsul and Fernando Arrellán Barajas carried out the attack, which was masterminded by Commander Hernán Darío Velásquez (aka El Paisa) and sanctioned by the FARC's Secretariat. Velásquez, who did not demobilize in 2016, was killed in Venezuela's western department of Apuré in 2021.
2. Andreas E. Feldmann, "Revolutionary Terror in the Colombian Civil War," *Studies in Conflict & Terrorism* 41, no. 10 (2018): 35–52.
3. Other insurgent groups combine for 1,753 acts, disaggregated as follows: the ELN (1,455), the Popular Liberation Army (EPL) (204), Revolutionary Patriotic Army (ERP) (eighty-two), M-19 (eight), Quintín Lamé (six), Jaime Bateman Cayón Group (six). The Simón Bolívar Guerrilla Coordinating Board accounts for forty-two.
4. The Colombian Truth Commission reports that the FARC was behind 29,410 cases, or 24 percent, of the total number of attacks that could the traced to an armed party. Comisión para el Esclarecimiento de la Verdad la Convivencia y la No Repetición, "Hallazgos y Recomendaciones," 2022, 139, https://www.comisiondelaverdad.co/hallazgos-y-recomendaciones-1.
5. Centro Nacional, "¡Basta Ya! Colombia: Memorias de guerra y dignidad," 2013, 161, https://www.centrodememoriahistorica.gov.co/descargas/informes2013/bastaYa/resumen-ejecutivo-basta-ya.pdf.
6. Centro Nacional, "¡Basta Ya!," 134–35.
7. Ian Beckett, *Encyclopedia of Guerrilla Warfare* (Santa Barbara: ABC-CLIO, 1999), ix.
8. Timothy Wickham-Crowley, *Guerrillas and Revolution in Latin America: A Comparative Study of Insurgents and Regimes Since 1956* (Princeton, NJ: Princeton University Press, 1992), 3.

9. Mao Zedong, *On Guerrilla Warfare* (New York: Anchor Press, 1978); Richard Clutterback, *Terrorism and Guerrilla Warfare* (London: Routledge, 1990).
10. Robert Asprey, *War in the Shadows: The Guerrilla in History* (New York: Harper Collins, 1994).
11. Walter Laqueur, *Guerrilla Warfare: A Historical and Critical Study* (New Brunswick, NJ: Transaction Publishers, 1998).
12. Eduardo Pizarro, *Las FARC 1949-2011: De guerrilla campesina a máquina de guerra* (Bogotá: Norma, 2012), 38.
13. Daniel Pécaut, *Las FARC ¿Una Guerrilla Sin Fin o Sin Fines?* (Bogotá: Norma, 2008).
14. Richard Gott, *Guerrilla Movements in Latin America* (New York: Doubleday, 1971).
15. Pizarro, *Las FARC 1949-2011*, 40–44.
16. Jorge Giraldo, *Las ideas en la guerra: Justificación y crítica en la Colombia contemporánea* (Bogotá: Debate, 2015), 72–74.
17. Eric Hobsbawn, "The Revolutionary Situation in Colombia," *World Today* 19, June (1963): 248–58.
18. Others included Riochiquito, Sumapaz, El Pato, Guayabero, Tequendama, and 26 de Septiembre.
19. Centro Nacional, "Guerrilla y población civil: La trayectoria de las FARC 1949–2013," 2014, 45–46, https://centrodememoriahistorica.gov.co/wp-content/uploads/2020/01/Guerrilla-y-poblaci%C3%B3n-civil.-Trayectoria-de-las-FARC-1949-2013-1.pdf.
20. Lars Schoultz, *Beneath the United States: A History of US Policy Towards Latin America* (Cambridge, MA: Harvard University Press, 1999).
21. Eduardo Pizarro, *De la guerra a la paz: Las fuerzas militares entre 1996 y 2018* (Bogotá: Planeta, 2019).
22. Centro Nacional, "¡Basta Ya!," 61. Other founding members included Jaime Guaracas, Rogelio Díaz, Glicerio González, Fermín Charry, Laurentino Perdomo, and Rigoberto Lozada.
23. Giohanny Olave, "El eterno retorno de Marquetalia: Sobre el Mito Fundacional de las FARC-EP," *Segunda Época* 37 (2013): 149–65.
24. Miguel Ángel Beltrán, *Las FARC-EP (1950-2015): Lucha de ira y esperanza* (Bogotá: Ediciones Desde Abajo, 2015), 145–46; see also María Victoria Uribe, *Salvo el poder todo es ilusión* (Bogotá: Universidad Javeriana, 2009), 229–34.
25. *Fariana* is the colloquial way FARC members refer to the organization. Cited in Juan Guillermo Ferro and Graciela Uribe, *El órden de la guerra: Las FARC-EP entre la organización y la política* (Bogotá: Pontificia Universidad Javeriana, 2002), 27 (translation by the author).
26. Carlos Arango, *FARC: Veinte años de Marquetalia a la Uribe*, 5th ed. (Bogotá: Ediciones Aurora, 1984), 111 (translation by the author).
27. Jeff Goodwin, "A Theory of Categorical Terrorism," *Social Forces* 84, no. 4 (2006): 2027–46.
28. Ana Arjona, *Rebelocracy: Social Order in the Colombian Civil War* (New York: Cambridge University Press, 2016), 181–90.
29. Gary Leech, *The FARC: The Longest Insurgency* (London: ZED Books, 2011).

30. Giraldo, *Las ideas en la guerra,* chap. 3.
31. On the construct, Pierre Gassmann, "Colombia: Persuading Belligerents to Comply with International Norms," in *Civilians in War,* ed. Simon Chesterman (Boulder, CO: Lynne Rienner, 2001), 67–92. While reflecting on this matter, Pierre Gassmann, who was the head of the International Committee of the Red Cross's mission in Colombia (1996–2000), points out that FARC commanders who vocally rejected IHL as a matter of principle would often plead with humanitarian organizations to protect their captured members. On the reality of war, Ferro and Uribe, *El Orden,* 134–36.
32. Pécaut, *Las FARC.*
33. Gott, *Guerrilla Movements.*
34. Ferro and Uribe, *El órden de la guerra,* 63.
35. Jacobo Arenas, *Cese al fuego: Una historia política de las FARC* (Bogotá: Oveja Negra, 1985).
36. Ferro and Uribe, *El órden de la guerra,* 124 (translation by the author).
37. Pizarro, *Las FARC 1949–2011,* 191.
38. Pécaut, *Las FARC.*
39. Ferro and Uribe, *El órden de la guerra,* 124–25.
40. Timothy Wickham-Crowley, "Two Waves of Guerrilla Movement Organizing in Latin America, 1956–1990," *Comparative Studies in Society and History* 56, no. 1 (2014): 215–42.
41. John A. Booth, "Socioeconomic and Political Roots of National Revolts in Central America," *Latin American Research Review* 26, no. 1 (1991): 33–73.
42. Rafael Pardo, *La Historia de Las Guerras* (Bogotá: Vergara, 2004), 465–66.
43. Bolívar's thinking was complex and combined liberal notions of freedom and the separation of power with republicanism, the rejection of monarchy, nationalism, and some conservative notions regarding societal order. Over the years, many sectors (conservative and progressive) have appropriated certain of his ideas. The best articulation of his philosophy may be found in the famous "Discurso de Angostura" (the Angostura Address) to the Venezuelan Congress in 1819. See Simón Bolívar, "Discurso pronunciado por Simón Bolívar ante el Congreso de Venezuela en Angostura, 15 de febrero de 1819," *Co-Herencia,* 16, no. 31 (2019): 397–424.
44. Jorge Castañeda, *Utopia Unarmed: The Latin American Left After the Cold War* (New York: Vintage Books, 2003).
45. Álvaro Camacho, interview by the author, Bogotá, February 2009.
46. International Institute for Strategic Studies, *The FARC Files: Venezuela, Ecuador, and the Secret Archive of Raúl Reyes* (London: International Institute for Strategic Studies, 2011).
47. Francisco Gutiérrez-Sanín, "Criminal Rebels? A Discussion of Civil War and Criminality from the Colombian Perspective," *Politics & Society* 32, no. 2 (2004): 257–85.
48. Albert Bandura, "Moral Disengagement in the Perpetration of Inhumanities," *Personality and Social Psychology Review* 3, no. 3 (1999): 193–209.

49. On the FARC's organizational structure, see Ferro and Uribe, *El órden de la guerra*, 40–54.
50. Centro Nacional, "¡Basta Ya!," 75–78.
51. Jorge Giraldo, *Las ideas en la guerra: Justificación y crítica en la Colombia contemporánea* (Bogotá: Debate, 2015), 47–52.
52. Pardo, *La Historia*, 459–65.
53. David Bushnell, *The Making of Modern Colombia: A Nation in Spite of Itself* (Berkeley: University of California Press, 1993), 256–57.
54. Despite advocating for violence, Guillén opposed unnecessary carnage and excessive force. See Abraham Guillén, *El error militar de las izquierdas* (Buenos Aires: Editorial Hacer, 1980).
55. Pécaut, "From Banality." The author also claims M-19 tactics influenced the repertoire of the Medellín Cartel.
56. Walter Laqueur, *The Age of Terrorism* (Boston: Little Brown, 1987), 247–48.
57. Alfredo Briceño (aka Mono Jojoy), the feared top military commander of the FARC, once famously said that if the oligarchy was not interested in the fate of captured military personnel in FARC custody, the group would need to snatch some politicians to use as bargaining chips to secure the release of imprisoned guerrillas. See María Alejandra Villamizar, "El Mono Jojoy: Perfil de Un Hombre Malo," *El Tiempo*, September 23, 2010, https://www.eltiempo.com/don-juan/historias/el-mono-jojoy-perfil-de-un-hombre-malo-7961621.
58. The FARC took responsibility for the abduction of Harold Eder, a landowner in Valle del Cauca, in late 1965.
59. Claire Metelits, *Inside Insurgency: Violence, Civilians and Revolutionary Group Behavior* (New York: New York University Press, 2010).
60. See Arango, *FARC*, 52–54.
61. The abduction of high-profile politicians such as former senator and presidential candidate Ingrid Betancourt is a case in point. On the history of abductions in Colombia, see Mauricio Rubio, "Del rapto a la pesca milagrosa: Breve historia del secuestro en Colombia," *Universidad de los Andes*, Documento de Trabajo 36 CEDE, 2003, http://hdl.handle.net/1992/8647.
62. In a detailed analysis of kidnapping patterns, the Centro Nacional de Memoria Histórica offers a useful periodization of this practice: emergence (1970–1989), intensification (1990–1995), massification (1996–2000), containment (2001–2005), and realignment (2006–2010). See Centro Nacional, "Memoria y Población Civil." Its data analysis accord with CINEP's, although it presents higher incident numbers.
63. The database contains 1,019 cases of abduction for which CINEP could not independently verify the responsible party.
64. Centro de Nacional de Memoria Histórica shows the same trend, attributing a slightly higher percentage (33 percent) of the total abduction cases between 1981 and 2012 to the FARC. Centro Nacional, "Una Sociedad Secuestrada," 65.
65. Centro Nacional, "¡Basta Ya!" 52.

66. Ernesto Guevara, *Guerrilla Warfare* (Lincoln: University of Nebraska Press, 1985).
67. Carlos Ardila-Castro, Eduardo Gamez, and Petrona Tirado, "Los artefactos explosivos improvisados AEI: Una amenaza para el Estado colombiano," in *Desafíos para la seguridad y defensa nacional de Colombia: Teoría y praxis*, ed. Jaime Cubides and Jonnathan Jiménez (Bogotá: Escuela Superior de Guerra, 2017), 279–81.
68. Interview by the author, Bogotá, May 2018.
69. International Institute for Strategic Studies, *The FARC Files*, 33.
70. Román D. Ortiz, "La Guerrilla Mutante," In *La Encrucijada: Colombia en el siglo XXI*, ed., Francisco Leal Buitrago, 323–56 (Bogotá: Norma, 2006).
71. Consejo de Estado Colombia, "Rodrigo Márquez Tejeda y Otros v/s Nación-Ministerio de Defensa-Policía Nacional y otros," 2018, https://www.funcionpublica.gov.co/eva/gestornormativo/norma.php?i=88139.
72. The excerpt is part of Genesis, a detailed report by military intelligence and the office of the Colombian Prosecutor's Office (Fiscalía) handed to the Truth Commission in 2018. Radio Cadena Nacional, "Farc pretendían asesinar a generales y ministros en el atentado a El Nogal," September 5, 2018, https://www.lafm.com.co/judicial/farc-pretendian-asesinar-generales-y-ministros-en-el-atentado-el-nogal (translation by the author).
73. They include Bogotá, Cali, Medellín, Barranquilla, Quibdó, Valledupar, Neiva, Montería, Villavicencio, Tumaco, Puerto Asís, Ibagué, and Tame.
74. They include Abriquí, Apartadó, Yarumal and Yondó in Antioquia; Araquita in Arauca; Riosucio in Caldas; Agustín Codazzi in Cesar; La Palma en Cundinamarca; El Retorno in Guaviare; Paujil and San Vicente del Caguán in Caquetá; El Carmen de Bolívar in Bolívar; and Argelia, Miranda, and Santander de Quilichao in Cauca.
75. Comisión para el Esclarecimiento, "Hallazgos y Recomendaciones," 155. A previous report by the Centro Nacional de Memoria Histórica has found that sixty thousand people disappeared in Colombia between 1970 and 2015. See Centro Nacional, "Hasta encontrarlos el drama de la desaparición forzada en Colombia," 2016, 18, https://centrodememoriahistorica.gov.co/descargas/informes2016/hasta-encontrarlos/hastaencontrarlos-drama-de-la-desaparicion-forzada-en-colombia.pdf.
76. Comisión para el Esclarecimiento, "Hallazgos," 157.
77. Pizarro, *Las FARC 1949–2011*, 194–96.
78. Jineth Bedoya, *Vida y muerte del Mono Jojoy* (Bogotá: Intermedio Editores, 2010)
79. International Institute for Strategic Studies, *The FARC files*, 26.
80. InSight Crime, "Víctor Julio Suárez Rojas, Alias Mono Jojoy," March 10, 2017, https://insightcrime.org/colombiaorganized-crime-news/jorge-briceno-suarez-mono-jojoy.
81. Killings were linked to the Medellín Cartel bosses, including José Gonzalo Rodríguez Gacha and Fidel Castaño, who were operating with help from the Colombian security forces.
82. Jaime Arenas, *Cese al fuego* (Bogotá: Oveja Negra, 1985). Steven Dudley convincingly claims that Jacobo Arenas instrumentalized the UP in his overall strategy to

topple the government by using the new political party to distract the FARC's enemies while the group kept on fighting militarily. Steven Dudley, *Armas y Urnas: Historia de un genocidio político* (Bogotá: Planeta, 2008).

83. Juan Enrique Botero, "LAS FARC-EP ante el nuevo gobierno: Entrevista a Alfonso Cano," *El Tiempo*, June 8, 2002, https://www.nodo50.org/pretextos/farc5.htm (translation by the author).

84. Pizarro, *Las FARC 1949-2011*, 229–34.

85. Centro Nacional, "Guerrilla y población civil: La trayectoria de las FARC 1949–2013," 2014, https://centrodememoriahistorica.gov.co/wp-content/uploads/2020/01/Guerrilla-y-poblaci%C3%B3n-civil.-Trayectoria-de-las-FARC-1949-2013-1.pdf.

86. Camilo Echandía, "Expansión Territorial de Las Guerrillas Colombianas: Geografía, Economía y Violencia," in *Reconocer la guerra para construir la paz*, ed. Malcolm Deas and María Victoria Llorente (Bogotá: Uniandes-Cerc-Norma, 1999), 105–108.

87. Juan E. Ugarriza and Nathalie Pabón, *Militares y Guerrillas: La memoria histórica del conflicto armado en Colombia desde los archivos militares 1958-2016*, 2nd ed. (Bogotá: Universidad del Rosario, 2018), 322.

88. Pécaut, *Las FARC*.

89. Andreas E. Feldmann and Victor J. Hinojosa, "Terrorism in Colombia: Logic and Sources of a Multidimensional and Ubiquitous Phenomenon," *Terrorism and Political Violence* 21, no. 1 (2009): 42–61.

90. Metelits, *Inside Insurgency*.

91. Targeted assassination is the most employed tactic among Colombian armed parties: the database registers 8,832 cases, corresponding to 65.8 percent of the total terrorist events attributed to a known source in the sample. Analysts speculate that this practice is consistently used across armed parties because it is very efficient and cost-effective in comparison with other terrorist tactics. Justicia Especial para la Paz magistrate, interview by the author via Zoom, December 2020.

92. Giohanny Olave, *El discurso de las Farc-EP: Identidad guerrillera y lucha armada en Colombia* (Bucaramanga: Universidad Industrial de Santander, 2022).

93. Centro Nacional, "¡Basta Ya!," chap. 1, 55.

94. Andrés Suárez's investigation of massacres in Urabá, the most complete study on massacres using overkill, reports only a handful of FARC cases concentrated during a short period (1995–1997). He states that paramilitaries committed three times the number of massacres with sevicia than guerrillas. Andrés Suárez, "La sevicia en las masacres de la guerra colombiana," *Análisis Político* 63 (May/August 2008): 59–77.

95. Stathis N. Kalyvas, *The Logic of Violence in Civil War* (Cambridge: Cambridge University Press, 2006).

96. In nineteen municipalities, the FARC disputed territory with paramilitary groups, in three with the army, in sixteen with paramilitaries and the army, in nine with paramilitaries and the ELN, and in twenty-two with paramilitaries, the CSSF, and the ELN simultaneously.

4. The ELN: From *Foquismo* Warfare to Terrorism

1. The Cali Supreme Tribunal (Tribunal Superior de Cali) found members of the ELN's Central Command guilty of masterminding the attack. These leaders included the top commander Nicolás Rodríguez Bautista (aka Gabino), Eliécer Erlinto Chamorro (aka Antonio García), Fernando Sánchez (aka Élite), and Carlos Arturo Restrepo Sánchez (aka Marcos). See Centro Nacional, "Iglesia La María 20 años del secuestro del ELN," 2019, https://centrodememoriahistorica.gov.co/iglesia-la-maria-20-anos-delsecuestro-del-eln.
2. Jorge Giraldo, *Las ideas en la guerra: Justificación y crítica en la Colombia contemporánea* (Bogotá: Debate, 2015).
3. Timothy Wickham-Crowley, "Two Waves of Guerrilla Movement Organizing in Latin America, 1956–1990," *Comparative Studies in Society and History* 56, no. 1 (2014): 219–22.
4. On the history of ELN, see Carlos Medina Gallego, *Ejército de Liberación Nacional: Historia de las ideas políticas (1958-2018)* (Bogotá: Universidad Nacional de Colombia, 2019).
5. Román D. Ortiz, "La Guerrilla Mutante," in *La Encrucijada: Colombia en el siglo XXI*, ed. Francisco Leal Buitrago (Bogotá: Norma, 2006), 325.
6. Medina Gallego, *Ejército de Liberación Nacional*, chap. 1.
7. Andrés Peñate, "El sendero estratégico del ELN: Del idealismo guevarista al clientelismo Armado," in *Reconocer La Guerra Para Construir La Paz*, ed. Malcolm Deas and María Victoria Llorente (Bogotá: Uniandes-Cerc-Norma, 1999), 66–67.
8. Carlos Medina Gallego, *ELN: Una historia contada dos veces* (Bogotá: Rodríguez Quito Editores, 1996), 46–48.
9. Medina Gallego, *ELN*, 47.
10. Milton Hernández, *Rojo y negro: Historia del ELN* (Tafalla País Vasco: Txalaparta, 2006), 229.
11. Peñate, "El Sendero," 73.
12. Mario Aguilera, "ELN: Entre las armas y la política." in *Nuestra guerra sin nombre: Transformaciones del conflicto en Colombia*, ed. Francisco Gutiérrez-Sanín, María Emma Willis, and Gonzalo Sánchez (Bogotá: IEPRI/Norma, 2006), 212–13.
13. Peñate, "El sendero estratégico del ELN," 74.
14. Aguilera, "ELN: Entre," 218–20.
15. Peñate, "El sendero estratégico del ELN," 82–86.
16. Charles Larratt-Smith, "Navigating Formal and Informal Processes: Civic Organizations, Armed Nonstate Actors, and Nested Governance in Colombia," *Latin American Politics and Society* 62, no. 2 (2020): 75–98.
17. Andreas E. Feldmann, "Revolutionary Terror in the Colombian Civil War," *Studies in Conflict & Terrorism* 41, no. 10 (2018): 832.
18. Peñate, "El sendero estratégico del ELN," 94–96.
19. James Rochlin, *Vanguard Revolutionaries in Latin America: Peru, Colombia, Mexico* (Boulder, CO: Lynne Rienner, 2003).

20. Camilo Echandía, "Expansión territorial de las guerrillas Colombianas: Geografía, economía y violencia," in *Reconocer la guerra para construir la paz*, ed. Malcolm Deas and María Victoria Llorente (Bogotá: Uniandes-Cerc-Norma, 1999), 99–149.
21. Ortiz, "La Guerrilla Mutante," 339–40.
22. Fernando Cubides, interview by the author, Bogotá, February 2014.
23. For an analysis on the relationship between the two groups, see Luis Miguel Buitrago, "La relación entre las FARC y el ELN: Guerra sin cuartel y confraternidad revolucionaría (2005–2010)" (master's thesis, Universidad Nacional de Colombia, 2016), https://repositorio.unal.edu.co/bitstream/handle/unal/59463/1023916755.2017.pdf.
24. Camilo Echandía, "Auge y declive del Ejército de Liberación Nacional: Análisis de la evolución militar y territorial de cara a la negociación," *Fundación Ideas para la Paz*, Informe 21, November 2013, https://www.files.ethz.ch/isn/175224/529debc8a48fa.pdf.
25. Joshua Collins, "Colombia Peace Talks with ELN Rebels Resume Amid Tensions," Aljazeera, February 13, 2023, https://www.aljazeera.com/news/2023/2/13/colombia-peace-talks-with-eln-rebels-set-to-resume-amid-tensions.
26. InSight Crime, "Ejército de Liberación Nacional (ELN)," May 2, 2023, https://insightcrime.org/tag/eln.
27. Juan Diego Posada and Chris Dalby, "What Will Gabino's Departure Mean for the ELN?," InSight Crime, June 24, 2021, https://insightcrime.org/news/what-will-gabino-retirement-mean-for-eln.
28. International Crisis Group, "Tackling Colombia's Next Generation in Arms," January 27, 2022, https://www.crisisgroup.org/latin-america-caribbean/andes/colombia/tackling-colombias-next-generation-arms.
29. Juan Diego Posada, "ELN Show of Force Confirms Its Unmatched Criminal Presence in Colombia." InSight Crime, March 2, 2022, https://insightcrime.org/news/eln-show-of-force-confirms-its-unmatched-criminal-presence-in-colombia.
30. Cited in Rafael Pardo, *La Historia de Las Guerras* (Bogotá: Vergara, 2004), 426.
31. Cited in Peñate, "El sendero estratégico del ELN," 65.
32. Medina Gallego, *ELN*, 38, 71.
33. Barbara Gruber and Jan Pospisil, "'Ser Eleno:' Insurgent Identity in the ELN," *Small Arms and Insurgencies* 26, no. 2 (2015): 227.
34. Medina Gallego, *ELN*, 170.
35. Jorge Castañeda, *Compañero: The Life and Death of Che Guevara* (New York: Vintage Books, 1998).
36. Gruber and Pospisil, "Ser Eleno," 232.
37. Gruber and Pospisil, "Ser Eleno," 229–31; Medina Gallego, *ELN*, 108.
38. Scott Mainwaring, *The Progressive Church in Latin America* (Notre Dame, IN: University of Notre Dame Press, 1989).
39. Medina Gallego, *ELN*, 129.
40. Peñate, "El sendero estratégico del ELN," 212–13.
41. Medina Gallego, *ELN*, 108, 226.

42. Carlos Medina Gallego, *Ejército de Liberación Nacional: Historia de las ideas políticas (1958-2018)* (Bogotá: Universidad Nacional de Colombia, 2019).
43. Medina Gallego, *ELN*, 226–27.
44. Medina Gallego, *ELN*.
45. Thomas Wright, *Latin America in the Era of the Cuban Revolution* (New York: Praeger, 1991), 100–101.
46. Pardo, *La Historia de Las Guerras*, 455–56.
47. Aguilera, "ELN: Entre," 227–28.
48. Cited in Rochlin, *Vanguard Revolutionaries*, 125
49. Jeff Goodwin, "A Theory of Categorical Terrorism," *Social Forces* 84, no. 4 (2006): 2027–46.
50. Medina Gallego, *ELN*, 89–97.
51. Pierre Gassmann, "Colombia: Persuading Belligerents to Comply with International Norms," in *Civilians in War*, ed. Simon Chesterman (Boulder, CO: Lynne Rienner, 2001), 79–80.
52. The ELN's central command is composed of five members: the military commander and head of the organization; three commanders in charge of political, financial, and international affairs; and one last person in charge of liaising between the central command and the organization's seven main fronts. On the ELN's organizational structure, see Fundación Ideas para la Paz, "¿Qué Hacer Con El ELN? Opciones Para No Cerrar La Puerta a Una Salida Negociada." January 28, 2020, https://ideaspaz.org/publicaciones/investigaciones-analisis/2020-01/que-hacer-con-el-eln-opciones-para-no-cerrar-la-puerta-a-una-salida-negociada.
53. Aguilera, "ELN: Entre," 241.
54. Medina Gallego, *ELN*, 178–80.
55. Medina Gallego, *ELN*, 58.
56. Peñate, "El sendero estratégico del ELN," 68–71.
57. Medina Gallego, *ELN*, 60–61.
58. In a sign of the strong relationships Torres developed over the years with these groups, the Montoneros in Argentina named a command after the slain priest Hernán Brienza, *Camilo Torres: Sacristán de la guerrilla* (Buenos Aires: Capital Intelectual, 2008), 12.
59. Feldmann, "Revolutionary Terror."
60. Gassmann, "Colombia: Persuading Belligerents."
61. The execution of several commanders and of the *Bertulfos elenos* in charge of the organization's work in urban areas is a case in point. See Medina Gallego, *Ejército*, chap. 2.
62. Jaime Arenas, *La Guerrilla por dentro* (Bogotá: Tercer Mundo, 1971).
63. Aguilera, "ELN: Entre," 222.
64. Medina Gallego, *ELN*, 44.
65. Centro Nacional, "¡Basta Ya! Colombia: Memorias de guerra y dignidad," 2013, 33, https://www.centrodememoriahistorica.gov.co/descargas/informes2013/bastaYa/resumen-ejecutivo-basta-ya.pdf.

66. The targeting of mayors and other state officers challenging the group would become official organizational policy in the 3rd National Congress in 1996, when the organization declared that these were military targets due to their role financing a dirty war carried out against insurgent groups and their supporters. Camilo Echandía, "Auge y declive del ELN: Análisis de la evolución militar y territorial de cara a la negociación," Fundación Ideas para la Paz, Informe 21, November 2013, 8, https://www.files.ethz.ch/isn/175224/529debc8a48fa.pdf.
67. Medina Gallego, *ELN*, 236.
68. Similar trends can be found in Centro Nacional, "Una Sociedad Secuestrada," 33, https://issuu.com/centronacionalmemoriahistorica/docs/una-sociedad-secuestrada
69. Camilo Echandía, Universidad del Externado, interview with the author, Bogotá, May 2017.
70. Aguilera, "ELN: Entre," 222.
71. Peñate, "El sendero estratégico del ELN," 88–91.
72. Carlos Ardila-Castro, Eduardo Gamez, and Petrona Tirado, "Los artefactos explosivos improvisados AEI: Una amenaza para el Estado colombiano," in *Desafíos para la seguridad y defensa nacional de Colombia: Teoría y praxis*, ed. Jaime Cubides and Jonnathan Jiménez (Bogotá: Escuela Superior de Guerra, 2017), 289–81.
73. Echandía, *Expansión*, 110–88.
74. Aguilera, "ELN: Entre," 226.
75. On the effects of these policies, see Kent Eaton, "Subnational Economic Nationalism? The Contradictory Effects of Decentralization in Peru," *Third World Quarterly* 31, no. 7 (2010): 1205–22.
76. Ortiz, "La Guerrilla Mutante," 328.
77. Peñate, "El sendero estratégico del ELN," 79–80.
78. Echandía, "Auge y Declive," 13.
79. Andreas E. Feldmann and Victor J. Hinojosa, "Terrorism in Colombia: Logic and Sources of a Multidimensional and Ubiquitous Phenomenon," *Terrorism and Political Violence* 21, no. 1 (2009): 51–53.
80. Ortiz, "La Guerrilla Mutante," 331–32.
81. Aguilera, "ELN: Entre," 212.
82. Centro Nacional, "¡Basta Ya!," 55. In 2015, following an incident in which members of the ELN displayed an enemy soldier's severed limb, the central command issued a communiqué indicating that any combatant would face revolutionary justice and would be prosecuted if found responsible of overkill. The group also asserted that it did not welcome "criminals and those responsible for massacres as those gathering and celebrating in military clubs." Agencia EFE, "La guerrilla del ELN advierte que juzgará a los subversivos que humillen al enemigo," May 9, 2015, https://quepasamedia.com/noticias/mundo/mexico/laguerrilla-del-eln-advierte-que-juzgara-a-los-subversivos-que-humillen-al (translation by the author).
83. Suárez, "La Sevicia"; see also María Victoria Uribe, *Antropología de la inhumanidad: Un ensayo interpretativo sobre el terror en Colombia* (Bogotá: Grupo Editorial Norma, 2004).

84. On the programmatic principles of the ELN, see Medina Gallego, *ELN*, 67–69. This view was corroborated by an International Committee of the Red Cross delegate regularly in touch with ELN commanders. The source conveyed that ELN commanders explained that this practice was banned something that was explicitly stated in an internal communique. Interview by the author, Villavicencio, Meta, February 2012.
85. In eight municipalities, the ELN disputed territory with paramilitary groups; in eight with paramilitaries and the army; and in twenty-seven with paramilitaries, the army, and FARC simultaneously.
86. The FARC and ELN account for 3,860 (83.6 percent) of the total attacks (4,617) traced to guerrilla groups.

5. Paramilitary Terrorism: The Fusion of Counterinsurgency and Criminality

1. Centro Nacional, *La Rochela: Memorias de un crimen contra la justicia* (Bogotá: Ediciones Semana, 2011), 57.
2. See Bruce B. Campbell, "Death Squads: Definition, Problems and Historical Context," in *Death Squads in Global Perspective: Murder with Deniability*, ed. Bruce B. Campbell and Arthur D. Brenner (New York: St. Martin's Press, 2000), 1–26.
3. Julie Mazzei, *Death Squads or Self-Defense Forces? How Paramilitary Groups Emerge and Challenge Democracy in Latin America* (Chapel Hill: University of North Carolina Press, 2009), 4.
4. Sabine C. Carey, and Neil J. Mitchell, "Progovernment Militias," *Annual Review of Political Science* 20 (2017): 127–47.
5. Ana Arjona and Stathis N. Kalyvas, "Paramilitarismo: Una perspectiva teórica," in *El Poder Paramilitar*, ed. Alfredo Rangel (Bogotá: Fundación Seguridad y Democracia, 2005), 31–34.
6. Nonconventional warfare refers to military confrontations that do not involve large formations, utilize heavy weapons (aircraft, artillery), and generally do not have a definable start or end. See Jack Levy and William Thompson, *The Arc of War: Origins, Escalation and Transformation* (Chicago: University of Chicago Press, 2011), 202–203.
7. Francisco Gutiérrez-Sanín, *Clientelistic Warfare: Paramilitaries and the State in Colombia (1982-2007)* (Oxford: Peter Lang, 2019), 108.
8. Fernando Cubides, "From Private to Public Violence: The Paramilitaries," in *Violence in Colombia: Waging War and Negotiating Peace*, ed. Charles Bergquist, Ricardo Peñaranda, and Gonzalo G. Sánchez (Wilmington, DE: SR Books, 2001), 123–46.
9. Raúl Zelik, *Paramilitarismo, violencia y transformación social, política y económica en Colombia* (Bogotá: Siglo del Hombre, Fescol, Goethe Institut, 2015).

10. Human Rights Watch, "Colombia's Killer Networks: The Military Partnership and the United States," November 1996, https://www.hrw.org/reports/1996/killer2.htm.
11. Inter-American Court on Human Rights, "Caso de la Masacre de La Rochela Vs. Colombia, Sentencia, Reparaciones y Costas," May 11, 2007, https://www.corteidh.or.cr/docs/casos/articulos/seriec_163_esp.pdf. Similar rulings include 19 Comerciantes (2004), Mapiripán (2005), and Pueblo Bello (2006).
12. Gutiérrez-Sanín, *Clientelistic Warfare*, 91.
13. Gustavo Duncan, *Los señores de la guerra: De paramilitares, mafiosos y autodefensas en Colombia* (Bogotá: Planeta, 2006).
14. Centro Nacional, "Paramilitarismo," 2018, 41, https://centrodememoriahistorica.gov.co/wp-content/uploads/2020/01/PARAMILITARISMO.pdf
15. Gutiérrez-Sanín, *Clientelistic Warfare*, 71
16. These include Decreto 3398 (1965), Ley 48 (1968).
17. Jennifer Holmes and Sheila Amin-Gutiérrez de Piñares, "Violence and the State: Lessons from Colombia," *Small Wars and Insurgencies* 25, no. 2 (2014): 372–403.
18. Rafael Pardo, *La Historia de Las Guerras* (Bogotá: Vergara, 2004), 459–65.
19. Mauricio Romero, *Paramilitares y autodefensas, 1982-2003* (Bogotá: IEPR Universidad Nacional de Colombia, 2003).
20. Jorge Melo, "Los paramilitares y sus impactos sobre la política," in *Al filo del caos: Crisis política en la Colombia de los Años 80*, ed. Francisco Leal and León Zamosc (Bogotá: IEPRI, 1990), 493.
21. Human Rights Watch, "Colombia's Killer Networks."
22. Centro Nacional, "Paramilitarismo," 175–84.
23. Duncan, *Los Señores de la guerra*.
24. Alejandro Reyes, "Compra de tierras por narcotraficantes," in *Drogas ilícitas en Colombia: Su impacto político, económico y social*, ed. Francisco Thoumi, 279–346 (Bogotá: Ariel, 1997).
25. Cubides, "From Private to Public Violence," 157.
26. Verdad Abierta, "Muerte a Secuestradores MAS: Los orígenes del paramilitarismo," Septiembre 23, 2011, https://verdadabierta.com/muerte-a-secuestradores-mas-los-origenes-del-paramilitarismo.
27. Gutiérrez-Sanín, *Clientelistic Warfare*, 73.
28. Steven Dudley, *Armas y urnas: Historia de un genocidio político* (Bogotá: Planeta, 2008), 186–87.
29. Centro Nacional, "Isaza, el clan paramilitar: Las autodefensas campesinas del Magdalena Medio," 2020, https://centrodememoriahistorica.gov.co/wp-content/uploads/2020/10/Pdf-Isaza-el-clanparamilitar.pdf.
30. Gutiérrez-Sanín, *Clientelistic Warfare*, 73.
31. It comprised the Cali Cartel, former Medellín Cartel operatives who fell out of favor with Escobar such as Diego Murillo (aka Don Berna). Los PEPES was unofficially aided by an elite task force of state security officers known as *Grupo de Búsqueda*

(Search Unit) and the Drug Enforcement Agency. See Marc Bowden, *Killing Pablo: The Hunt for the World's Greatest Outlaw* (New York: Grove Press, 2001).
32. A fascinating account of the Castaño family is given by Manuel Castaño Gil—brother of Vicente, Fidel, and Carlos—in an interview reproduced in "Entrevista Completa a Manuel Castaño Gil En Semblanzas Con Toño Sánchez Jr.," *Semblanzas 2018*, https://www.vidoevo.com/video/RjZlU2xKcWuRpUFh5ZXc/semblanzas-con-too-snchez-jr-crnica-sobre-el-sitio-donde-cay-carlos-castao-gil (video no longer available).
33. Gutiérrez-Sanín, *Clientelistic Warfare*, 79–81; Dudley, *Armas y urnas*, 113.
34. Centro Nacional, "Paramilitarismo," 62
35. Gutiérrez-Sanín, *Clientelistic Warfare*, 81.
36. Duncan, *Los Señores de la guerra*, 277.
37. Nazih Richani, "Caudillos and the Crisis of the Colombian State: Fragmented Sovereignty, the War System and the Privatization of Counterinsurgency in Colombia," *Third World Quarterly* 28, no. 2 (2007): 407.
38. Gustavo Duncan, *Beyond Plata o Plomo: Drugs and State Reconfiguration in Colombia*. (New York: Cambridge University Press, 2022).
39. Enzo Nussio, "Learning from Shortcomings: The Demobilisation of Paramilitaries in Colombia," *Journal of Peacebuilding & Development* 6, no. 2 (2011): 88–92.
40. Groups include the Wayuu Counterinsurgency Front, the Peasant Self-Defense of Casanare, the South Putumayo Front, Self-defenses of Meta and Vichada, the Anti-communist Popular Revolutionary Army, and splinter groups of the Central Bolívar Bloc (e.g., Pacific, North, South, and Elmer Cárdenas).
41. Kimberly Inksater and Paola Jiménez, "The Organization of American States Mission to Support the Peace Process in Colombia," (Stockholm: International Institute for Democracy and Electoral Assistance, 2016), https://www.idea.int/sites/default/files/publications/the-organization-of-american-states-mission-to-support-the-peace-process-in-colombia.pdf.
42. Sarah Z. Daly, *Organized Violence After Civil War: The Geography of Recruitment in Latin America* (Cambridge: Cambridge University Press, 2016), 4.
43. Human Rights Watch, "Paramilitary Heirs: The New Face of Violence in Colombia," February 3, 2010, https://www.hrw.org/report/2010/02/03/paramilitaries-heirs/new-face-violence-colombia.
44. International Crisis Group, "Colombia's Armed Groups Battle for the Spoils of Peace," Latin America & Caribbean Report no. 63, October 19, 2017, https://www.crisisgroup.org/latin-america-caribbean/andes/colombia/63-colombias-armed-groups-battle-spoils-peace.
45. United Nations High Commissioner on Human Rights, "Situation of Human Rights Report of the United Nations High Commissioner for Human Rights," A/HRC/46/76, February 10, 2021, https://reliefweb.int/report/colombia/situation-human-rights-colombia-report-united-nations-high-commissioner-human-0.
46. Alfredo Rangel, ed., *El poder paramilitar* (Bogotá: Planeta, 2005), 11.

47. Francisco Gutiérrez-Sanín and Elizabeth Jean Wood, "Ideology in Civil War: Instrumental Adoption and Beyond," *Journal of Peace Research* 51, no. 2 (2014): 218.
48. Duncan, *Los Señores de la guerra*, 281.
49. Daniel Castaño and Gabriel Ruíz, "La construcción del discurso contrainsurgente como legitimador del poder paramilitar en Colombia," *Estudios Políticos* 51 (2017): 153–74.
50. Eduardo Pizarro, *Una democracia asediada* (Bogotá: Norma, 2004), 124.
51. Carlos Medina Gallego, *Autodefensas, paramilitares y narcotráfico en Colombia. Origen, desarrollo y consolidación: El caso 'Puerto Boyacá'* (Bogotá: Editorial Documentos Periodísticos, 1990), 195–219.
52. Francisco Gutiérrez-Sanín, "Telling the Difference: Guerrillas and Paramilitaries in the Colombian War," *Politics & Society* 36, no. 1 (2008): 3–34.
53. Gustavo Duncan, private exchange with the author, June 2020.
54. Fernando Cubides, interview by the author, Bogotá, February 18, 2009.
55. Duncan, *Los Señores de la guerra*, 244–45.
56. Some members of the armed forces joined the ranks of paramilitarism for economic reasons. See Nazih Richani, *Systems of Violence: The Political Economy of War and Peace in Colombia*, 2nd ed. (Albany: State University of New York Press, 2013), 53.
57. Puerto Boyacá would boast of being the anti-subversive capital of Colombia. See Verdad Abierta, "Pablo Emilio Guarín," 2009, https://www.youtube.com/watch?v=IOqZn0eTnp4.
58. A *bloque* (block) refers to a large and autonomous military structure with its own leadership operating within the AUC confederation.
59. Congreso Internacional Para No Volver a la Guerra, "Mejores momentos Ernesto Báez: Congreso internacional para no volver a la guerra," 2020, https://www.youtube.com/watch?v=BJuCKHwSYVE.
60. María Teresa Ronderos, *Guerras recicladas, una historia periodística del paramilitarismo en Colombia* (Bogotá: Aguilar, 2014), 284 (translation by the author). Other paramilitary commanders, such as Rodrigo Pérez Alzate (aka Julián Bolívar) of the Bloque Central Bolívar, displayed more moderate views. In an interview, Pérez stated that he never held strong political views, that he did not consider himself an ultrarightist, and that while in prison he met several guerrilla commanders with whom he shared views. See Verdad Abierta, "Entrevista con Julián Bolívar," 2016, https://www.youtube.com/watch?v=NOIxEMUbSMY.
61. Autodefensas Unidas de Colombia. "Discurso autodefensa: Comandantes Carlos Castaño, Salvatore Mancuso y Adolfo Paz," 2004, YouTube video, minute 7.44, https://www.youtube.com/watch?v=LgMbz3coo04.
62. Fernando Londoño, "Lo Que Murió con Castaño." *El Colombiano*, April 30, 2013, https://prensarural.org/spip/spip.php?article10765, second para. (translation by the author).
63. David Bushnell, *The Making of Modern Colombia: A Nation in Spite of Itself* (Berkeley: University of California Press, 1993), 262–63.

5. PARAMILITARY TERRORISM

64. On the sociological aspects of narcotrafficking, see Álvaro Camacho, "De narcos, paracracias y mafias," in *En la encrucijada: Colombia en el siglo XXI*, ed. Francisco Leal Buitrago (Bogotá: Norma, 2006), 387–419.
65. Autodefensas Unidas, "Discurso autodefensa," minute 2.40 (translation by the author).
66. Ricardo Vargas, "State and *Espírit* Mafioso and Armed Conflict in Colombia," in *Politics in the Andes: Identity, Politics, Reform*, ed. Jo Marie Burt and Phillip Mauceri, 107–25 (Pittsburgh: University of Pittsburgh Press, 2004).
67. For example, Gutiérrez-Sanín asserts that up to one-third of the Bloque Cacique Nutibará were linked to the drug industry. Gutiérrez-Sanín, "Telling the Difference," 12.
68. Duncan, *Los Señores de la guerra*, 280.
69. Gutiérrez-Sanín, *Clientelistic Warfare*, 123.
70. Vadim Volkov, *Violent Entrepreneurs: The Use of Force in the Making of Russian Capitalism* (Ithaca, NY: Cornell University Press, 2002).
71. Gustavo Duncan, "Historia de una subordinación. ¿Cómo los guerreros sometieron a los narcotraficantes?," in *El Desarrollo: Perspectivas y Dimensiones: Aportes Interdisciplinarios*, ed. Carlos Zorro Sánchez (Bogotá: Ediciones Uniandes, 2007), 433–52.
72. Pardo, *Las Guerras*, 606–607.
73. Duncan, "Historia de una subordinación," 441.
74. Cubides, "From Private to Public Violence."
75. Duncan, *Los Señores de la guerra*, 361
76. Richani, "Caudillos and the Crisis."
77. Gutiérrez-Sanín, *Clientelistic Warfare*, 87.
78. Centro Nacional, "Paramilitarismo," 87.
79. Human Rights Watch, "Killer Networks."
80. Eric Lair, "El terror, recurso estratégico de los actores armados: Reflexiones en torno al conflicto colombiano," *Análisis Político* 37 (May/August 1999): 69.
81. Francisco Gutiérrez-Sanín and Mauricio Barón. "Estado, control territorial paramilitar y orden político en Colombia. Notas para una economía política de paramilitarismo, 1978–2004," in *Nuestra guerra sin nombre: Transformaciones del conflicto en Colombia*, ed., Francisco Gutiérrez Sanín, María Emma Wills, and Gonzalo Sánchez (Bogotá: IEPRI Universidad Nacional de Colombia, 2006), 288.
82. Olga Behar and Carolina Ardila, *El caso Klein. El origen del paramilitarismo* (Bogotá: Icono Editorial, 2012).
83. David Navarro, *Por acá se entra, pero no se sale.' Análisis de Los Centros de Entrenamiento Paramilitar* (Madrid: Editorial Académica Española, 2017), 24–27.
84. Verdad Abierta, "La 'Universidad Paramilitar' de Ernesto Báez," June 4, 2012, https://verdadabierta.com/la-universidad-paramilitar-de-ernesto-baez.
85. Tribunal Superior de Bogotá, "Sentencia, Salvatore Mancuso y otros," November 20, 2014, 160, https://ilg2.files.wordpress.com/2015/04/mancuso-et-al-judgement.pdf.
86. Verdad Abierta, "La Universidad."

87. Dudley, *Armas y urnas*, 184–87.
88. Verdad Abierta, "La Universidad."
89. Centro Nacional, "¡Basta Ya!," 45.
90. Duncan, *Los señores de la guerra*, 247. The Inter-American court finds a similar pattern. See Inter-American Court,"Caso de la Masacre de La Rochela Vs. Colombia."
91. People offering goods and services to guerrillas were particularly vulnerable to attacks. Gustavo Duncan, private conversation.
92. Dudley provides a very detailed account of one guerrilla commander known as El Negro Vladimir who deserted and became an implacable paramilitary commander. Dudley, *Armas y urnas*, chaps. 5, 9.
93. Tribunal Superior de Bogotá, "Sentencia Freddy Rendón Herrera," August 4, 2020, 990–91, https://www.ramajudicial.gov.co/documents/6342975/46525367/2020.08.04+Fredy+Rendon+Herrera_Libertad_a_Prueba_2a_Instancia.pdf/f0fcb031-9bd4-4d58-a670-61a414b6234e.
94. Tribunal Superior de Bogotá, "Sentencia, Salvatore Mancuso y otros," 987–88, 994, 1046.
95. Several studies have underscored the relevance of massacres in the modi operandi of paramilitary groups. See Centro Nacional, "Paramilitarismo," part 4, 171–92.
96. Data by the National Commission of Historical Memory provide a similar count: they attribute 59 percent of the total number of massacres perpetrated between 1980 and 2012 to paramilitaries. See Centro Nacional, "¡Basta Ya!," 47.
97. See Comisión Colombiana de Juristas, *Colombia Derechos Humanos y Derecho Humanitario: 1997-2001*, vol. 1 (Bogotá: Comisión Colombiana de Juristas, 2005).
98. Gutiérrez-Sanín, *Clientelistic Warfare*, 88.
99. Duncan, *Los Señores de la guerra*, 247–49.
100. Centro Nacional, *Masacre El Tigre, Putumayo* (Bogotá: Pro-offset Editorial, 2011), 94 (translation by the author).
101. Gustavo Gallón, director Comisión Colombiana de Juristas, interview by the author, Bogotá, April 2018.
102. The analysis also reveals that massacres and executions were often used in tandem.
103. Richani, "Caudillos and the Crisis," 411–13.
104. Duncan, *Los señores de la guerra*, 247.
105. In fifteen municipalities, paramilitaries disputed territory with the FARC in five, the ELN in two, and the FARC and the ELN simultaneously in eight.
106. Centro Nacional, "¡Basta Ya!," 54–55.
107. Andrés Suárez, "La sevicia en las masacres de la guerra colombiana," *Análisis Político* 63 (May/August 2008): 59–77.
108. Comisión Colombiana, *Colombia Derechos*, 26–27.
109. Centro Nacional, "¡Basta Ya!," 55
110. On armed parties, Jeremy M. Weinstein, *Inside Rebellion: The Politics of Insurgent Violence* (Cambridge: Cambridge University Press, 2007), 127–40; on a central command, Gutiérrez Sanín, *Clientelistic Warfare*, 135.

111. Iván Orozco, *Sobre los límites de la conciencia humanitaria: Dilemas de la paz y la justicia en América Latina* (Bogotá: Editorial Temis, 2005).
112. Mauricio Aranguren, *Mi confesión: Carlos Castaño revela sus secretos* (Bogotá: Oveja Negra, 2001), 109.
113. Tribunal Superior de Bogotá, "Sentencia Freddy Rendón."
114. Verdad Abierta, "Las escuelas para matar de los 'paras,' " October 28, 2009, https://verdadabierta.com/las-escuelas-para-matar-de-los-paras.
115. Tribunal Superior de Bogotá, "Sentencia, Salvatore Mancuso," 160.
116. A graphic account of how these gruesome practices were taught can be found in the testimony of a paramilitary trainee, Francisco Villalba (aka Cristián Barrientos), one of the confessed perpetrators of the el Aro massacre. He told the Colombian Prosecutor's Office about the special role played by Carlos Mauricio García (aka Doble Cero), a former Green Beret and leader of the feared Bloque Metro, in this atrocity. *El Tiempo*, "Se entrenaban para matar picando campesinos vivos," April 23, 2007, https://www.eltiempo.com/archivo/documento/CMS-3525024.
117. Centro Nacional, "¡Basta Ya!," 56.
118. Diego Gambetta, *Codes of the Underworld: How Criminals Communicate* (Princeton, NJ: Princeton University Press, 2009).
119. Special Prosecutor Justicia Especial para la Paz, interview by the author via Zoom, July 2022.
120. Gutiérrez-Sanín, *Clientelistic Warfare*, 157.
121. Special Prosecutor Justicia Especial para la Paz, interview.
122. *Semana*, "Guerra de rehenes," September 1, 1996, https://www.semana.com/nacion/articulo/guerra-de-rehenes/29982-3.
123. The Medellín Cartel under Pablo Escobar regularly employed kidnappings during its war against the state. He borrowed this tactic from guerilla operatives, particularly members of M-19. On Escobar's relationship with M-19. See Dudley, *Armas*, 120–21.
124. Aranguren, *Mi Confesión*, 208.
125. Aranguren, *Mi Confesión*, 140.
126. Aranguren, *Mi Confesión*, 195.
127. Centro Nacional, "Paramilitarismo, "90.
128. See United Nations General Assembly, *International Convention for the Protection of All Persons from Enforced Disappearance*, December 10, 2010, Article 2, https://www.ohchr.org/en/instruments-mechanisms/instruments/international-convention-protection-all-persons-enforced.
129. Karina Ansolabehere, Barbara Frey, and Laigh A. Payne, "Introduction," in *Disappearances in the Post-Transition Era in Latin America*, ed. Karina Ansolabehere, Barbara Frey, and Laigh A. Payne, 1–29 (Oxford: Oxford University Press, 2021).
130. Centro Nacional, "Desaparición forzada," 56, https://centrodememoriahistorica.gov.co/wpcontent/uploads/2020/01/BALANCE_DESAPARICION_FORZADA.pdf.
131. On concealing bodies, victims' relatives in Juan Frio, a village in the outskirts of Cúcuta, Norte de Santander, reported that paramilitaries of the Bloque Catatumbo

cremated bodies to conceal their whereabouts. Interview by the author, June 23, 2023. On accurate estimates, see Centro Nacional, "Desaparición forzada," 57–58.

132. Comisión para el Esclarecimiento de la Verdad la Convivencia y la No Repetición, "Hallazgos y Recomendaciones," 2022, 137–39, https://www.comisiondelaverdad.co/hallazgos-y-recomendaciones-1.

6. State Terror in the Colombian Civil War

1. United Nations Human Rights Council, "Report of the Special Rapporteur on Extrajudicial, Summary, or Arbitrary Executions: Mission to Colombia," A/HRC/14/24/Add 2, March 31, 2010, 3, https://www.refworld.org/docid/4c0763db2.html.
2. Justicia Especial para la Paz, "Audiencia de Reconocimiento por 'falsos positivos' en el Catatumbo," April 26, 2022, https://www.youtube.com/watch?v=g2gqn62VkgQ (translation by the author).
3. Christopher Mitchell, George Lopez, David Carleton, and Michael Stohl, "State Terrorism: Issues of Concept and Measurement," in *Government Violence and Repression: An Agenda for Research*, ed. Michael Stohl and George Lopez (New York: Greenwood Press, 1986), 5.
4. Michael Walzer, "Five Questions About Terrorism," *Dissent* 49, no. 1 (2002), 5.
5. On this criticism, see the discussion offered by Tim Wilson, "State Terrorism," in *The Oxford Handbook of Terrorism*, ed. Erica Chenoweth et al. (Oxford: Oxford University Press, 2019), 332.
6. Erica Chenoweth and Pauline E. Moore, *The Politics of Terror* (Oxford: Oxford University Press, 2018), 29.
7. Bradley McAllister and Alex Schmid, "Theories of Terrorism," in *The Routledge Handbook of Terrorism Research*, ed. Alex P. Schmid (London: Routledge, 2011), 203.
8. Erica Chenoweth and Pauline E. Moore, *The Politics of Terror* (Oxford: Oxford University Press, 2018), 258–63.
9. Bruce Hoffman, *Inside Terrorism* (New York: Columbia University Press, 2006). For this study, I do not make such a distinction and use terrorism generically for both sets of actors.
10. Hoffman, *Inside Terrorism*, 253–58.
11. A useful distinction between state and nonstate types of violence is offered by Charles Tilly, who contrasts "state-sponsored" violence (perpetrators of violence are authorized by and benefit from the protection and material support of the state) from "state-incited" violence (groups might be spurred to violence but have no access to state power, although they explicitly claim it). Charles Tilly, "State Incited Violence, 1900–1999," in *Political Power and Social Theory*, ed. Diane E. Davis and Howard Kimeldorf (Greenwich, CT: JAI Press, 1995), 164.
12. Ruth Blakeley, "State Violence as State Terror," in *The Ashgate Research Companion to Political Violence*, ed. Marie Breen-Smyth (London: Ashgate, 2012), 63–78; for an overview of this literature, see Jarvis Lee and Michael Lister, "State Terrorism

Research and Critical Terrorism Studies: An Assessment," *Critical Studies on Terrorism* 7, no. 1 (2014): 43–61.
13. Wilson, "State Terrorism," 335.
14. Juan Corradi, Patricia Weiss Fagen, and Manuel Antonio Garretón, eds., *Fear at the Edge: State Terror and Resistance in Latin America* (Berkeley: University of California Press, 1992).
15. Jorge Mendoza García, "Reconstructing the Collective Memory of Mexico's Dirty War: Ideologization, Clandestine Detention, and Torture," *Latin American Perspectives* 43, no. 6 (2016): 124–40.
16. Ruth Blakeley, *State Terrorism and Neoliberalism: The North in the South* (London: Routledge, 2009).
17. David Claridge, "State Terrorism? Applying a Definitional Model," *Terrorism and Political Violence* 8, no. 3 (1996): 52–53.
18. On state terror in Peru, see Comisión de la Verdad y Reconciliación, "Reporte Final," 2004, vol. II, 260–68, 286–358, https://www.cverdad.org.pe/ifinal.
19. For the most comprehensive and evenhanded analysis of the Colombian military and police, see Francisco Leal Buitrago, *El oficio de la guerra: Seguridad nacional en Colombia* (Bogotá: Tercer Mundo Editores-IEPRI, 1994). For an updated, excellent analysis, see Juan E. Ugarriza and Nathalie Pabón, *Militares y Guerrillas: La memoria histórica del conflicto armado en Colombia desde los archivos militares 1958-2016*, 2nd ed. (Bogotá: Universidad del Rosario, 2018).
20. By 1888, the National Army, including the National Police, had on average 6,500 members. Numbers would increase during times of domestic disturbances. See Frank Safford and Marco Palacio. *Colombia: País fragmentado, sociedad dividida* (Bogotá: Norma, 2002), 463.
21. Hillel Soifer, *State Building in Latin America* (Cambridge: Cambridge University Press, 2015), 41–45.
22. Leal Buitrago, *El oficio de la guerra*, 45. From time to time, the military would intervene in politics through symbolic "saber rattling" to pressure politicians to reach agreements if deadlock was threatening the normal functioning of the critical activities. Nazih Richani, *Systems of Violence: The Political Economy of War and Peace in Colombia*, 2nd ed. (Albany: State University of New York Press, 2013), 36.
23. Daniel Premo, "Coping with Insurgency: The Politics of Pacification in Colombia and Venezuela," in *Democracy in Latin America: Colombia and Venezuela*, ed. Donald L. Herman (New York: Praeger, 1988), 227–28.
24. Rafael Pardo, *La historia de las guerras* (Bogotá: Vergara, 2004), 411.
25. Eduardo Pizarro, *De la guerra a la paz: Las fuerzas militares entre 1996 y 2018* (Bogotá: Planeta, 2019), 92.
26. Leal Buitrago, *El oficio de la guerra*, 78.
27. Leal Buitrago, *El oficio de la guerra*, 71–75. For an alternative view arguing that the military sought to control public order, see Andrés Dávila, *El juego del poder: Historia, armas y votos* (Bogotá: CERC, Ediciones Uniandes, 1998).
28. Ugarizza and Pabón, *Militares*, 55.

29. Richani, *Systems of Violence*, 45.
30. Leal Buitrago, *El oficio de la guerra*, 79.
31. Pardo, *La historia de las guerras*, 448–59.
32. Álvaro Valencia Tovar, *Historia de las fuerzas militares de Colombia* (Bogotá: Planeta, 1993) vol. III, 124. On the military vision of those days, see Alberto Ruiz Novoa, *El gran desafío* (Bogotá: Tercer Mundo, 1965).
33. Leal Buitrago, *El oficio de la guerra*, 82.
34. Pizarro, *De la guerra*, 58–59. In the case of the FARC, the army missed an opportunity when Ciro Trujillo, FARC's second in command, was killed in 1967, pushing the group to the brink of collapse. As for the ELN, the army let it regroup after almost destroying it with attacks such as the so-called assault in Anorí (1973), see Milton Hernández, *Rojo y negro: Historia del ELN* (Tafalla País Vasco: Txalaparta, 2006), 229.
35. See Carlos Ospina Ovalle, *Los años en que Colombia recuperó la esperanza* (Medellín: Editorial Universidad Pontificia Bolivariana, 2014).
36. Fernando Cubides, interview by the author, Bogotá, May 2017.
37. One of the most important was Decree 3398 of 1965, which, in addition to redefining the contours of security, reorganized the structure and responsibilities of state agencies. Leal Buitrago reports that between 1948 and 1991, Colombia was under a quasi-permanent state of emergency (Estado de Conmoción Interior). Leal Buitrago, *El oficio de la guerra*, 87–89.
38. Robin Kirk, *More Terrible Than Death: Massacres, Drugs, and the America's War in Colombia* (New York: Public Affairs, 2003).
39. Premo, "Coping with Insurgency," 232.
40. Marco Palacio, *Entre La Legitimidad y La Violencia 1875-1944* (Bogotá: Norma, 1995), 270–2.
41. Harvey Kline, *State Building and Conflict Resolution in Colombia, 1986-1999* (Tuscaloosa: University of Alabama Press, 1999), 15.
42. Leal Buitrago, *El oficio de la guerra*, 99–104. Many human rights violations are attributed to intelligence units within the army such as the Brigade of Military Institutes and the Intelligence and Counterintelligence Battalion. On human rights abuses during the Turbay-Ayala administration, see Daniel Pécaut, *Crónica de cuatro décadas de política colombiana* (Bogotá: Norma, 2006), 289–98.
43. John Dugas, "The Colombian Nightmare: Human Rights Abuses and the Contradictory Effects of U.S. Foreign Policy," in *When States Kill: Latin America, the US and Technologies of Terror*, ed. Cecilia Menjívar and Néstor Rodríguez (Austin: University of Texas Press, 2005), 232–33.
44. Jorge Delgado, "Colombian Military Thinking and the Fight Against the FARC-EP Insurgency, 2002-2014," *Journal of Strategic Studies* 38 (2015): 839.
45. Ugarriza and Pabón, *Militares y guerrillas*, 199–219.
46. The attack on la Casa Verde, the headquarters of the FARC in 1991 is a case in point.
47. Up 70 percent of the budget was used to finance salaries and pensions. See Richani, *Systems of Violence*, 40.

48. Leal Buitrago, *El oficio de la guerra*, 112.
49. The Rojas Pinilla administration created the Colombian Administrative Department of Intelligence Services in 1953. This service, which was placed under the aegis of the military, became the first intelligence agency in the country. Seven years later, during the Lleras Camargo administration, the intelligence agency was restructured, creating DAS. The agency was dissolved in 2011.
50. Richani, *Systems of Violence*, 52–53.
51. Guerrilla groups included including M-19, the Movimiento Armado Quintín Lamé, the Workers Revolutionary Party (Partido Revolucionario de los Trabajadores), and a segment of the Popular Liberation Army. These groups had signed a peace agreement with the Barco administration in 1990, although negotiations started before the start of President Betancur's term.
52. New institutions included the Constitutional Court and the Office of the Attorney General (Fiscalía), while the most consequential instrument was the *recurso de tutela*, a habeas corpus action.
53. Leal Buitrago, *El oficio de la guerra*, 129.
54. Dugas, "Colombian Nightmare," 236.
55. One example was the creation of the National Defense Superior Council Permanent Executive Secretariat (Secretaría Ejecutiva Permanente del Consejo Superior de la Defensa Nacional).
56. Leal Buitrago, *El oficio de la guerra*, 130–35.
57. Pardo, *La historia de las guerras*, 532–41.
58. Pizarro, *De la guerra a la paz*, 51–53.
59. Pardo, *La historia de las guerras*, 541–46.
60. Román D. Ortiz, "Insurgent Strategies in the Post-Cold War: The Case of the Revolutionary Armed Forces of Colombia," *Studies in Conflict & Terrorism* 25, no. 2 (2002): 127–43.
61. Around 2000, the FARC reached the zenith of its power, with eighteen to twenty thousand members and an established presence in half of Colombia's municipalities. International Institute of Strategic Studies, *The FARC Files: Venezuela, Ecuador, and the Secret Archive of Raúl Reyes* (London: International Institute for Strategic Studies, 2011).
62. Carlos Ospina, "Insights from Colombia's 'Prolonged War,'" *Joint Force Quarterly* 42, no. 3 (2006): 60.
63. The CSSF coordinated operations among different branches by creating a Joint Operational Taskforce (Fuerzas de Tarea Conjunta). Pizarro, *De la guerra a la paz*, 187.
64. Jonathan D. Rosen, *The Losing War: Plan Colombia and Beyond* (Albany: State University of New York Press, 2014).
65. For an analysis, see Ann Mason, "Colombia's Democratic Security Agenda: Public Order in the Security Tripod," *Security Dialogue* 34, no. 4 (2003): 391–409.
66. Comisión para el Esclarecimiento de la Verdad la Convivencia y la No Repetición, "Hallazgos y Recomendaciones," 2022, 496–97, https://www.comisiondelaverdad.co/hallazgos-y-recomendaciones-1.

67. See Presidencia de la República Colombia, "Política de Defensa y Seguridad Democrática," June 16, 2003, https://www.oas.org/csh/spanish/documentos/colombia.pdf.
68. Pizarro, *De la guerra a la paz*, 208.
69. Ugarriza and Pabón, *Militares y guerrillas*, 357–61.
70. Pizarro, *De la guerra a la paz*, 247–86.
71. On regaining superiority over the FARC, see Mark Peceny and Michael Durnan, "The Farc's Best Friend: US Anti-Drug Policies and the Deepening of Colombia's Civil War in the 1990s," *Latin American Politics and Society* 48, no. 2 (2006): 95–116. On the killings, captures, and desertions, see International Institute for Strategic Studies, *The FARC Files: Venezuela, Ecuador, and the Secret Archive of Raúl Reyes* (London: International Institute for Strategic Studies, 2011).
72. Francisco Leal Buitrago, *La inseguridad de la seguridad: Colombia 1958-2005* (Bogotá: Planeta, 2006).
73. See Howard J. Wiarda, *The Soul of Latin America* (New Haven, CT: Yale University Press, 2003). For a classic discussion of the role of the military in society, see Samuel Huntington, *The Soldier and the State; The Theory and Practice of Civil Military Relations* (Cambridge, MA: Harvard University Press, 1957).
74. Barry Ames, "Military and Society in Latin America," *Latin American Research Review* 23, no. 2 (1988): 157–69.
75. Guillermo O'Donnell, *Modernization and Bureaucratic Authoritarianism: Studies in South American Politics* (Berkeley: University of California Institute for International Studies, 1973); Alfred Stepan, *Rethinking Military Politics: Brazil and the Southern Cone* (Princeton, NJ: Princeton University Press, 1988).
76. Erich Ludendorff, *The Nation at War* (London: Hutchinson, 1936).
77. Genaro Arriagada, *El pensamiento político de los militares: Estudios sobre Argentina, Brasil, Chile y Uruguay* (Santiago de Chile: Editorial Aconcagua, 1986). On the Colombian military, see Richani, *Systems of Violence*, 51.
78. Renán Vega, "La dimensión internacional del conflicto social y armado en Colombia Injerencia de los Estados Unidos, contrainsurgencia y terrorismo de estado," *Espacio Crítico*, February 10, 2015, 10–11, https://www.corteidh.or.cr/tablas/r33458.pdf.
79. Francisco Gutiérrez-Sanín and Elizabeth Jean Wood, "Ideology in Civil War: Instrumental Adoption and Beyond," *Journal of Peace Research* 51, no. 2 (2014): 215.
80. Hal Brands, *Latin America's Cold War* (Cambridge, MA: Harvard University Press, 2010), 72–73.
81. David Pion-Berlin, *The Ideology of State Terror: Economic Doctrine and Political Repression in Argentina and Peru* (Boulder, CO: Lynne Rienner, 1989), 98. Although all states are security driven, DNS views security as the ultimate yardstick against which all public policies ought to be measured.
82. Pion-Berlin, *Ideology of State Terror*, 98.
83. Brian Loveman, *Por la Patria: Politics and the Armed Forces in Latin America* (Wilmington, DE: SR Books, 1999), 151.

84. Brands, *Latin America*, 73
85. Brands, *Latin America*, 84.
86. Pion-Berlin, *Ideology of State Terror*.
87. Cecilia Menjívar and Rodríguez Néstor, eds., *When States Kill: Latin America, the U.S., and Technologies of Terror* (Austin: University of Texas Press, 2005).
88. Pion-Berlin, *Ideology of State Terror*, 413–15.
89. Pablo Nieto, "El reformismo doctrinario en el Ejército colombiano: Una nueva aproximación para enfrentar la violencia, 1960–1965," *Historia Crítica* 53 (May/August 2014): 155–76. For an illuminating account differentiating between a traditionalist wing influenced by the Prussian tradition and a population-centric wing advocating for civic-military action and espoused by combatants in the Korean War. See Delgado, *Colombian Military*, 834–37.
90. Quoted in Elsa Blair Trujillo, *Las Fuerzas Armadas: Una mirada civil* (Bogotá: CINEP, 1993), 95 (translation by the author).
91. Blair Trujillo, 126. For an alternative view arguing Colombia's repressive record matches those in the Southern Cone, see Dugas, "Colombian Nightmare."
92. Leal Buitrago, *El oficio de la guerra*, 43–56.
93. Comisión para el Esclarecimiento, *Hallazgos*, 475.
94. These include the Inter-American Treaty of Reciprocal Assistance (1947) (the Rio Treaty) and the Treaty for the Prohibition of Nuclear Weapons in the Americas (Tlatelocolo Treaty).
95. Lars Schoultz, *Beneath the United States: A History of US Policy Towards Latin America* (Cambridge, MA: Harvard University Press, 1999).
96. David Mares, "The United States' Impact on Latin America's Security Environment: The Complexities of Power Disparity," in *The Routledge Handbook of Latin American Security*, ed. Arie Kacowicz, 302–13 (London: Routledge, 2015).
97. David Bushnell, *The Making of Modern Colombia: A Nation in Spite of Itself* (Berkeley: University of California Press, 1993), 83–85.
98. See Rodrigo Pardo and Juan G. Tokatlián, *Política exterior colombiana: ¿De la subordinación a la autonomía?* (Bogotá: Tercer Mundo Editores-IEPRI, 1988).
99. Blair Trujillo, *Las Fuerzas*, 74–75.
100. Leal Buitrago, *El oficio de la guerra*, 83.
101. Adolfo Atehortúa, "Colombia en la guerra de Corea," *Folios* 27 (2008): 63–76.
102. Cited in Leal Buitrago, *El oficio de la guerra*, 69.
103. Forrest Hylton, "Plan Colombia: The Measure of Success," *Brown Journal of World Affairs* 17, no. 2 (2010): 99.
104. Dugas, "Colombian Nightmare," 240.
105. Dennis Rempe, *The Past as Prologue? A History of U.S. Counterinsurgency Policy in Colombia, 1958-1966* (Washington DC: Strategic Studies Institute, 2002).
106. Arie Kacowicz, "Latin America in the Contemporary World Security Architecture," in *Routledge Handbook of Latin American Security Studies*, ed. David Mares Arie Kacowicz (London: Routledge, 2015), 336–47.

107. Michael Shifter, "Plan Colombia: A Retrospective," *America's Quarterly*, July 18, 2012, https://www.americasquarterly.org/fulltextarticle/plan-colombia-a-retrospective.
108. Emma Björnehed, "Narco-Terrorism: The Merger of the War on Drugs and the War on Terror," *Global Crime* 6, no. 3-4 (2004): 305–24.
109. Legislation that prohibited providing counternarcotic assistance to units engaging in human rights violations, the so-called Leahy amendment, constituted an important initiative, see Víctor J. Hinojosa, *Domestic Politics, and International Narcotics Control: US Relations with Mexico and Colombia 1989-2000* (New York: Routledge, 2007).
110. Strategies are deliberated, planned, and developed by the Colombian Military Forces Central Command (Comando General de las Fuerzas Militares). For an overview on the structure and operation of the Colombian Armed Forces, see Ministerio Nacional de Defensa Colombia. "Organigrama," May 17, 2023, https://cgfm.mil.co/es/conocenos/organigrama.
111. Security expert, interview by the author, Bogotá, May 2018.
112. María Teresa Ronderos, "Harold Bedoya de la guerra a la política," *El Tiempo*, May 10, 1998, para. 30, https://www.eltiempo.com/archivo/documento/MAM-785005 (translation by the author).
113. GAULA groups, created through a formal Law decree 282 of 1996, are interinstitutional units composed of members of the Army, Navy, Intelligence Service National Police, the Prosecutors Office. See Colombian Defense Ministry, "Grupos GAULA," 2023, https://www.cgfm.mil.co/es/atencion-alciudadano/direccion-nacional-de-gaula-militares.
114. Magistrate Special Peace Tribunal, interview by the author via Zoom, July 21, 2022.
115. Ospina, "Insights from Colombia."
116. Leal Buitrago, *La inseguridad*.
117. Rempe, *The Past as Prologue*, 22–28.
118. General William Yarborough, founder of the Green Berets and head of the U.S. Army Special Warfare at Fort Bragg (now Fort Liberty).
119. Cited in Hylton, "Plan Colombia," 105.
120. Human Rights Watch, "Colombia's Killer Networks: The Military Partnership and the United States," November 1996, 83–87, https://www.hrw.org/reports/1996/killer2.htm.
121. Centro Nacional, "¡Basta Ya! Colombia: Memorias de guerra y dignidad," 2013, 54–55, https://www.centrodememoriahistorica.gov.co/descargas/informes2013/bastaYa/resumen-ejecutivo-basta-ya.pdf.
122. On the role of military leadership in this case, see Human Rights Watch, "El rol de los altos mandos."
123. Gustavo Duncan, *Los señores de la guerra: De paramilitares, mafiosos y autodefensas en Colombia* (Bogotá: Planeta, 2006), 247.
124. His sworn evidence before the Special Tribunal for Peace is available at Revista Semana, "General (r) Rito Alejo Del Río entrega versión ante la JEP," 2021, https://www.youtube.com/watch?v=QDrT2Sa89Hg.

125. The CSSF disputed territory with the FARC in thirteen municipalities, with the ELN in five, and with the FARC and the ELN simultaneously in one. No evidence indicated confrontation with paramilitary groups.
126. Comisión para el Esclarecimiento, "Hallazgos," 157.
127. Interestingly, abductions also account for 12 percent of terrorist acts committed by paramilitary groups.
128. Magistrate Special Peace Tribunal, interview by the author via Zoom, July 21, 2022. GAULA groups would also offer their services to criminal organizations to secure the release of their members or guarantee the payment of outstanding debts. On the links of GAULA groups and paramilitary and narcotrafficking groups, see Verdad Abierta, "El Gaula y 'Don Berna' Cercaron a Vicente Castaño: 'Don Mario,'" May 13, 2010, https://verdadabierta.com/el-gaula-y-don-berna-cercaron-a-vicente-castano-don-mario.

7. Terrorism in Criminal Wars

1. Renata Segura, and Delphine Mechoulan, "Made in Havana: How Colombia and the FARC Decided to End the War," International Peace Institute, February 27, 2017, https://www.ipinst.org/2017/02/how-colombia-and-the-farc-ended-the-war.
2. David Gagne, "InSight Crime Homicide Rate 2016 Round-Up," InSight Crime, January 16, 2017, https://insightcrime.org/news/analysis/insight-crime-2016-homicide-round-up.
3. In 2022, homicides for the year totaled 12,221 (26.1 per hundred thousand). See Peter Applebe et al., "InSight Crime's 2022 Homicide Round-Up," InSight Crime, February 8, 2023, https://insightcrime.org/news/insight-crime-2022-homicide-round-up; Universidad del Externado, "12.221 homicidios en Colombia durante el 2022," May 18, 2023, https://www.uexternado.edu.co/delfos-centro-analisis-datos/homicidios-en-colombia-durante-el-2022.
4. These include the Gaitanista Self-Defense Forces of Colombia, Oficina de Envigado, Urabeños, Rastrojos, the Norte del Valle Cartel, the Popular Revolutionary Anti-Terrorist Army of Colombia, and the Popular Liberation Army.
5. Juan Diego Posada, "ELN Show of Force Confirms Its Unmatched Criminal Presence in Colombia," InSight Crime, March 2, 2022, https://insightcrime.org/news/eln-show-of-force-confirms-its-unmatched-criminal-presence-in-colombia.
6. The Colombian government refers to FARC dissident groups as Residual Organized Armed Groups (Grupos Armados Organizados Residuales). They include several groups that either refused to demobilize or remobilized after the peace accord was signed. They are, for the most part, linked to former fronts or commanders and divided geographically. However, unlike in the past, they do not operate as a structured organization but rather as a loose confederation of groups claiming allegiance to the FARC. They are divided into two main wings or factions: the self-proclaimed Central General Staff (Estado Mayor Central) led by Néstor Gregorio

Vera Fernández (aka Iván Mordisco) and Segunda Marquetalia under the command of Luciano Marín Arango (aka Iván Marquez). Other smaller structures are operating independently, including the 36th Front in Antioquia and the Oliver Sinisterra Front active in Nariño, which has expanded its presence in Ecuador. See InSight Crime, "Colombia Criminal Groups," June 3, 2023. https://insightcrime.org/colombia-organized-crime-news.

7. Juan Trujillo, "Autoridades alertan sobre el renacimiento de frente de las FARC en Sumapaz," *El País*, April 21, 2023, https://www.elpais.com.co/judicial/autoridades-alertan-sobre-el-renacimiento-de-frente-de-las-farc-en-sumapaz.html.
8. International Crisis Group, "Tackling Colombia's Next Generation in Arms," January 27, 2022, https://www.crisisgroup.org/latin-america-caribbean/andes/colombia/tackling-colombias-next-generation-arms.
9. Francisco Gutiérrez-Sanín, *¿Un Nuevo Ciclo de La Guerra En Colombia?* (Bogotá: Debate, 2020), 14–15.
10. Angelika Rettberg, "Peace-Making Amidst an Unfinished Social Contract: The Case of Colombia," *Journal of Intervention and Statebuilding* 14, no. 1 (2020): 84–100.
11. CentroNacional,"Paramilitarismo,"2018,113–20,https://centrodememoriahistorica.gov.co/wp-content/uploads/2020/01/PARAMILITARISMO.pdf
12. InSight Crime, "Ex FARC Mafia," February 16, 2023, https://es.insightcrime.org/noticias-crimen-organizado-colombia/ex-farc-mafia.
13. InSight Crime, "Ejército de Liberación Nacional (ELN)," May 2, 2023, https://insightcrime.org/tag/eln.
14. InSight Crime, "EPL," July 15, 2022, https://www.insightcrime.org/colombia-organized-crimenews/epl.
15. Rettberg, "Peace Making." This view was corroborated by many of the sources I interviewed.
16. Johan Vibe, Norwegian ambassador to Colombia; Todd Howland, head of the UN Office for Human Rights; and Christoph Harnisch, head of the International Committee of the Red Cross delegation, interviews by the author, Bogotá, April 2017.
17. Julie Turkewitz, "Deep in Colombia, Rebels and Soldiers Fight for the Same Prize: Drugs," *New York Times*, April 20, 2022, para. 10, https://www.nytimes.com/2022/04/20/world/americas/colombia-comandos-armed-groups.html.
18. Instituto de Estudios para el Desarrollo y la Paz, "El primer asesinato de un líder social en Colombia ocurrió al mediodía del 1 de enero de 2021," January 2, 2021, https://www.infobae.com/america/colombia/2021/01/02/el-primer-asesinato-de-un-lider-social-en-colombia-ocurrio-al-mediodia-del-1-de-enero-de-2021/#.
19. Carlos Negret, ombusman, interview by the author, Bogotá, May 2018.
20. On deaths per year, Therése Pettersson, Shawn Davies, Amber Deniz, Garoun Engström, Nanar Hawach, Stina Högbladh, and Margareta Sollenberg Magnus Öberg, "Organized Violence 1989–2020, with a Special Emphasis on Syria," *Journal of Peace Research* 58, no. 4 (2021): 809–25; on state capture, Andreas E. Feldmann and Juan Pablo Luna, *Criminal Politics and Botched Development in Contemporary Latin America* (Cambridge: Cambridge University Press, 2023), 15, 24.

21. Andreas E. Feldmann and Juan Pablo Luna, "Criminal Governance and the Crisis of Contemporary Latin American States," *Annual Review of Sociology* 48, no. 1 (2022), 441–45.
22. Juan Albarracín, "Criminalized Electoral Politics in Brazilian Urban Peripheries," *Crime, Law, and Social Change* 69, no. 4 (2018): 553–75.
23. David Smilde, Verónica Zubillaga, and Rebecca Hanson, eds., *The Paradox of Violence in Venezuela: Crime and Revolution* (Pittsburgh, PA: Pittsburgh University Press, 2022).
24. David Shirk and Joel Wallman, "Understanding Mexico's Drug Violence," *Journal of Conflict Resolution* 59, no. 8 (2015): 1348–76.
25. Petterson et al., "Organized Violence."
26. Michael W. Doyle and Nicholas Sambanis, *Making War & Building Peace: United Nations Peace Operations* (Princeton, NJ: Princeton University Press, 2006).
27. Jorge Mantilla and Andreas E. Feldmann, "Criminal Governance in Latin America," in *The Oxford Encyclopedia of International Criminology*, ed. Edna Eretz and Peter Ibarra (Oxford: Oxford University Press, 2021), 214.
28. On clear boundaries, Stathis N. Kalyvas, "How Civil Wars Help Explain Organized Crime- and How They Do No," *Journal of Conflict Resolution* 59, no. 8 (2015): 15–40; on governance as intertwined, Enrique Desmond Arias, *Criminal Enterprises and Governance in Latin America and the Caribbean* (Cambridge: Cambridge University Press, 2017).
29. Benjamin Lessing, "Logic of Violence in Criminal War," *Journal of Conflict Resolution* 59, no. 8 (2015): 486–516.
30. Benjamin Lessing, *Making Peace in Drug Wars: Crackdowns and Cartels in Latin America* (Cambridge: Cambridge University Press, 2017), 42–46.
31. Guillermo Trejo and Sandra Ley, *Votes, Drugs and Violence: The Political Logic of Criminal Wars in Mexico* (New York: Cambridge University Press, 2020), 58.
32. Trejo and Ley, *Votes, Drugs and Violence*, 23. For an overview of the conceptualization of criminal wars, see Raúl Zepeda, "Conceptualising Criminal Wars in Latin America," *Third World Quarterly* 44, no. 4 (2022): 776–94.
33. José Miguel Cruz and Angélica Durán-Martínez, "Hiding Violence to Deal with the State: Criminal Pacts in El Salvador and Medellín," *Journal of Peace Research* 53 no. 2 (2016): 197–210.
34. InSight Crime, "Ejército de Liberación."
35. This section expands on previous work by the author. See Andreas E. Feldmann and Marc Lopez, "Repertoires of Terrorism in Mexico's Criminal War," *Perspectives on Terrorism* 16, no. 2 (2022): 4–13.
36. Guillermo Trejo, "Mexico's Illegal Democratic Trap," in *Divisive Politics and Democratic Dangers in Latin America*, ed. Tom Carothers and Andreas E. Feldmann (Washington, DC: Carnegie Endowment for International Peace, 2021), 24.
37. Karina Ansolabehere, Barbara Frey, and Laigh A. Payne, introduction to *Disappearances in the Post-Transition Era in Latin America*, ed. Karina Ansolabehere, Barbara Frey, and Laigh A. Payne (Oxford: Oxford University Press 2021), 1–29.

38. Xóchitl Bada and Andreas E. Feldmann, "Mexico's Michoacán State: Mixed Migration Flows and Transnational Links," *Forced Migration Review* 56 (2017): 12–14.
39. Trejo and Ley, *Votes, Drugs, and Violence*.
40. John Gerring, *Case Study Research Principles and Practices*, 2nd ed. (Cambridge: Cambridge University Press, 2007), 20. For a solid review on shadow cases, see Hillel Soifer, "Shadow Cases in Comparative Research," *Qualitative and Multi-Method Research* 18, no. 2 (2020): 9–18.
41. See Cynthia Arnson, and Eric Olson, eds., *One Goal Two Struggles: Confronting Crime and Violence in Mexico and Colombia* (Washington, DC: Woodrow Wilson International Center for Scholars, 2014), https://www.wilsoncenter.org/sites/default/files/media/documents/publication/Colombia_Mexico_Final.pdf.
42. Alan Knight, "Narco Violence and the State in Mexico," in *Violence, Coercion and State Making in Twentieth Century Mexico: The Other Half of the Centaur*, ed. Wil Pansters, 115–34 (Stanford, CA: Stanford University Press, 2012).
43. Jane Esberg, "More than Cartels: Counting Mexico's Crime Ring," International Crisis Group, May 8, 2020, https://www.crisisgroup.org/latin-america-caribbean/mexico/more-cartels-counting-mexicos-crime-rings.
44. Alejandro Anaya Muñoz and Barbara Frey, eds., *Mexico's Human Rights Crisis* (Philadelphia: University of Pennsylvania Press, 2020).
45. Michael J. Wolff, "Insurgent Vigilantism and Drug War in Mexico," *Journal of Politics in Latin America* 12, no. 1 (2020): 32–52.
46. Presidentes Muncipales (mayors) of municipalities in Tierra Caliente, a zone particularly affected by violence, underscored that such acts of violence had indeed the intent of terrorizing people. Morelia Michoacán, interview by the author, December 2017.
47. See Pamela Bunker, Lisa Campbell, and Robert Bunker, "Torture, Beheadings and Narcocultos," *Small Arms and Insurgencies* 21 (2010): 145–78.
48. Howard Campbell and Tobin Hansen, "Is Narco-Violence in Mexico Terrorism?" *Bulletin of Latin American Research* 33, no. 2 (2013): 158–73; Brian J. Phillips, "Terror Tactics by Criminal Organizations: The Mexican Case," *Perspectives on Terrorism* 12, no. 1 (2018): 46–63.
49. Daniel Wilkinson, "Mexico: Violence and Opacity," Human Rights Watch, October 17, 2020, https://www.hrw.org/news/2018/10/17/mexico-violence-and-opacity.
50. Catalina Pérez, Carlos Silva, and Rodrigo Gutiérrez, "Deadly Forces: Use of Lethal Force by Mexican Security Forces 2007–2015," in *Mexico's Human Rights Crisis*, ed. Alejandro Anaya-Muñoz and Barbara Frey (Philadelphia: University of Pennsylvania Press, 2019), 23–42.
51. José Antonio Guevara, "Amid Brutality and Impunity: Atrocious Crimes Committed Under the Militarized Security Strategy" (Mexico City: Comisión Mexicana de Defensa y Promoción de los Derechos Humanos, 2020), 53, https://www.cmdpdh.org/publicaciones-pdf/cmdpdh-amid-brutality-and-impunity.pdf.
52. Anaya-Muñoz and Frey, *Mexico's Human Rights Crisis*, 1.

53. I thank Guillermo Trejo for persuasively bringing up this important point.
54. Eduardo Moncada, "Resisting Protection: Rackets, Resistance, and State Building," *Comparative Politics* 51, no. 2 (2019): 321–39.
55. Wolff, "Insurgent Vigilantism."
56. Esberg, "More Than Cartels."
57. On guerrillas in Guerrero see Mark R. Wrighte, "The Real Mexican Terrorists: A Group Profile of the Popular Revolutionary Army (EPR)," *Studies in Conflict & Terrorism*, 25 no. 4 (2002): 207–25.
58. Chris Kyle, "Violence and Insecurity in Guerrero." Briefing Paper Series Wilson Center, January 15, 2015. https://www.wilsoncenter.org/publication/violence-and-insecurity-guerrero.
59. Vanda Felbab-Brown, "The Rise of Militias in Mexico: Citizens' Security or Further Conflict Escalation?" *Prism* 5, no. 4 (2016), 174, 178.
60. Comisión Nacional de Derechos Humanos México. "Informe especial de los grupos de autodefensa en el estado de Michoacán y las violaciones a los derechos humanos relacionadas con el conflicto," 2015, 230, https://www.cndh.org.mx/documento/informe-especialsobre-los-grupos-de-autodefensa-en-el-estado-de-michoacan-y-las-0.
61. Wolff, "Insurgent Vigilantism."
62. International Crisis Group, "Justice at the Barrel of a Gun: Vigilante Militias in Mexico," Latin America Briefing 29, May 28, 2013, https://www.crisisgroup.org/latin-america-caribbean/mexico/justice-barrel-gun-vigilante-militias-mexico.
63. Some of these actions, including torture and executions, are graphically captured in the documentary *Cartel Land*.
64. Kyle, "Violence and Insecurity," 44–45.
65. In 2023, major OCGs included Sinaloa, Los Zetas, Tijuana/AFO, Juárez/CFO, Beltrán Leyva, Gulf, La Familia Michoacana, the Knights Templar, and Cartel Jalisco Nuevo Generación.
66. On security specialists, see José Miguel Cruz, "Criminal Violence and Democratization in Central America: The Survival of the Violent State," *Latin American Politics and Society* 53, no. 4 (2011): 1–33.
67. Brian J. Phillips, "Terror Tactics by Criminal Organizations: The Mexican Case," *Perspectives on Terrorism* 12, no. 1 (2018): 46–63.
68. Brian J. Phillips and Viridiana Ríos, "Narco-Messages: Competition and Public Communication by Criminal Groups," *Latin American Politics and Society* 62, no. 1 (2020): 1–24.
69. Ana Villarreal, "Fear and Spectacular Drug Violence in Monterrey," in *Violence and the Urban Margins*, ed. Javier Auyero, Philippe Bourgois, and Nancy Scheper-Hughes, 135–61 (Oxford: Oxford University Press, 2015).
70. *La Jornada*, "Arrojan 5 cabezas humanas en centro nocturno de Uruapán," September 7, 2006, https://www.jornada.com.mx/2006/09/07/index.php?section=estados&article=037n1est.

71. Investigations established that groups apparently adopted these tactics from jihadist groups such as Daesh (ISIS). Secretaría de Gobernación security officer, interview by the author, Mexico City, September 2012.
72. Phil Williams, "The Terrorism Debate Over Mexican Drug Trafficking Violence," *Terrorism and Political Violence* 24, no. 2 (2012): 260.
73. Marco Sassòli, and Antoine A. Bouvier, *How Does Law Protect in War* (Geneva: International Committee of the Red Cross, 1999), 123. The other requisite, wearing a distinctive sign, which is often not met in the Mexican setting, is trumped by the fact that DTO operatives carry their weapons openly.
74. Sassòli and Bouvier, *How Does Law Protect*.
75. On these groups modus operandi see Ioan Grillo, *El Narco: Inside Mexico's Criminal Insurgency* (New York: Bloomsbury Press, 2011). Distinctions are difficult to make as there are clearly gray areas, including whether individuals working for DTOs such as so-called *halcones* (falcons)—people guarding strongholds—should be considered combatants. These people, including teenagers, food vendors, and taxi drivers are normally not armed but indirectly participate in these organizations' armed activities by serving as their eyes and ears. In addition, it is debatable whether minors actively participating as contract killers, enforcers, and operatives should be considered combatants, see Ken Elingwood, "The Grim Glossary of the Narcoworld," *Los Angeles Times*, September 16, 2014, https://www.latimes.com/la-fg-narco-glossary28-2009oct28-story.html
76. Trejo and Ley, *Votes, Drugs, and Violence*.
77. Lessing, "Logic of Violence."
78. Lessing, "Logic of Violence," 1506.
79. Richard Snyder and Angelica Durán-Martínez, "Does Illegality Breed Violence? Drug Trafficking and State Sponsored Protection Rackets," *Crime, Law, and Social Change* 52 (2009): 253–73.
80. Grillo, *El Narco*, 102.
81. Angélica Durán-Martínez, *The Politics of Drug Violence: Criminals, Cops and Politicians in Colombia and Mexico* (Oxford: Oxford University Press, 2018), 182–83.
82. Trejo and Ley, *Votes, Drugs, and Violence*, 77.
83. An alternative account arguing that Mexican DTOs eschewed terrorism because they sought to maintain civilian support. See Steward Scott. "Why Don't Mexico's Cartles use Vehicle Bombs," Stratfor, January 14, 2020, https://worldview.stratfor.com/article/mexico-drug-cartel-violence-car-bombs.
84. Roland Sánchez, "The Gulf Cartel: Profile, History, Methods, Practices and Geo-Politics" (master's thesis, University of Texas Rio Grande Valley, 2018).
85. Grillo, *El Narco*.
86. Tom Dart, "Mexican Cartel Team Used Elaborate Tactics to Hunt Murdered Rival in Texas," *The Guardian*, April 26, 2016, https://www.theguardian.com/world/2016/apr/26/mexico-drug-gulf-cartel-revenge-murder-texas-hunt-juan-jesus-guerrero-chapa.

87. Raúl Flores Martínez, "Dan 143 Años de Cárcel a Secuestradores Del Cártel Del Golfo," *Excelsior*, March 2, 2020, https://www.excelsior.com.mx/nacional/dan-143-anos-de-carcel-a-secuestradores-del-cartel-del-golfo/1435572.
88. Fernando Escalante, "Crimen Organizado: La Dimensión Imaginaria," *Nexos* 15008 (2002): 12–19.
89. Juan Paullier, "México: Así Ocurrió La Brutal y Olvidada Masacre de Allende, Una de Las Más Sangrientas de Los Zetas," BBC Mundo, October 10, 2016, https://www.bbc.com/mundo/noticias-america-latina-37614215.
90. Michael Evans, "The Allende Massacre in Mexico: A Decade of Impunity," National Security Archive, March 18, 2021, https://nsarchive.gwu.edu/briefing-book/mexico/2021-03-18/allende-massacre-decade-impunity.
91. George Greyson, "Los Zetas: The Ruthless Army Spawned by a Mexican Drug Cartel," Foreign Policy Research Institute, May 13, 2008, https://www.fpri.org/article/2008/05/los-zetas-the-ruthless-army-spawned-by-a-mexican-drug-cartel.
92. Claudio Lomnitz, "Los Caballeros Templarios de Michoacán: An Ethnography," *Representations* 147, no. 1 (2019): 96–123.
93. Trejo and Ley, *Votes, Drugs, and Violence*, 193–98.
94. Ioan Grillo, *Gangster Warlords: Drug Dollars, Killing Fields, and the New Politics of Latin America* (London: Bloomsbury Press, 2016).
95. Mayor of Nueva Italia, interview by the author, Morelia Michoacán, December 2017.
96. InSight Crime, "Jalisco Cartel New Generation," July 8, 2020, https://insightcrime.org/mexico-organized-crime-news/jalisco-cartel-new-generation.
97. Vanda Felbab-Brown, "Criminal Violence, Politics and State Capture in Michoacán" (Washington, DC: Brookings Institution, September 24, 2021), https://www.brookings.edu/opinions/criminal-violence-politics-and-state-capture-in-michoacan.

Conclusion

1. Jessica A. Stanton, "Terrorism in the Context of Civil War," *Journal of Politics* 75, no. 4 (2013): 1009–22.
2. Nicholas Sambanis, "Terrorism and Civil War," in *Terrorism, Economic Development, and Political Openness*, ed. Philip Keefer and Norman Loyza, 174–206 (Cambridge: Cambridge University Press, 2008).
3. These violations are considered war crimes or crimes against humanity (when systematic and widespread). See Theodor Meron, *The Humanization of International Law* (Leiden: Brill Nihjoff, 2006).
4. Bruce Hoffman, *Inside Terrorism* (New York: Columbia University Press, 2006).
5. Carl Von Clausewitz, *On War* (Princeton, NJ: Princeton University Press, 1976).
6. Alex P. Schmid, and Janny de Graaf, *Violence as Communication: Insurgent Terrorism and the Western News Media* (London: Sage, 1982).

7. Stanton, "Terrorism and Civil War."
8. Eugen Victor Walter, *Terror and Resistance* (Oxford: Oxford University Press, 1969).
9. Hugo Slim, *Killing Civilians: Method, Madness, and Morality in War* (New York: Columbia University Press, 2008).
10. Benjamin Lessing, "Logic of Violence in Criminal War," *Journal of Conflict Resolution* 59, no. 8 (2015): 486–516.
11. Jonathan Leader Maynard, "Ideology and Armed Conflict," *Journal of Peace Research* 56, no. 5 (2019): 635–49.
12. Pierre Gassmann, "Colombia: Persuading Belligerents to Comply with International Norms," in *Civilians in War*, ed. Simon Chesterman, 67–92 (Boulder, CO: Lynne Rienner, 2001).
13. Ami Carpenter, "Civilian Protection in Mexico & Guatemala: Humanitarian Engagement with Druglords & Gangs," *Homeland Security Review* 6, no. 2 (2012): 111.
14. Elena Lucchi and Schuberth Moritz, "Negotiating Humanitarian Space with Criminal Armed Groups in Urban Latin America," *Disasters* 47, no. 3 (2022): 700–24, https://doi.org/10.1111/disa.12569.
15. José Miguel Cruz and Angélica Durán-Martínez, "Hiding Violence to Deal with the State: Criminal Pacts in El Salvador and Medellín," *Journal of Peace Research* 53, no. 2 (2016): 197–210; International Crisis Group, "Protecting Colombia's Most Vulnerable on the Road to Total Peace," Latin America Report no. 38, February 24, 2023, https://www.crisisgroup.org/latin-america-caribbean/andes/colombia/98-protecting-colombias-most-vulnerable-road-total-peace.
16. Francisco Gutiérrez-Sanín and Elizabeth Jean Wood, "Ideology in Civil War: Instrumental Adoption and Beyond," *Journal of Peace Research* 51, no. 2 (2014): 218.
17. Tamara Makarenko, "The Crime-Terror Continuum: Tracing the Interplay Between Transnational Organised Crime and Terrorism," *Global Crime* 6, no. 1 (2004): 129–45.
18. Benjamin Lessing, "Conceptualizing Criminal Governance," *Perspectives on Politics* 19, no. 3 (2020): 856.
19. Lucchi and Schuberth, "Negotiating Humanitarian Space."
20. Marco Sassòli, "Taking Armed Groups Seriously: Ways to Improve Their Compliance with International Humanitarian Law," *Journal of International Humanitarian Legal Studies* 1, no. 1 (2010): 5–51.
21. Benjamin Lessing, *Making Peace in Drug Wars: Crackdowns and Cartels in Latin America* (Cambridge: Cambridge University Press, 2017).
22. Juan Camilo Castillo and Dorothy Kronick, "The Logic of Violence in Drug War," *American Political Science Review* 114, no. 3 (2020): 874–87.
23. Jenna Jordan, *Leadership Decapitation: Strategic Targeting of Terrorist Organizations* (Stanford, CA: Stanford University Press, 2019).

Bibliography

Abdelal, Rawi, Yoshiko M. Herrera, Alastair Iain Johnston, and Rose McDermott "Identity as a Variable." *Perspectives on Politics* 4, no. 4 (2006): 695–711.
Adler, Emmanuel. "Seizing the Middle Ground: Constructivism in World Politics." *European Journal of International Relations* 3, no. 3 (2015): 319–63.
Agencia EFE. "La guerrilla del ELN advierte que juzgará a los subversivos que humillen al enemigo." May 9, 2015. https://quepasamedia.com/noticias/mundo/mexico/laguerrilla-del-eln-advierte-que-juzgara-a-los-subversivos-que-humillen-al.
Aguilera, Mario. "ELN: Entre las armas y la política." In *Nuestra guerra sin nombre: Transformaciones del conflicto en Colombia*, ed. Francisco Gutiérrez-Sanín, María Emma Willis, and Gonzalo Sánchez, 209–66. Bogotá: IEPRI/Norma, 2006.
Albarracín, Juan. "Criminalized Electoral Politics in Brazilian Urban Peripheries." *Crime, Law, and Social Change* 69, no. 4 (2018): 553–75.
Albert, Stuart, and David A. Whetten. "Organizational Identity." *Research in Organizational Behavior* no. 7 (1985): 263–285.
Albertus, Michael, and Oliver Kaplan. "Land Reform as a Counterinsurgency Policy: Evidence from Colombia." *Journal of Conflict Resolution* 57, no. 2 (2013): 198–231.
Ames, Barry. "Military and Society in Latin America." *Latin American Research Review* 23, no. 2 (1988): 157–69.
Anaya Muñoz, Alejandro and Barbara Frey, eds. *Mexico's Human Rights Crisis*. Philadelphia: University of Pennsylvania Press, 2020.
Anderson, Elijah. *Code of the Street: Decency, Violence, and the Moral Life of the Inner City*. New York: Norton, 1999.
Appleby, Peter, Chris Dalby, Sean Doherty, Scott Mistler-Ferguson, and Henry Shuldiner. "InSight Crime's 2022 Homicide Round-Up." InSight Crime, February 8, 2023. https://insightcrime.org/news/insight-crime-2022-homicide-round-up.

Ansolabehere, Karina, Barbara Frey, and Laigh A. Payne. Introduction to *Disappearances in the Post-Transition Era in Latin America*, ed. Karina Ansolabehere, Barbara Frey, and Laigh A. Payne, 1–29. Oxford: Oxford University Press 2021.

Arango, Carlos. *FARC: Veinte años de Marquetalia a la Uribe*. 5th ed. Bogotá: Ediciones Aurora, 1984.

Aranguren, Mauricio. *Mi confesión: Carlos Castaño revela sus secretos*. Bogotá: Oveja Negra, 2001.

Ardila-Castro, Carlos, Eduardo Gamez, and Petrona Tirado. "Los artefactos explosivos improvisados AEI: Una amenaza para el Estado colombiano." In *Desafíos para la seguridad y defensa nacional de Colombia: Teoría y praxis*, ed. Jaime Cubides and Jonnathan Jiménez, 255–309. Bogotá: Escuela Superior de Guerra, 2017.

Arenas, Jacobo. *Cese al fuego: Una historia política de las FARC*. Bogotá: Oveja Negra, 1985.

Arenas, Jaime. *La Guerrilla por dentro*. Bogotá: Tercer Mundo, 1971.

Arias, Enrique Desmond. *Criminal Enterprises and Governance in Latin America and the Caribbean*. Cambridge: Cambridge University Press, 2017.

Arjona, Ana. *Rebelocracy: Social Order in the Colombian Civil War*. New York: Cambridge University Press, 2016.

Arjona, Ana, and Stathis N. Kalyvas. "Paramilitarismo: Una perspectiva teórica," in *El poder paramilitar*, ed. Alfredo Rangel, 25–45. Bogotá: Fundación Seguridad y Democracia, 2005.

Arnson, Cynthia, and Eric Olson, eds. *One Goal Two Struggles: Confronting Crime and Violence in Mexico and Colombia*. Washington, DC: Woodrow Wilson International Center for Scholars, 2014. https://www.wilsoncenter.org/sites/default/files/media/documents/publication/Colombia_Mexico_Final.pdf.

Arriagada, Genaro. *El pensamiento político de los militares: Estudios sobre Argentina, Brasil, Chile y Uruguay*. Santiago de Chile: Editorial Aconcagua, 1986.

Asprey, Robert. *War in the Shadows: The Guerrilla in History*. New York: Harper Collins, 1994.

Atehortúa, Adolfo. "Colombia en la guerra de Corea." *Folios* 27 (2008): 63–76.

Auger, Vincent. "Right-Wing Terror." *Perspectives on Terrorism* 14, no. 3 (2020): 87–97.

Autodefensas Unidas de Colombia. "Discurso autodefensa: Comandantes Carlos Castaño, Salvatore Mancuso y Adolfo Paz." 2004. https://www.youtube.com/watch?v=LgMbz3coo04.

Bada, Xóchitl, and Andreas E. Feldmann. "Mexico's Michoacán State: Mixed Migration Flows and Transnational Links." *Forced Migration Review* 56 (2017): 12–14.

BBC Mundo. "De qué se acusa Álvaro Uribe y por qué su arresto domiciliario es histórico en Colombia." August 4, 2020. https://www.bbc.com/mundo/noticias-america-latina-53658947.

Balcells, Laia. "Rivalry and Revenge: Violence Against Civilians in Civil War." *International Studies Quarterly* 54, no. 2 (2010): 291–313.

Balcells, Laia, and Jessica A. Stanton. "Violence Against Civilians During Armed Conflict: Moving Beyond the Macro- and Micro-Level Divide." *Annual Review of Political Science* 24, no. 1 (2021): 45–69.

Bandura, Albert. "Moral Disengagement in the Perpetration of Inhumanities." *Personality and Social Psychology Review* 3, no. 3 (1999): 193–209.

Beckett, Ian. *Encyclopedia of Guerrilla Warfare*. Santa Barbara, CA: ABC-CLIO, 1999.
Bedoya, Jineth. *Vida y muerte del Mono Jojoy*. Bogotá: Intermedio Editores, 2010.
Behar, Olga, and Carolina Ardilla. *El caso Klein. El origen del paramilitarismo*. Bogotá: Icono Editorial, 2012.
Bell-Martin, Rebecca V., and Jerome F. Marston Jr. "Confronting Selection Bias: The Normative and Empirical Risks of Data Collection in Violent Contexts." *Geopolitics* 26, no. 1 (2019): 159–92.
Bellamy, Alex. *Massacres and Morality: Mass Atrocities in an Age of Civilian Immunity*. Oxford: Oxford University Press, 2012.
Beltrán, Miguel Ángel. *Las FARC-EP (1950-2015): Lucha de ira y esperanza*. Bogotá: Ediciones Desde Abajo, 2015.
Berenskoetter, Felix. "Identity in International Relations." In *The International Studies Encyclopedia*, ed. Robert A. Denmark and Renée Marlin-Bennett, 3594–611. Oxford University Press, 2017.
Björnehed, Emma. "Narco-Terrorism: The Merger of the War on Drugs and the War on Terror." *Global Crime* 6, no. 3–4 (2004): 305–24.
Blair Trujillo, Elsa. *Las Fuerzas Armadas: Una mirada civil*. Bogotá: CINEP, 1993.
Blakeley, Ruth. *State Terrorism and Neoliberalism: The North in the South*. London: Routledge, 2009.
———. "State Violence as State Terror." In *The Ashgate Research Companion to Political Violence*, ed. Marie Breen-Smyth, 63–78. London: Ashgate, 2012.
Blombäck, Anna, and Olof Brunninge. "Corporate Identity Manifested Through Historical References." *Corporate Communications: An International Journal* 14, no. 4 (2009): 404–19.
Bloom, Mia. *Bombshell: Women and Terrorism*. Philadelphia: University of Pennsylvania Press, 2011.
Bolívar, Simón. "Discurso pronunciado por Simón Bolívar ante el Congreso de Venezuela en Angostura, 15 de febrero de 1819." *Co-Herencia*, 16 no. 31 (2019): 397–424.
Booth, John A. "Socioeconomic and Political Roots of National Revolts in Central America." *Latin America Research Review* 26, no. 1 (1991): 33–73.
Botero, Juan Enrique. "LAS FARC-EP ante el nuevo gobierno: Entrevista a Alfonso Cano." *El Tiempo*, June 8, 2002.
Bowden, Marc. *Killing Pablo: The Hunt for the World's Greatest Outlaw*. New York: Grove Press, 2001.
Brands, Hal. *Latin America's Cold War*. Cambridge, MA: Harvard University Press, 2010.
Brienza, Hernán. *Camilo Torres: Sacristán de la guerrilla*. Buenos Aires: Capital Intelectual SA., 2008.
Brubaker, Rogers, and Frederick Cooper. "Beyond 'Identity.'" *Theory and Society* 29, no. 1 (2000): 1–47.
Bucher, Bernd, and Ursula Jasper. "Revisiting 'Identity.'" In International Relations: From Identity as Substance to Identifications in Action." *European Journal of International Relations* 23, no. 2 (2016): 391–415.
Bueno de Mesquita, Ethan. "Conciliation, Counterterrorism, and Patterns of Terrorist Violence." *International Organization* 59, no. 1 (2005): 145–76.

Bugnion, François. *The International Committee of the Red Cross and the Protection of War Victims*. Oxford: MacMillan for the International Committee of the Red Cross, 2003.

Buitrago, Luis Miguel. "La relación entre las FARC y el ELN: Guerra sin cuartel y confraternidad revolucionaría (2005–2010)." MA thesis, Instituto de Estudios Políticos, Universidad Nacional de Colombia, 2016. https://repositorio.unal.edu.co/bitstream/handle/unal/59463/1023916755.2017.pdf.

Bull, Hedley. *The Anarchical Society*. New York: Columbia University Press, 1984.

Bunker, Pamela, Lisa Campbell, and Robert Bunker. "Torture, Beheadings and Narcocultos." *Small Arms and Insurgencies* 21 (2010): 145–78.

Bushnell, David. *The Making of Modern Colombia: A Nation in Spite of Itself*. Berkeley: University of California Press, 1993.

Butcher, Charity. "Civil War and Terrorism: A Call for Further Theory Building." *Oxford Research Encyclopedia Politics* August (2017): 1–24.

Camacho, Álvaro. "De narcos, paracracias y mafias." In *En la encrucijada: Colombia en el siglo XXI*, ed. Francisco Leal, 387–419. Bogotá: Norma, 2006.

Campbell, Bruce B. "Death Squads: Definition, Problems and Historical Context." In *Death Squads in Global Perspective: Murder with Deniability*, ed. Bruce B. Campbell and Arthur D. Brenner, 1–26. New York: St. Martin Press, 2000.

Carey, Sabine C., and Neil J. Mitchell. "Progovernment Militias." *Annual Review of Political Science* 20 (2017): 127–47.

Carpenter, Ami. "Civilian Protection in Mexico & Guatemala: Humanitarian Engagement with Druglords & Gangs." *Homeland Security Review* 6, no. 2 (2012): 109–36.

Castañeda, Jorge. *Compañero: The Life and Death of Che Guevara*. New York: Vintage Books, 1998.

———. *Utopia Unarmed: The Latin American Left after the Cold War*. New York: Vintage Books, 2003.

Castaño, Daniel, and Gabriel Ruíz. "La construcción del discurso contrainsurgente como legitimador del poder paramilitar en Colombia." *Estudios Políticos* 51 (2017): 153–74.

Castillo, Juan Camilo, and Dorothy Kronick. "The Logic of Violence in Drug War." *American Political Science Review* 114, no. 3 (2020): 874–87.

Centro de Investigación y Educación Popular. "Banco de Datos." *Revista Noche y Niebla*, no. 67. September 27, 2023. https://www.nocheyniebla.org.

Centro Nacional de Memoria Histórica (Centro Nacional). "¡Basta Ya! Colombia: Memorias de guerra y dignidad." 2013. https://www.centrodememoriahistorica.gov.co/descargas/informes2013/bastaYa/resumen-ejecutivo-basta-ya.pdf.

———. "Desaparición forzada." 2018. https://centrodememoriahistorica.gov.co/wp-content/uploads/2020/01/BALANCE_DESAPARICION_FORZADA.pdf.

———. "Guerrilla y población civil: La trayectoria de las FARC 1949–2013." 2014. https://centrodememoriahistorica.gov.co/wp-content/uploads/2020/01/Guerrilla-y-poblaci%C3%B3n-civil.-Trayectoria-de-las-FARC-1949-2013-1.pdf.

———. "Hasta encontrarlos el drama de la desaparición forzada en Colombia." 2016. https://centrodememoriahistorica.gov.co/descargas/informes2016/hasta-encontrarlos/hastaencontrarlos-drama-de-la-desaparicion-forzada-en-colombia.pdf.

———. "Iglesia La María 20 años del secuestro del ELN." 2019. https://centrodememoria-historica.gov.co/iglesia-la-maria-20-anos-delsecuestro-del-eln.
———. "Isaza, el clan paramilitar: Las autodefensas campesinas del Magdalena Medio." 2020. https://centrodememoriahistorica.gov.co/isaza-el-clan-paramilitar.
———. *La Rochela: Memorias de un crimen contra la justicia*. Bogotá: Ediciones Semana, 2011.
———. *Masacre El Tigre, Putumayo*. Bogotá: Pro-offset Editorial, 2011.
———. "Paramilitarismo." 2018. https://centrodememoriahistorica.gov.co/wp-content/uploads/2020/01/PARAMILITARISMO.pdf.
———. "Una sociedad secuestrada." 2013. https://issuu.com/centronacionalmemoriahistorica/docs/una-sociedad-secuestrada.
Checkel, Jeffrey T. "Socialization and Violence: Introduction and Framework." *Journal of Peace Research* 54, no. 5 (2017): 592–605.
Chenoweth, Erica. "Democratic Competition and Terrorist Activity." *Journal of Politics* 71, no. 1 (2010): 16–30.
———. "Terrorism and Democracy." *Annual Review of Political Science* 16: 355–78.
Chenoweth, Erica, and Pauline E. Moore. *The Politics of Terror*. Oxford: Oxford University Press, 2018.
Chenoweth, Erica, Richard English, Andreas Gofas, and Stathis N. Kalyvas, eds. *The Oxford Handbook of Terrorism*. Oxford: Oxford University Press, 2019.
Claridge, David. "State Terrorism? Applying a Definitional Model." *Terrorism and Political Violence* 8, no. 3 (1996): 47–63.
Clutterback, Richard. *Terrorism and Guerrilla Warfare*. London: Routledge, 1990.
Cohen, Dara Kay. "The Ties That Bind: How Armed Groups Use Violence to Socialize Fighters." *Journal of Peace Research* 54, no. 5 (2017): 701–14.
Collins, Joshua. "Colombia Peace Talks with ELN Rebels Resume Amid Tensions." Aljazeera, February 13, 2023. https://www.aljazeera.com/news/2023/2/13/colombia-peace-talks-with-eln-rebels-set-to-resume-amid-tensions.
Colombian Defense Ministry. "Grupos GAULA." 2023. https://www.cgfm.mil.co/es/atencion-alciudadano/direccion-nacional-de-gaula-militares.
Comisión Colombiana de Juristas. *Colombia Derechos Humanos y Derecho Humanitario: 1997-2001*, Vol. 1. Bogotá: Comisión Colombiana de Juristas, 2005.
Comisión de la Verdad y Reconciliación. "Reporte Final." 2004. https://www.cverdad.org.pe/ifinal.
Comisión Nacional de Derechos Humanos México. "Informe Especial de los grupos de autodefensa en el estado de Michoacán y las violaciones a los derechos humanos relacionadas con el conflicto." 2015. https://www.cndh.org.mx/documento/informe-especialsobre-los-grupos-de-autodefensa-en-el-estado-de-michoacan-y-las-0.
Comisión Nacional de Verdad y Reconciliación. "Informe de la Comisión Nacional de Verdad y Reconciliación." No. de Inscripción 98.498. December 1996. https://bibliotecadigital.indh.cl/bitstream/handle/123456789/170/tomo1.pdf.
Comisión para el Esclarecimiento de la Verdad la Convivencia y la No Repetición. "Hallazgos y Recomendaciones." 2022. https://www.comisiondelaverdad.co/hallazgos-y-recomendaciones-1.

Congreso Internacional Para No Volver a la Guerra. "Mejores momentos Ernesto Báez: Congreso internacional para no V=volver a la guerra." 2020. https://www.youtube.com/watch?v=BJuCKHwSYVE.

Consejo de Estado Colombia. "Rodrigo Márquez Tejeda y Otros v/s Nación-Ministerio de Defensa-Policía Nacional y otros." 2018. https://www.funcionpublica.gov.co/eva/gestornormativo/norma.php?i=88139.

Corradi, Juan, Patricia Weiss Fagen, and Manuel Antonio Garretón, eds. *Fear at the Edge: State Terror and Resistance in Latin America*. Berkeley: University of California Press, 1992.

Cosoy, Natalio. "Why Has Colombia Seen an Increase in Activist Murders." BBC World, May 19, 2017. https://www.bbc.com/news/world-latin-america-39717336.

Crenshaw, Martha. "The Causes of Terrorism." *Comparative Politics* 13, no. 4 (1981): 379–99.

———. *Revolutionary Terrorism: The FLN in Algeria 1954–1962*. Stanford, CA: Hoover Institution, 1978.

Cruz, José Miguel. "Criminal Violence and Democratization in Central America: The Survival of the Violent State." *Latin American Politics and Society* 53, no. 4 (2011): 1–33.

Cruz, José Miguel, and Angélica Durán-Martínez. "Hiding Violence to Deal with the State: Criminal Pacts in El Salvador and Medellín." *Journal of Peace Research* 53 no. 2 (2016): 197–210.

Cubides, Fernando. "From Private to Public Violence: The Paramilitaries." In *Violence in Colombia 1990–2000: Waging War and Negotiating Peace*, ed. Charles Bergquist, Ricardo Peñaranda, and Gonzalo Sánchez, 127–49. Wilmington, DE: SR Books, 2001.

Daly, Sarah Z. *Organized Violence After Civil War: The Geography of Recruitment in Latin America*. Cambridge: Cambridge University Press, 2016.

Dart, Tom. "Mexican Cartel Team Used Elaborate Tactics to Hunt Murdered Rival in Texas." *The Guardian*, April 26, 2016. https://www.theguardian.com/world/2016/apr/26/mexico-drug-gulf-cartel-revenge-murder-texas-hunt-juan-jesus-guerrero-chapa.

Dávila, Andrés. *El juego del poder: Historia, armas y votos*. Bogotá: CERC, Ediciones Uniandes, 1998.

De la Calle, Luis, and Ignacio Sánchez-Cuenca. "Rebels without a Territory: An Analysis of Nonterritorial Conflicts in the World, 1970–1997." *Journal of Conflict Resolution* 56, no. 4 (2012): 580–603.

———. "What We Talk About When We Talk About Terrorism." *Politics & Society* 39, no. 3 (2011): 451–72.

Delgado, Jorge. 2015. "Colombian Military Thinking and the Fight Against the FARC-EP Insurgency, 2002–2014." *Journal of Strategic Studies* 38 (2015): 826–51.

Della Porta, Donatella. *Social Movements, Political Violence, and the State: A Comparative Analysis of Italy and Germany*. Cambridge: Cambridge University Press, 2006.

Dieterich, Antje. "Are FARC Militias a Wild Card in Colombia Peace Process?" InSight Crime, September 15, 2016. https://insightcrime.org/news/brief/are-farc-militias-a-wild-card-in-colombia-peace-process.

Dishman, Chris. "Terrorism, Crime and Transformation." *Studies in Conflict & Terrorism* 24, no. 1 (2001): 43–58.

Doctor Austin C. "Rebel Leadership and the Specialization of Rebel Operations." *Civil Wars*, April (2021): 1–32.

Doyle, Michael W., and Nicholas Sambanis. *Making War & Building Peace: United Nations Peace Operations*. Princeton, NJ: Princeton University Press, 2006.

Drake, C. J. M. 1998. "The Role of Ideology in Terrorists' Target Selection." *Terrorism and Political Violence* 10, no. 2 (1998): 53–85.

Dudley, Steven. *Armas y urnas: Historia de un genocidio político*. Bogotá: Planeta, 2008.

Dugas, John. "The Colombian Nightmare: Human Rights Abuses and the Contradictory Effects of US Foreign Policy." In *When States Kill: Latin America, the US, and Technologies of Terror*, ed. Cecilia Menjívar and Néstor Rodríguez, 227–51. Austin: University of Texas Press, 2005.

Duncan, Gustavo. *Beyond Plata o Plomo: Drugs and State Reconfiguration in Colombia*. New York: Cambridge University Press, 2022.

———. "Exclusión, insurrección y crimen." In *Contribución al entendimiento del conflicto armado en Colombia*, ed. Comisión Histórica del Conflicto y sus Víctimas, 249–94. Bogotá: Ediciones Desde Abajo, 2015.

———. "Historia de una subordinación. ¿Cómo los guerreros sometieron a los narcotraficantes?" In *el desarrollo: Perspectivas y dimensiones, aportes interdisciplinarios*, ed. Carlos Zorro Sánchez, 433–52. Bogotá: Ediciones Uniandes, 2007.

———. *Los señores de la guerra: De paramilitares, mafiosos y autodefensas en Colombia*. Bogotá: Planeta, 2006.

———. *Más plata que plomo: El poder político del narcotráfico en Colombia y México*. Bogotá: Debate, 2015.

Duncan, Gustavo, Santiago Sosa, and José Antonio Fortou. "Terrorism and Organized Crime in Colombia." In *The Nexus Between Organized Crime and Terrorism*, ed. Letizia Paoli, Cyrille Fijnaut, and Jan Wouters, 412–32. Cheltenham, UK: Edward Elgar, 2022.

Durán-Martínez, Angélica. *The Politics of Drug Violence: Criminals, Cops and Politicians in Colombia and Mexico*. Oxford: Oxford University Press, 2018.

Eaton, Kent. "Subnational Economic Nationalism? The Contradictory Effects of Decentralization in Peru." *Third World Quarterly* 31, no. 7 (2010): 1205–22.

Echandía, Camilo. "Auge y declive del Ejército de Liberación Nacional: Análisis de la evolución militar y territorial de cara a la negociación." Fundación Ideas para la Paz, Informe 21, Noviembre, 2013. https://www.files.ethz.ch/isn/175224/529debc8a48fa.pdf.

———. *Dos décadas de escalamiento del conflicto armado en Colombia 1986-2006*. Bogotá: Universidad del Externado, 2006.

———. "Expansión territorial de las guerrillas colombianas: Geografía, Eeconomía y violencia." In *Reconocer la guerra para construir la paz*, ed. Malcolm Deas and María Victoria Llorente, 99–149. Bogotá: Uniandes-Cerc-Norma, 1999.

Eck, Kristine, and Lisa Hultman. "One-Sided Violence Against Civilians in War: Insights from New Fatality Data." *Journal of Peace Research* 44, no. 2 (2007): 233–46.

Elingwood, Ken. "The Grim Glossary of the Narcoworld." *Los Angeles Times*, September 16, 2014. https://www.latimes.com/la-fg-narco-glossary28-2009oct28-story.html.

El Tiempo. "En combates murió autor intelectual de secuestro de avión de Avianca." February 16, 2015. https://www.eltiempo.com/archivo/documento/CMS-15259155.

———. "Se cumplen 18 años del atentado del Nogal." February 7, 2021. https://www.eltiempo.com/justicia/jep-colombia/atentado-al-club-el-nogal-se-cumplen-18-anos-del-carro-bomba-en-que-va-el-proceso-judicial-565243.

———. "Se entrenaban para matar picando campesinos vivos." April 23, 2007. https://www.eltiempo.com/archivo/documento/CMS-3525024.

Enders, Walter and Todd, Sandler. *The Political Economy of Terrorism*. Cambridge: Cambridge University Press, 2006.

Esberg, Jane. "More Than Cartels: Counting Mexico's Crime Rings." International Crisis Group, May 8, 2020. https://www.crisisgroup.org/latin-america-caribbean/mexico/more-cartels-counting-mexicos-crime-rings.

Escalante, Fernando. "Crimen organizado: La dimensión imaginaria." *Nexos* 15008 (2002): 12–19.

Evans, Michael. "The Allende Massacre in Mexico: A Decade of Impunity." National Security Archive, March 18, 2021. https://nsarchive.gwu.edu/briefing-book/mexico/2021-03-18/allende-massacre-decade-impunity.

Fearon, James. "What Is Identity? (As We Now Use the Word)." Unpublished paper, Stanford University, 1999. https://web.stanford.edu/group/fearon-research/cgi-bin/wordpress/wp-content/uploads/2013/10/What-is-Identity-as-we-now-use-the-word-.pdf.

Fearon, James, and David Laitin. 2003. "Ethnicity, Insurgency and Civil War." *American Political Science Review* 97, no. 1 (2003): 75–90.

Felbab-Brown, Vanda. "Criminal Violence, Politics and State Capture in Michoacán." Washington, DC: Brookings Institution, September 24, 2021. https://www.brookings.edu/opinions/criminal-violence-politics-and-state-capture-in-michoacan.

———. "The Rise of Militias in Mexico: Citizens' Security or Further Conflict Escalation?" *Prism* 5, no. 4 (2016): 173–86.

Feldmann, Andreas E. "Colombia's Polarization Peace Efforts." In *Divided Democracy: The Global Challenge of Political Polarizations*, ed. Tom Carothers and Andrew O'Donohue, 153–74. Washington, DC: Brookings Institution Press, 2019.

———. "Measuring the Colombian Success Story." *Revista de Ciencia Política* 32, no. 3 (2012): 739–52.

———. "Revolutionary Terror in the Colombian Civil War." *Studies in Conflict & Terrorism* 41, no. 10 (2018): 35–52.

———. "A Shift in the Paradigm of Violence: Non-Governmental Terrorism in Latin America Since the End of the Cold War." *Revista de Ciencia Política* 25, no. 2 (2005): 3–35.

Feldmann, Andreas E., and Marc Lopez. "Repertoires of Terrorism in Mexico's Criminal War." *Perspectives on Terrorism* 16, no. 2 (2022): 4–13.

Feldmann, Andreas E., and Juan Pablo Luna. "Criminal Governance and the Crisis of Contemporary Latin American States." *Annual Review of Sociology* 48, no. 1 (2022): 441–61.

———. *Criminal Politics and Botched Development in Contemporary Latin America.* Cambridge: Cambridge University Press, 2023.

Feldmann, Andreas E., and Victor J. Hinojosa. "Terrorism in Colombia: Logic and Sources of a Multidimensional and Ubiquitous Phenomenon." *Terrorism and Political Violence* 21, no. 1 (2009): 42–61.

Feldmann, Andreas E., and Maiju Perälä. "Reassessing the Causes of Nongovernmental Terrorism in Latin America." *Latin American Politics and Society* 46, no. 2 (2004): 101–32.

Ferro, Juan Guillermo, and Graciela Uribe. *El órden de la guerra: Las FARC-EP entre la organización y la política.* Bogotá: Pontificia Universidad Javeriana, 2002.

Fielding, David, and Anja Shortland. "The Dynamics of Terror During the Peruvian Civil War." *Journal of Peace Research* 49, no. 6 (2012): 847–62.

Finnemore, Martha. *National Interests in International Society.* Ithaca, NY: Cornell University Press, 1996.

Fjelde, Hanne, and Lisa Hultman. "Weakening the Enemy: A Disaggregated Study of Violence Against Civilians in Africa." *Journal of Conflict Resolution* 58, no. 7 (2013): 230–57.

Flores Martínez, Raúl. "Dan 143 años de cárcel a secuestradores del Cártel Del Golfo." *Excelsior*, March 2, 2020. https://www.excelsior.com.mx/nacional/dan-143-anos-de-carcel-a-secuestradores-del-cartel-del-golfo/1435572.

Forero, Juan. "Blast at Social Club Struck at Colombia's Elite." *New York Times*, February 9, 2003. https://www.nytimes.com/2003/02/09/world/blast-at-social-club-struck-at-colombia-s-elite.html.

Forest, James J. F. *Teaching Terror: Strategic and Tactical Learning in the Terrorist World.* Lanham, MD: Rowman and Littlefield, 2006.

Fortou, José Antonio, Sandra Lillian Johansson, and Juan Carlos Muñoz Mora. "Control, Dispute, and Concentration of Land During Civil War: Evidence from Colombia." *International Interactions*, 49, no. 2 (2023): 201–36.

Franchetti, Leopoldo. *Condizioni Politiche e Amministrative Della Sicilia.* Rome: Donzelli Editore, 1993.

Fujii, Lee Ann. *Killing Neighbors: Webs of Violence in Rwanda.* Ithaca, NY: Cornell University Press, 2009.

Fundación Ideas para la Paz. "¿Qué hacer con el ELN? Opciones para no cerrar la puerta a una salida negociada." January 28, 2020. https://ideaspaz.org/publicaciones/investigaciones-analisis/2020-01/que-hacer-con-el-eln-opciones-para-no-cerrar-la-puerta-a-una-salida-negociada.

Gagne, David. "InSight Crime Homicide Rate 2016 Round-Up." InSight Crime, January 16, 2017. https://insightcrime.org/news/analysis/insight-crime-2016-homicide-round-up.

Gambetta, Diego. *Codes of the Underworld: How Criminals Communicate*. Princeton, NJ: Princeton University Press, 2011.

——. *The Sicilian Mafia: The Business of Private Protection*. Cambridge, MA: Harvard University Press, 1996.

García Pinzón, Viviana, and Jorge Mantilla. "Contested Borders: Organized Crime, Governance, and Bordering Practices in Colombia-Venezuela Borderlands." *Trends in Organized Crime* 24 (2021): 265–81.

Gassmann, Pierre. "Colombia: Persuading Belligerents to Comply with International Norms." In *Civilians in War*, ed. Simon Chesterman, 67–92. Boulder, CO: Lynne Rienner, 2001.

George, Alexander, and Andrew Bennett. *Case Studies and Theory Development in the Social Sciences*. Cambridge, MA: MIT Press, 2005.

Gerring, John. *Case Study Research*. Cambridge: Cambridge University Press, 2007.

Giraldo, Jorge. *Las ideas en la guerra: Justificación y crítica en la Colombia contemporánea*. Bogotá: Debate, 2015.

Gilbert, Danielle. "The Logic of Kidnapping in Civil War: Evidence from Colombia." *American Political Science Review* 116, no. 4 (2022): 1226–41.

Goodwin, Jeff. "The Causes of Terrorism." In Chenoweth et al., *The Oxford Handbook of Terrorism*, 253–67, 2019.

——. "A Theory of Categorical Terrorism." *Social Forces* 84, no. 4 (2006): 2027–46.

Gott, Richard. *Guerrilla Movements in Latin America*. New York: Doubleday, 1971.

Grabosky, Peter, and Michael Stohl. *Crime and Terrorism*. London: Sage, 2010.

Greyson, George. "Los Zetas: The Ruthless Army Spawned by a Mexican Drug Cartel." *Foreign Policy Research Institute*, May 13, 2008. https://www.fpri.org/article/2008/05/los-zetas-the-ruthless-army-spawned-by-a-mexican-drug-cartel.

Grillo, Ioan. *El Narco: Inside Mexico's Criminal Insurgency*. New York: Bloomsbury Press, 2011.

——. *Gangster Warlords: Drug Dollars, Killing Fields, and the New Politics of Latin America*. London: Bloomsbury Press, 2016.

Gruber, Barbara, and Jan Pospisil. 2015. "'Ser Eleno:' Insurgent Identity in the ELN." *Small Arms and Insurgencies* 26, no. 2 (2015): 226–47.

Guembe María José and Helena Olea, "No Justice, No Peace: Discussion of the Legal Framework Regarding Demobilization of Non-State Groups in Colombia." In *Transitional Justice in the New Millennium: Beyond Truth and Reconciliation*, ed. Naomi Roth-Arriaza and Javier Mariezcurrena, 120–42. Cambridge: Cambridge University Press, 2006.

Guevara, Ernesto. *Guerrilla Warfare*. Lincoln: University of Nebraska Press, 1985.

Guevara, José Antonio. "Amid Brutality and Impunity: Atrocious Crimes Committed Under the Militarized Security Strategy." Mexico City: Comisión Mexicana de Defensa y Promoción de los Derechos Humanos, 2020. https://www.cmdpdh.org/publicaciones-pdf/cmdpdh-amid-brutality-and-impunity.pdf.

Guillén, Abraham. *El error militar de las izquierdas*. Buenos Aires: Editorial Hacer, 1980.

Gurr, Ted Robert. *Minorities at Risk: A Global View of Ethnopolitical Conflicts*. Washington, DC: United States Institute of Peace Press, 2003.

———. "Terrorism in Democracies: Its Social and Political Basis." In *Origins of Terrorism: Psychologies, Ideologies, Theologies, States of Mind*, 2nd ed., ed. Walter Reich, 86–102. Washington, DC: The Woodrow Wilson Center Press; Baltimore, MD: Johns Hopkins University Press, 1998.

Gutiérrez-Sanín, Francisco. *Clientelistic Warfare: Paramilitaries and the State in Colombia (1982–2007)*. Oxford: Peter Lang, 2019.

———. "Criminal Rebels? A Discussion of Civil War and Criminality from the Colombian Perspective." *Politics & Society* 32, no. 2 (2004): 257–85.

———. "Internal Conflict, Terrorism and Crime in Colombia." *Journal of International Development* 18, no. 1 (2006): 137–50.

———. "Telling the Difference: Guerrillas and Paramilitaries in the Colombian War." *Politics & Society* 36, no. 1 (2008): 3–34.

———. *¿Un nuevo ciclo de la guerra en Colombia?* Bogotá: Debate, 2020.

Gutiérrez-Sanín, Francisco, and Mauricio Barón. "Estado, control territorial paramilitar y orden político en Colombia. Notas para una economía política de paramilitarismo, 1978–2004." In *Nuestra guerra sin nombre: Transformaciones del conflicto en Colombia*, ed. Francisco Gutiérrez-Sanín, María Emma Willis, and Gonzalo Sánchez, 267–311. Bogotá: IEPRI Universidad Nacional de Colombia, 2006.

Gutiérrez-Sanín, Francisco, and Elizabeth Jean Wood. "Ideology in Civil War: Instrumental Adoption and Beyond." *Journal of Peace Research* 51, no. 2 (2014): 213–26.

———. "What Should We Mean by 'Pattern of Political Violence?' Repertoire, Targeting, Frequency, and Technique." *Perspectives on Politics* 15, no. 1 (2017): 20–41.

Hartlyn, Jonathan. *The Politics of Coalition Rule in Colombia*. Cambridge: Cambridge University Press, 1988.

Hernández, Milton. *Rojo y negro: Historia del ELN*. Tafalla País Vasco: Txalaparta, 2006.

Hinojosa, Victor J. *Domestic Politics, and International Narcotics Control: IS Relations with Mexico and Colombia 1989–2000*. Routledge. New York, 2007.

Hobsbawn, Eric. "The Revolutionary Situation in Colombia." *World Today* 19, June (1963): 248–58.

Hoffman, Bruce. *Inside Terrorism*. New York: Columbia University Press, 2006.

Holmes, Jennifer, and Sheila Amin-Gutiérrez de Piñares. "Violence and the State: Lessons from Colombia." *Small Wars and Insurgencies* 25, no. 2 (2014): 372–403.

Holsti, Kalevi. *State War and the State of War*. Cambridge: Cambridge University Press.

Hoover Green, Amelia. *The Commander's Dilemma: Violence and Restraint in Wartime*. Ithaca, NY: Cornell University Press, 2018.

Hopf, Ted. 1998. "The Promise of Constructivism in International Relations Theory." *International Security* 23, no. 1 (1998): 171–200.

Horowitz, Donald. *Ethnic Groups in Conflict*. Los Angeles: University of California Press, 2000.

Horowitz, Michael C. "Nonstate Actors and the Diffusion of Innovations: The Case of Suicide Terrorism." *International Organization* 64, no. 1 (2010): 33–64.

Hultman, Lisa "Violence Against Civilians." In *Routledge Handbook of Civil Wars*, ed. Edward Newman and Karl DeRouen Jr., 289–99. London: Routledge, 2014.

Human Rights Watch. "Colombia's Killer Networks: The Military Partnership and the United States." November 1996. https://www.hrw.org/reports/1996/killer2.htm.
———. "El rol de los altos mandos en falsos positivos." June 23, 2015. https://www.hrw.org/es/report/2015/06/23/el-rol-de-los-altos-mandos-en-falsos-positivos/evidencias-de-responsabilidad-de#.
———. "Mexico: Lessons from a Human Rights Catastrophe." January 15, 2019. https://www.hrw.org/blog-feed/mexico-lessons-human-rights-catastrophe#.
———. "Paramilitary Heirs: The New Face of Violence in Colombia." February 3, 2010. https://www.hrw.org/report/2010/02/03/paramilitaries-heirs/new-face-violence-colombia.
Humphreys, Macartan N., and Jeremy M. Weinstein. "Handling and Manhandling Civilians in Civil War." *American Political Science Review* 100, no. 3 (2006): 429–47.
Huntington, Samuel. *The Soldier and the State; The Theory and Practice of Civil Military Relations.* Cambridge, MA: Harvard University Press, 1957.
Hutchinson, Steven, and Pat O'Malley. "A Crime-Terror Nexus? Thinking on Some of the Links Between Terrorism and Criminality." *Studies in Conflict and Terrorism* 30, no. 12 (2007): 1095–107.
Hylton, Forrest. "Plan Colombia: The Measure of Success." *Brown Journal of World Affairs* 17, no. 2 (2010): 99–116.
Inksater, Kimberly, and Paola Jiménez. "The Organization of American States Mission to Support the Peace Process in Colombia." Stockholm: International Institute for Democracy and Electoral Assistance, 2016. https://www.idea.int/sites/default/files/publications/the-organization-of-american-states-mission-to-support-the-peace-process-in-colombia.pdf.
Inkster, Nigel, and Virginia Comolli. *Drugs Insecurity and Failed States: The Problems of Prohibition.* London: Routledge for the International Institute for Strategic Studies, 2012.
InSight Crime. "Colombia Profile." January 1, 2023. https://www.insightcrime.org/colombia-organizedcrime-news/colombia.
———. "Ejército de Liberación Nacional (ELN)." May 2, 2023. https://insightcrime.org/tag/eln.
———. "EPL." July 15, 2022. https://www.insightcrime.org/colombia-organized-crimenews/epl.
———. "Ex FARC Mafia." February 16. 2023. https://es.insightcrime.org/noticias-crimen-organizado-colombia/ex-farc-mafia.
———. "Jalisco Cartel New Generation." July 8, 2020. https://insightcrime.org/mexico-organized-crime-news/jalisco-cartel-new-generation.
———. "Víctor Julio Suárez Rojas, Alias Mono Jojoy." March 10, 2017. https://insightcrime.org/colombiaorganized-crime-news/jorge-briceno-suarez-mono-jojoy.
Instituto de Estudios para el Desarrollo y la Paz. 2021. "El primer asesinato de un líder social en Colombia ocurrió al mediodía del 1 de enero de 2021." January 2, 2021.

https://www.infobae.com/america/colombia/2021/01/02/el-primer-asesinato-de-un-lider-social-en-colombia-ocurrio-al-mediodia-del-1-de-enero-de-2021/#.

Inter-American Court on Human Rights. "Caso de la Masacre de La Rochela Vs. Colombia. Sentencia, Reparaciones y Costas." May 11, 2007. https://www.corteidh.or.cr/docs/casos/articulos/seriec_163_esp.pdf.

———. "Masacre Mapiripán v/s Colombia. Sentencia." September 15, 2005. https://www.corteidh.or.cr/docs/casos/articulos/seriec_134_esp.pdf.

International Crisis Group. "Colombia's Armed Groups Battle for the Spoils of Peace." Latin America & Caribbean Report no. 63, October 19, 2017. https://www.crisisgroup.org/latin-america-caribbean/andes/colombia/63-colombias-armed-groups-battle-spoils-peace.

———. "Justice at the Barrel of a Gun: Vigilante Militias in Mexico." Latin America & Caribbean Briefing no. 29, May 28, 2013. https://www.crisisgroup.org/latin-america-caribbean/mexico/justice-barrel-gun-vigilante-militias-mexico.

———. "Protecting Colombia's Most Vulnerable on the Road to Total Peace." Latin America Report no. 38, February 24, 2023. https://www.crisisgroup.org/latin-america-caribbean/andes/colombia/98-protecting-colombias-most-vulnerable-road-total-peace.

———. "Tackling Colombia's Next Generation in Arms." January 27, 2022. https://www.crisisgroup.org/latin-america-caribbean/andes/colombia/tackling-colombias-next-generation-arms.

International Institute for Strategic Studies. *The Armed Conflict Survey*. London: Routledge for the International Institute for Strategic Studies, 2020.

———. *The FARC Files: Venezuela, Ecuador, and the Secret Archive of Raúl Reyes*. London: International Institute for Strategic Studies, 2011.

Jackson, Richard. "The Ghosts of State Terror: Knowledge, Politics and Terrorism Studies." *Critical Studies on Terrorism* 1, no. 3 (2008): 377–92.

Jentzsch, Corinna, Stathis N. Kalyvas, and Livia Isabella Schubinger. "Militias in Civil Wars." *Journal of Conflict Resolution* 59, no. 5 (2015): 755–69.

Jo, Hyeran. *Compliant Rebels: Rebel Groups and International Law in World Politics*. Cambridge: Cambridge University Press, 2015.

Jordan, Jenna. *Leadership Decapitation: Strategic Targeting of Terrorist Organizations*. Stanford, CA: Stanford University Press, 2019.

La Jornada. "Arrojan 5 cabezas humanas en centro nocturno de Uruapán." September 7, 2006. https://www.jornada.com.mx/2006/09/07/index.php?section=estados&article=037n1est.

Justicia Especial para la Paz. "Audiencia de reconocimiento por 'falsos positivos' en el Catatumbo." April 26, 2022. https://www.youtube.com/watch?v=g2gqn62VkgQ.

Kacowicz, Arie. "Latin America in the Contemporary World Security Architecture." In *Routledge Handbook of Latin American Security Studies*, ed. David Mares and Arie Kacowicz, 336–47. London: Routledge, 2015.

Kaldor, Mary. *New and Old Wars*. Stanford, CA: Stanford University Press, 2001.

Kalyvas, Stathis N. "How Civil Wars Help Explain Organized Crime—and How They Do Not." *Journal of Conflict Resolution* 59, no. 8 (2015): 15–40.
——. "The Landscape of Political Violence." In Chenoweth et al., *The Oxford Handbook of Terrorism*, 11–33, 2019.
——. *The Logic of Violence in Civil War.* Cambridge: Cambridge University Press, 2006.
——. "'New' and 'Old' Civil Wars: Valid Distinctions?" *World Politics* 54, no. 1 (2001): 99–118.
——. "Wanton and Senseless: The Logic of Massacres in Algeria." *Rationality and Society* 11, no. 3 (1999): 243–85.
Kalyvas, Stathis N., and Laia Balcells. "International System Technologies of Rebellion: How the End of the Cold War Shaped Internal Conflict." *American Political Science Review* 104, no. 3 (2010): 415–29.
Koufa, Kalliopi. "Specific Human Rights Issues: New Priorities, in Particular Terrorism and Counterterrorism." Final Report of the Special Rapporteur on Human Rights and Terrorism. E/CN.4/Sub.2/31. New York: United Nations Economic and Social Council. June 25, 2004. https://documents-dds-ny.un.org/doc/UNDOC/GEN/G04/146/77/PDF/G0414677.pdf.
Kavrakis, Konstantinos. "Identity and Ideology Through the Frames of Al-Qaeda and Islamic State." *Terrorism and Political Violence* 35 (2022): 1235–52.
Keen, David. *The Economic Functions of Violence in Civil Wars.* Adelphi Paper. Oxford: Oxford University Press for the International Institute for Strategic Studies, 1996.
Kirk, Robin. *More Terrible Than Death: Massacres, Drugs, and the America's War in Colombia.* New York: Public Affairs, 2003.
Kline, Harvey. *State Building and Conflict Resolution in Colombia, 1986–1999.* Tuscaloosa: University of Alabama Press, 1999.
Knight, Alan. "Narco Violence and the State in Mexico." In *Violence, Coercion and State Making in Twentieth Century Mexico: The Other Half of the Centaur,* ed. Wil Pansters, 115–34. Stanford, CA: Stanford University Press, 2012.
Kohl, James, and John Litt. *Urban Guerrilla Warfare.* Cambridge, MA: MIT Press, 1974.
Kraushaar, Wolfgang. *Die RAF und der Linke Terrorismus.* Hamburg: HIS Verlag, 2006.
Kydd, Andrew, and Barbara Walter. "The Strategies of Terrorism." *International Security* 31, no. 1 (2006): 49–80.
Kyle, Chris. "Violence and Insecurity in Guerrero." Briefing Paper. Washington, DC: Wilson Center Mexico Institute, January 15, 2015. https://www.wilsoncenter.org/publication/violence-and-insecurity-guerrero.
Lair, Eric. "El terror, recurso estratégico de los actores armados: Reflexiones en torno al conflicto colombiano." *Análisis Político* 37 (May/August 1999): 60–72.
Lake, David A. "Rational Extremism: Understanding Terrorism in the Twenty-First Century." *Dialogue IO* 1, no. 1 (2002): 15–28.
Laqueur, Walter. *The Age of Terrorism.* Boston: Little Brown, 1987.
——. *Guerrilla Warfare: A Historical and Critical Study.* New Brunswick, NJ: Transaction Publishers, 1998.

———. *New Terrorism: Fanaticism and the Arms of Mass Destruction.* New York: Oxford University Press, 2000.

Larratt-Smith, Charles. "Navigating Formal and Informal Processes: Civic Organizations, Armed Nonstate Actors, and Nested Governance in Colombia." *Latin American Politics and Society* 62, no. 2 (2020): 75–98.

Leal Buitrago, Francisco. *El oficio de la guerra: Seguridad nacional en Colombia.* Bogotá: Tercer Mundo Editores-IEPRI, 1994.

———. "El surgimiento, auge y crisis de la Doctrina Nacional de Seguridad en América Latina y Colombia." *Análisis Político* 15, no. Enero-Abril (1992): 6–34.

———. *La inseguridad de la seguridad: Colombia 1958-2005.* Bogotá: Planeta, 2006.

Lee, Jarvis, and Michael Lister. "State Terrorism Research and Critical Terrorism Studies: An Assessment." *Critical Studies on Terrorism* 7, no. 1 (2014): 43–61.

Leech, Gary. *The FARC: The Longest Insurgency.* London: ZED Books, 2011.

LeGrand, Catherine. *Frontier Expansion and Peasant Protest in Colombia 1850-1936.* Albuquerque: University of New Mexico Press, 1986.

Lessing, Benjamin. "Conceptualizing Criminal Politics." *Perspectives in Politics* 19, no. 3 (2020): 854–73.

———. "Logic of Violence in Criminal War." *Journal of Conflict Resolution* 59, no. 8 (2015): 1486–1516.

———. *Making Peace in Drug Wars: Crackdowns and Cartels in Latin America.* Cambridge: Cambridge University Press, 2017.

Levy, Jack. "Case Studies: Types, Designs, and Logics of Inference." *Conflict Management and Peace Studies,* 25, no. 1 (2008): 1–18.

Levy, Jack, and William Thompson. *The Arc of War: Origins, Escalation and Transformation.* Chicago: University of Chicago Press, 2011.

Littman, Rebecca, and Elizabeth Levy Paluck. "The Cycle of Violence: Understanding Individual Participation in Collective Violence." *Political Psychology* 36, no. 1 (2015): 79–99.

Lomnitz, Claudio. 2019. "Los Caballeros Templarios de Michoacán: An Ethnography." *Representations* 147, no. 1 (2019): 96–123.

Londoño, Fernando. "Lo que murió con Castaño." *El Colombiano,* April 30, 2013. https://prensarural.org/spip/spip.php?article10765.

Lopez, George. "National Security Ideology as an Impetus to State Violence and State Terror." In *Government Violence and Repression: An Agenda for Research,* ed. Michael Stohl and George Lopez, 73–95. Westport, CT: Praeger, 1986.

———. "Terrorism in Latin America." In *The Politics of Terrorism,* ed. Michael Stohl, 497–524. New York: Marcel Dekker, 1988.

Loveman, Brian. *Por la Patria: Politics and the Armed Forces in Latin America.* Wilmington, DE: SR Books, 1999.

Lucchi, Elena, and Moritz Schuberth. "Negotiating Humanitarian Space with Criminal Armed Groups in Urban Latin America." *Disasters* 47, no. 3 (2022): 700–24.

Ludendorff, Erich. *The Nation at War.* London: Hutchinson, 1936.

Mahadevan, Prem. "The Maoist Insurgency in India: Between Crime and Revolution." *Small Wars & Insurgencies* 23, no. 2 (2012): 203–20.

Mainwaring, Scott. *The Progressive Church in Latin America*. Notre Dame, IN: University of Notre Dame Press, 1989.

Makarenko, Tamara. 2004. "The Crime-Terror Continuum: Tracing the Interplay Between Transnational Organised Crime and Terrorism." *Global Crime* 6, no. 1 (2004): 129–45.

Manekin, Devorah. "Violence Against Civilians in the Second Intifada: The Moderating Effect of Armed Group Structure on Opportunistic Violence." *Comparative Political Studies* 46, no. 10 (2013): 1273–300.

Mann, Michael. *The Sources of Social Power: A History of Power from the Beginning to AD 1760*. Cambridge: Cambridge University Press, 1986.

Mantilla, Jorge, and Andreas E. Feldmann. "Criminal Governance in Latin America." In *The Oxford Encyclopedia of International Criminology*, ed. Edna Eretz and Peter Ibarra, 212–32. Oxford: Oxford University Press, 2021.

Mardsen, Sarah V., and Alex P. Schmid. "Typologies of Terrorism and Political Violence." In *The Routledge Handbook of Terrorism Research*, ed. Alex P. Schmid, 158–200. London: Routledge, 2011.

Mares, David. "The United States' Impact on Latin America's Security Environment: The Complexities of Power Disparity." In *The Routledge Handbook of Latin American Security*, ed. Arie Kacowicz, 302–13. London: Routledge, 2015.

Marighella, Carlos. *Minimanual of Urban Guerrilla*. Chapel Hill: North Carolina University Press Documentary Publications, 1985.

Martin, Susanne, and Leonard Weinberg. *The Role of Terrorism in Twenty-First-Century Warfare*. Manchester, UK: Manchester University Press, 2017.

———. "Terrorism in an Era of Unconventional Warfare." *Terrorism and Political Violence* 28, no. 2 (2016): 236–53.

Mason, Ann. "Colombia's Democratic Security Agenda: Public Order in the Security Tripod." *Security Dialogue* 34, no. 4 (2003): 391–409.

Matard-Bonucci, Marie Anne. *Histoire de La Mafia*. Brussels: Editones Complexe, 1994.

Maynard, Jonathan Leader. "Ideology and Armed Conflict." *Journal of Peace Research* 56, no. 5 (2019): 635–49.

Mazzei, Julie. *Death Squads or Self-Defense Forces? How Paramilitary Groups Emerge and Challenge Democracy in Latin America*. Chapel Hill: University of North Carolina Press, 2009.

McAllister, Bradley, and Alex P. Schmid. "Theories of Terrorism." In *The Routledge Handbook of Terrorism Research*, ed. Alex P. Schmid, 201–71. London: Routledge, 2011.

Medina Gallego, Carlos. *Ejército de Liberación Nacional: Historia de las ideas políticas (1958–2018)*. Bogotá: Universidad Nacional de Colombia, 2019.

———. *ELN: Una historia contada dos veces*. Bogotá: Rodríguez Quito Editores, 1996.

Menjívar Cecilia, Rodríguez Néstor, eds. *When States Kill: Latin America, the U.S., and Technologies of Terror*. Austin: University of Texas Press, 2005.

Merari, Ariel. 1993. "Terrorism as a Strategy of Insurgency." *Terrorism and Political Violence* 5, no. 4 (1993): 213–51.

Meron, Theodor. *The Humanization of International Law*. Leiden: Brill Nihjoff, 2006.
Metelits, Claire. *Inside Insurgency: Violence, Civilians and Revolutionary Group Behavior*. New York: New York University Press, 2010.
Milhaupt, Courtis and Mark D. West. "The Dark Side of Private Ordering: An Institutional and Empirical Analysis of Organized Crime." *University of Chicago Law Review* 67, no. 1 (2000): 41–98.
Ministerio Nacional de Defensa Colombia. "Organigrama." May 17, 2023. https://cgfm.mil.co/es/conocenos/organigrama
Mitchell, Christopher, George Lopez, David Carleton, and Michael Stohl. "State Terrorism: Issues of Concept and Measurement." In *Government Violence and Repression: An Agenda for Research*, ed. Michael Stohl and George Lopez, 1–26. New York: Greenwood Press, 1986.
Mitton, Kieran. "Irrational Actors and the Process of Brutalisation: Understanding Atrocity in the Sierra Leonean Conflict (1991–2002)." *Civil Wars* 14, no. 1 (2012): 104–22.
Moncada, Eduardo. "The Politics of Crime in Latin America: New Insights, Future Challenges." *Latin American Politics and Society* 63, no. 1 (2021): 165–73.
———. "Resisting Protection: Rackets, Resistance, and State Building." *Comparative Politics* 51, no. 2 (2019): 321–39.
Moro, Francesco N. 2017. "Organizing Emotions and Ideology in Collective Armed Mobilization." *PS: Political Science & Politics* 50, no. 4 (2017): 944–47.
Nasi, Carlo, and Angelika Rettberg. "Colombia's Farewell to Civil War." In *How Negotiations End*, ed. William Zartman, 62–82. Cambridge: Cambridge University Press, 2019.
National Consortium for the Study of Terrorism and Responses to Terrorism Global Terrorism. "Global Terrorism Database: Colombia." 2023. https://www.start.umd.edu/gtd/search/Results.aspx?chart=overtime&search=Colombia
Navarro, David. *Por acá se entra, pero no se sale.' Análisis de los centros de entrenamiento paramilitar*. Madrid: Editorial Académica Española, 2017.
Newman, Edward, and Karl DeRouen Jr., eds. *Routledge Handbook of Civil Wars*. London: Routledge, 2014.
Nieto, Pablo. "El reformismo doctrinario en el Ejército Colombiano: Una nueva aproximación para enfrentar la Violencia, 1960–1965." *Historia Crítica* 53 (May/August 2014): 155–76.
Nussio, Enzo. "Learning from Shortcomings: The Demobilisation of Paramilitaries in Colombia." *Journal of Peacebuilding & Development* 6, no. 2 (2011): 88–92.
O'Donnell, Guillermo. *Modernization and Bureaucratic Authoritarianism: Studies in South American Politics*. Berkeley: University of California Institute for International Studies, 1973.
Olave, Giohanny. *El discurso de las Farc-EP: Identidad guerrillera y lucha armada en Colombia*. Bucaramanga: Universidad Industrial de Santander, 2022.
———. "El eterno retorno de Marquetalia: Sobre el mito fundacional de las FARC-EP." *Segunda Época* 37 (2013): 149–65.

Onuf, Nicholas. *World of Our Making: Rules and Rule in Social Theory and International Relations*. London: Routledge, 2012.

Oquist, Paul. *Violence Conflict and Politics in Colombia*. New York: Academia, 1980.

Orozco, Iván. 2005. *Sobre los límites de la conciencia humanitaria: Dilemas de la paz y la justicia en América Latina*. Bogotá: Editorial Temis, 2005.

Ortiz, Román D. "Insurgent Strategies in the Post-Cold War: The Case of the Revolutionary Armed Forces of Colombia." *Studies in Conflict & Terrorism* 25, no. 2 (2002): 127–43.

———. "La guerrilla mutante." In *La Encrucijada: Colombia en el siglo XXI*, ed. Francisco Leal Buitrago, 323–56. Bogotá: Norma, 2006.

Ospina Ovalle, Carlos. *Los años en que Colombia recuperó la esperanza*. Medellín: Editorial Universidad Pontificia Bolivariana, 2014.

———. "Insights from Colombia's 'Prolonged War.'" *Joint Force Quarterly* 42, no. 3 (2006): 57–62.

Palacio, Marco. *Violencia pública en Colombia 1958-2010*. Ciudad de México: Fondo de Cultura Económica, 2012.

Pape, Robert. "The Strategic Logic of Suicide Terrorism." *American Political Science Review* 97, no. 3 (2003): 343–61.

Pardo, Rafael. *La historia de las guerras*. Bogotá: Vergara, 2004.

Pardo, Rodrigo, and Juan G. Tokatlián. *Política exterior colombiana: De la subordinación a la autonomía?* Bogotá: Tercer Mundo Editores-IEPRI, 1988.

Paullier, Juan. "México: así ocurrió la brutal y olvidada masacre de Allende, una de las más sangrientas de Los Zetas." BBC Mundo, October 10, 2016. https://www.bbc.com/mundo/noticias-america-latina-37614215.

Pécaut, Daniel. *Crónica de cuatro décadas de política colombiana*. Bogotá: Norma, 2006.

———. "From Banality of Violence to Real Terror: The Case of Colombia." In *Societies in Fear: The Legacy of Civil War, Violence and Terror in Latin America*, ed. Kees Kooning and Dirk Kruijt, 141–68. London: Zed Books, 1999.

———. *Guerra contra la sociedad*. Bogotá: ESPASA, 2012.

———. *Las FARC ¿Una Guerrilla Sin Fin o Sin Fines?* Bogotá: Norma, 2008.

Peceny, Mark and Michael Durnan. "The Farc's Best Friend: US Anti-Drug Policies and the Deepening of Colombia's Civil War in the 1990s." *Latin American Politics and Society* 48, no. 2 (2006): 95–116.

Pedahzur, Ami and Leonard Weinberg. "Modern European Democracy and Its Enemies: The Threat of the Extreme Right." *Totalitarian Movements and Political Religions* 2, no. 1 (2001): 52–72.

Peñate, Andrés. 1999. "El sendero estratégico del ELN: Del idealismo guevarista al clientelismo armado." In *Reconocer La Guerra Para Construir La Paz*, ed. Malcolm Deas and María Victoria Llorente, 53–98. Bogotá: Uniandes-Cerc-Norma, 1999.

Pérez, Catalina, Carlos Silva, and Rodrigo Gutiérrez. "Deadly Forces: Use of Lethal Force by Mexican Security Forces 2007–2015." In *Mexico's Human Rights Crisis*, ed. Alejandro Anaya-Muñoz and Barbara Frey, 23–42. Philadelphia: University of Pennsylvania Press, 2019.

Pettersson, Therése, Shawn Davies, Amber Deniz, Garoun Engström, Nanar Hawach, Stina Högbladh, and Margareta Sollenberg Magnus Öberg. "Organized Violence 1989–2020, with a Special Emphasis on Syria." *Journal of Peace Research* 58, no. 4 (2021): 809–25.

Phillips, Brian J. "Terror Tactics by Criminal Organizations: The Mexican Case." *Perspectives on Terrorism* 12, no. 1 (2018): 46–63.

Phillips, Brian J., and Viridiana Ríos. "Narco-Messages: Competition and Public Communication by Criminal Groups." *Latin American Politics and Society* 62, no. 1 (2020): 1–24.

Pion-Berlin, David. *The Ideology of State Terror: Economic Doctrine and Political Repression in Argentina and Peru*. Boulder, CO: Lynne Rienner, 1989.

———. "The National Security Doctrine: Military Threat Perception and the Dirty War in Argentina." *Comparative Political Studies* 21, no 3. (1988): 382–407.

Pizarro, Eduardo. *De la guerra a la paz: Las fuerzas militares entre 1996 y 2018*. Bogotá: Planeta, 2019.

———. *Las FARC 1949–2011: De guerrilla campesina a máquina de guerra*. Bogotá: Norma, 2012.

Polo, Sara MT, and Kristian Skrede Gleditsch. "Twisting Arms and Sending Messages: Terrorist Tactics in Civil War." *Journal of Peace Research* 53, no. 6 (2016): 815–29.

Posada, Juan Diego. "ELN Show of Force Confirms Its Unmatched Criminal Presence in Colombia." InSight Crime, March 2, 2022. https://insightcrime.org/news/eln-show-of-force-confirms-its-unmatched-criminal-presence-in-colombia.

Post, Jerrold M. "Terrorist Psycho-Logic: Terrorist Behavior as Product of Psychological Forces." In *Origins of Terrorism: Psychologies, Ideologies, Theologies, States of Mind*, 2nd ed., ed. Walter Reich, 25–40. Washington, DC: Woodrow Wilson Center Press, 1988.

Premo, Daniel. "Coping with Insurgency: The Politics of Pacification in Colombia and Venezuela.'" In *Democracy in Latin America: Colombia and Venezuela*, ed. Donald L. Herman, 224–41. New York: Praeger, 1988.

Presidencia de la República Colombia. "Política de Defensa y Seguridad Democrática." June 16, 2003. https://www.oas.org/csh/spanish/documentos/colombia.pdf.

Price, Richard, and Christian Reus-Smit. "Dangerous Liaisons? Critical International Theory and Constructivism." *European Journal of International Relations* 4, no. 3 (1998): 259–94.

Radio Cadena Nacional. "Farc pretendían asesinar a generales y ministros en el atentado a El Nogal." September 5, 2018. https://www.lafm.com.co/judicial/farc-pretendian-asesinar-generales-y-ministros-en-el-atentado-el-nogal.

Ramírez, Socorro and Luis Alberto Restrepo. *Actores en conflicto por la paz: El proceso de paz durante el gobierno de Belisario Betancur (1982–1986)*. Bogotá: Siglo XXI, 1989.

Rangel, Alfredo, ed. *El poder paramilitar*. Bogotá: Planeta, 2005.

Rapoport, David C. *Waves of Global Terrorism: From 1879 to the Present*. New York: Columbia University Press, 2022

Ratliff, William. "Revolutionary Warfare." In *Violence and Latin American Revolutionaries*, ed. Michael Radu, 15–36. New Brunswick: Transaction, 1988.

Raymond, Gregory. "The Evolving Strategies of Political Terrorism." In *The New Global Terrorism: Characteristics, Causes and Control*, ed. Charles W. Kegley Jr., 71–83. Upper Saddle River, NJ: Prentice Hall, 2003.

Rempe, Dennis. *The Past as Prologue? A History of U.S. Counterinsurgency Policy in Colombia, 1958-1966*. Washington, DC: Strategic Studies Institute, 2002.

Rettberg, Angelika. "From Old Battles to New Challenges in Colombia." In *Divisive Politics and Democratic Dangers in Latin America*, ed. Tom Carothers and Andreas E. Feldmann, 18–23. Washington, DC: Carnegie Endowment for International Peace Press, 2020.

———. "Peace-Making Amidst an Unfinished Social Contract: The Case of Colombia." *Journal of Intervention and Statebuilding* 14, no. 1 (2020): 84–100.

Revista Semana. "General (r) Rito Alejo Del Río entrega versión ante la JEP." 2021. https://www.youtube.com/watch?v=QDrT2Sa89Hg.

Reyes, Alejandro. "Compra de tierras por narcotraficantes." In *Drogas ilícitas en Colombia: Su impacto político, económico y social*, ed. Francisco Thoumi, 279–346. Bogotá: Ariel., 1997.

Reyes, Alejandro, and Liliana Duica. *Guerreros y campesinos: El despojo de la tierra en Colombia*. Buenos Aires: Norma, 2009.

Richani, Nazih. "Caudillos and the Crisis of the Colombian State: Fragmented Sovereignty, the War System and the Privatization of Counterinsurgency in Colombia." *Third World Quarterly* 28, no. 2 (2007): 403–17.

———. *Systems of Violence: The Political Economy of War and Peace in Colombia*, 2nd ed. Albany: State University of New York Press, 2013.

Roberts, Adam. "The Civilian in Modern War." In *The Changing Character of War*, ed. Hew Strachan and Sibylle Scheipers, 357–81. Oxford: Oxford University Press, 2011.

Rochlin, James. *Vanguard Revolutionaries in Latin America: Peru, Colombia, Mexico*. Boulder, CO: Lynne Rienner, 2003.

Rodgers, Dennis. "Bróders in Arms: Gangs and the Socialization of Violence in Nicaragua." *Journal of Peace Research* 54, no. 5 (2017): 648–60.

Romero, Mauricio. *Paramilitares y autodefensas, 1982-2003*. Bogotá: IEPR Universidad Nacional de Colombia, 2003.

Ruggie, John "What Makes the World Hang Together? Neo-utiliarianism and the Social Constructivist Challenge," *International Organization* 54, no. 4 (1998): 855–85.

Ronderos, María Teresa. *Guerras recicladas, una historia periodística del paramilitarismo en Colombia*. Bogotá: Aguilar, 2014.

———. "Harold Bedoya de La Guerra a La Política." *El Tiempo*, May 10, 1998. https://www.eltiempo.com/archivo/documento/MAM-785005.

Rosen, Jonathan D. *The Losing War: Plan Colombia and Beyond*. Albany: State University of New York Press, 2014.

Rubin, Barnett R. *Afghanistan from the Cold War Through the War on Terror*. Oxford: Oxford University Press, 2013.

Rubio, Mauricio. "Del rapto a la pesca milagrosa: Breve historia del secuestro en Colombia." *Universidad de los Andes*, Documento de trabajo 36 CEDE, 2003. http://hdl.handle.net/1992/8647.

Ruiz Novoa, Alberto. *El gran desafío*. Bogotá: Tercer Mundo, 1965.

Safford, Frank, and Marco Palacio. *Colombia: País fragmentado, sociedad dividida*. Bogotá: Norma, 2002.

Salehyan, Idean, David Siroky, and Reed M. Wood. "External Rebel Sponsorship and Civilian Abuse: A Principal-Agent Analysis of Wartime Atrocities." *International Organization* 68, no. 3 (2014): 633–61.

Sambanis, Nicholas. "Terrorism and Civil War." In *Terrorism, Economic Development, and Political Openness*, ed. Philip Keefer and Norman Loyza, 174–206. Cambridge: Cambridge University Press, 2008.

———. "What Is Civil War? Conceptual and Empirical Complexities of an Operational Definition." *Journal of Conflict Resolution* 48, no. 6 (2004): 814–58.

Sánchez, Gonzalo, and Donny Meertens. *Bandoleros, gamonales y campesinos: El caso de La Violencia en Colombia*. Bogotá: IEPRI Universidad Nacional de Colombia, 1983.

Sánchez, Roland. *The Gulf Cartel: Profile, History, Methods, Practices and Geo-Politics*. MA thesis, University of Texas Rio Grande Valley, 2018.

Sánchez, Toño Jr. "Entrevista cCompleta a Manuel Castaño Gil en Semblanzas con Toño Sánchez Jr." *Semblanzas* 2018. https://www.youtube.com/watch?v=1AjRNoBV4 a.m.

Sanderson, Thomas M. "Transnational Terror and Organized Crime. Blurring the Lines." *SAIS Review* 24, no. 1 (2004): 49–61.

Sassòli, Marco. *International Humanitarian Law: Rules, Controversies, and Solutions to Problems Arising in Warfare*. Cheltenham, UK: Edward Elgar, 2019.

Sassòli, Marco and Antoine A. Bouvier. *How Does Law Protect in War*. Geneva: International Committee of the Red Cross, 1999.

Saviano, Roberto, *Zero, Zero, Zero*. New York: Penguin Books, 2015.

Scharpf, Adam. "Ideology and State Terror: How Officers Beliefs Shaped Repression during Argentina's 'Dirty War.'" *Journal of Peace Research* 55, no. 2 (2018): 206–21.

Schlichte, Klaus. *In the Shadow of Violence: The Politics of Armed Groups*. Frankfurt-am-Main: Campus Verlag, 2009.

Schmid, Alex P. "Links Between Transnational Organized Crime and Terrorist Crimes." *Transnational Organized Crime* 2, no. 4 (1996): 40–82.

Schmid, Alex P. "The Definition of Terrorism." In *The Routledge Handbook of Terrorism Research*, ed. Alex P. Schmid, 39–98. London: Routledge, 2011.

Schmid, Alex P., and Neil G Bowie. "Data Bases on Terrorism." In *The Routledge Handbook of Terrorism Research*, ed. Alex P. Schmid, 295–340. London: Routledge, 2011.

Schmid, Alex P. and Janny de Graaf. *Violence as Communication: Insurgent Terrorism and the Western News Media*. London: Sage, 1982.

Schmid, Alex P., Albert Jongman, and Michael Stohl, eds. *Political Terrorism: A New Guide to Actors, Authors, Concepts, Data Bases, Theories, and Literature*. New Brunswick, NJ: Transaction Publishers, 1988.

Schoultz, Lars. *Beneath the United States: A History of US Policy towards Latin America*. Cambridge, MA: Harvard University Press, 1999.

Scott, Steward. "Why Don't Mexico's Cartles use Vehicle Bombs." Stratfor, January 14, 2020. https://worldview.stratfor.com/article/mexico-drug-cartel-violence-car-bombs.

Seawright, Jason. Review of *Measuring Identity: A Guide for Social Scientists*, ed. Rawi Abdelal, Yoshiko M. Herrera, Alastair Ian Johnston, Rose McDermott. *Perspectives on Politics* 9, no. 2 (2011): 454–56.

Segura, Renata, and Delphine Mechoulan. "Made in Havana: How Colombia and the FARC Decided to End the War." *International Peace Institute*, February 27, 2017. https://www.ipinst.org/2017/02/how-colombia-and-the-farc-ended-the-war.

Selznick, Phillipe. *Leadership in Administration: A Sociological Interpretation*. Evanston, IL: Row Peterson, 1957.

Semana. "Guerra de rehenes." September 1, 1996. https://www.semana.com/nacion/articulo/guerra-de-rehenes/29982-3.

Sergi, Anna. *From Mafia to Organised Crime. Critical Criminological Perspectives*. New York: Palgrave, 2017.

Shelley, Louise. *Dirty Entanglements: Corruption, Crime and Terrorism*. Cambridge: Cambridge University Press, 2014.

Shelley, Louise, and John Picarelli. "The Diversity of Crime Terror Interaction." *International Annals of Criminology* 43 (2005): 51–81.

Shesterinina, Anastasia. *Mobilizing in Uncertainty: Collective Identities and War in Abkhazia*. Ithaca, NY: Cornell University Press, 2021.

Shifter, Michael. "Plan Colombia: A Retrospective." *Americas Quarterly*, July 18, 2012. https://www.americasquarterly.org/fulltextarticle/plan-colombia-a-retrospective.

Shirk, David, and Joel Wallman. "Understanding Mexico's Drug Violence." *Journal of Conflict Resolution* 59, no. 8 (2015): 1348–76.

Slim, Hugo H. *Killing Civilians: Method, Madness, and Morality in War*. New York: Columbia University Press, 2008.

Smilde, David, Verónica Zubillaga, and Rebecca Hanson, eds. *The Paradox of Violence in Venezuela: Crime and Revolution*. Pittsburgh, PA: Pittsburgh University Press, 2022.

Smith, Roger, "Identities, Interests, and the Future of Political Science," *Perspectives on Politics* 2, no. 2 (2004): 301–12.

Snow, David A, and Scott Byrd. "Identities, Interests, and the Future of Political Science." *Perspectives on Politics* 2, no. 2 (2004): 301–12.

Snyder, Richard, and Angélica Durán-Martínez. "Does Illegality Breed Violence? Drug Trafficking and State Sponsored Protection Rackets." *Crime, Law, and Social Change* 52 (2009): 253–73.

Soifer, Hillel. "Shadow Cases in Comparative Research." *Qualitative and Multi-Method Research* 18, no. 2 (2020): 9–18.

——. *State Building in Latin America*. Cambridge: Cambridge University Press, 2015.

Sprinzak, Ehud. "The Psychopolitical Formation of Extreme Left Terrorism in a Democracy: The Case of the Weatherman." In *Origins of Terrorism: Psychologies, Ideologies,*

Theologies, States of Mind, 2nd ed., ed. Walter Reich, 65–85. Washington, DC: Woodrow Wilson Center Press, 1998.

———. "Right-wing Terrorism in a Comparative Perspective: The Case of Split Delegitimization." *Terrorism and Political Violence* 7, no. 1 (1995): 17–43.

Staniland, Paul. *Networks of Rebellion: Explaining Insurgent Cohesion and Collapse*. Ithaca, NY: Cornell University Press, 2013.

Stanton, Jessica A. "Terrorism, Civil War and Insurgency." In Chenoweth et al., *The Oxford Handbook of Terrorism*, 348–65, 2019.

———. "Terrorism in the Context of Civil War." *Journal of Politics* 75, no. 4 (2013): 1009–22.

———. *Violence and Restraint in Civil War: Civilian Targeting in the Shadow of International Law*. Cambridge: Cambridge University Press, 2016.

Stepan, Alfred. *Rethinking Military Politics: Brazil and the Southern Cone*. Princeton, NJ: Princeton University Press, 1988.

Stepanova, Ekaterina. *Terrorism in Asymmetrical Conflict: Ideological and Structural Aspects*. Oxford: Oxford University Press, 2008.

Stohl, Michael. *The Politics of Terrorism*. New York: Marcel Dekker, 1988.

———. "The State as Terrorist: Insights and Implications." *Democracy and Security* 2, June (2006): 1–25.

Suárez, Andrés. "La sevicia en las masacres de la guerra colombiana." *Análisis Político* 63 (May/August 2008): 59–77.

Sullivan, Christopher M. "Undermining Resistance: Mobilization, Repression, and the Enforcement of Political Order." *Journal of Conflict Resolution* 60, no. 7 (2015): 1163–90.

Thaler, Mathias. *Naming Violence: A Critical Theory of Genocide, Torture, and Terrorism*. New York: Columbia University Press, 2018.

Themnér, Lotta, and Peter Wallensteen. "Armed Conflict 1946–2012." *Journal of Peace Research* 50, no. 4 (2013): 509–21.

Thompson, Peter G. *Armed Groups The 21st Century Threat*. Boulder, CO: Rowman Littlefield, 2014.

Thornton, Thomas. "Terror as a Weapon of Political Agitation." In *Internal War*, ed. Harry Eckstein, 71–99. New York: Free Press, 1964.

Tilly, Charles. "Contentious Repertoires in Great Britain, 1758–1834." *Social Science History* 17, no. 2 (1993): 253–80.

———. "State Incited Violence, 1900–1999." In *Political Power and Social Theory*, ed. Diane E. Davis and Howard Kimeldorf, 161–79. Greenwich, CT: JAI Press, 1995.

———. "Terror, Terrorism, Terrorists." *Sociological Theory* 22, no. 1 (2004): 5–13.

Trejo, Guillermo. "Mexico's Illegal Democratic Trap." In *Divisive Politics and Democratic Dangers in Latin America*, ed. Tom Carothers and Andreas E. Feldmann, 22–26. Washington, DC: Carnegie Endowment for International Peace, 2021.

Trejo, Guillermo, and Sandra Ley. *Votes, Drugs and Violence: The Political Logic of Criminal Wars in Mexico*. New York: Cambridge University Press, 2020.

Tribunal Superior de Bogotá. "Sentencia, Freddy Rendón Herrera." 2011. https://www.ramajudicial.gov.co/documents/6342975/46525367/2020.08.04+Fredy+Rendon

+Herrera_Libertad_a_Prueba_2a_Instancia.pdf/f0fcb031-9bd4-4d58-a670-61a414b6234e.

———. "Sentencia, Salvatore Mancuso y otros." November 20, 2014. https://ilg2.files.wordpress.com/2015/04/mancuso-et-al-judgement.pdf.

Trujillo, Juan. "Autoridades alertan sobre el renacimiento de frente de las FARC en Sumapaz." *El País*, April 21, 2023. https://www.elpais.com.co/judicial/autoridades-alertan-sobre-el-renacimiento-de-frente-de-las-farc-en-sumapaz.html.

Turkewitz, Julie. "Deep in Colombia, Rebels and Soldiers Fight for the Same Prize: Drugs." *New York Times*, April 20, 2022. https://www.nytimes.com/2022/04/20/world/americas/colombia-comandos-armed-groups.html.

Ugarriza, Juan E., and Matthew J. Craig. "The Relevance of Ideology to Contemporary Armed Conflict: A Quantitative Analysis of Former Combatants in Colombia." *Journal of Conflict Resolution* 57, no. 3 (2012): 445–77.

Ugarriza, Juan E., and Nathalie Pabón. *Militares y Guerrillas: La memoria histórica del conflicto armado en Colombia desde los archivos militares 1958-2016*, 2nd ed. Bogotá: Universidad del Rosario, 2018.

United Nations Human Rights Council. "Report of the Special Rapporteur on Extrajudicial, Summary or Arbitrary Executions: Mission to Colombia." A/HRC/14/24/Add 2, March 31, 2010. https://www.refworld.org/docid/4c0763db2.html.

United Nations General Assembly. *International Convention for the Protection of All Persons from Enforced Disappearance*. December 10, 2010. https://www.ohchr.org/en/instruments-mechanisms/instruments/international-convention-protection-all-persons-enforced.

United Nations High Commissioner on Human Rights. "Situation of Human Rights Report pf the United Nations High Commissioner for Human Rights." A/HRC/46/76, February 10, 2021. https://reliefweb.int/report/colombia/situation-human-rights-colombia-report-united-nations-high-commissioner-human-0.

United Nations Office of Drugs and Crime. "Colombia Coca Cultivation Survey 2013." June, 2014. https://www.unodc.org/documents/crop-monitoring/Colombia/Colombia_coca_cultivation_survey_2013.pdf

Universidad del Externado. "12.221 homicidios en Colombia durante el 2022." Delfos Centro de Análisis de Datos. May 18, 2023. https://www.uexternado.edu.co/delfos-centro-analisis-datos/homicidios-en-colombia-durante-el-2022/

Uribe, María Victoria. *Antropología de la inhumanidad: Un ensayo interpretativo sobre el terror en Colombia*. Bogotá: Grupo Editorial Norma, 2004.

U.S. Congress. "The 9/11 Commission Report: Final Report of the National Commission on Terrorist Attacks Upon the United States." Y3.2:27/2/FINAL. July 22, 2004. https://www.govinfo.gov/app/details/GPO-911REPORT.

Valencia Tovar, Álvaro. *Historia de las fuerzas militares de Colombia*. Bogotá: Planeta, 1993.

Valentino, Benjamin. *Final Solutions, Mass Killings and Genocide in the Twentieth Century*. Ithaca, NY: Cornell University Press, 2004.

Valentino, Benjamin, Paul Huth, and Dylan Balch-Lindsay. "'Draining the Sea': Mass Killing and Guerrilla Warfare." *International Organization* 58, no. 2 (2004): 375–407.

Varese, Federico. "What Is Organized Crime." In *What Is Organised Crime? Redefining Organised Crime: A Challenge for the European Union*, ed. Stefania Carnevale, Serena Forlati, and Orsetta Giolo, 27–53. Oxford: Hart Publishing, 2017.

Vargas, Gonzalo. "Urban Irregular Warfare and Violence Against Civilians: Evidence from a Colombian City." *Terrorism and Political Violence* 21, no. 1 (2009): 110–32.

Vega, Renán. "La dimensión internacional del conflicto social y armado en Colombia: Injerencia de los Estados Unidos, contrainsurgencia y terrorismo de estado." *Espacio Crítico*, February 10, 2015. https://www.corteidh.or.cr/tablas/r33458.pdf.

Verdad Abierta. "El Gaula y 'Don Berna' cercaron a Vicente Castaño: 'Don Mario.'" May 13, 2010. https://verdadabierta.com/el-gaula-y-don-berna-cercaron-a-vicente-castano-don-mario.

——. "Entrevista con Julián Bolívar." 2016. https://www.youtube.com/watch?v=NOIxEMUbSMY.

——. "Las escuelas para matar de los 'paras.'" October 28, 2009. https://verdadabierta.com/las-escuelas-para-matar-de-los-paras.

——. "La 'universidad paramilitar' de Ernesto Báez." June 4, 2012. https://verdadabierta.com/la-universidad-paramilitar-de-ernesto-baez.

——. "Muerte a Secuestradores MAS: Los orígenes del paramilitarismo." September 23, 2011. https://verdadabierta.com/muerte-a-secuestradores-mas-los-origenes-del-paramilitarismo.

——. "Pablo Emilio Guarín." 2009. https://www.youtube.com/watch?v=IOqZn0eTnp4.

Villamizar, María Alejandra. "El Mono Jojoy: Perfil de un hombre malo." *El Tiempo*, September 23, 2010. https://www.eltiempo.com/don-juan/historias/el-mono-jojoy-perfil-de-un-hombre-malo-7961621.

Villarreal, Ana. "Fear and Spectacular Drug Violence in Monterrey." In *Violence and the Urban Margins*, ed. Javier Auyero, Philippe Bourgois, and Nancy Scheper-Hughes, 135–61. Oxford: Oxford University Press, 2015.

Volkov, Vadim. *Violent Entrepreneurs: The Use of Force in the Making of Russian Capitalism*. Ithaca, NY: Cornell University Press, 2002.

Von Clausewitz, Carl. *On War*. Princeton, NJ: Princeton University Press, 1976.

Walter, Eugen Victor. *Terror and Resistance*. Oxford: Oxford University Press, 1969.

Walzer, Michael. "Five Questions About Terrorism." *Dissent* 49, no. 1 (2002): 5–11.

Weinberg, Leonard, Ami Pedahzur, and Sivan Hirsch-Hoeffler. "The Challenges of Conceptualizing Terrorism." *Terrorism and Political Violence* 16, no.4 (2004): 777–794.

Weinstein, Jeremy M. *Inside Rebellion: The Politics of Insurgent Violence*. Cambridge: Cambridge University Press, 2007.

Weiss Fagen, Patricia. "Repression and State Security." In *Fear at the Edge: State Terror and Resistance in Latin America*, ed. Juan Corradi, Patricia Weiss Fagen, and Manuel Antonio Garretón, 39–89. Berkeley: University of California Press, 1992.

Wendt, Alexander. "Anarchy Is What States Make of It: The Social Construction of Power Politics." *International Organization* 46, no. 2 (1992): 391–425.

——. "The Agent-Structure in International Relations Theory." *International Organization* 41, no. 3 (1987): 335–70.

———. "Collective Identity Formation and the International State." *American Political Science Review* 88, no. 2 (1994): 384–96.

Whetten, David. "Albert and Whetten Revisited Strengthening the Concept of Organizational Identity." *Journal of Management Inquiry* 15, no. 3 (2006): 219–34.

Wiarda, Howard J. *The Soul of Latin America*. New Haven, CT: Yale University Press, 2003.

Wickham-Crowley, Timothy. *Guerrillas and Revolution in Latin America: A Comparative Study of Insurgents and Regimes Since 1956*. Princeton, NJ: Princeton University Press, 1992.

———. "Terror and Guerrilla Warfare in Latin America, 1956–1970." *Comparative Studies in Society and History* 32, no. 2 (1990): 201–37.

———. "Two Waves of Guerrilla Movement Organizing in Latin America, 1956–1990." *Comparative Studies in Society and History* 56, no. 1 (2014): 215–42.

Wilkinson, Daniel. "Mexico: Violence and Opacity." Human Rights Watch, October 17, 2020. https://www.hrw.org/news/2018/10/17/mexico-violence-and-opacity.

Williams, Phil. "The Terrorism Debate Over Mexican Drug Trafficking Violence." *Terrorism and Political Violence* 24, no. 2 (2012): 259–78.

Wilson, Tim. "State Terrorism." In Chenoweth et al., *The Oxford Handbook of Terrorism*, 331–47, 2019.

Wolff, Michael J. "Insurgent Vigilantism and Drug War in Mexico." *Journal of Politics in Latin America* 12, no. 1 (2020): 32–52.

Wood, Elisabeth Jean. *Insurgent Collective Action and Civil War in El Salvador*. Cambridge: Cambridge University Press, 2003.

———. "The Social Processes of Civil War: The Wartime Transformation of Social Networks." *Annual Review of Political Science* 11, no. 1 (2008): 539–61.

———. "Variation in Sexual Violence During War." *Politics & Society* 34, no. 3 (2006): 307–42.

Wood, Reed M., and Jacob D. Kathman. "Too Much of a Bad Thing? Civilian Victimization and Intrastate Conflicts." *British Journal of Political Science* 44, no. 3 (2014): 685–706.

Wright, Thomas. *Latin America in the Era of the Cuban Revolution*. New York: Praeger, 1991.

Wrighte, Mark, "The Real Mexican Terrorists: A Group Profile of the Popular Revolutionary Army (EPR)," *Studies in Conflict & Terrorism* 25, no. 4 (2002): 207–225.

Zedong, Mao. *On Guerrilla Warfare*. New York: Anchor Press, 1978.

Zelik, Raúl. *Paramilitarismo, violencia y transformación social, política y económica en Colombia*. Bogotá: Siglo del Hombre, Fescol, Goethe Institut, 2015.

Zepeda, Raúl. "Conceptualising Criminal Wars in Latin America." *Third World Quarterly* 44, no. 4 (2022): 776–94.

Index

Note: Page numbers in *italics* refer to tables and figures.

Abdelal, Rawi, 36
abduction: as agitational and coercive strategy, 14, 15, 46; CSSF and, 3, 157, 158, *159*, 183, 185; ELN and, 2, 22, 99, 100, *101*, 102, 113–115, *114*, 125; FARC and, 21, 73, *74*, 83–86, *85*, *86*, 91, 98, 123; mass abductions, 2, 99; OCGs and, 200, 203, 205, *206*; paramilitaries and, 3, 5, 15–16, 59, 62, 128, *128*, 152–156, *153*, *154*; in post-peace agreement Colombia, 69, 194, *194*, 197; research design and, 19
Afghanistan, 48, 49, 169
agitational strategies, 13–16; abduction and, 14, 46; CSSF and, 183; defining and categorizing, 13; ELN and, 22, 99, 102, 112, 117, 123, 125, 212; FARC and, 21, 71–72, 82–84, 89, 98, 211, 212; paramilitaries and, 142, 152, 156
Algeria, 35, 173
al-Qaeda, 42
anarchism, 13, 34, 42

Anaya Muñoz, Alejandro, 198
Anorí assault (1973), 104, 105, 112, 275n34
April 19 Movement (M-19), 61, 141; impact of, 83, 109, 165; Palacio de Justicia siege, 166–167; peace negotiations, 132; repertoires of terrorism used by, 87, 133; revisionist second wave insurgency and, 83, 165
Arellán, Fernando, 87
Arenas, Jacobo, 80, 84, 90
Arenas, Jaime, 107, 112
Argentina, 42, 84, 162
Arjona, Ana, 28, 130, 240n12, 242n38
Armed Movement Quintín Lamé, 165, 253n51
Asociación de Campesinos y Ganaderos del Magdalena Medio (ACDEGAM), 133–134
Asociaciones Comunitarias de Vigilancia, 63–64

316 INDEX

Autodefensas Unidas de Colombia (AUC), 1, 54, 63, 64–65, 127, 171, 187; Bloque Central Bolívar, 139, *224*; demobilization of, 70, 137, 144, 187; founding of, 54, 63, 127, 135; Mapiripán dispute, 1; overkill policy and practices, 151; peace negotiations, 66; repertoires of terrorism, 154, 232n9; training schools and, 143–144
Avianca plane hijacking, 2, 99

Baez, Ernesto, 139, 143
Balcells, Laia, 34
bandolerism, 54
Bandura, Albert, 82
Barco, Virgilio, 167, 276n51
Batallón Colombia, 165, 168, 177
Bateman Cayón, Jaime, 83
Betancur, Belisario, 60, 61, 90, 132, 166, 167
bin Laden, Osama, 42
Blakeley, Ruth, 162
bodies, desecrating and displaying: Mexican criminal wars and, 197, 200; *narcomantas,* 200; ruthlessness and, 50. See also *sevicia*
Bolívar, Simón, 81, 83
Bolivarianism, 81
Bolivia, 46, 80, 83, 135
bombings, 3–4, *4*; as agitational and coercive strategy, 15; avoided by CSSF, 158, *159*, 183, 185; avoided by paramilitaries, 60, 61–62, *128*, 156; ELN and, 100, *101*, 115, *116*, 123, *124*, 125; El Nogal Club bombing, 2, 71–72, 87; FARC and, 2, 21, 71–72, 73, *74*, 85–89, *88*, 98, *124*; OCGs and, 200, 203, 204–205, *206*; in post-peace agreement Colombia, 69, 193–194, *194*, 197; research design and, 19; suicide bombings, 10
Brands, Hal, 277n80, 278nn84–85
Brazil: Comando Vermelho, 189–190, 191; criminal wars and violence, 6, 48, 189–190, 191; Primeiro Comando da Capital, 189–190, 191
Brazilian Action for National Liberation (Ação Libertadora Nacional), 13, 82–83
Briceño, Alfredo, 89, 90, 259n47
Bull, Hedley, 28

Caicedo, Fernando, 81
Cali church kidnapping, 2, 99
Cano, Alfonso, 87, 90, 154
Castaño, Carlos, 5, 63, 64, 134–135; on abduction, 5, 154; assassination of, 139; AUC created by, 63, 135; on cruelty, 151; on paramilitary goals, 139, 141–142; training schools and, 143
Castaño, Fidel, 63, 134–135, 260n81
Castaño, Vicente, 63, 134–135
Castaño Clan, 132, 134–135
Castro, Fidel, 57, 80, 173, 211–212
categorical terrorism, 41, 79, 110
Centro de Investigación y Educación Popular (CINEP), 19, 119, 155, 158, 191
Chapa, Juan Jesús Guerrero, 203
Charry Rincón, Fermin, 77
Checkel, Jeffrey, 44
Chenoweth, Erica, 30
civilian targeting: forms of, 29–30; lethal and nonlethal, 29–30; terrorism and, 30–32
civil war: conceptualizing terrorism during, 27–29, 209–211; criminal wars compared with, 189–192; defining, 27–28; forms of violence during, 29–32; identity transformation and, 36–37; international humanitarian law and, 28–29, 52, 210; international human law and, 17; as state-building process, 190; terrorism's role in, 5–10
Colombian Battalion, 165, 168, 177
Colombian state security forces (CSSF), 157–160; abductions, 3, 157, 158, *159*, 183, 185; agitational strategies, 183; assassinations, 178, 180, 181,

185; bombings avoided by, 158, *159*, 183, 185; conceptualization of state terrorism, 160–162; disappearances, 158, 170, 177, 182–183, 185; DSP and peace agreement, 168–171; executions, 16, *159*, 170, 177, 178–180, *179*, 181, 182; expansion of counterinsurgency, 164–168; geographic dimensions of terrorism, 182, *182*; as guardians of social order, 171–174; ideology and identity, 212; La Violencia and, 162, 163–164; leadership, 176–177; massacres, 3, 159, 170, *180*, 180–183, *181*, *185*; military autonomy, 163–164; National Front and, 162, 163; origins and history of, 162–171; post-conflict phase, *193*, 194, *194*; in post-peace agreement Colombia, 193, 194, *194*; repertoires of terrorism, 176–183; socialization, 176–177; torture, 158, 162, 166, 170, 175, 183, 185; U.S. influence on, 174–176
Colombian Truth Commission, 17, 89, 155, 177, 182
Colombian War of Independence, 39–40, 54, 55, 69
Colombo American Institute bombing, 115
Comisión para el Esclarecimiento de la Verdad la Convivencia y la No Repetición, 17, 89, 155, 177, 182
Communist Party of Colombia (PCC), 76–77, 80, 84, 109
comparative politics, 6, 7, 18, 30, 32–33, 36–37
complicity, 41, 79
constructivism, 7–8, 35–36, 37, 38–39, 45
Cooperatives of Rural Security (CONVIVIR), 63–64, 254n62
Coordinadora Guerrillera Simón Bolívar, 81
Coronado Gámez, Paulino, 158
COVID-19 pandemic, 204
Crenshaw, Martha, 35
crime-terrorism nexus, 49, 62, 213

criminal codes of conduct, 49–50, 93, 213
criminal ethos, 8–9, 23, 38, *39*, 43, 48–51; paramilitaries and, 140–142
criminal wars, 189–191; defining, 190–191; in Mexico, 190, 195–206; as state-building process, 190; terrorism and, 213—214
Critical Terrorism Studies School, 161
Cuban Revolution, 40, 56, 57, 77, 80, 101, 102, 125
Cubides, Fernando, 130

dau tranh (insurgency method), 47, 59, 89
Death to Kidnappers, 133, 154
de Graaf, Janny, 241n23, 244n62, 286n6
dehumanization, 17, 18, 41–42, 70, 90, 143
de la Calle, Luis, 30
Democratic Security Policy, 65–67, 72, 118, 162, 168–171
dirty wars, 14, 162, 198, 207
disappearances, 5, 12; CSSF and, 16, 158, 170, 177, 182–183, 185; ELN and, 45, 112, 121; FARC and, 45, 73, 79, 89, 112, 121; in Mexico, 195, 198; paramilitaries and, 15, 16, 47, 127, 137, 144, 154–155; as pro-regime terrorism, *13*, 14, 15; statistics, 17, 195, 198
Dishman, Chris, 48
dispossession, 12, 31, 32, 52, 211
doctrine of national security (DNS), 138, 143, 160, 172–174, 185
Domingo Laín Front, 60, 102, 105, 108, 112, 117, 125
drug trafficking. *See* narcotrafficking
Duncan, Gustavo, 62, 64, 135, 136, 138, 141, 144
Duque Escobar, Iván (aka Ernesto Baez), 139, 143
Durán-Martínez, Angélica, 51

Echandía, Camilo, 251n22, 253n48, 255n79, 261n86, 263n20, 263n24, 265n66, 265n69

Ecuador, 82, 187
Eisenhower, Dwight D., 177
Ejército de Liberación Nacional (National Liberation Army, ELN), 2, 4, *4*, 99–102; abductions, 2, 22, 99, 100, *101*, 102, 113–115, *114*, *124*, 125; agitational strategies, 22, 99, 102, 112, 117, 123, 125, 212; armed clientelism, 117; armed proselytism, 117; bombings, 100, *101*, 115, *116*, 123, *124*, 125; comparison of FARC and ELN terrorism, 123–125; disappearances, 45, 112, 121; executions, 100, *101*, 107, 112, 118–119, *119*, *121*, 123; founding and early history, 102–107; geographic dimensions of terrorism, *122*, 122–123; ideology and identity, 107–110, 211–212; leadership and repertoires of terrorism, 110–116; massacres, 4, 101, *101*, 117, 119–121, *121*, 123, *124*; paramilitaries and, 118; in post-peace agreement Colombia, 186–187, 188, 192, *193*, 194, *194*; territorial terrorism, 117–123
Ejército Popular de Liberación (EPL), 56–57, 63, 135, 143, 188
El Billar, Caquetá attack, 168
elites: CSSF and, 172; economic elites, 58, 132; land distribution resisted by, 187; landed elites, 2, 4, 58, 68, 132, 140, 187; paramilitaries and, 65, 131, 132–133, 136, 137–139; political elites, 59, 132–133; self-defense groups and, 198; state-building resisted by, 163
El Nogal Club bombing, 2, 71–72, 87
El Salvador, 34, 36–37; criminal groups in, 191; Farabundo Martí Liberation Front (Frente de Liberación Farabundo Martí), 81, 91, 104–105, 108, 109; state violence in, 162
Escobar, Pablo, 51, 59, 61, 63, 133–135, 139–140, 190, 267–268n31
esprit mafioso, 140, 141, 195. *See also* criminal ethos
ethnic cleansing, 12, 26, 29–30, 31, 52, 211

executions, 3–4; as agitational and coercive strategy, 15; categories of terrorism and, 13, 14, 15; CSSF and, 16, *159*, 170, 177, 178–180, *179*, 181, 182; ELN and, 100, *101*, 107, 112, 118–119, *119*, *121*, 123; FARC and, 73, *74*, 80, 84, 91–93, *92*, 95; in Mexico, 197–198, 199, 200, 202, 203; paramilitaries and, 16, *128*, 144–146, *145*, 148–149, 150, 156; in post-peace agreement Colombia, *194*; research design and, 19; statistics, 148, 237n74
extremism, 31–32, 41, 42–43, 90

falsos positivos (false positives) scandal, 67, 157–158, 178
Familia Michoacana, 51
fariana culture, 78
Felbab-Brown, Vanda, 284n59, 286n97
forced recruitment, 12, 17, 30, 89, 137, 200, 204
Forest, James, 47
foundational myths, 8, 39–40
Frey, Barbara, 198
Fríes, Bertha Lucía, 71
Fuerzas Armadas Revolucionarias de Colombia (FARC), 2, 4, *4*, 15, 71–76, *73*; abductions, 21, 73, *74*, 83–86, *85*, *86*, 91, 98, 123, *124*; agitational strategies, 21, 71–72, 82–84, 89, 98, 211, 212; bombings, 2, 21, 71–72, 73, *74*, 85–89, *88*, 98, *124*; comparison of ELN and FARC terrorism, 123–125; *dau tranh* insurgency method used by, 59; disappearances, 45, 73, 79, 89, 112, 121; distribution of terror attacks by Fronts, *97*; dynamics of territorial terrorism, 95, *96*; executions, 73, *74*, 80, 84, 91–93, *92*, 95, *124*; founding and historical foundation, 76–78; geographic dimensions of terrorism, 95–97, *96*; *gramaje* (protection tax), 91; ideology and identity, 78–82, 211;

La Violencia and, 74, 77; leadership and repertoires of terrorism, 82–89; massacres, 73, 74, 93–95, 94, 124; New Operational Form (Nueva Forma de Operar), 89–90; Patriotic Union, 60, 75, 90; in post-peace agreement phase, 187–188, 192, 193, 193, 194, 194–195; repertoires of terrorism, 74; Secretariat, 74, 82, 87, 154, 187; Seventh National Conference (1982), 15, 59, 89; Sixth National Conference (1978), 84; territorial terrorism, 89–97; torture, 1, 73, 79–80, 89

Gabino. *See* Rodríguez Bautista, Nicolás
Gaitán, Jorge Eliécer, 55–56, 62, 86
Gambetta, Diego, 249n150, 249n154, 249n156, 272n118
Garcés, Julián, 80
Gaviria, César, 63, 168
genocide, 26, 30, 31, 37, 42, 52, 211
Georgian civil war, 37
Gerring, John, 196
Giraldo, Gustavo Aníbal (aka Pablito), 105, 112
Giraldo, Jorge, 79, 251n17, 257n16, 258n30, 259n51, 262n2
Goodwin, Jeff, 41, 79, 240n9, 241n22, 246n101, 257n27, 264n49
Green, Amelia Hoover, 34, 44, 45
Guarín, Pablo, 138–139
Guatemala, 32, 83–84, 109, 162
Guatemalan National Revolutionary Unity, 109
Guatemalan Revolutionary Armed Forces, 83–84
guerrilla groups, 72–73, 79, 132–133, 139, 166. *See also* Ejército de Liberación Nacional; Fuerzas Armadas Revolucionarias de Colombia
guerrilla warfare, defining, 75
Guevara, Ernesto "Che," 46, 80, 107, 108, 115; *Guerra de Guerrillas*, 85

Guillén, Abraham, 46, 83, 109
Gulf Cartel, 202–203, 205, 206
Gurr, Ted Robert, 42
Gutiérrez, Gustavo, 112
Gutiérrez, Néstor Guillermo, 158
Gutiérrez-Sanín, Francisco: on Bloque Cacique Nutibará, 270n67; on ideology, 8, 40, 41, 82, 137–138, 172; on third cycle of violence, 187; on violence blueprints, 32

hacienda system, 54, 55
Hobsbawm, Eric, 56, 77
Hoffman, Bruce, 12
homicide rates, 186
Horowitz, Michael, 47
hors de combat, 28
Human Rights Watch, 178, 239n95, 252n35, 267n10, 267n21, 268n43, 270n79, 279n120, 279n122, 283n49
Hylton, Forrest, 177

identity. *See* organizational identity
ideology: defining, 8; ELN and, 107–110, 211–212; FARC and, 78–82, 211; organizational identity and, 37–38, 39, 40–43; paramilitaries and, 137–140
Independent Peasant Republics, 40, 56, 74, 97–98, 164
indoctrination, 9, 44, 60, 76, 102, 111, 156
informants, 21, 23, 43, 90, 112, 203, 204, I 0
insurgent (anti-regime) terrorism, 12–13, 13, 14, 16, 62; ELN and, 102, 113, 124, 125; FARC and, 73, 84, 93, 96, 98; M-19 and, 61. *See also* abduction; bombings
Inter-American Court of Human Rights, 1, 19, 126
International Committee of the Red Cross, 19, 99, 215, 258n31, 266n84
International Criminal Court, 29
International Crisis Group, 196

international humanitarian law (IHL), 28–29; civil war and, 28–29, 52, 210; Colombian civil war breaches of, 17; distinction principle, 3, 28, 162; ELN and, 110; FARC and, 79, 258n31; organized crime groups and, 201; proportionality principle, 28, 162; purpose of, 28–29; terrorism and, 3, 29, 52, 211, 240n18
International Institute for Strategic Studies, 249n144, 252n39, 258n46, 260n69, 260n79, 276n61, 277n71
Irish Republican Army, 47–48, 87
Isaza, Ramón, 134, 143

Jalisco Cartel New Generation (Cartel Jalisco Nueva Generación, CJNG), 202, 204–205, *206*
Jongman, Albert, 10–11, 235n45
Justice and Peace (Justicia y Paz), 19–20, 239n97

Kaldor, Mary, 32–33, 242n41
Kalyvas, Stathis, 27–28, 30, 32–33, 130, 238–239n94
Keen, David, 31
Kennedy, John F., 78, 172
kidnapping. *See* abduction
Knights Templar Cartel, 202, 203–205, *206*
Korean War, 104, 165, 174, 175, 177
Koufa, Kalliopi, 10, 234

Laqueur, Walter, 48
Lara Bonilla, Rodrigo, 61, 167
La Rochela massacre, 126
La Violencia, 40, 55–56, 74, 77, 103, 162–164
Leal Buitrago, Francisco, 250n5, 253n52, 274n19, 274n22, 275n33, 275n37, 275n42, 277n72
Lee, Ann Fujii, 37
Legislative Decree 1923 (Estatuto de Seguridad), 166

LeGrand, Catherine, 54
Lehder, Carlos, 61, 133
Lessing, Benjamin, 51, 190
Ley, Sandra, 190–191, 202
Libardo Mora Toro Front, 188
Liberal Revolutionary Movement, 56
Lleras Camargo, Alberto, 77–78, 164, 177
Lleras Restrepo, Carlos, 58, 132
Lloreda, Rodrigo, 169
Londoño, Bernando, 139
López Michelsen, Alfonso, 56, 102–103
Los Zetas, 200, 202–205, *206*
Ludendorff, Erich, 277n76

M-19. *See* April 19 Movement
mafia. *See* Organized Criminal Groups
maiming, deliberate, 49, 50
Makarenko, Tamara, 49
Mancuso, Salvatore, 139, 143, 151
Maoism, 17, 47, 56–57, 89, 188
Mao Tse-Tung, 47
Mapiripán massacre, 1
Marighella, Carlos, 13, 46, 47, 83, 109; *Mini Manual of the Urban Guerrilla,* 13
Marín, Pedro Antonio (aka Tirofijo or "sure shot"). *See* Marulanda, Manuel
Marín Arango, Luciano (aka Iván Marquez), 87, 187, 280–281n6
Márques, Iván, 87, 187, 280–281n6
Marulanda, Manuel, 21, 56, 78–79, 89, 90
Marxism, 22, 40, 65; ELN and, 104, 107; FARC and, 76, 80–81, 109, 211; paramilitaries and, 40, 65. *See also* Cuban Revolution
massacres, 3–4, *4*; CSSF and, 3, 159, 170, *180,* 180–183, *181, 185*; ELN and, 4, 101, *101,* 117, 119–121, *121,* 123, *124*; FARC and, 73, *74,* 93–95, *94*; Mexican armed parties and, 200, 202, 203, 204, 205, *206*; OCGs and, 200, 203, 204, *206*; paramilitaries and, 3, 4, 59, 128, *128,* 144, 146–150, *147, 148,* 156; in post-peace agreement Colombia, 69, 188, 194, *194,* 197;

research design and, 19; statistics, 73, 93; as territorial terrorism, *13*, 15–16
Maynard, Jonathan, 41
Mazzei, Julie, 130
McAllister, Bradley, 235n47, 273n7
Medellín Cartel, 59, 61, 134–135, 141, 167, 174
Medina Gallego, Carlos, 111, 138
Meron, Theodor, 240n17, 286n3
Metelits, Claire, 242n42, 251n23, 259n59, 261n90
Mexican National Human Rights Commission, 199
Mexican Revolution, 195
Mexico: armed parties' repertoires of terrorism, 195–206, *206*; community policing (Policía Comunitaria), 198; criminal wars and violence, 190, 195–206; drug trafficking organizations (DTO), 201–202; Organized Criminal Groups, 200–206; security forces, 197–198; self-defense groups *(auto-defensas)*, 197, 198–200; strategic and contested plazas, 196, 202–203; variation in repertoires of terrorism, 33; "war on drugs," 195
Mitchell, Christopher, 11
money laundering, 48, 49, 59, 133
Mora, Enrique, 169
moral disengagement, 82
Morantes, Luis (aka Jacobo Arenas), 80, 84, 90
Moro, Francesco, 8, 39
Muerte a Secuestradores (MAS), 133, 154
Murillo, Diego (aka Don Berna), 63, 140, 267–268n31

narcoterrorism, 176
narcotrafficking: antinarcotic and counternarcotic operations, 158, 167, 168, 176, 197; Democratic Security Policy and, 65; ELN and, 108; Leahy amendment and, 279n109; national security and, 174; paramilitary groups and, 133, 141–142; reaction to guerrillas' abductions, 4; rise in violence, 59; terrorism and, 62. *See also* Medellín Cartel
National Center of Historic Memory (Centro Nacional de Memoria Histórica), 19, 119, 132, 150
National Front, 56, 77, 162, 163, 164
National Liberation Army. *See* Ejército de Liberación Nacional
National Popular Alliance (Alianza Nacional Popular), 83
Nazi Germany, 31
new wars thesis, 32–33
Noche y Niebla, 19–20, 239nn95–97

Ochoa, Martha Nieves, 133
Ochoa Vásquez, Jorge Luis, 61
O'Donnell, Guillermo, 171
organizational identity, 7–10, 37–51; criminal ethos and, 8–9, 48–51; defining, 6–7; flexibility of, 7; historical context of armed parties, 39–40; ideology and, 8, 37–38, *39*, 40–43; leadership and, 43–47; repertoires of action and, 35; repertoires of terrorism and, 7, 38–39, *39*; as social category, 7; transnational diffusion of ideas and, 47–48; violence and, 211–213
Organization of American States, 136, 175, 186
Organized Criminal Groups (OCGs), 190–191, 200–207; abductions, 200, 203, 205, *206*; assassinations, 203, 204–205, *206*; bombings, 200, 203, 204–205, *206*; massacres, 200, 203, 204, *206*; overkill, 205; repertoires of terrorism, 200–207
overkill. See *sevicia*

Pablito, 105, 112
Palacio, Marco, 61, 166

Panama, 175, 177, *226, 227*
paramilitarism and paramilitaries, 2–5, *4,* 126–129; abductions, 3, 5, 15–16, 59, 62, 128, *128,* 152–156, *153, 154*; agitational strategies and, 142, 152, 156; bombings avoided by, 60, 61–62, *128,* 156; criminal ethos, 140–142; defining, 129–131; disappearances, 47, 127, 137, 144, 154–155; emergence of Colombian paramilitary groups, 131–137; emergence of paramilitary groups, 57–62; Escuelas de Formación (training schools), 143; executions, 16, *128,* 144–146, *145,* 148–149, 150, 156; geographic dimensions of terrorism, 155–156; ideology and identity, 137–140, 212; leadership, 142–143; massacres, 3, 4, 59, 128, *128,* 144, 146–150, *147, 148,* 156; overkill used by, 150–152, *151*; in post-peace agreement Colombia, 192, *193,* 194, *194*; pro-regime terrorism of, 15; repertoires of terrorism, 142–150; socialization, 143; torture, 15, 59, 127, 143, 144, 151
Pardo, Rafael, 141, 168
Pastrana, Andrés, 64, 72, 105, 168–169, 170, 254n71
Patriotic Union, 60, 75, 90
Peace Accord (2016), 20, 24, 54, 67–68, 69, 186. See also post-peace agreement Colombia
Peace Communities, 94
Peasant Association of Cattle Ranchers and Agriculturalists of Magdalena Medio, 133–134
Peasant Self-Defense Forces of Córdoba and Urabá (ACCU), 63, 135
Pécaut, Daniel, 62, 83
People's Alternative Revolutionary Force, 53
Pérez, Henry, 126, 143
Pérez, Manuel (aka El Cura Pérez), 104, 108, 113

Pérez Alzate, Rodrigo (aka Julian Bolívar), 269n60
Pérez Cardon, José Efrain, 143–144
Persecuted by Pablo Escobar (Perseguidos por Pablo Escobar), 63, 134, 140, 267–268n31
Personal Liberty Unified Action Groups (Grupos de Acción Unificada por la Libertad Personal) GAULA, 99, 177, 183, 279n113, 280n128
Peru, 33, 37, 83, 162; Center for Higher Military Studies (Centro de Altos Estudios Militares), 173; Tupac Amaru Revolutionary Movement (Movimiento Revolucionario Tupac Amaru), 33, 109; variation in repertoires of terrorism, 33
Peruvian-Colombian war, 163
Petro, Gustavo, 69, 106
Pion-Berlin, David, 173
Pizarro, Eduardo, 77, 138
Plan Colombia, 65, 72, 105, 118, 169, 176
Plan Consolidación, 170, 174
Plan Espada de Honor (Sword of Honor), 170
Plan Lazo, 164–165, 174
Plan Patriota, 170
policy: conditions of violence and, 216–217; humanitarian considerations, 214–216
political training. See indoctrination
Post, Jerrold, 42
post-peace agreement Colombia, 67–69, 191–195; abduction, 69, 194, *194,* 197; abductions, 194, 197; armed group's repertoires of terrorism, 191–195, *194*; bombings, 69, 193–194, *194,* 197; CSSF and, *193,* 194, *194*; ELN and, 186–187, 188, 192, *193,* 194, *194*; executions, *194*; FARC and, 187–188, 192, 193, *193, 194,* 194–195; massacres, 69, 188, 194, *194,* 197; paramilitaries, 192, *193,* 194, *194*; terrorism in, 186–189, *192*; terrorist

attacks by group, *193*; terrorist attacks by municipality, *193*
Prolonged Popular War (PPW) doctrine, 102, 105, 112
pro-regime terrorism, *13*, 13–14, 15, 16; CSSF and, 178, 185, 205; Mexican state security forces and, 178, 185, 205; paramilitaries and, 22, 144, 156. *See also* disappearances; torture
Provisional Irish Republican Army, 47–48, 87

racketeering, 48, 49, 202, 237n73
radicalism, political, 34
radicalization, 37, 42–43, 74
Rangel, Rafael, 56, 103
rape, 30, 45, 199, 200, 204
Rapoport, David, 34, 41–42, 46, 243n59, 246n103
Raymond, Gregory, 12–13
Rempe, Dennis, 177
Rendón Herrera, Freddy (aka El Alemán), 145, 151
repertoires of contention, 5
repertoires of terrorism, 12–16, *13*; of armed groups in post-conflict Colombia, 191–195; CSSF and, 176–183; ELN and, 110–116; FARC and, 82–97; insurgent (anti-regime) terrorism, 12–13; in Mexico's criminal war, 195–206; organizational identity and, 7; paramilitaries and, 142–155; in post-peace agreement Colombia, 191–195; pro-regime terrorism, 13–14; territorial terrorism, 14; variation in, 32–37. *See also* agitational strategies; territorial terrorism
Research Center for Investigation and Popular Education, 19, 119, 155, 158, 191
Research Center for Investigation and Popular Education, 19–20, 89
Rettberg, Angelika, 255n87, 255n90, 281n10, 281n15

Revolutionary Armed Forces of Colombia. *See* Fuerzas Armadas Revolucionarias de Colombia
Reyes, Raúl, 82, 90
Richani, Nazih, 164
Ríos, Iván, 78, 80, 81
Rodríguez Bautista, Nicolás (aka Gabino), 103, 104, 106, 107–108, 111, 112, 194–195, 262n1
Rodríguez Gacha, Gonzalo (aka El Mexicano), 59, 61, 62, 260n81
Rojas Pinilla, Gustavo, 56, 77, 83, 163, 276n49
Rueda, Alberto, 174
Ruiz Novoa, Alberto, 164–165, 175
Russia, 5–6, 48
ruthlessness, 50, 111, 133
Rwanda, 31, 37

Safford, Frank, 274n20
Salvadoran civil war. *See* El Salvador
Sambanis, Nicholas, 27, 233n21, 240n4, 240n20, 282n26, 286n2
Samper, Ernesto, 63–64
Sánchez-Cuenca, Ignacio, 30
Santafé de Ralito Peace Accord (2006), 66, 136, 139, 140
Santos, Juan Manuel, 67, 171, 186
Sassòli, Marco, 216
Saviano, Roberto, 50
Schlichte, Klaus, 38
Schmid, Alex, 10–11, 235n45, 235n47, 241n23, 244n62, 286n6
Segunda Marquetalia, 187, 280–281n6
self-determination, 27, 42, 109
September 11, 2001, attacks of, 42, 174, 176
sevicia (overkill), 150–152; definition of, 4, 93; ELN and, 4, 121; FARC and, 93; in Mexican criminal wars, 205–206, *206*; paramilitaries and, 4, 150, 261n94
sexual violence, 12, 17, 49, 197, 200
Shesterinina, Anastasia, 37
Sierra Leone, 37, 49

Simón Bolívar National Guerrilla Coordination, 81
Sinaloa Cartel, 202, 204
smuggling, 48, 49, 106; drug smuggling, 61; emerald smuggling, 59, 133; gasoline smuggling, 188; human smuggling, 68
socialization, 44; CSSF and, 176–177; hazing and, 9, 44; initiation rituals and, 9, 44; leadership and, 44; paramilitaries and, 143
Spanish civil war, 34
Special Jurisdiction for Peace (Jurisdicción Especial Para la Paz), 67–68, 157, 186
Special Tribunal for Peace (Tribunal Especial para la Paz), 19
Sprinzak, Ehud, 41, 243n57, 246n100
Sri Lanka, 37
Staniland, Paul, 28
Stanton, Jessica, 31, 34
state-incited violence, 11–12
state-sponsored violence, 11–12
state terrorism, civil war and, 160–162. *See also* Colombian state security forces
Stepan, Alfred, 171
Stohl, Michael, 10–11, 235n45
Strauss, Richard, 84
Suárez, Andrés, 150
Suárez Rojas, Victor (aka Alfredo Briceño, Mono Jojoy), 89, 90, 259n47
Surveillance and Private Security Associations, 63–64

Taliban, 49
Tapias, Fernando, 169
Teófilo Forero Mobile Column, 71, *97*
territorial terrorism, 14–16; CSSF and, 181–182, *182*; ELN and, 102, 117–118, 121, 122–123, 125; FARC and, 74, 76, 89, 91, 93, 95, *96*, *97*, 98; paramilitaries and, 144, *149*, 156. *See also* massacres

terrorism: attacks in Colombian civil war, *3*; attacks in post-peace agreement Colombia, 191–195, *192*, *193*; civilian targeting and, 29–32; civil war and, 27–29, 209–211; defining, 10–12, 28, 201; goals of, 10; ideological theories of, 34; rationalist theories of, 35; role of in civil wars, 5–10; state versus nonstate terrorism, 11; terror versus, 12; wave theory of, 34–35, 41–42, 46. *See also* repertoires of terrorism
testimony, 5, 18–20, 146–147, 272n116
Tilly, Charles, 5, 11, 35, 273n11
Torres, Camilo, 103, 104, 108, 111–112, 264n58
torture: CSSF and, 158, 162, 166, 170, 175, 183, 185; "enhanced interrogation" methods, 48, 143; FARC and, 1, 73, 79–80; Mexican armed parties and, 197, 198, 199, 200, 205, *206*; paramilitaries and, 15, 59, 127, 143, 144, 151; as pro-regime terrorism, *13*, 14, 15, 16; ruthlessness and, 50; used in Mexican criminal war, 200, 205, *207*
Total Peace (Paz Total), 69
Trejo, Guillermo, 190–191, 202
Turbay Ayala, Julio César, 61, 79, 162, 166, 174
Turkey, 31

Ugarizza, Juan, 231n1, 251n19, 254n70, 261n87, 274n19
Ukraine, 5–6
Unidad Revolucionaria Nacional Guatemalteca, 109
United Nations High Commissioner for Refugees, 19
United Nations Office of the High Commissioner for Human Rights, 19
United Nations Special Rapporteur on Human Rights and Terrorism, 10

United Self-Defense Forces of Colombia. *See* Autodefensas Unidas de Colombia
Uribe, Álvaro, 54, 65–67, 136, 169–170
Uruguay, 82, 84, 162
useful fools, 23, 43, 129, 138

Valencia, Guillermo León, 58, 78, 132, 164
Varese, Federico, 50
Vargas, Ricardo, 50
Vásquez Castaño, Fabio, 103, 104, 111–112
Velandia, José Juvenal (aka Iván Ríos), 78, 80, 81
Venezuela: abductions, 84; Colombian geography and, 54, 63. 68, 184; criminal organizations, 190; ELN and, 67, 106; paramilitaries and, 155, 184; Revolutionary Leftist Movement, 82
veredas (rural villages), 2, 144
Viet Cong, 21, 81, 85, 89, 91, 105, 109, 112, 118

Villarreal, Ana, 200
Volkov, Vadim, 141

Walter, Eugen Victor, 31
Walzer, Michael, 161
Weinstein, Jeremy, 33
Wendt, Alexander, 233n25, 245n83, 245n86
Whetten, David, 244n66
Wickham-Crowley, Timothy, 75
Wilson, Tim, 162
Wood, Elisabeth: on civilian victimization, 45; on identity transformation and civil war, 36–37; on ideology, 8, 40, 41, 82, 137–138, 172; on socialization in military organizations, 44; on violence blueprints, 32

Yugoslavia, 49

GPSR Authorized Representative: Easy Access System Europe, Mustamäe tee
50, 10621 Tallinn, Estonia, gpsr.requests@easproject.com